# Beyond Versailles

# Europe, 1923

Iceland

Norway

Sweden

Finland

Petro

Baltic Sea

Estonia

Latvia

Lithuania

Danzig

Belar
SS

Denmark

East Prussia

Ireland

United
Kingdom

London

Netherlands

The Hague

Berlin

Warsaw

Brest-Litov

Germany

Poland

Belgium

Prague

Upper Silesia

Teschen

Paris

Czechoslovakia

Vienna

Budapest

France

Switzerland

Austria

Hungary

Romani

Geneva

South
Tyrol

Trieste

Fiume

Italy

Yugoslavia

Bulga

Portugal

Madrid

Rome

Albania

Lisbon

Spain

Greece

Spanish Zone

Mediterranean

Morocco

French West Africa

Tunis

Tripoli

Tripolitania

Libya

Cyrenaic

Fezzan

1,000

Kilometers

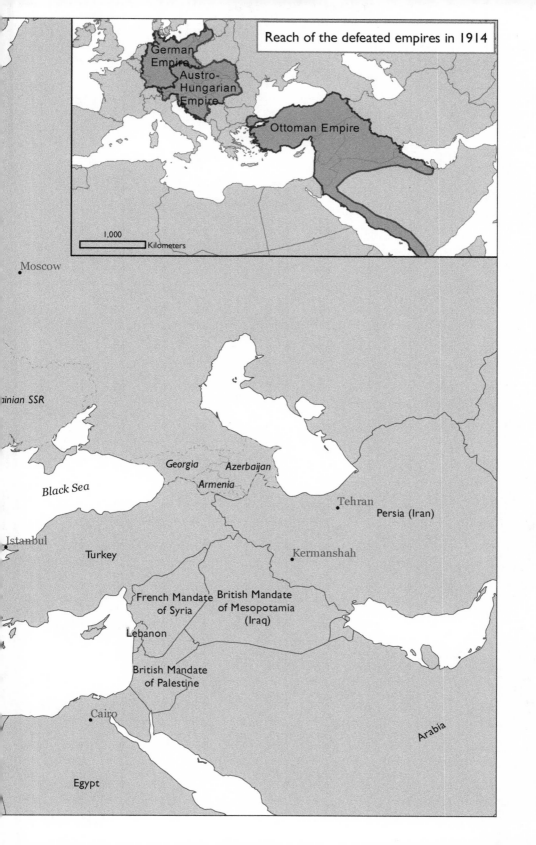

Reach of the defeated empires in 1914

German Empire

Austro-Hungarian Empire

Ottoman Empire

1,000 Kilometers

Moscow

Ukrainian SSR

Georgia

Azerbaijan

Black Sea

Armenia

Tehran

Persia (Iran)

Istanbul

Turkey

Kermanshah

French Mandate of Syria

British Mandate of Mesopotamia (Iraq)

Lebanon

British Mandate of Palestine

Cairo

Arabia

Egypt

EDITED BY MARCUS M. PAYK
AND ROBERTA PERGHER

# Beyond Versailles

## Sovereignty, Legitimacy, and the Formation of New Polities after the Great War

INDIANA UNIVERSITY PRESS

This book is a publication of

Indiana University Press
Office of Scholarly Publishing
Herman B Wells Library 350
1320 East 10th Street
Bloomington, Indiana 47405 USA

iupress.indiana.edu

Library of Congress Cataloging-in-Publication Data

Names: Payk, Marcus M., editor. | Pergher, Roberta., editor.
Title: Beyond Versailles : Sovereignty, Legitimacy, and the Formation of New
    Polities After the Great War / edited by Marcus M. Payk and Roberta Pergher.
Description: Bloomington, Indiana : Indiana University Press, 2018. |
    Includes bibliographical references and index.
Identifiers: LCCN 2018049712 (print) | LCCN 2018052054 (ebook) | ISBN
    9780253040947 (e-book) | ISBN 9780253040909 (cl : alk. paper) | ISBN
    9780253040916 (pbk. : alk. paper)
Subjects:  LCSH: Europe—Politics and government—1918-1945.
Classification: LCC D727 (ebook) | LCC D727 .B47 2018 (print) | DDC
    940.5/1—dc23
LC record available at https://lccn.loc.gov/2018049712

1  2  3  4  5    24  23  22  21  20  19

# Contents

# Acknowledgments

The idea for this project was born over coffee and cookies at the Institute for Advanced Study in Princeton in the spring of 2013, when the two editors were fellows at the institute's School for Historical Studies. Our plan for a conference exploring the emergence of a new world order "beyond Versailles" was realized in May 2015 at Humboldt University of Berlin. More than twenty scholars presented their work, offering new interpretations about the implementation and afterlife of the Paris peace settlements following the First World War. The lively and collegial discussions at the conference reverberate in these pages. We would like to thank all the participants, including those not represented in this volume.

The organization of the conference and the preparation of this book were made possible by the generous support of the Fritz Thyssen Foundation; a Mellon Innovating International Research, Teaching, and Collaboration Grant from Indiana University, Bloomington; and the Kosmos-Programm of the Humboldt-Universität zu Berlin. Sophie Abramowicz, Karin Trieloff, and Timo Walz helped with all conference arrangements and the preparation of the book manuscript. Eva Schissler translated chapters 2 and 10 and provided editorial assistance. Theresa Quill, map librarian at Indiana University, created the map used for the frontispiece. We are grateful to the two anonymous reviewers for their helpful and constructive suggestions. Finally, we thank Jennika Baines and Kate Schramm at Indiana University Press for their unwavering support and their continuous guidance.

Marcus M. Payk (*Hamburg*)
Roberta Pergher (*Bloomington, Indiana*)

Beyond Versailles

# Introduction

## Marcus M. Payk and Roberta Pergher

Commenting on the difficulty of enforcing the policies and principles formulated at the Paris Peace Conference, Chief of the British Imperial General Staff
Henry Wilson complained in June 1919 to British premier David Lloyd George:
"The root of evil is that the Paris writ does not run."[1] Wilson was right in many
respects. Agreeing on what should go into the Paris peace treaties was only half
the battle. The terms of the treaty had to be implemented and enforced, and the
peacemakers' reach was not limitless—to the contrary. War, insurrection, and
civil strife continued to shake eastern Europe; the vanquished nations opposed
the peace terms with increasing strength and defiance; unrest and discontent
spread in the colonial world; the great powers felt deeply threatened by the
Russian revolution and yet unsure how to respond—and these were just a few
of the challenges that bedeviled the statesmen assembled in Paris. Often enough
the peacemakers themselves did not want to invest any further resources into far-
away places. The public too soon grew impatient with what it perceived as drawn-
out diplomatic parlor games and shaky compromises concocted in ornate and
smoke-filled salons. Before long, the impression of an irreconcilable chasm between the lofty ideals of peacemaking and the grim realities of a chaotic and un-
resolvable postwar situation took hold in the popular mind.

Even so, the Paris writ ran further and deeper than Henry Wilson acknowledged. What politicians, experts, and administrators discussed and decided on
in Paris mattered greatly. If ideas of national self-determination, minority rights,
and colonial emancipation were older than the Great War, Paris imbued them
with new energy, afforded them new legitimacy, and indeed made them seem the
constituent principles of an emerging new world order. This book is about that
Paris writ: about the partly codified, but partly unwritten principles and promises of a new normative international regime, principles and promises that resonated a long way from Paris—from Polish borderlands to Portuguese colonies,
from the city of Vienna to those of Cairo and Tehran. What did individuals and
groups in places where the peace treaties were to be executed understand the new
norms of sovereignty and legitimacy to mean? How, for instance, did people who
voted in plebiscites make sense of the principle of national self-determination?
As former imperial provinces became new nations, how did the new Paris norms

affect notions of citizenship and belonging? How, in other words, was the Paris writ reinterpreted on the ground, across Europe and in the colonies?

The point is not simply to shift the spotlight from the metropole to the periphery. Rather, this volume explores the interplay between what was decided at the peace conference and what unfolded beyond, between allegedly universal principles and particular understandings in particular places. For whatever intentions guided the peace-makers, the settlement they produced was in turn interpreted and adapted locally and regionally, as well as nationally and internationally. New postwar tenets such as self-determination as an inherent right of peoples took on a life of their own, conflicting with more traditional doctrines of sovereignty or hitherto inviolable assumptions about the colonial right to rule. At times they gave rise to visions of the international order that were the very opposite of what the peacemakers had originally intended. This volume explores the complex force field of discourses and policies that emerged in the wake of the peace treaties.

## The Paris Settlement in an Unsettled World

Seldom has the map of empires, nations, and peoples been so open to redrawing as during the deliberations of the Paris Peace Conference in 1919. Taken together, the Treaties of Versailles, Saint-Germain, Trianon, Neuilly, and Sèvres, not to mention several dozen related agreements and conventions, sealed the end of the German and Austrian Empires, redrew state borders across Europe and the Near East, and validated the emergence of new states from unruly Poland to stillborn Armenia. The settlement also established the self-determination of people as the core principle of legitimate government, created a new framework for the international order in the form of the League of Nations, and introduced new protections for peoples that were not self-governing nations—be it in the mandate system as a "progressive" form of colonial rule or in minority rights enshrined in the treaties with the vanquished and their successor states.

That these innovations and structural changes in international affairs would nevertheless be eclipsed by the settlement's failures, was a sign of the enormous challenges faced by the peacemakers in Paris. On top of the immediate demands of the peace negotiations, there was the daunting task of a comprehensive reordering of the world. The management and conduct of the conference was haphazard at best, burdened by overly ambitious and partly incoherent goals and by deliberations that were at times protracted, at times all too rushed. The international press corps objected to the persistence of "secret diplomacy" and negotiations behind closed doors. The small nations felt snubbed by the great powers' exclusive deal making. Even a major player, the Italians, temporarily walked out in a bitter dispute in late April 1919, smarting at being shortchanged in their territorial ambitions. The Japanese, too, felt rebuffed, especially after the United States and Great Britain rejected their proposed clause of racial equality as an amendment to the League Covenant.

A sign of how intractable global reordering would prove was that even as the victorious nations convened in Paris, elsewhere in much of central and eastern

Europe, in the Middle East, and in other parts of the colonial world, conflict and violence continued unabated or intensified. Border skirmishes and ethnic cleansing, revolutionary upheaval and firebrand nationalism formed an explosive mixture that deeply shook engrained power structures. Large swaths of land in Europe and its peripheries descended into political and economic chaos, sometimes accompanied by the rise of uncompromising warlords, sometimes giving way to authoritarian cadres of a Bolshevik or a fascist stripe who rejected all the Allied postwar arrangements.[2]

The following years saw repeated diplomatic failures. The Americans' unwillingness to ratify the treaties was only the most obvious sign of a general tendency to reject the Paris compromises.[3] Among the defeated nations, responses to the peace treaties ranged from contempt to outrage, but even among the victors, there was growing disillusionment and resentment. From Lausanne to Locarno, a whole slate of new accords was signed in the course of the 1920s because the original ones proved impractical or inadequate or failed to settle old disputes. The new institutions created by Paris, namely the League of Nations, its councils, and its commissions, had a hard time fulfilling their core mission. Keeping international peace proved to be impossible, especially when the aggression emanated from permanent members of the League Council, as in the case of Japan in Manchuria in 1931 or Italy in Abyssinia in 1935.

## Scholars and the Treaties

No wonder then, that when scholars talked about Paris and its aftermath, they tended to highlight failure. Henry Wilson's assessment of a Paris writ without legs seems prescient. The settlement clearly failed to bring about lasting peace. Indeed, in the popular mind the treaties' punitive elements still bear much of the blame for the interwar crises that led to the Second World War while the noble ideals underwriting them seem illusory and naive. Though explanations for the treaties' shortcomings have varied, the standard narrative quickly emerged of a fatally flawed peace settlement that like its notorious near contemporaries, the *Titanic* and the *Hindenburg* airship, was destined for disaster.

Already in December 1919, John Maynard Keynes's scathing critique in *The Economic Consequences of the Peace* laid the foundations for the perception that the peace settlement was, and could be, nothing but a dramatic failure.[4] Hundreds of books, sometimes more or less subtly promoted by the revisionist Kriegsschuldreferat (Center for the Study of the Causes of the War) in the German Foreign Ministry, repeated the basic tenets of Keynes polemic, from bitter disappointment with Woodrow Wilson's alleged naiveté to rejection of Georges Clemenceau's unyielding lust for vengeance. These interpretations fell on fertile ground in many nations and especially in the United States and Great Britain. Dissatisfaction with the treaties was, however, greatest in France, where the German settlement was deemed too soft and Allied support for French security concerns too halfhearted. In the end, all sides easily agreed on the master narrative of a "failed peace," a narrative firmly established years before the out-break of the Second World War in 1939.[5]

From the 1960s onward, a new wave of scholarship revisited the Paris Peace Conference of 1919–20, seeking to move beyond the narrative of inevitable disas-ter.[6] The traditional accounts of high-level diplomacy, often written by partici-pants in the negotiations or other contemporaries, were now followed by analyses of the newly instituted organs charged with maintaining the peace and creating a new basis for international relations. A younger generation of scholars began to highlight the diversity of interests and plurality of actors on an international as well as transnational stage, recognizing that states are not the sole agents of world politics and arguing for the open-endedness of a process often perceived as a one-way street to the Second World War. The economic aspects of the peace, as well as the vexed question of reparations, found new interest and more so-phisticated interpretations, with studies from Charles Maier, Peter Krüger, or Georges-Henri Soutou as the most prominent examples.[7] In the same context, the virulent debate over Germany's ostensible war guilt was given a new perspective, stressing less the moralistic arrogance of the victors than the responsibility— or irresponsibility—of the defeated elites who had whipped up public outrage to reject any accountability for the war and its conduct.[8]

Over the last ten years, historians have begun to pay greater attention to the power of expectations raised by Paris and its influence on the institutional and normative regime that ensued. For all their shortcomings, the peace treaties were understood by their drafters as well as by a global audience to be inaugurating a new world order.[9] The gathering of the victorious powers in Paris was seen in many societies as a singular historic moment where the entire world would be re-made.[10] There were good reasons for this belief. Drafting a skeleton treaty as early as late December 1918, American delegates, for instance, believed the negotia-tions would result in a single "world treaty" of enormous proportions signed by all belligerent and neutral nations of the world and shaping the affairs of a global state society for years to come.[11] In countless variations, ideas were circulating of a world predicated on international collaboration, cooperation, and peace; na-tional sovereignty and self-determination; democracy; minority rights; and the prospect of successive emancipation for subject peoples around the globe.

Historians have rightly begun to emphasize the resonance of such ideas, even if they were honored more in the breach than in the observance. For all the broken promises of self-determination or the doublespeak of the mandate system, it is clear that the relationship between sovereignty and legitimacy was changing rap-idly.[12] Erez Manela, for instance, has famously spoken of a "Wilsonian moment," when the idea of self-determination stirred independence movements around the world, causing the European colonial powers much discomfort.[13] In a similar vein, Susan Pedersen has highlighted how shortsighted it would be to view the mandates simply as an arbitrary imperialism thinly veiled with empty rhetoric of humanitarian concerns and benign paternalism. Rather, she argues that by in-stituting a mandate system the Allies acknowledged, albeit perhaps unwittingly, that emancipation and national independence should be the international norm and would prevail in the long run. At least implicitly, this pledge fundamentally altered the relationship between imperial powers and subject peoples.[14] And for all the failure to prevent or tackle the world economic crisis, we now know that the League of Nations created important institutions that were rethinking the relationship between economic and political stability.[15]

Of course, the fact that the ideas of Paris enjoyed real resonance does not mean that the impact of those ideas was unambiguously positive. Eric Weitz, for example, sees Paris as a watershed moment in the use of population politics to establish claims of sovereignty. Whereas traditional conceptions of peacemaking, epitomized in the Vienna system of the 1814–15 settlement, centered on territorial adjustments and the equilibrium of powers, the Paris system was based on populations defined by their alleged nationality or ethnicity.[16] Creating homogeneous collectives with clear-cut borders was the new imperative. While this may have had antecedents in prewar experiments at creating "national" classes of imperial subject—as in the "national compromises" in Habsburg Moravia (1905), Bukovina (1910), or Galicia (1914)—the idea that nations with identifiable, clearly defined populations were the bedrock of both domestic and international affairs took hold only after 1918.[17] This premise gave rise not only to the principle of national self-determination but also to population policies ranging from minority protection to forced deportation. Only nation-states free from any restless minorities with irredentist ambitions promised to be guarantors of peace—a notion that, paradoxically, may have paved the way for ethnic cleansing and racial extermination.[18] As the "aftershocks" of the war and the swirling maelstrom of violence, unrest, and anarchy in the "shatterzones" of empire showed, the principles that undergirded the peace negotiations could equally lead to violence and conflict.[19]

## Beyond Versailles

The contributions to this volume share two key assumptions that enable them to offer new perspectives on the Paris treaties. The first, in line with recent scholarship and already intimated in this introduction, is that the postwar treaties were influential not simply in redrawing the map of Europe, empowering the victors, and restraining the vanquished but also in contributing to a broader, subtler transformation of the international order. Following the cataclysms of a war that had shaken up all the societies and polities involved and had brought European dominance around the world to a critical juncture, core principles of sovereignty and legitimacy were being redefined. In this context, the Paris system should be understood not as some programmatic "Wilsonianism" but as an informal, dynamic combination of various related promises, practices, and proclamations. Incoherent, piecemeal, and dysfunctional as the treaties proved to be in hindsight, they merged older ideas of sovereignty and legitimacy with early twentieth-century concepts of public consent, population politics, state responsibility, and universal interdependence, creating, or at least contributing to, a new understanding of how a stable international order ought to operate in the future.

Understood thus, the Paris principles shaped the various pathways from war to peace that went well beyond the actual treaties. They provided a new language and understanding of nationalism and internationalism, sovereignty and territoriality, ethnicity and popular participation.

The volume's second starting point is more distinctive—namely, that the victorious powers were never really in control of the ideas and institutions of the Paris system, even if they thought otherwise. The forging of a postwar order was not a linear process emanating from a single center of political power and built on a coherent strategy. Nor was the postwar order merely the sum of separate local deals, dominated by local concerns and considerations. Rather, it was the result of multifaceted, competitive, and often contradictory practices within a shared matrix of formal and informal obligations, ideas, and ambitions. If previous research has pursued these phenomena, then mostly with regard to the official German resistance to and avoidance of the responsibilities arising out of the Versailles treaty.[20] Too often the diplomacy of negotiating and concluding an agreement has retained center stage, while the world beyond the immediate signatories has remained under-illuminated. Yet as the individual case studies in this volume show, elites around the globe, in the defeated as well as the victorious nations, were soon well versed in speaking the new language of national sovereignty and international order—rapidly adopting, adapting, and rejecting its vocabulary as circumstances allowed and political interests dictated. This process had important precursors in the late nineteenth century, when Western understandings of international law and international society were appropriated by indigenous political leaders and intellectuals to find advantageous ground vis-à-vis the colonial powers.[21] But as the new norms rapidly gained traction in the years following the Great War, it is all the more important to shift attention closer to the ground, to the multiple readings of the Paris writ and the space for interpretation it allowed. Wherever the decisions of Paris were implemented, they overlapped with local interests and imaginations and were adopted as well as subverted in the process—whether in Silesia, Teschen, or Danzig, or in Austria, Egypt, or Iran.

Chapters 1 through 3 explore the way in which new borders in eastern Europe were imagined, endorsed, and implemented—only to be challenged anew. In theory, the principle of national self-determination promised a more democratic world, in which people would decide which state they belong to. Nationalists, and indeed the peacemakers, now saw multilingual, mixed ethnic identities or ethnically and linguistically diverse territories as anomalies and ethnically homogenous nation-states as the norm. Heterogeneous regions thus required a clear national designation.[22] In other words, the scaffolding of legitimation changed from one where dynasties ruled over diverse populations to one where homogeneous peoples determined the shape and form of sovereign territories. In reality, the redrawing of state borders after the First World War was rarely "willed" by the people, nor did the "people's will," in the few instances it was consulted, necessarily align with the expectations of experts and diplomats who envisioned a vote along clear ethnographic lines.[23] Thus, while "the people" were indispensable to legitimizing this new order, they rarely, if ever, determined it.

As Brendan Karch shows in chapter 1, the decision to hold a plebiscite to establish the national identity of particular territories depended on a number of considerations. In many contested central and eastern European borderlands, the shape of states was in fact decided by continuing warfare and the lobbying efforts of national elites. The peacemakers approved plebiscites in only six mixed-language regions, all of which had belonged to the vanquished German and Austrian Empires. The largest and most contested vote took place in Upper Silesia on the German-Polish border in March 1921. Though plebiscites were premised on the idea that people have a clear, innate national identity and that they would vote accordingly, Karch shows that they rarely offered a simple measure of national allegiance. In the case of Upper Silesia it was not a presumed national identity that found expression in the democratic process of "self-determination" but rather people's desire for security and order in a highly volatile and violent postwar transition. Analysis of plebiscite propaganda on both the German and the Polish side reveals that even nationalist activists believed that instrumental considerations, rather than an intrinsic and deeply felt sense of ethnicity, would carry the day.

The peacemakers came to regard a plebiscite as the most expedient solution to a border conflict also in the former Austrian duchy of Teschen. Initially, the border between the new nations of Poland and Czechoslovakia was supposed to be drawn in Paris, but after a 1919 border skirmish, the decision was delegated to the people of Teschen. In chapter 2, Isabelle Davion examines France's stance in the conflict, including the actions of its representatives on the ground in Teschen, as they sought to forge new alliances in central and eastern Europe. She shows that the planned plebiscite emerged not out of "Wilsonian idealism" but out of great power impotence. It was opportunistically embraced by Polish and Czechoslovakian delegations, but only as long as each side thought that they would win. Technical expertise and the reliance on objective criteria were supposed to take emotions out of the debate and move decisions about the plebiscite's organization into the administrative sphere. Yet violence on the ground became unmanageable, and soon enough both Poles and Czechs started to have doubts about the outcome. In the end, the plebiscite was abandoned.

Though state borders were generally gerrymandered from above rather than willed by the people, the new European order of nation-states demanded the alignment of state boundaries, on the one hand, and national groups—understood increasingly as biological entities, defined by descent—on the other. In chapter 3, Jesse Kauffman takes us into the decades following the Paris settlement, when a new slate of scholarship sought to assert exclusive national claims to particular territories. True, this scholarship rested on earlier work and prerogatives, but Kauffman identifies a new, broader "völkisch turn" after the First World War that was very much invigorated and given legitimacy by the new postwar norms. The notion of national self-determination became the essential ingredient in the language of political legitimacy deployed not only by Germany but also by the newly established Polish state and was used to lay claim to various disputed territories after the Great War such as Posen/Poznań and Schlesien/Śląnsk, where a plebiscite had in fact taken place. By comparing Germany and Poland, the chapter shows that Germany was not unique or distinctive but that Poles too advanced their claims using ideas and categories of the Paris system, which they reinterpreted and subverted in the process.

One of the central ironies revealed by the first three chapters is that although the role of popular will in giving shape to the new postwar polities was extremely circumscribed, the notion of "the people" was becoming central to defining the nation-state as the "natural" and "self-determining" polity. Chapters 4 through 6 look at how the nation-state came to be understood as natural and inevitable and hence as the preferred unit in the new international order. For all the nation-state's seeming inevitability, these chapters demonstrate how complex and contested were the efforts to rethink imperial spaces and relationships as national ones. As the chapters examine the transformation of state bureaucracies and the recasting of imperial repertoires of inclusion and exclusion to the needs of nation-states, they reveal the importance of local concerns, selective interests, and competing actors. They also show the continuing importance and appeal of imperial political formations.

In chapter 4, Aimee Genell explores evolving conceptions of Egypt's status and sovereignty. The British confronted this question at the onset of the war as they considered how the Ottoman Empire's entry into the war on the side of the Central powers would affect Britain's control over Egypt. Britain would clearly be forced to take a stand on its occupation and formalize Egypt's position either as protectorate or as proper colony. Genell shows that the conflicting stances taken by different British officials prefigured later discussions about the mandate system. After evaluating the importance of popular opinion and the support of Egyptian elites, Britain opted to declare a protectorate, but the issue of Egypt's status returned with a vengeance at the end of the war. In their demands for emancipation and independence from Britain, Egyptian nationalists began to use the language of the Paris peacemakers. They also invoked the institutions of Paris, namely the mandate system, to argue that their current position as a British protectorate put Egypt, which had actively supported Britain in the war, at a disadvantage compared to all the other former Ottoman territories, which had fought against it. Their demands led to Egypt's gaining nominal independence in 1922.

Expanding on Genell's analysis of Egyptians' demands for independence, Jeffrey Culang explores in chapter 5 how the legal category of the Egyptian national was up for grabs both before and after the war. As a territory under British protection, Egypt was subject to neither the postwar treaties nor the mandate system, and it did not join the League of Nations until 1937. Yet as Culang argues, Paris left an unmistakable imprint on Egyptian law, politics, and society. To illustrate this point, he analyzes the evolving meaning and usage of the term "Egyptian national," paying particular attention to the way in which religion was politicized, as Western concepts of majority and minority were grafted onto religious groups. Egyptian jurists debated who counted as an "Egyptian national" as opposed to the legal categories of "Ottoman national" and "foreigner." In the process, they also pondered who the "true Egyptians" were and who counted as a "minority" in this nation-state in the making.

The creation of national subjects out of formerly imperial ones is also the topic tackled in chapter 6 by John Deak in the context of the re-formation of Austria as a small republic between 1918 and 1925. In a long, painful transition that lasted nearly a decade, the state bureaucracy was stripped of the multinational heritage of the Habsburg Monarchy, as the former imperial center had to reinvent itself as a nation and decide what defined and tied the new state together. For instance, employment in the new republic was contingent on being "Austrian," even though no one knew what that really meant. Commissions were set up to determine nationality and force out of state employment those who did not fit the bill. Deak mines civil servants' files for the arguments they put forth in claiming Austrian nationality and analyzes the verdicts of the commissions that had to adjudicate who was eligible to serve the new state. In the end, the republic ham-fistedly forced a former imperial center of "national indifference," populated by hybrids and code-switchers, into a new, and supposedly natural, national order.

In chapter 7, Roberta Pergher explores tensions between imperial and national rule. Using the case of Italy, she examines the place of "others" in the colonial realm and inside the nation. After the Great War, Italy incorporated into the nation new multiethnic territories acquired from the defunct Habsburg Empire in the north. At the same time, it sought to strengthen its hold on recently conquered colonial possessions in North Africa. Both realms, Pergher argues, posed similar challenges to Italian sovereignty. The Paris principles of colonial emancipation and of minority rights found resonance among the non-Italian populations in these contested territories and forced the Italian government, by 1922 in the hands of the Fascists, to respond. While the Fascists conformed to the Paris mold in their embrace of the homogeneous nation-state model, they felt constantly at odds with other principles of the postwar order, not least its mandate of colonial emancipation and the protection of minorities. Eventually, the Fascists created their own hybrid variant of a nationalized space that included former imperial realms and established new hierarchies of membership.

Although a "world of nations" came to be seen as the only effective guarantee of international peace after the cataclysms of war and revolution, this seeming consensus in fact concealed a number of alternative visions of what constituted a just and peaceful international order. Japan's proposal for racial equality had unexpected and unsettling reverberations throughout the European empires, while the rise of bolshevism and the Comintern directly challenged the Paris order, especially in countries at the margins of Western influence. Moreover, the postwar settlement itself did not always adhere to its own fundamental principles. The peacemakers at times strayed from the nation-state model, only to find themselves confronted by the very nationalist ideals that they elsewhere endorsed. For example, the creation of nonnational zones like the Free City of Danzig or the

Saarland, a solution debated also for the contested city of Fiume, did not fit easily into the Paris vision of an international order composed of nation-states. The final chapters explore various alternative understandings of how to reconcile national self-determination, power politics, and peaceful relations in a newly forged international order.

The immediate postwar period witnessed a proliferation of internationalist agendas. The Wilsonian vision for peace, predicated on institutionalism and self-determination, became particularly influential. Yet as the peace conference was taking place, individuals and organizations of a variety of political leanings gathered in Paris to promote their own ideas for a new world order based on international agreements and institutions. Focusing on the particularly contentious question of racial equality, Caio Simões de Araújo examines in chapter 8 how the racial question entered the realm of formal diplomacy via a Japanese proposal for racial equality presented at the peace conference, only to be left out of the Paris settlement. Nevertheless, prominent black personalities, such as the African American W. E. B. Du Bois, continued to challenge the dominant internationalist order. As Simões de Araújo shows, the ideas discussed at Pan-African Congresses in the early 1920s, organized by members of the African diaspora, found resonance in the colonial world, especially in the Portuguese Empire. Racial belonging—the experience of being black—served as an increasingly powerful common denominator in internationalist agendas. At the same time, race was constantly in tension with more divisive and territorially bound loyalties, such as belonging to a nation or an empire. This chapter highlights how the quest for racial equality, as well as the diplomatic and political debates it engendered, linked a series of global concerns: the intensification of racial differentiations inside nation-states, the challenge to European colonialism in Africa and Asia, and the emergence of non-Western powers.

While Iran is not commonly included in accounts of the First World War, Timothy Nunan in chapter 9 shows that ideas for a new postwar order became very important for Iranian intellectuals seeking to advance the creation of an independent Iranian nation-state. Drawing on Persian, Russian, and German sources, he follows the intellectual engagements of Iranian nationalists associated with the newspaper *Kāveh* as they sought to guide Iran's entrance into a post-imperial international order. From 1916 to 1921, these nationalists reflected on successive visions of self-determination emerging, for example, in the context of the Treaty of Brest-Litovsk, Woodrow Wilson's offer of "peace without victory," and Vladimir Lenin's vision of socialist anti-imperialism. Nunan argues that Iranian nationalists' view of Iran's place in a post-imperial world is best understood as an outgrowth of the "market in ideas" on self-determination that flourished beyond Versailles—between Berlin, Tehran, and Petrograd already during the Great War—and in its aftermath.

One of the peculiarities of the Paris treaties was the invention of new international and legal institution like the Free City of Danzig. The German port was declared a semiautonomous city-state under the protection of the League of Nations. At the same time, it was bound to the newly established Polish Republic through a customs union and placed under a special treaty regime, guaranteeing Poland access to the sea. But as Marcus Payk shows in chapter 10, that compromise opened more questions than it solved, making ever more convoluted legal arrangements necessary to establish Danzig's sovereignty under international control. The limits of this approach became apparent when the Polish postal service positioned ten letterboxes throughout the city in 1925. The Danzig government reacted with strong objections and an appeal to the high commissioner, successively involving the League Council in Geneva and the Permanent Court of International Justice in The Hague. Payk examines the fierce struggle over a Polish postal service in Danzig as an example of how the Paris settlement tried to solve or at least defuse political and territorial disputes with juridical schemes and legal agreements.

The contributors to this volume come from different historical traditions and fields—some are specialists in the history of nation-states, others in that of empires. Placing them in dialogue here allows a fruitful discussion to emerge about nation-states as historical constructs and about the rethinking of imperial precepts in an age of "nation." Because war and international crisis bring established modes into question, they provide useful moments to observe the reinterpretation of such ostensibly timeless concepts as "sovereignty," "legitimacy," "state," "nation," and "international order."[24] They also allow us to observe the underlying forces and ideas around which new international regimes coalesce and challenge our established assumptions about the natural order of the world. In the aftermath of World War I, a European order of nation-states emerged that is still very much with us and that with the dismantling of the colonial empires and the end of the Cold War, has attained renewed global legitimacy and naturalness. By adopting a localized yet comparative perspective, the contributions together question our understanding of the nation-state as the inevitable, natural, and preferred outcome of the cataclysms of war and anarchy after 1918, and examine—from above as well as from below—the ideas and practices by which a "world of nations" came into being.

## Notes

1. Henry Wilson, *Field-Marshal Sir Henry Wilson: His Life and Diaries*, 2 vols., ed. Charles E. Callwell (London: Cassell, 1927), 2:197.

2. Robert Gerwarth, *The Vanquished: Why the First World War Failed to End, 1917–1923* (London: Allen Lane, 2016); Jochen Böhler, "Enduring Violence: The Postwar Struggles in East-Central Europe, 1917–21," *Journal of Contemporary History* 50, no. 1 (2014): 58–77.

3. Patrick O. Cohrs, *The Unfinished Peace after World War I: America, Britain and the Stabilisation of Europe, 1919–1932* (Cambridge: Cambridge University Press, 2006).

4. John Maynard Keynes, *The Economic Consequences of the Peace* (New York: Harper, 1920). For a recent account of Keynes's position, see the two-part article by Stephen A. Schuker, "J. M. Keynes and the Personal Politics of Reparations," *Diplomacy & Statecraft* 25, no. 3 (2014): 453–71 and no. 4 (2014): 579–91.

5. Sally Marks, "Mistakes and Myths: The Allies, Germany, and the Versailles Treaty, 1918–1921," *Journal of Modern History* 85, no. 3 (2013): 632–59.

6. Manfred F. Boemeke, Gerald D. Feldman, and Elisabeth Glaser, eds., *The Treaty of Versailles: A Reassessment after 75 Years* (New York: Cambridge University Press, 1998); Marc Trachtenberg, "Versailles after Sixty Years," *Journal of Contemporary History* 17, no. 3 (1982): 487–506.

7. Charles S. Maier, *Recasting Bourgeois Europe: Stabilization in France, Germany, and Italy in the Decade after World War I* (Princeton, NJ: Princeton University Press, 1975); Peter Krüger, *Deutschland und die Reparationen 1918/19: Die Genesis des Reparationsproblems in Deutschland zwischen Waffenstillstand und Versailler Friedensschluß* (Stuttgart: Deutsche Verlags-Anstalt, 1973); Georges-Henri Soutou, *L'or et le sang: Les buts de guerre économiques de la Première Guerre mondiale* (Paris: Fayard, 1989).

8. John Horne and Alan Kramer, *German Atrocities, 1914: A History of Denial* (New Haven: Yale University Press, 2001); Ulrich Heinemann, *Die verdrängte Niederlage: Politische Öffentlichkeit und Kriegsschuldfrage in der Weimarer Republik* (Göttingen: Vandenhoeck & Ruprecht, 1983).

9. Adam Tooze, *The Deluge: The Great War and the Remaking of Global Order, 1916–1931* (London: Allen Lane, 2014); Alan Sharp, *The Versailles Settlement: Peacemaking after the First World War, 1919–1923* (Basingstoke: Palgrave Macmillan, 2008); Margaret MacMillan, *Peacemakers: The Paris Conference of 1919 and Its Attempt to End War* (London: Murray, 2001).

10. See Jörn Leonhard, *Der überforderte Frieden. Versailles und die Welt 1918-1923* (Munich: C.H. Beck, 2018) and Eckart Conze, *Die große Illusion: Versailles 1919 und die Neuordnung der Welt* (Munich: Siedler, 2018).

11. *Papers Relating to the Foreign Relations of the United States: The Paris Peace Conference, 1919*, 13 vols. (Washington, DC: US Government Printing Office, 1942–47), 1:298–324.

12. A publication that appeared too recently be properly acknowledged in this volume is Leonard V. Smith, *Sovereignty at the Paris Peace Conference of 1919* (Oxford: Oxford University Press, 2018).

13. Erez Manela, *The Wilsonian Moment: Self-Determination and the International Origins of Anticolonial Nationalism* (Oxford: Oxford University Press, 2007).

14. Susan Pedersen, *The Guardians: The League of Nations and the Crisis of Empire* (Oxford; New York: Oxford Univ. Press, 2015). See also Leonard V. Smith, "Empires at the Paris Peace Conference," in *Empires at War: 1911–1923*, ed. Robert Gerwarth and Erez Manela (Oxford: Oxford University Press, 2014), 254–76.

15. Patricia Clavin, *Securing the World Economy: The Reinvention of the League of Nations, 1920–1946* (Oxford: Oxford University Press, 2013).

16. Eric D. Weitz, "From the Vienna to the Paris System. International Politics and the Entangled Histories of Human Rights, Forced Deportations, and Civilizing Missions," *American Historical Review* 113, no. 5 (2008): 1313–43.

17. Pieter M. Judson, *The Habsburg Empire. A New History* (Cambridge, MA: Belknap Press of Harvard University Press, 2016), 315–16, 376–77; Börries Kuzmany, "Habsburg Austria: Experiments in Non-Territorial Autonomy," *Ethnopolitics* 15, no. 1 (2016): 43–65.

18. Norman M. Naimark, *Fires of Hatred: Ethnic Cleansing in Twentieth-Century Europe* (Cambridge, MA: Harvard University Press, 2001); Aviel Roshwald, *Ethnic Nationalism and the Fall of Empires: Central Europe, Russia, and the Middle East, 1914–1923* (London: Routledge, 2001). See also Umut Özsu, *Formalizing Displacement: International Law and Population Transfers* (Oxford: Oxford University Press, 2015).

19.  Julia Eichenberg and John P. Newman, "Aftershocks: Violence in Dissolving Empires after the First World War," *Contemporary European History* 19, no. 3 (2010): 183–94; Omer Bartov and Eric D. Weitz, eds., *Shatterzone of Empires: Coexistence and Violence in the German, Habsburg, Russian, and Ottoman Borderlands* (Bloomington: Indiana University Press, 2013).

20.  See case studies in Conan Fischer and Alan Sharp, eds., *After the Versailles Treaty: Enforcement, Compliance, Contested Identities* (London: Routledge, 2008).

21.  Arnulf Becker Lorca, *Mestizo International Law: A Global Intellectual History 1842–1933* (Cambridge: Cambridge University Press, 2015). A good example would be Japan; see Douglas Howland, *International Law and Japanese Sovereignty: The Emerging Global Order in the 19th Century* (New York: Palgrave Macmillan, 2016).

22.  Jörg Fisch, *Das Selbstbestimmungsrecht der Völker. Die Domestizierung einer Illusion* (München: C. H. Beck, 2010); Carole Fink, *Defending the Rights of Others: The Great Powers, the Jews, and International Minority Protection, 1878–1938* (New York: Cambridge University Press, 2006).

23.  Volker Prott, *The Politics of Self-Determination: Remaking Territories and National Identities in Europe, 1917–1923* (Oxford: Oxford University Press, 2016).

24.  Glenda Sluga and Patricia Clavin, eds., *Internationalisms: A Twentieth-Century History* (Cambridge; New York: Cambridge University Press, 2016); Glenda Sluga, *Internationalism in the Age of Nationalism*, Pennsylvania Studies in Human Rights (Philadelphia: University of Pennsylvania Press, 2013); Isabella Löhr and Roland Wenzlhuemer, eds., *The Nation State and Beyond: Governing Globalization Processes in the Nineteenth and Early Twentieth Centuries* (Berlin: Springer, 2013).

# Bibliography

Bartov, Omer, and Eric D. Weitz, eds. *Shatterzone of Empires: Coexistence and Violence in the German, Habsburg, Russian, and Ottoman Borderlands*. Bloomington: Indiana University Press, 2013.

Becker Lorca, Arnulf. *Mestizo International Law: A Global Intellectual History 1842–1933*. Cambridge: Cambridge University Press, 2015.

Boemeke, Manfred F., Gerald D. Feldman, and Elisabeth Glaser, eds. *The Treaty of Versailles: A Reassessment after 75 Years*. New York: Cambridge University Press, 1998.

Böhler, Jochen. "Enduring Violence: The Postwar Struggles in East-Central Europe, 1917–21." *Journal of Contemporary History* 50, no. 1 (2014): 58–77.

Clavin, Patricia. *Securing the World Economy: The Reinvention of the League of Nations, 1920–1946*. Oxford: Oxford University Press, 2013.

Cohrs, Patrick O. *The Unfinished Peace after World War I: America, Britain and the Stabilisation of Europe, 1919–1932*. Cambridge: Cambridge University Press, 2006.

Conze, Eckart. *Die große Illusion: Versailles 1919 und die Neuordnung der Welt*. Munich: Siedler, 2018.

Eichenberg, Julia, and John P. Newman. "Aftershocks: Violence in Dissolving Empires after the First World War." *Contemporary European History* 19, no. 3 (2010): 183–94.

Fink, Carole. *Defending the Rights of Others: The Great Powers, the Jews, and International Minority Protection, 1878–1938*. New York: Cambridge University Press, 2006.

Fisch, Jörg. *Das Selbstbestimmungsrecht der Völker. Die Domestizierung einer Illusion*. Munich: C. H. Beck, 2010.

Fischer, Conan, and Alan Sharp, eds. *After the Versailles Treaty: Enforcement, Compliance, Contested Identities.* London; New York: Routledge, 2008.

Gerwarth, Robert. *The Vanquished: Why the First World War Failed to End, 1917–1923.* London: Allen Lane, 2016.

Heinemann, Ulrich. *Die verdrängte Niederlage: Politische Öffentlichkeit und Kriegsschuldfrage in der Weimarer Republik.* Göttingen: Vandenhoeck & Ruprecht, 1983.

Horne, John, and Alan Kramer. *German Atrocities, 1914: A History of Denial.* New Haven: Yale University Press, 2001.

Howland, Douglas. *International Law and Japanese Sovereignty: The Emerging Global Order in the 19th Century.* New York: Palgrave Macmillan, 2016.

Judson, Pieter M. *The Habsburg Empire. A New History.* Cambridge, MA: Belknap Press of Harvard University Press, 2016.

Keynes, John Maynard. *The Economic Consequences of the Peace.* New York: Harper, 1920.

Krüger, Peter. *Deutschland und die Reparationen 1918/19: Die Genesis des Reparationsproblems in Deutschland zwischen Waffenstillstand und Versailler Friedensschluß.* Stuttgart: Deutsche Verlags-Anstalt, 1973.

Kuzmany, Börries. "Habsburg Austria: Experiments in Non-Territorial Autonomy." *Ethnopolitics* 15, no. 1 (2016): 43–65.

Leonhard, Jörn. *Der überforderte Frieden. Versailles und die Welt 1918-1923.* Munich: C.H. Beck, 2018.

Löhr, Isabella, and Roland Wenzlhuemer, eds. *The Nation State and Beyond: Governing Globalization Processes in the Nineteenth and Early Twentieth Centuries.* Berlin: Springer, 2013.

MacMillan, Margaret. *Peacemakers: The Paris Conference of 1919 and Its Attempt to End War.* London: Murray, 2001.

Maier, Charles S. *Recasting Bourgeois Europe: Stabilization in France, Germany, and Italy in the Decade after World War I.* Princeton, NJ: Princeton University Press, 1975.

Manela, Erez. *The Wilsonian Moment: Self-Determination and the International Origins of Anticolonial Nationalism.* Oxford: Oxford University Press, 2007.

Marks, Sally. "Mistakes and Myths: The Allies, Germany, and the Versailles Treaty, 1918–1921." *Journal of Modern History* 85, no. 3 (2013): 632–59.

Naimark, Norman M. *Fires of Hatred: Ethnic Cleansing in Twentieth-Century Europe.* Cambridge, MA: Harvard University Press, 2001.

Özsu, Umut. *Formalizing Displacement: International Law and Population Transfers.* Oxford: Oxford University Press, 2015.

*Papers Relating to the Foreign Relations of the United States: The Paris Peace Conference, 1919.* 13 vols. Washington, DC: US Government Printing Office, 1942–47.

Pedersen, Susan. *The Guardians: The League of Nations and the Crisis of Empire.* Oxford: Oxford University Press, 2015.

Prott, Volker. *The Politics of Self-Determination: Remaking Territories and National Identities in Europe, 1917–1923.* Oxford: Oxford University Press, 2016.

Roshwald, Aviel. *Ethnic Nationalism and the Fall of Empires: Central Europe, Russia, and the Middle East, 1914–1923.* London: Routledge, 2001.

Schuker, Stephen A. "J. M. Keynes and the Personal Politics of Reparations." *Diplomacy & Statecraft* 25, no. 3 (2014): 453–71; no. 4 (2014): 579–91.

Sharp, Alan. *The Versailles Settlement: Peacemaking after the First World War, 1919–1923.* Basingstoke, UK: Palgrave Macmillan, 2008.

Sluga, Glenda, and Patricia Clavin, eds. *Internationalisms: A Twentieth-Century History.* Cambridge: Cambridge University Press, 2016.

———. *Internationalism in the Age of Nationalism.* Pennsylvania Studies in Human Rights. Philadelphia: University of Pennsylvania Press, 2013.

Smith, Leonard V. *Sovereignty at the Paris Peace Conference of 1919.* Oxford: Oxford University Press, 2018.

———. "Empires at the Paris Peace Conference." In *Empires at War: 1911–1923*, edited by Robert Gerwarth and Erez Manela, 254–76. Oxford: Oxford University Press, 2014.

Soutou, Georges-Henri. *L'or et le sang: Les buts de guerre économiques de la Première Guerre mondiale.* Paris: Fayard, 1989.

Tooze, Adam. *The Deluge: The Great War and the Remaking of Global Order, 1916–1931.* London: Allen Lane, 2014.

Trachtenberg, Marc. "Versailles after Sixty Years." *Journal of Contemporary History* 17, no. 3 (1982): 487–506.

Weitz, Eric D. "From the Vienna to the Paris System. International Politics and the Entangled Histories of Human Rights, Forced Deportations, and Civilizing Missions." *American Historical Review* 113, no. 5 (2008): 1313–43.

Wilson, Henry. *Field-Marshall Sir Henry Wilson: His Life and Diaries.* 2 vols. Edited by Charles E. Callwell. London: Cassell, 1927.

MARCUS M. PAYK is Professor of Modern History at Helmut Schmidt University in Hamburg. He is author of *Frieden durch Recht? Der Aufstieg des modernen Völkerrechts und der Friedensschluss nach dem Ersten Weltkrieg.*

ROBERTA PERGHER is Associate Professor of History at Indiana University Bloomington. She is author of *Mussolini's Nation-Empire: Sovereignty and Settlement in Italy's Borderlands, 1922–1943.*

# 1   Plebiscites and Postwar Legitimacy

Brendan Karch

## Introduction

As the curtain fell on the First World War in November 1918, most of the Continent east of Paris lay in disarray. Millions of hungry Europeans lacked a functioning government. The redrawing of borders and reestablishment of order from Alsace to Anatolia would take five more years, cost many millions more lives, and require extensive diplomatic wrangling. While most borders were decided by military force or Allied dictate, local citizens in five disputed border regions were given an electoral choice over which state to join. Roughly two million Europeans participated in this new democratic experiment. In Upper Silesia and parts of East and West Prussia, Germany and Poland competed for votes. In Schleswig-Holstein, the Danes sought to take back lands ceded a half century earlier to Prussia. And on the ruins of the Habsburg Empire, votes were cast in Carinthia and Sopron to decide Austria's borders with its Yugoslav and Hungarian neighbors. These were the plebiscites—a series of voting exercises invoked by the Allied powers to decide national boundaries in contested borderlands.[1]

In the aftermath of the First World War, plebiscites became popularly discussed as one form, among many, of forging democratic legitimacy on the ruins of fallen empires. Far from the Paris negotiations, competing notions of legitimacy were being tried out on the ground for the first time. The epicenter of experimentation was central and eastern Europe. Citizens voted for constitutional conventions, assembled in mass protest, or embraced socialist or national revolutions. Much of this democratic energy was homegrown and preceded the caesura of 1918. Principles of self-determination were not simply a foreign import of Woodrow Wilson's imagination. The Habsburg, German, and British Empires—along with Bolshevists and Austro-Marxists—all proposed various forms of self-determination under federal or socialist principles.[2] The plebiscites were far from a comprehensive solution to the problems of European order. But as mechanisms for resolving specific borderland disputes in central Europe, they very much fit the spirit of the age.

This spirit of 1918, as I argue, was one of profound contradictions. These voting exercises brought democratic promise to the call for a landscape of nation-states in postwar Europe. Yet while the plebiscites were discussed as a continent-wide measure to settle national loyalties and boundaries, their use was limited by Allied realpolitik to just a few key zones, all involving Austrian or German borders. A desire to draw borders along clear ethnonational lines competed against many other factors: historical boundaries, secret treaties, military force, reward for war victors or punishment for its losers, anti-Bolshevist sentiment, colonial hubris, or avoidance of international embarrassment. The Allies were willing to resort to democratic practice in border drawing only in a small number of cases where the outcome was of marginal importance to the postwar order. Elite nationalist activists and statesmen generally defined the "self" in national self-determination as the collective body enumerated by "objective" ethnolinguistic statistics rather than a community bound by democratic wishes. This interpretation further blunted the will to call for plebiscites.

The most surprising contradiction, however, revealed itself when plebiscites were implemented: the greatest stumbling block to creating a democratic nation-state order was the will of voters. The more one analyzes the motivations, propaganda, voting behavior, and outcome of the plebiscites, the harder it becomes to support the logic that a well-ordered democratic continent was best divided along national lines. In this chapter special emphasis is placed on Upper Silesia, where the 1.19 million votes cast made it larger than the other four plebiscites combined.[3] Voters in Upper Silesia and other contested borderlands experienced the post-1918 period as one of material deprivation and loss of trust in government and fellow citizens. These new grievances were not always channeled into pre-scripted national boundaries. Plebiscite propaganda often invoked an instrumentalist attitude toward national belonging by emphasizing material and social benefits over ethnolinguistic ties. National identity—insofar as borderland residents even possessed such identities—emerged as only one consideration among many as plebiscite voters decided on their future state citizenships. As the plebiscites showed, the closer one approached the democratic practice of self-determination in central and eastern Europe, the less national self-determination appeared a coherent blueprint for order.

## Plebiscites in the Postwar Political Landscape

Amid the scramble to redraw borders after November 1918, national governments or international bodies discussed the use of plebiscites for a panoply of European regions, including Alsace, the Banat, Bessarabia, Burgenland, Dalmatia, Danzig, parts of East Prussia, Eupen and Malmedy, Fiume, Eastern Galicia, Klagenfurt, the Saar, Schleswig-Holstein, Smyrna, South Tirol, Teschen, western Thrace, Transylvania, and Upper Silesia. Nearly all were contested territories situated on the ruins of central and eastern Europe's four fallen empires. The plebiscite became one technique among many to establish the legitimacy of the nation-state in this political vacuum and was applied only to cases involving one of the defeated Central powers, Germany or Austria. To understand why, it is necessary to examine the range of diplomatic solutions invoked by Allied peacemakers as piecemeal solutions for a fractured continent.

The Allied powers alone commanded enough authority on the international stage to adjudicate matters of peace between any two competing countries' territorial claims. The principle of legitimacy for post-1918 Europe was most famously outlined by Wilson's Fourteen Points. Yet Wilson never uttered the term *national self-determination* in his speech and generally avoided using it.[4] The term is more directly traceable to David Lloyd George, who, in January 1918, declared "national self-determination" along with "no annexations" the core principles of any peace settlement.[5] While Wilson had long positioned himself as an anti-autocratic liberal internationalist, western European leaders were largely responding to central and eastern European calls for self-determination. In April 1917, democratic revolutionaries in Russia called for "the establishment of permanent peace on the basis of the self-determination of peoples."[6] A year prior, Lenin had articulated the right to self-determination as a tool for undermining capitalism by freeing subject peoples from their imperial chains.[7] During earlier war occupations, eastern front armies had dangled promises of autonomy in front of subject peoples. The Germans declared their intent to resurrect a new Poland in November 1916. Although seen by many Poles as a cheap ploy to recruit more of their people as cannon fodder, Germany backed up their plan with "nation-building" measures such as new Polish-speaking schools and local elections.[8] These wartime measures in turn were partly inspired by prewar nationalist politics in the Habsburg Empire, where Austro-Marxists, Czech nationalists, and others had theorized and enacted policies to promote sustainable national "bodies" on a multiethnic territory.[9] Wilson and Lloyd George followed the lead of these empire breakers and reformers in central and eastern Europe.

Until 1918, few nationalists, especially in Austria-Hungary, called for full nation-state sovereignty. Many Polish or Czech nationalists foresaw continued imperial domination and bet on the victory of the Habsburg state in the First World War. They often collaborated with authorities in the hopes of winning concessions or autonomy, rather than independence, after victory.[10] Only the collapse of major powers on all sides of the war—Russia as well as the Central powers and the Ottoman Empire—created the political vacuum that could be filled by a nation-state order. Even then, experts and politicians played a greater role in determining borders than did voters. Armed with prewar census statistics and ethnographic maps that conveniently bolstered their causes, leaders such as Edvard Beneš and Roman Dmowski convinced negotiators in Paris to draw state boundaries that advantaged Czech and Polish national claims. The vast majority of Europeans east of Berlin did not choose their new citizenships. Their most meaningful form of democratic engagement came, rather, in universal suffrage and the ability to shape constitutional conventions. Millions of "optants" voted with their feet to join their new national "homelands" or were forced to do so by ethnic cleansing. Those who stayed became minorities, promised the protection of an ultimately ineffective League of Nations minority system.[11] These provisions affected millions of Europeans who had no choice in the drawing of borders.

Plebiscites were only to be used in limited areas that were "objectively" contestable based on specific political or ethnographic criteria. The Allies' logic, as expressed to Germany in a June 1919 memorandum, proved deceptively simple: "Where the affinities of the population are undoubted, there is no necessity for a plebiscite; where they are in doubt, there is a plebiscite enjoined."[12] But this statement already revealed cracks in the theoretical foundation of the nation-state order. Affinities could be in doubt for two main reasons. First, many regions counted several languages and ethnicities among their populations. Very often local ethnic boundaries—insofar as they existed—followed urban-rural or class divides. In Upper Silesia, for example, cities were dominated by a German-speaking bourgeoisie, while urban workers and rural peasants mostly spoke a Polish-leaning dialect known as *schlonsak* (though most were at least minimally bilingual). Plebiscites meant to disentangle loyalties in these multilingual borderlands were destined by Allied logic to be majoritarian exercises, in which the numerically stronger ethnicity could dictate the region's fate to the minority. By acknowledging the necessity of such plebiscites, the Allied powers admitted the impossibility of drawing neat nation-state borders. Moreover, given the ethnolinguistic diversity of the Continent, nearly every border zone in central and eastern Europe, according to the Allies' standard of doubt, was potentially up for grabs.

A second, deeper unease further undermined the logic of the plebiscites: that people's "affinities" might not line up with their ethnicity or language use. This suspicion proved the raison d'être for the plebiscites in the first place. Allied peacemakers, led in this instance by Lloyd George, slowly came to realize that ethnic traits did not predetermine voting behavior and that census statistics alone were not sufficient for drawing borders. But it was a realization that was only selectively applied. The plebiscites in Marienwerder/East Prussia and in Upper Silesia were called because Germany defiantly insisted that Polish speakers, although a majority in both regions, preferred to remain in their German homeland rather than join the new Poland. In both plebiscites, German claims were proven right, as Germany garnered the majority of votes. Hundreds of thousands voted against their supposed ethnolinguistic belonging. If "affinities" could run so contradictory to ethnic self-identification in these disputed border regions, then one could easily foresee equally confounding results across the multiethnic landscape of eastern Europe. To preserve the neatness of the Wilsonian ideal in central Europe and to privilege the claims of allies, it was wise to limit the use of the plebiscite in order to keep the democratic genie in the ethnonational bottle.

Several other political imperatives also interceded to limit the use of a plebiscite. The Allied powers declared some regions simply too important nationally or strategically to leave to the whims of voters. In the Treaty of Versailles, the Allies awarded Belgium two bordering counties from western Germany: Eupen and Malmedy. Eupen was snatched away for its valuable forest and zinc resources despite being majority German speaking.[13] France, meanwhile, sought retribution against Germany by retaking Alsace-Lorraine, which had been lost in the

Franco-Prussian War of 1870–71. The French strenuously objected to German entreaties for a plebiscite in Alsace. They instead occupied the area by force and imposed harsh assimilatory measures to erase any German imprint, including purges, trials, and racial classification schemes.[14] With Italy, the Allies felt partially beholden to the secretive Treaty of London from 1915, which had promised Italy war spoils from the losing powers. The Italians gained South Tirol, along the Austrian border, but not the Yugoslav or Ottoman territories the Allies promised.

The Allies' military capacities and self-conceived moral authority also put limits on the use of plebiscites. Since the plebiscites required Allied troops to occupy the regions to ensure a fair vote, this precluded votes in ongoing war zones such as the eastern Polish borderlands, Russia, or the former Ottoman lands. Anti-Bolshevist sentiment also prevented the Allies from promoting any territorial settlements—democratic or otherwise—that would benefit the Soviets. In the former Ottoman Empire, old colonial modes of rule were modernized and turned into a "mandates" system that, despite lofty rhetoric of eventual liberation, avoided the practice of national self-determination.[15] Most of eastern Europe and Anatolia were thus precluded from plebiscite settlements on ideological or military grounds.

The Allied powers balked at most territorial concessions that would have benefited prostrate Germany or Austria. As early as October 1918, Austrian politicians called for national unification of German-speaking Austria with Germany.[16] Vienna's socialist-minded proposal for a Deutsch-Österreich included large German-speaking sections of Czechoslovakia. Yet no level of lobbying could convince the Allied powers to enhance the stature and power of the First World War's losers through mergers. Similarly, in the mountainous western Austrian province of Vorarlberg, separatists voted in May 1919 to join Switzerland. But Swiss and Allied resistance quashed any territorial cession.[17] Western powers, notably, felt less comfortable projecting their authority when the two conflicting sides in a territorial dispute were both friendly states in the postwar settlement. Poland and Czechoslovakia met in deadly clashes over three small regions along their new shared border (Cieszyn, Spiš, and Orava). As Isabelle Davion explores in chapter 2, the Allies agreed to call a plebiscite in September 1919, but it was never carried out due to continued violence.[18] The Allies proved unwilling to intervene with force in a conflict between two powers where each was deemed an ally, as in the case of Poland and Czechoslovakia, but had few qualms dictating settlement terms to Germany or Austria.

The limitation of plebiscites to German and Austrian border zones was thus born of postwar political imperatives that often overrode principled dedication to national self-determination. But the limitation also made sense in terms of the macro region's political development. The plebiscite zones shared two features: well-developed (if not always popular) nationalist movements and prior democratic practice. For citizens to be able to cast a vote for competing nation-states, nationalist movements and arguments of ethnonational belonging had to make sense to the local populations. Upper Silesians or East Prussians understood, at least rhetorically, the difference between being a German or Polish national, but peasants in much of Ukraine had no analogous national understanding of being a Ukrainian or a Russian.[19] The vocabulary of national belonging had permeated central European societies enough for a plebiscite vote to make sense. Likewise, central European plebiscite voters were accustomed to electoral practices from the prewar era. Universal male suffrage in national and imperial parliaments came to Germany in 1871 and Austria in 1907. Widespread female suffrage and new liberal constitutions made postwar central Europe, at least by certain metrics, more democratic than France or Britain. Central Europe was, in short, "developed" enough to serve as an experimental zone for new democratic nation-state politics. Farther to the east or south, a lack of electoral tradition or nationalist movements—combined with widespread violence—foreclosed the possibility of plebiscites. Farther to the west, strategic advantage and national pride made contested regions too important to hold to a vote. The plebiscites were thus fated to be a central European phenomenon.

## Calling Plebiscites

Most of the future plebiscite zones along German and Austrian borders emerged as politically contested territories only after the end of the First World War. During the war, territorial revisions in Germany's eastern districts of Upper Silesia or East Prussia were scarcely imaginable. With Germany occupying large stretches of eastern Europe from 1915 to 1918, the loss of core Prussian lands would have seemed implausible.[20] Meanwhile, the two future plebiscite zones in Austria were internal imperial "language frontiers" between German speakers and Slovenes or Hungarians.[21] The contestation of these lands made sense only in the wake of Habsburg collapse and partition. Nor did local citizens in future plebiscite zones rise up to seek their national independence during the First World War. Polish-speaking soldiers from both East Prussia and Upper Silesia were almost uniformly loyal to the Prussian army. Cases of disobedience or desertion proved exceedingly rare.[22] In Schleswig-Holstein, over thirty thousand Danish speakers served loyally for Germany in the war.[23]

Even after defeat and revolution, the new socialist German and Austrian states were surprised to learn the extent of the territorial losses proposed by the Allies. At the Paris Peace Conference, Polish politicians lobbied successfully for the cession of Posen, West Prussia, Danzig, Upper Silesia, and parts of East Prussia to Poland.[24] They were backed by Allied technical experts, who used 1910 Prussian language statistics to collapse the concept of national self-determination into a matter of "objectively" defined ethnicity.[25] In the draft peace treaty, a plebiscite was called only for the Allenstein district of East Prussia because the Polish speakers there were heavily Protestant. Many Germans saw this as a blatant violation of national self-determination. Protests erupted in Upper Silesia and other affected areas. Over 20,000 protestors took to the streets in Upper Silesia's district capital of Oppeln. A local Catholic newspaper announced, in a glaring headline, "Germany's Death Sentence—Wilson's Colossal Moral Defeat."[26] Vigorous German counter-lobbying earned the sympathetic ear of Lloyd George. In a heated debate, Lloyd George challenged Wilson's reliance on "ethnographical facts" as contrary to the true principle of self-determination, which the British leader insisted rested in the people's will, not in demographic expertise.[27] Wilson acceded to Lloyd George's logic, leading to the provision for an Upper Silesian plebiscite in the final Treaty of Versailles. Roughly 1.2 million Upper Silesians would vote on their border. Lloyd George also successfully pushed for over-turning Danzig's cession to Poland in favor of a "Free City" administered by the League of Nations, and for expanding the East Prussian plebiscite to include the Marienwerder district of West Prussia. These were the only major concessions granted to Germany.[28]

Meanwhile, neither of the two plebiscites involving Austria was motivated by an Austrian desire to reclaim lost territory. In Carinthia, a plebiscite was called in May 1919 primarily as a tool to overcome an intra-Allied stalemate after Yugoslav troops had occupied the Austrian region.[29] The Hungarian city and county of Sopron, meanwhile, were initially granted to Austria by the Treaties of St. Ger-main and Trianon, but Hungarian officials supplied insurgents that prevented the Austrian takeover, prompting a mediated settlement for a plebiscite in Oc-tober 1921.[30] Thus, while plebiscites were called largely as a method of resolving diplomatic impasses, they more commonly served to allay diplomatic tensions among Allied or defeated powers. Only Upper Silesia's plebiscite stood as a di-rect concession to Germany or Austria. Rather than farsighted applications of principles of self-determination, most plebiscites emerged as hasty compromises amid stalemates in postwar diplomacy and border drawing.

After the plebiscites were commissioned and before voting could take place, the Allied powers agreed to place troops in the contested plebiscite areas. These Inter-Allied Commissions (IACs), as they were known, were meant to secure the peace deemed necessary for fair voting. This itself marked a democratic ad-vance, as it recognized that a legitimate democratic outcome required elimi-nating levers of intimidation or voter suppression, such as police censorship or employers' threats. Yet the IACs did not always achieve order and in some cases exacerbated the disorder of the postwar years. In the process, they led many pleb-iscite zone voters to distance themselves from the national commitments that had produced conditions of violence.

Nowhere was the presence of Allied troops more damaging to peace than in Upper Silesia. Over the previous fifteen years, the largely Polish-speaking and bi-lingual population of Upper Silesia had been drawn suddenly and overwhelm-ingly to the Polish nationalist party. Upper Silesia thus had a recent history of national division—even if these divisions were most prominent in politics and did not structure everyday social life. By the end of the First World War, hun-ger, burdensome wage and labor controls, and ongoing class conflict sank Up-per Silesia—especially its eastern industrial stretches—into disorder. The social radicalization of 1917–19, as massive strikes and uprisings gripped the district, had the potential to split the region into violently divided Polish and German camps. Yet this social conflict was only partially defined in national terms. Pol-ish nationalist activists argued that the worker and peasant uprisings were a sign of the imminent collapse of German national authority. But in the eastern mining region, plagued by wildcat strikes, it was never entirely clear whether Polish nationalism or communism proved the greater motivator. Arkadiusz Bożek, a leading interwar Polish nationalist in the region, described himself as "a conglomerate of a socialist, a Spartacist, and a conservative" during the 1918 German Revolution.[31] His descriptions of resistors reveal a mix of languages and faiths. Class loyalties sometimes overlapped with national ones, especially in the coal-belt eastern stretches of Upper Silesia: Germans were the military majors and factory owners, Poles the workers and socialists.[32] But social conflict did not transform itself into a popular national uprising.

This was the volatile environment that the IAC occupation forces entered, only to worsen conditions by their presence. In February 1920, Germany ceded control of the Upper Silesian plebiscite zone to the IAC under the direction of French commissioner Henri LeRond, backed by roughly thirteen thousand troops, eleven thousand of them French.[33] The new troop presence precipitated a descent into conditions resembling civil war. The new, blatantly Polonophile French-led force overturned traditional structures of governance and policing in Upper Silesia but did not replace them with effective new ones.[34] Some regional unrest was directed against the occupying force. For example, the fatal shooting of a local bartender by a drunken French soldier in the district capital of Oppeln sparked a six-thousand-person street protest.[35] French troops fired shots to control the protestors and instituted a three-day evening curfew.[36] Far greater unrest was caused by the failure of IAC forces to ensure local security among Upper Silesians. Ahead of the May 3, 1920, anniversary of the 1791 Polish constitution, nationalists planned parades throughout the province. As news of the planned Polish march spread, a group of mostly working-class, pro-German citizens in Oppeln blockaded the main roads into town. A mass brawl erupted in which shots were fired and eight people seriously injured.[37] For the next year, Upper Silesia descended into chaos. IAC troops were generally isolated in garrisons or simply refused to enforce order, especially in favor of Germans.

Much of this bloodshed resulted directly from national strife over the plebiscite, with roving bands of Polish and German partisans terrorizing villages and hoping to scare locals into one national camp or another. A regional Polish uprising in August 1920, led by a mix of local Polish activists and insurgents from Poland, swept westward across more than half of Upper Silesia. During the uprising, scattered cells of Polish nationalist fighters threw hand grenades through the windows of their targets, stole official symbols of power, and issued death threats.[38] Nationalist violence was not limited to periods of major uprisings. Hundreds of incidents came to mark a new daily reality of violence in communities across the region. One historian has estimated an average of seven to eight deaths per day during the thirteen-month occupation leading up to the plebiscite—and this figure excludes deaths during the Polish uprising of August 1920.[39]

Yet at the local level, this violence was experienced largely as a breakdown of community. While neighbors became enemies, the lack of trust also pitted local communities against outsiders. A glut of weapons after the war and the

Upper Silesian IAC's inability to suppress violence cast a wider net of fear and distrust than could be captured by national antipathy. Riots against excessive police force, bombings of factories, and violent robberies marked the breakdown of social order.[40] Some communities set up local self-defense forces whose primary aim was protecting the local peace against outsiders regardless of nationality. Local officials often interpreted violent acts as nationally defined, but in some cases, the evidence pointed in other directions. One such scuffle took place in Ellguth-Turawa on July 20, 1920, when some men refused to pay the cover charge for a dance hall, were expelled, and then returned with guns ablaze.[41] Police insisted on defining it as Polish nationalist agitation, even though local eyewitnesses claimed otherwise.

Violence ruled the Upper Silesian plebiscite region in 1920–21 in a way it never had before. For locals, Upper Silesia's civil war tore apart communities more than the Great War. The nationalist battle between Germany and Poland over the region created the conditions in which near anarchy could thrive, but the everyday effects of that anarchy were not necessarily experienced or made sense of through nationalist divisions. In other plebiscite regions, violence was also framed at times in nonnational terms. The East Prussian plebiscite vote in July 1920 coincided with the Soviet advance on Warsaw during the Polish-Soviet War. Fears of Bolshevik conquest and violence loomed large for voters, regardless of national affinities.[42] In the two Austrian plebiscites, the zones were controlled partially by militaries or paramilitaries from opponent states (Hungary and Yugoslavia), with violent clashes leaving many injured or dead.[43] These occupations did not endear the supposed national liberators to local citizens. Food shortages, administrative dysfunction, and severed economic links prompted many to reject their occupiers. Violence created new divisions and animosities but did not necessarily reinforce national divides.

If local and regional violence muddied national dividing lines as much as it clarified them, then plebiscite propaganda demonstrated that governments acknowledged how weak national loyalties were in contested borders. In the months leading up to each plebiscite vote, borderland citizens were flooded with newspapers, magazines, satirical publications, placards, pamphlets, speeches, debates, and priestly sermons seeking their vote. Upper Silesia, as the most heavily contested region, also produced the greatest volume and widest range of propaganda. The battle for the loyalty of Upper Silesians could have easily hinged on racialist or integralist arguments over national identity: true Poles should vote for Poland and true Germans for Germany. Although negative stereotyping of the enemy was pervasive, there were relatively few positive appeals to national identity. Propaganda by German and Polish nationalists, with its focus on pragmatic, material concerns, revealed activists' belief that the nationally ambiguous Upper Silesians would be driven to their "national" choices through instrumentalist cultural or material calculations. Just as the content of propaganda aimed to reach Upper Silesians without clear national commitment, so too did the form: both Polish and German propaganda pieces often featured versions in both languages.

On the economic plane, Germany's war defeat and the onerous reparations dictated by the Versailles Treaty offered Poles a powerful line of attack in propaganda. The *Kocynder*, a Polish humor magazine in Upper Silesia, compared German and Polish debts through the imagery of weightlifting in one cartoon. While the German figure, decrepit and sweating under the weight of a giant barbell, holds out a cup asking for donations, a healthy Polish bodybuilder clutches a small weight with one hand, announcing: "These are my debts."[44] Another pro-Polish cartoon from 1919 shows a portly, supine German tied up with a hand pump attached to his stomach. The Allies pump gold from his belly (worth 725 billion marks), claiming that they will pump him empty.[45] The relentless focus on German debts was combined with Polish criticism of the tax burdens of the German welfare state.[46]

The pro-Polish camp also built on decades of social antagonism, especially related to land ownership, where in the eastern stretches of Upper Silesia a few noblemen controlled vast estates. Promises of land reform spread through the Polish press.[47] German propaganda countered with appeals to robust welfare-state benefits buttressed by new socialist promises for worker equality.[48] German propaganda also rode the reputation of a strong Reichsmark to stoke fears of poor purchasing power and future inflation for the Polish marka.[49] This fed into more general alarms about economic disparities between Germany and Poland. German propaganda warned of a flood of workers from across Poland migrating to a Polish Upper Silesia, bringing down wages.[50] This sort of comparative economics easily slid into long-held negative German stereotypes against allegedly incompetent and corrupt *polnische Wirtschaft* (Polish economics), as well as broad national biases against Poles as weak or unproductive.[51]

Economic arguments, while the most prominent, were far from the only appeals made in Upper Silesian propaganda. Military service (required in Poland but not in Germany) was used in German propaganda to address a war-weary populace. Appeals were made especially to women as the protectors of family integrity. One pro-German pamphlet showed a mother tearfully sending her child off to war with the caption: "Mothers consider: Poland has mandatory military service!"[52] During the Polish-Soviet War, German propaganda capitalized on fears of a Bolshevik takeover of Poland, warning (in the Polish language) that "if you are going to vote for Poland, you are giving your country not to Poland, but rather to Russia and Moscow."[53] The promise of order and prosperity was juxtaposed with the fear of disorder, violence, or foreign occupation.

Direct appeals were also made to Upper Silesians as a distinct regional group. For the German side in particular, the concept of *Heimat*, or homeland, worked as an established idiom through which to temper nationalist claims by appealing to the local. In this frame, Upper Silesia was allowed to have its unique Polish-German cultural characteristics yet still join the panoply of culturally and historically diverse regions that made up greater Germany. Hence the claim in one German pamphlet: "Upper Silesia is not Polish, but rather <u>Silesian</u> land."[54] Religion also became a key theme ahead of the plebiscite. German propagandists, fearing Upper Silesians would be enticed to join a Catholic-dominated

Poland, pinned their hopes on the new, more socially activist Catholic Party and on promises for regional autonomy.[55]

Most of the same instrumentalist arguments that Germany and Poland used in Upper Silesia were easily applied in other cases. In East Prussia, many of the Polish speakers were Protestants, which allowed Germany to use religion as a wedge to attract local citizens who felt no religious sympathy with Catholic Poland.[56] Along the contested Austrian-Hungarian border, it was easy for both sides to stoke fears among conservative peasants that their votes might result in domination by "Red Vienna" or communist Hungary.[57] Even when some camps in the plebiscites, such as the Danes or Yugoslavs, made common direct appeals to national belonging, the opposing sides highlighted historical links and the economic benefits of their social welfare states.[58]

As the weight of propaganda suggests, the need to sway undecided voters in these borderlands relied heavily on the muddling of national rhetoric or on filtering it through alternative cultural and material arguments. The propaganda also conveys that voters were largely being swayed to vote for state rather than national belonging. The logic of democratic choice in the plebiscite forced activists to reconfigure the language of national appeals. Before the plebiscite, nationalist activists had typically framed national belonging as an inherent trait, determined by ethnicity, to which one owed full loyalty. But during the plebiscite, the script was temporarily flipped. The language of national duties was replaced with that of privileges, sacrifices were tossed in favor of benefits, loyalty was less important than satisfaction and flourishing. Rather than harp on the burdens or responsibilities of national belonging, propaganda had to present the clear benefits of state membership, for the choice now rested with the people. The plebiscite inverted the agency that underlay discourses of ethnic nationalism. Now, instead of asking what you can do for the nation, the plebiscite forced the question: What can the state do for you? Answers to this question would come, ultimately, at the ballot box.

## The People's Voice

As plebiscite ballots were cast across central Europe, voters sometimes confirmed their supposed ethnic belonging at the polls but often did not. Turnout was almost universally high, ranging from around 84 percent in East Prussia to over 95 percent in Upper Silesia and Carinthia. Violence was also practically nonexistent, thanks to Allied diplomacy that insisted on delaying voting dates— sometimes for many months—until relative peace could be secured. The plebiscite in Schleswig-Holstein, which was split into two zones, accorded most closely to ethnonational statistics. The northern, heavily Danish-speaking zone turned out a 74 percent majority for Denmark, while the southern, German-dominated zone returned a 79 percent majority for Germany.[59] In Carinthia and East Prussia, however, Slavic-speaking voters cast ballots for their German-speaking historical rulers in large numbers. One Yugoslav activist on the Inter-Allied Commission blamed the results in Carinthia on Slovene national "wobblers" who had been psychologically crushed into a "subordinate condition" by their German "hereditary lords and superiors" and thus voted for the wrong side.[60] In the Allenstein district of East Prussia, the ethnonational "betrayal" was stark: the overall vote was 97.8 percent for Germany and just 2.2 percent for Poland despite 1910 language statistics showing almost half the population spoke Polish or the local Slavic Masurian dialect. In the county of Johannisburg, over 83 percent of schoolchildren spoke Polish or Masurian, but just 0.04 percent of adults voted for Poland.[61] Here the Protestant faith of many local Polish speakers was seen as responsible for driving widespread German patriotism and hostility to Catholic Poland.

Voting in Upper Silesia produced the most contestable outcome. The regional results showed almost precisely 60 percent support for remaining in Germany, and 40 percent for joining Poland. This massive voting exercise showed predictable geographic and social divisions at work. Voters in the heavily Polish-speaking southeastern rural counties of Pleß and Rybnik tallied the largest majorities, of 74 and 65 percent, respectively, for the Poles. Meanwhile, the city of Oppeln, dominated by civil servants and German-speaking artisan and working classes, tallied a 95 percent vote for Germany. Is it possible that, once at the ballot box, Upper Silesians simply voted according to ethnic identification?

The Upper Silesian plebiscite results reveal new layers of complexity at the geographic microlevel that challenge an ethnonational reading. This proved especially true for Upper Silesians in the rural county of Oppeln, who voted for Germany with a 70 percent majority. This represented an inversion compared to 1910 Prussian language statistics, which counted 78 percent of locals as Polish speaking or bilingual.[62] Zooming into the village level reveals stark variations that cannot be accounted for by ethnic difference. In Chmiellowitz, near Oppeln, 87 percent declared themselves Polish-speaking or bilingual in the 1910 census, yet only 16 percent voted for Poland in the plebiscite. However, just down the road in Folwark, a town that was counted 97 percent Polish-speaking or bilingual in the same census, the vote for Poland reached 67 percent.[63] Language statistics failed to correlate with the plebiscite vote. Local plebiscite results in Upper Silesia instead hinged largely on village-level national or social relations, such as the presence of a strong prosocialist working class (generally pro-German), or the leadership of rural nationalist activists (typically pro-Polish).

For all of the importance laid on the voting process and for all the bloodshed, the plebiscites did not always bind the Allied powers to specific outcomes. In some cases, particularly along the German-Polish border, the plebiscites remained "advisory" on the final border decision. Exact borders depended on whether the original plebiscite treaty had called for the entire region to be ceded to the majority winner or had given the Allied powers leeway to draw borders across internal county or communal lines. In Carinthia, the entire region was given to Austria because the treaty demanded an all-or-nothing transfer of territory. But in Allenstein, even though the overall vote was 97.8 percent in favor of Germany, a few small pro-Polish communes along the border were ceded to Poland.[64]

The Upper Silesian case, with its geographic checkerboard of Polish and German votes, left no clear mandate for ceding the entire region to one state or the other. Both German and Polish parties returned to lobbying and violence after the plebiscite to seek the most advantageous solution. Within Germany, national leaders still hoped for complete territorial control given the 20 percent margin of victory. Wojciech Korfanty, head of the regional Polish delegation, suggested a partition that would have ceded around 60 percent of the land and 70 percent of the people to Poland. The French backed a slightly less pro-Polish boundary that still included the entire eastern industrial area, while the Italian and British delegations countered with far more pro-German boundaries. Korfanty, fearing the British-Italian line, organized an uprising in the hope of forcing a solution on the ground. With the support of the Polish army, he launched a full-scale insurrection on May 3, 1921, Poland's national holiday.[65] The resulting mini-war, known as the Third Silesian Uprising, was by far the largest and bloodiest of the plebiscite era. It pitted around fifty thousand pro-Polish fighters against thirty-five thousand German loyalists, with rough estimates of nearly four thousand killed in the fighting.[66] On June 26, a ceasefire brought the battle to a close, but tensions remained enormously high. Many Upper Silesians experienced the Third Uprising as a horrifically distilled version of the violence they had witnessed in the year of disorder, 1920. Korfanty had failed to preempt the plebiscite results. Partition seemed inevitable to most of the parties involved; the politics now centered on where to draw the line.

To solve the impasse among the Allies over Upper Silesia's border, the League of Nations tasked the Committee of Four, created from countries deemed neutral—Belgium, China, Spain, and Brazil—to resolve the dispute. The committee recommended a partition line that split the eastern industrial zone but gave Poland a distinct majority of Upper Silesia's mineral riches and factories, including 90 percent of its coal deposits.[67] Germany received 71 percent of the land and 53 percent of the population. German protests that the partition line would economically traumatize Germany did not reverse the result.

## Plebiscite Legacies

The partitions and territorial cessions, far from resolving competing national claims, allowed them to fester and infect interwar regional politics. Upper Silesia proved the deepest wound for all sides. As the League of Nations' October 1921 report noted, the "mixture of racial elements" made it impossible to draw a neat ethnonational border. Forty-four percent of Upper Silesians in the Polish partition, and 23 percent in the German partition, had voted for the other state.[68] Historians have estimated that around 150,000 Upper Silesians moved across the new border to Germany and 60,000 to 70,000 moved to Poland, though chaotic conditions make the figures inexact.[69] Many who remained simply valued their communities, homelands, families, property, and relationships more than their national belonging. Yet they would often be treated as unwelcome fifth columns by suspicious governments in the decades that followed.

The politics of the interwar period throughout central Europe would be defined largely by two unresolved inevitabilities of the plebiscites: the presence of minorities and a mutual desire for border revision. The plebiscites thus failed, at the most fundamental level, to achieve their aim of resolving national questions in borderlands. In the case of Upper Silesia, a majority of local citizens developed an ever-increasing instrumental attitude toward national belonging as the battles over their region intensified in the 1930s and 1940s. Wary of the dangers of belonging to the "wrong" nationality, they hedged their bets against regime change by crafting an ambiguous identity that allowed them to pass as loyal Germans or Poles. Meanwhile, each state radicalized its claims of revision. Germany and Poland both downplayed the democratic legitimacy of the plebiscite and played up the heroism of its uprisings (in Poland) or self-defense forces (in Germany).[70] The implication was that future revision required force, not ballots. The democratic promise of national self-determination in Upper Silesia yielded not two happy nations divided peacefully but rather two antagonistic nations, with an instrumentally minded regional group caught in the crossfire. With the cataclysm of the Second World War, the German-Polish plebiscites in Upper Silesia and East Prussia would be overturned amid Nazi racial violence and the subsequent expulsion of Germans.[71]

Based on the German-Polish cases alone, the plebiscites can be seen as producing partial solutions. Rather than resolving national tensions, the plebiscite outcomes legitimated the logic of ethnic nationalism and provoked "full solutions" of territorial conquest, expulsion, and murder. On the other hand, the territorial settlements of three other plebiscites—in Schleswig-Holstein, Sopron, and Carinthia—were maintained in the post–1945 period. When Yugoslavia demanded parts of Carinthia in 1945–47, the western Allies rejected the claim by arguing that the issue had been settled democratically after the First World War.[72] The enduring legitimacy created by fair democratic voting was used here as a shield against territorial revision.

A quieter legacy of the plebiscites was to raise general standards for fair voting by guaranteeing conditions of peace under international guidance and control. In nearly every plebiscite treaty, elaborate Allied clauses sought to eliminate the most predictable forms of coercion ahead of the vote. Police and military power was vested in international commissions that controlled justice, expulsions, voter registration, and election monitoring. Secret ballots, far from standard in 1918, were ensured in every plebiscite. In Schleswig-Holstein a 10,000 mark fine was instituted for any attempt to tamper with ballots, violate secrecy, or cast multiple votes.[73] Some of the most elaborate rules were designed to control propaganda or political meetings, which in many zones required police surveillance or twenty-four-hour notice. The Sopron plebiscite even technically banned all voter propaganda, although this proved unenforceable.[74] After voting occurred, unsatisfied voters were promised the right to move across the border if they chose, with full compensation for their property. These provisions largely worked. Complaints of unfair election practices proved unsubstantiated or else minute in scale. Not only did these provisions raise expectations for fair voting, but the international nature of democratic oversight also arguably provided a precedent for the common practice of internationally monitored or supervised elections.[75]

A darker legacy of the plebiscite also emerged in the interwar period—the use of referenda, above all in Nazi Germany, to legitimate undemocratic governments and their actions. In most cases, Nazi plebiscites were called as spectacles to rally public support for a fait accompli. Major votes were commissioned in 1934, to approve Hitler naming himself Führer after President Paul von Hindenburg's death; in 1936, to approve the reoccupation of the Rhineland; and in 1938, to approve the Anschluss with Austria. Nazi voters were marched to polls to cast their votes publicly, ballot boxes were stuffed, and dissenters punished with physical violence or imprisonment.[76] The Nazi plebiscites, with their implausible supermajorities, made a mockery of democratic accountability. Yet they also served as key moments of regime consolidation, as symbolic gestures of popular will that clearly mattered to the regime's leaders. The Nazi plebiscites perverted democratic norms that had been entrenched in post-1918 Europe but also used these norms to build up ritual public solidarity and legitimacy.

The Nazi regime also had the opportunity to participate in one of the last unresolved clauses of the Versailles Treaty—the plebiscite in the Saarland. France had originally wished to seize the mineral-rich German-speaking territory in 1919, but Wilson opposed a permanent seizure on national grounds. The resulting compromise led to French seizure of mines, rule by the League of Nations, and a fifteen-year delayed plebiscite.[77] No one in 1919 could predict the conditions in Germany in January 1935, when the vote was held. To ensure return to Germany, the Nazis funneled support to the Saar Deutsche Front, which established a semi-official parallel government under Nazi guidance. The Deutsche Front used tactics of voter intimidation and threats to pressure voters. To counter the Deutsche Front, a last-minute international force led by English and Italian troops was brought in, but these forces did little to affect the lopsided outcome. Over 477,000 voted for union with Germany compared with just 47,000 for League of Nations rule and 2,200 for union with France.[78] The Saar plebiscite reminded the embattled league that fair voting depended both on the strength of its own moral authority and on the commitment of interested governments on all sides to uphold democratic norms. These conditions, which had at least partially prevailed after World War I, proved lacking in 1935.

If the post-1918 plebiscites hardly bear mentioning in traditional narratives of Europe's twentieth century, it is largely by design. Paris peacemakers saw only limited use for applying what was arguably the most democratic means of drawing borders and deciding sovereignty on the ruins of empires. Self-determination after 1918 more commonly involved the privilege of war victors or elite lobbyists drawing inevitably imperfect ethnonational boundaries. The practice of democratic voting only further confounded this already impossible task of making nation-states, as voters often prioritized economic, religious, historical, regional, or personal ties over national belonging. Nationalist activists who had been convinced of the primacy of national loyalties had their ideologies cast into doubt by voters. Plebiscite propaganda often skirted the rhetoric of national duty in favor of appeals to safety or welfare-state benefits. The plebiscites disrupted the order envisioned both by Allied peacemakers and by most competing states, who were forced to seek votes on largely nonnational grounds.

The legacies of most of these plebiscites were buried amid the more violent remaking of central European borders between 1917 and 1945. But plebiscites have recently returned to the forefront of European politics, especially in the United Kingdom, where the referendum over Scottish independence failed in 2014 and Brexit narrowly succeeded in 2016. As after the First World War, votes often hinged on perceived economic benefits or drawbacks, and propaganda also dished out crude stereotypes. The surprise success of Brexit has even left some questioning the wisdom of democratic referenda on weighty decisions of sovereignty. National self-determination has returned as a rallying principle for opponents of a Brussels-led Europe—and just as a century ago, plebiscites remain only one means among many of contesting and resolving the sovereignty of government.

## Notes

1. Plebiscites have a long history dating back to Roman consultations of plebeians. In modern times, they are generally defined as a type of referendum meant to answer fundamental questions of governance, above all the issue of sovereignty. The first major modern use of plebiscites came during the French Revolution. Newly conquered French territories such as Papal Avignon would conduct votes, typically to affirm or reject their new rulers. Napoleon subsequently used plebiscites to enhance his authority by urging the people to confirm his major decisions. Some US southern states used plebiscites to secede during the Civil War. Several other isolated uses of plebiscites emerged before the First World War, most notably for Norwegian independence from Sweden. On definitions, see Johannes Mattern, *The Employment of the Plebiscite in the Determination of Sovereignty* (Baltimore: Johns Hopkins Press, 1920), 12–13. On French uses, see Lawrence T. Farley, *Plebiscites and Sovereignty: The Crisis of Political Illegitimacy* (Boulder, CO: Westview Press, 1986), 30–31; Jean A. Laponce, "National Self-Determination and Referendums: The Case for Territorial Revisionism," *Nationalism and Ethnic Politics* 7, no. 2 (2001): 38; Malcolm Crook, "The Uses of Democracy: Elections and Plebiscites in Napoleonic France," in *The French Experience from Republic to Monarchy, 1792–1824: New Dawns in Politics, Knowledge and Culture*, ed. Máire F. Cross (Basingstoke, UK: Palgrave, 2000), 58–71. Farley also covers the US Civil War, and Laponce discusses other cases in the nineteenth century.

2. For a historical discussion of self-determination from its original German Enlightenment context through the mid-twentieth century, see Eric D. Weitz, "Self-Determination: How a German Enlightenment Idea Became the Slogan of National Liberation and a Human Right," *American Historical Review* 120, no. 2 (April 1, 2015): 462–96.

3. There were roughly 476,000 votes in Allenstein-Marienwerder, 166,000 in Schleswig-Holstein, 38,000 in Carinthia, and 24,000 in Sopron. All figures are taken from

Sarah Wambaugh, *Plebiscites Since the World War: With a Collection of Official Documents,* vol. 1 (Washington: Carnegie Endowment for International Peace, 1933).

4. For an argument on the "myth" of Wilson's full embrace of national self-determination, see Trygve Throntveit, "The Fable of the Fourteen Points: Woodrow Wilson and National Self-Determination," *Diplomatic History* 35, no. 3 (June 1, 2011): 445–81.

5. Volker Prott, *The Politics of Self-Determination: Remaking Territories and National Identities in Europe, 1917–1923* (New York: Oxford University Press, 2016), 22.

6. Statement is taken from April 1917 war aims proclaimed by the Russian provisional government. Quoted in Erez Manela, *The Wilsonian Moment: Self-Determination and the International Origins of Anticolonial Nationalism* (New York: Oxford University Press, 2007), 37.

7. Ibid.

8. Jesse Kauffman, *Elusive Alliance: The German Occupation of Poland in World War I* (Cambridge, MA: Harvard University Press, 2015).

9. Karl Renner and Otto Bauer, two prominent Austro-Marxist theorists, advocated broad cultural autonomy within a class-based multiethnic revolutionary society. See Karl Renner, *Staat und Nation* (Vienna: J. Dietel, 1899); Otto Bauer, *Die Nationalitätenfrage und die Sozialdemokratie* (Vienna: I. Brand, 1907). On prewar efforts of Czech nationalists to reify Czech solidarities through schooling restrictions and electoral communalism, see Tara Zahra, *Kidnapped Souls: National Indifference and the Battle for Children in the Bohemian Lands* (Ithaca, NY: Cornell University Press, 2008), ch. 1.

10. For the contrasting political alliances of Poland's two main political figures in the First World War, Józef Piłsudski and Roman Dmowski, see Piotr S. Wandycz, *The Lands of Partitioned Poland, 1795–1918* (Seattle: University of Washington Press, 1974), ch. 16. On Adam Napieralski's conciliatory stance toward Germany in Upper Silesia, see James E. Bjork, "A Polish Mitteleuropa? Upper Silesia's Conciliationists and the Prospect of German Victory," *Nationalities Papers* 29, no. 3 (September 2001): 477–92. For the role of elite lobbying by Czech leaders during the First World War with the Entente powers, see Andrea Orzoff, *Battle for the Castle: The Myth of Czechoslovakia in Europe, 1914–1948* (New York: Oxford University Press, 2009), ch. 1.

11. Mark Mazower, "Minorities and the League of Nations in Interwar Europe," *Daedalus* 126, no. 2 (Spring 1997): 47–63.

12. Wambaugh, *Plebiscites Since the World War,* 1:108.

13. Vague concessions for "consulting the population" never led to a plebiscite, but instead a complaint process where local residents could contest the fait accompli (Wambaugh, 1:518–38).

14. Elizabeth Vlossak, *Marianne or Germania? Nationalizing Women in Alsace, 1870–1946* (Oxford: Oxford University Press, 2010), 210–15; Christopher J. Fischer, *Alsace to the Alsatians? Visions and Divisions of Alsatian Regionalism, 1870–1939* (New York: Berghahn Books, 2010), 132–33.

15. On the mandates system, see Susan Pedersen, *The Guardians: The League of Nations and the Crisis of Empire* (Oxford: Oxford University Press, 2015).

16. Otto Bauer, *Die österreichische Revolution* (Vienna: Wiener Volksbuchhandlung, 1923), 75–76; Marsha L. Rozenblit, *Reconstructing a National Identity: The Jews of Habsburg Austria during World War I* (Oxford: Oxford University Press, 2001), 132.

17. Wambaugh, *Plebiscites Since the World War,* 1:25–26.

18. In July 1920, Poland and Czechoslovakia agreed to submit themselves to the decision of the Allied Supreme Council, which decided heavily in the Czechs' favor. Neither

side was satisfied, however, and the area became a point of conflict between the two states throughout the entire interwar period (Wambaugh, 1:159–60).

19. Allied peacemakers ran into serious trouble applying self-determination to the drawing of Romanian borders, for example, since self-conscious "nations" hardly existed there. See Prott, *Politics of Self-Determination*, 119–31.

20. The two primary German zones produced substantially different occupation cultures. On the Ober-Ost, see Vejas Liulevicius, *War Land on the Eastern Front: Culture, National Identity and German Occupation in World War I* (Cambridge: Cambridge University Press, 2000). On the General Government, see Kauffman, *Elusive Alliance*.

21. On the ideological construction of bilingual and mixed-language spaces as "language frontiers," see Pieter M. Judson, *Guardians of the Nation: Activists on the Language Frontiers of Imperial Austria* (Cambridge, MA: Harvard University Press, 2006).

22. Polish-speaking soldiers from the Posen region provoked greater concern among Prussian officers. On the role of Polish soldiers fighting for Germany in the First World War, see Alexander Watson, "Fighting for Another Fatherland: The Polish Minority in the German Army, 1914–1918," *English Historical Review* 126, no. 522 (October 1, 2011): 1137–66; Ryszard Kaczmarek, *Polacy w armii kajzera na frontach pierwszej wojny światowej* (Krakow: Wydawnictwo Literackie, 2014).

23. Nina Jebsen and Martin Klatt, "The Negotiation of National and Regional Identity during the Schleswig-Plebiscite Following the First World War," *First World War Studies* 5, no. 2 (2014): 184.

24. Wambaugh, *Plebiscites Since the World War*, 1:103–5.

25. Prott, *Politics of Self-Determination*, ch. 1, 145.

26. *Oppelner Nachrichten*, May 10, 1919.

27. Prott, *Politics of Self-Determination*, 138–39.

28. Guido Hitze, *Carl Ulitzka (1873–1953), oder, Oberschlesien zwischen den Weltkriegen* (Düsseldorf: Droste, 2002), 212. The British feared that the loss of Upper Silesia's coal and mineral riches would disastrously weaken Germany's overall industrial capacity.

29. Webmag, *Plebiscites Since the World War*, 1:171–77.

30. John C. Swanson, "The Sopron Plebiscite of 1921: A Success Story," *East European Quarterly* 34, no. 1 (March 22, 2000): 82–83; Wambaugh, *Plebiscites Since the World War*, 1:276–80.

31. This statement is from Bożek's 1957 memoirs. Quoted in James E. Bjork, *Neither German nor Pole: Catholicism and National Indifference in a Central European Borderland* (Ann Arbor: University of Michigan Press, 2008), 195.

32. Rudolf Vogel, "Deutsche Presse und Propaganda des Abstimmungskampfes in Oberschlesien" (PhD diss., Universität Leipzig, 1931), 61.

33. Waldemar Grosch, *Deutsche und polnische Propaganda während der Volksabstimmung in Oberschlesien, 1919–1921* (Dortmund: Forschungsstelle Ostmitteleuropa, 2002), 28. Of these troops, only around four hundred were stationed in Oppeln and its surrounding county, with much larger forces stationed in the industrial area. See Prussian Interior Ministry report of March 1920, Geheimes Staatsarchiv preußischer Kulturbesitz [GStA PK], I. HA, Rep. 77, Tit. 856, Nr. 380.

34. The IAC could not, however, reasonably remake the entire bureaucracy overnight, and as such the German legal system, currency, and much of the police apparatus remained temporarily in place under direction of the IAC. See Hitze, *Carl Ulitzka*, 261.

35. The French soldier was eventually sentenced to ten years of forced labor and expelled from the military. See report of Hatzfeld to Prussian Interior Ministry, May 9, 1920,

in Kazimierz Popiołek, *Źródła do dziejów powstań śląskich* (Wrocław: Zakład Narodowy im. Ossolińskich, 1963), 169.

36. *Oppelner Nachrichten*, April 15 and 16, 1920.

37. Police reports of May 2 and 3, 1920, Archiwum Państwowe w Opolu [APO], Rejencja Opolska Biuro Prezydialne [ROBP], Syg. 299.

38. Report of Oppeln Landrat, September 10, 1920, APO, Starostwo Powiatowe w Opolu [SPO], Syg. 93. Rumors of French deliveries to Polish forces can be found in government reports throughout the same file, and also in APO, ROBP, Syg. 93.

39. Sigmund Karski, *Albert (Wojciech) Korfanty: Eine Biographie* (Dülmen: Laumann-Verlag, 1990), 308.

40. *Oppelner Nachrichten*, July 3, 1920; police report on incident of July 3, 1920, APO, ROBP, Syg. 302; *Oppelner Nachrichten*, July 2, 1920; police report on June 8, 1920 shooting, APO, ROBP, Syg. 301.

41. Police reports of July 21 and 22, 1920, APO, SPO, Syg. 93.

42. Richard Blanke, *Polish-Speaking Germans? Language and National Identity among the Masurians Since 1871* (Cologne: Böhlau, 2001), 181.

43. Wambaugh, *Plebiscites Since the World War*, 1:177.

44. Poster reprinted in Karski, *Albert (Wojciech) Korfanty*, 240.

45. Poster reprinted in Grosch, *Deutsche und polnische Propaganda*, 318.

46. Poster reprinted in Karski, *Albert (Wojciech) Korfanty*, 238.

47. Grosch, *Deutsche und polnische Propaganda*, 311–12.

48. Cartoon reprinted in Karski, *Albert (Wojciech) Korfanty*, 272.

49. Grosch, *Deutsche und polnische Propaganda*, 331.

50. Ibid., 346.

51. Poster reprinted in Grosch, *Deutsche und polnische Propaganda*, 302.

52. Reprinted in Grosch, *Deutsche und polnische Propaganda*, 213.

53. Grosch, *Deutsche und polnische Propaganda*, 216.

54. Ibid., 182. Emphasis in original.

55. See Bjork, *Neither German nor Pole*, ch. 5.

56. Blanke, *Polish-Speaking Germans?*, 147.

57. Wambaugh, *Plebiscites Since the World War*, 1:286–87.

58. On propaganda in Schleswig-Holstein, see Jebsen and Klatt, "Negotiation of National and Regional Identity." On Carinthia, see Wambaugh, *Plebiscites Since the World War*, 1:182–84.

59. Jebsen and Klatt, "Negotiation of National and Regional Identity," 185–86.

60. Wambaugh, *Plebiscites Since the World War*, 1:198–200. Quote from p. 203.

61. Blanke, *Polish-Speaking Germans?*, 187; Wambaugh, *Plebiscites Since the World War*, 1:134.

62. Local census results in APO, Rejencja Opolska [RO] I, Syg. 2096.

63. Results of the plebiscite at the county level can be found in APO, SPO, Syg. 134.

64. Blanke, *Polish-Speaking Germans?*, 191.

65. Wambaugh, *Plebiscites Since the World War*, 1:253–54.

66. Marek Czapliński et al., *Historia Śląska* (Wrocław: Wydawnistwo Uniwersytetu Wrocławskiego, 2002), 363–64.

67. Wambaugh, *Plebiscites Since the World War*, 1:257–60.

68. Figures from Czapliński et al., *Historia Śląska*, 365; Wambaugh, *Plebiscites Since the World War*, 1:267n2.

69. Various figures and estimates can be found in Danuta Berlińska, *Mniejszość niemiecka na Śląsku Opolskim w poszukiwaniu tożsamości* (Opole: Stowarzyszenie Instytut Śląski, 1999), 94–96.

70. For an examination of revanchist tactics and arguments, see Peter Polak-Springer, *Recovered Territory: A German-Polish Conflict over Land and Culture, 1919–89* (New York: Berghahn Books, 2015).

71. Amid the vast literature on German expulsions and border drawing, a valuable brief synopsis can be found in Norman M. Naimark, *Fires of Hatred: Ethnic Cleansing in Twentieth-Century Europe* (Cambridge, MA: Harvard University Press, 2001), ch. 4.

72. Robert Knight, "Ethnicity and Identity in the Cold War: The Carinthian Border Dispute, 1945–1949," *International History Review* 22, no. 2 (2000): 274–303.

73. Wambaugh, *Plebiscites Since the World War*, 2: doc. 5.

74. Ibid., 1:285–86.

75. Farley, *Plebiscites and Sovereignty*, 42.

76. Richard J. Evans, *The Third Reich in Power, 1933–1939* (New York: Penguin, 2005), 110–11, 637.

77. Wambaugh, *Plebiscites Since the World War*, 1:18.

78. C. J. Hill, "Great Britain and the Saar Plebiscite of 13 January 1935," *Journal of Contemporary History* 9, no. 2 (1974): 141.

# Bibliography

Bauer, Otto. *Die Nationalitätenfrage und die Sozialdemokratie*. Vienna: I. Brand, 1907.

———. *Die österreichische Revolution*. Vienna: Wiener Volksbuchhandlung, 1923.

Berlińska, Danuta. *Mniejszość niemiecka na Śląsku Opolskim w poszukiwaniu tożsamości*. Opole: Stowarzyszenie Instytut Śląski, 1999.

Bjork, James E. *Neither German nor Pole: Catholicism and National Indifference in a Central European Borderland*. Ann Arbor: University of Michigan Press, 2008.

———. "A Polish Mitteleuropa? Upper Silesia's Conciliationists and the Prospect of German Victory." *Nationalities Papers* 29, no. 3 (September 2001): 477–92.

Blanke, Richard. *Polish-Speaking Germans? Language and National Identity among the Masurians since 1871*. Cologne: Böhlau, 2001.

Crook, Malcolm. "The Uses of Democracy: Elections and Plebiscites in Napoleonic France." In *The French Experience from Republic to Monarchy, 1792–1824: New Dawns in Politics, Knowledge and Culture*, edited by Máire F. Cross, 58–71. Basingstoke, UK: Palgrave, 2000.

Czapliński, Marek, Elżbieta Kaszuba, Gabriela Wąs, and Rościsław Żerelik. *Historia Śląska*. Wrocław: Wydawnistwo Uniwersytetu Wrocławskiego, 2002.

Evans, Richard J. *The Third Reich in Power, 1933–1939*. New York: Penguin, 2005.

Farley, Lawrence T. *Plebiscites and Sovereignty: The Crisis of Political Illegitimacy*. Boulder, CO: Westview Press, 1986.

Fischer, Christopher J. *Alsace to the Alsatians? Visions and Divisions of Alsatian Regionalism, 1870–1939*. New York: Berghahn Books, 2010.

Grosch, Waldemar. *Deutsche und polnische Propaganda während der Volksabstimmung in Oberschlesien, 1919–1921*. Dortmund: Forschungsstelle Ostmitteleuropa, 2002.

Hill, C. J. "Great Britain and the Saar Plebiscite of 13 January 1935." *Journal of Contemporary History* 9, no. 2 (1974): 121–42.

Hitze, Guido. *Carl Ulitzka (1873–1953), oder, Oberschlesien zwischen den Weltkriegen.* Düsseldorf: Droste, 2002.

Jebsen, Nina, and Martin Klatt. "The Negotiation of National and Regional Identity during the Schleswig-Plebiscite Following the First World War." *First World War Studies* 5, no. 2 (2014): 181–211.

Judson, Pieter M. *Guardians of the Nation: Activists on the Language Frontiers of Imperial Austria.* Cambridge, MA: Harvard University Press, 2006.

Kaczmarek, Ryszard. *Polacy w armii kajzera na frontach pierwszej wojny światowej.* Krakow: Wydawnictwo Literackie, 2014.

Karski, Sigmund. *Albert (Wojciech) Korfanty: Eine Biographie.* Dülmen: Laumann-Verlag, 1990.

Kauffman, Jesse. *Elusive Alliance: The German Occupation of Poland in World War I.* Cambridge, MA: Harvard University Press, 2015.

Knight, Robert. "Ethnicity and Identity in the Cold War: The Carinthian Border Dispute, 1945–1949." *International History Review* 22, no. 2 (2000): 274–303.

Laponce, Jean A. "National Self-Determination and Referendums: The Case for Territorial Revisionism." *Nationalism and Ethnic Politics* 7, no. 2 (2001): 33–56.

Liulevicius, Vejas. *War Land on the Eastern Front: Culture, National Identity and German Occupation in World War I.* Cambridge, UK: Cambridge University Press, 2000.

Manela, Erez. *The Wilsonian Moment: Self-Determination and the International Origins of Anticolonial Nationalism.* New York: Oxford University Press, 2007.

Mattern, Johannes. *The Employment of the Plebiscite in the Determination of Sovereignty.* Baltimore: Johns Hopkins Press, 1920.

Mazower, Mark. "Minorities and the League of Nations in Interwar Europe." *Daedalus* 126, no. 2 (Spring 1997): 47–63.

Naimark, Norman M. *Fires of Hatred: Ethnic Cleansing in Twentieth-Century Europe.* Cambridge, MA: Harvard University Press, 2001.

Orzoff, Andrea. *Battle for the Castle: The Myth of Czechoslovakia in Europe, 1914–1948.* New York: Oxford University Press, 2009.

Pedersen, Susan. *The Guardians: The League of Nations and the Crisis of Empire.* Oxford: Oxford University Press, 2015.

Polak-Springer, Peter. *Recovered Territory: A German-Polish Conflict over Land and Culture, 1919–89.* New York: Berghahn Books, 2015.

Popiołek, Kazimierz. *Źródła do dziejów powstań śląskich.* Wrocław: Zakład Narodowy im. Ossolińskich, 1963.

Prott, Volker. *The Politics of Self-Determination: Remaking Territories and National Identities in Europe, 1917–1923.* New York: Oxford University Press, 2016.

Renner, Karl. *Staat und Nation.* Vienna: Josef Dietl, 1899.

Rozenblit, Marsha L. *Reconstructing a National Identity: The Jews of Habsburg Austria during World War I.* Oxford: Oxford University Press, 2001.

Swanson, John C. "The Sopron Plebiscite of 1921: A Success Story." *East European Quarterly* 34, no. 1 (March 22, 2000): 81–94.

Throntveit, Trygve. "The Fable of the Fourteen Points: Woodrow Wilson and National Self-Determination." *Diplomatic History* 35, no. 3 (June 1, 2011): 445–81.

Vlossak, Elizabeth. *Marianne or Germania? Nationalizing Women in Alsace, 1870–1946.* Oxford: Oxford University Press, 2010.

Vogel, Rudolf. *Deutsche Presse und Propaganda des Abstimmungskampfes in Oberschlesien.* PhD diss., Universität Leipzig, 1931.

Wambaugh, Sarah. *Plebiscites since the World War: With a Collection of Official Documents.* 2 vols. Washington, DC: Carnegie Endowment for International Peace, 1933.

Wandycz, Piotr S. *The Lands of Partitioned Poland, 1795–1918.* Seattle: University of Washington Press, 1974.

Watson, Alexander. "Fighting for Another Fatherland: The Polish Minority in the German Army, 1914–1918." *English Historical Review* 126, no. 522 (October 1, 2011): 1137–66.

Weitz, Eric D. "Self-Determination: How a German Enlightenment Idea Became the Slogan of National Liberation and a Human Right." *American Historical Review* 120, no. 2 (April 1, 2015): 462–96.

Zahra, Tara. *Kidnapped Souls: National Indifference and the Battle for Children in the Bohemian Lands, 1900—1948.* Ithaca, NY: Cornell University Press, 2008.

BRENDAN KARCH is Assistant Professor of History at Louisiana State University. He is author of *Nation and Loyalty in a German-Polish Borderland: Upper Silesia, 1848-1960.*

# 2   Teschen and Its Impossible Plebiscite

## *Can the Genie Be Put Back in the Bottle?*

Isabelle Davion

In the aftermath of the Great War, the two newly established nations of Czechoslovakia and Poland disputed the border between them. This particular conflict, which was part of the broader reordering of nations, polities, and peoples in central and eastern Europe, had international repercussions. The most serious clash broke out over the former Austrian duchy of Teschen, a territory of approximately 880 square miles. The dispute carried particular significance for France, which sought to establish new alliances in eastern Europe after the war.[1] Czechoslovakia and Poland had already settled on a provisional demarcation line in November 1918, but the agreement was built on the unspoken assumption on both sides that their claim to Teschen would find France's full support. Both claimants had good reasons for this expectation. The experts in the Quai d'Orsay had already endorsed Poland's "historical boundaries," whereas Stephen Pichon, the French minister of foreign affairs, had officially supported the "historical boundaries" of Bohemia.[2] The Teschen region had been highly contested for centuries. A 1910 Vienna census recording the *Umgangssprache* (language of daily use) showed a highly mixed population: 55 percent of the 426,667 inhabitants were Poles, 27 percent Czechs, 18 percent Germans, and the rest mostly Slonzaks, a Silesian population group speaking a variety of West Slavonic.[3]

Divided by a demarcation line and occupied by the Polish and Czechoslovakian armies in November 1918, Teschen and its division seemed one of the faits accomplis the Paris Peace Conference would simply have to resign itself to. After the breakup of the old multinational empires, both the Polish and the Czechoslovak government rested their claims on the triumph of a nationalist vision of statehood. As far as the local population was concerned, Polish claims on Teschen arguably were well founded—three out of the four districts were predominantly Polish speaking: Teschen, Frysztat, and Bielsko. Historically, however, Czechoslovakia could make a stronger case, as the region had more recently been ruled by the Bohemian crown rather than the Polish one. Much was at stake: the coal deposits of Teschen were among the richest in Europe (with 7.4 million tons of coal produced in 1913), and the Bohumín-Oderberg station was a major hub controlling the flow of traffic and communication with the Danubian, eastern, and Adriatic regions. The Polish delegation therefore argued that the region was vital to its economy—as did the Czechs, who saw it as the Škoda hinterland and as a strategic link between Bohemia and Slovakia.

That France was the most important ally and Western supporter of the Polish and Czechoslovak nations after 1918 is not surprising given the long-standing connections between Paris and these countries' respective independence movements, even years before the Great War. Although the peoples in central Europe shared a lot of history and culture, the different political standing of individuals living in the Austrian and Hungarian halves of the empire, their fights in the Imperial Parliament, and the diverging attitudes on pan-Slavism had created a lasting antagonism between Polish and Czech nationalists. This antagonism was widely publicized and therefore widespread within both countries.[4] Both sides tried to paper over this opposition during the war, trying to ensure future support from the Quai d'Orsay.[5] The French authorities, however, could not ignore that "there is a Polish-Czech conflict in existence!"[6] This tension was particularly significant given the French ambition to create an "eastern barrier," or "cordon sanitaire," in order to establish a stable state system in eastern Europe that would guarantee security for France and the whole continent.[7] There are relatively few signs for a similar interest in the Polish-Czech dispute among the other great powers. It was only after the escalation of the conflict in the spring of 1919 that Great Britain and to a lesser degree the United States and Italy began considering the problem of Teschen. In fact, American and Italian delegates remained mostly on the sidelines when the issue was debated in the Allied councils and at the Conference of Ambassadors.[8]

As this chapter will show, the case of Teschen Silesia offers a unique perspective on the use of plebiscites following the Great War. For one, the peacemakers originally had intended to decide on the Polish-Czechoslovakian border without consulting the local population. A plebiscite was improvised only in the spring of 1920. Secondly, Teschen is a rare case because the plebiscite's implementation was stopped in its tracks and hence the will of the people did not offer any guidance on the border drawing. Even the list of those eligible to vote was never completed. Finally, the conflict over Teschen illustrates the difficulties of demobilizing European societies and the contestation on the ground of Wilsonian ideas and principles of "new diplomacy."

The beginning of the twenty-first century has witnessed a reevaluation of Woodrow Wilson's ideas in general and the right to national self-determination in particular.[9] It is clear by now that the multiethnic empires had an internal "nationality problem" on their hands long before the war. However, after 1918 the prospect and promise of national self-determination released forces the great powers could hardly control. At the end of four years of brutal and existential conflict, the governments of the newly established states were not disposed to restrict themselves to "reasonable" claims. In fact, their territorial programs made full use of all historical, ethnic, linguistic, and other arguments that could legitimate nationalist claims and popular demands. Their position corresponded to the Wilsonian view that considered popular will as the supreme arbiter of a state's domestic affairs.[10] But given the violence unleashed, would it be possible to put the genie back in the bottle?

Since the 1960s, various historical studies have focused on Polish-Czechoslovak relations after 1918.[11] The pioneering work of Piotr Wandycz is still authoritative but, after fifty-five years, needs to be complemented in two respects. First, the Teschen conflict needs to be placed much more firmly in the context of the international system and investigated as an example of the systemic function (or dysfunction) of this system.[12] Secondly, previous research like that of Wandycz tends to neglect the importance of experts, who complemented the diplomatic field, in negotiating and drawing borders.[13] In the case of Teschen, it is particularly evident that the reliance on technical expertise was an attempt to take emotions out of the debate by using a certain set of "hard," scientific-like criteria that would move decisions into the administrative sphere.

The project of a referendum was supported by both the Polish and Czechoslovakian delegations as long as each thought that they would win. But both stymied its implementation as they began to lose confidence in the outcome. The democratic process that was supposed to inaugurate a new international order swiftly gave way to arbitrary decision-making. This chapter explores the nature and function of the failed plebiscite of Teschen: To what extent was it modeled on "Wilsonian idealism"? To what extent was it an instrument of realpolitik? When, why, and for how long did the parties involved argue for the right to self-determination? As we search for answers, two equally crucial aspects of peacemaking after the Great War come into view: the negotiations between the great powers and the successor states of the multinational empires and the relations between the successor states and their respective populations. After 1918, all central governments were overwhelmed by the dynamic nationalism on the ground, and the plebiscite shows the difficulty in finding common ground in highly divided societies.[14] The case of Teschen offers fascinating insights into the mixture of violence and votes, the tension between centralized diplomacy and local action, and the clash of new ideals and power politics that characterized border conflicts and plebiscites at the end of the war.

## From Hopes of a Compromise to the Plebiscite (November 1918–September 1919)

Throughout the last phase of the war, the Polish National Committee, as well as the Czechoslovakian National Council, made increasingly aggressive demands to gain full sovereignty over what it claimed as "its" territories.[15] Wilson's Fourteen Points, both governing bodies assumed, acknowledged the legitimacy of those claims—whether based on historical or ethnographic arguments—in principle, and the US entry into the conflict seemed to validate them as the foundation for future peace. The French government, mindful of the opportunity for future military alliances, made generous territorial promises to the leaders of the emergent nations in central Europe. Ultimately, both the Czechoslovakian and Polish committees believed Teschen had been "promised" to them and came to see it as an irrevocable spoil of war. However, the different criteria discussed by Allied experts from 1917 onward did not enable them to find a common position. Concerning Poland's western border, and hence Teschen's future nationality, France tended to support Polish interests.[16] Invoking arguments favoring an economic and strategic balance between continental nations, Great Britain backed Czechoslovakian claims. But the British were also keen to intervene as little as possible in eastern European disputes and argued for a compromise that would yield a stable solution.[17]

If the French and the British attached widely different importance to the question of Teschen, the American position was even more removed.[18] Lloyd George would later assert that the Polish-Americans had tried to convince Wilson to speak out in favor of Poland's position on Teschen.[19] Research in American archives has highlighted Washington's general support for Polish claims but has also shown how divided the American Commission to Negotiate Peace remained.[20] On the one hand, US experts on Austro-Hungarian and Polish questions defended ethnic arguments, which tended to favor the Polish cause in the Teschen case; on the other hand, many US delegates saw Czechoslovakia as a "modern" state, especially when it came to the treatment of minorities, and thus better suited to deal with mixed-population areas.[21] The Italian delegation, for its part, was in favor of Poland for reasons that actually had nothing to do with the Teschen quarrel. Rome opposed Czechoslovakia above all because of its informal alliance with the Kingdom of the Serbs, Croats, and Slovenes, Italy's main rival on the Adriatic shores.[22] In the end, Italian premier Vittorio Orlando attempted to form a Catholic bloc to gain more influence on the negotiations.[23]

As early as in the spring of 1918–19, violence was on the rise in Teschen. With Allied promises and the collapse of the central empires reinforcing public expectations, nationalist groups invoked the popular will in search for legitimacy. In the wake of the armistice of Salonica on September 29, 1918, a Czech National Council of Teschen (Národní Výbor à Ostrava) and a Polish National Council (Rada Narodowa Ksiestwa Cieszynskiego, located in Teschen too) were established. The governments in Prague and Warsaw subsequently recognized these local initiatives.[24] Participants mostly came from distinguished social backgrounds; they were former members of the Silesian Diet or hailed from medical and professional circles. The Polish Rada and the Czech Výbor both organized mass rallies, encouraging local residents to claim their "legitimate rights" and demonstrate their national commitment to the Allied powers at every opportunity available. On December 3, 1918, for instance, the "Reformed Evangelical Clergy" of Teschen demanded incorporation into Poland;[25] on May 15, 1919, six thousand members of the Polish Miners' Union declared their pro–Czech stance.[26] Yet the results of these patriotic demonstrations were mixed as they undercut the Paris calls for peace and raised distrust on the part of the Big Four.

Fears of a Bolshevik "contagion" in Eastern Silesia as well as anxieties over an anarchic situation with disarmed soldiers roaming the land had already forced both sides to look for an interim settlement to restore order. On November 5, 1918, a provisional agreement was signed, based on local initiatives and only tacitly accepted by the central governments.[27] The agreement drew an ethnographic line through Teschen buttressing Polish territorial claims: only one of four districts, Frýdek, was left to the Czech side (Frysztat was under mixed control). But in terms of economic power, the agreement favored the Czechs, who gained twenty-six out of thirty-six mines. Unsurprisingly, the compromise left both sides unsatisfied, and the Czechs soon assumed that the Poles were trying to preserve the provisional arrangement. The Poles were allegedly recruiting local soldiers for the Polish army and organizing elections to the Polish National Assembly (scheduled for January 26) in their districts. Consequently, the Czech authorities in Prague and Paris launched an intense diplomatic campaign with newspaper articles and memoranda to decry the Polish initiatives and demanded an Allied intervention.[28] In fact, both Czechs and Poles hoped for a strong French presence in the contested territories as they sought to showcase the support of the Quai d'Orsay for their respective demands. Most politicians in Paris, including Prime Minister Georges Clemenceau, were reluctant to do so and opted to maintain neutrality. Several French diplomats, however, wanted to abandon the position of passive onlooker in order to press the parties to reach a lasting agreement on Teschen.[29]

In this situation of uncertainty, an attack launched by Czech forces in January 1919 acted as a turning point. Despite warnings by French diplomats, the Prague government would and could not prevent the assault by Czech units that triggered the seven-day Polish-Czechoslovak War. On January 23, 1919, a Czech military delegation claimed to act on behalf of the Allies when it demanded that the commander in chief of the Polish forces, General Franciszek Latinik, evacuate the Polish-controlled territory up to the border of the district of Bielsko. After the Poles refused, fighting ensued on the left bank of the Olsa, mainly around Frysztat and the Oderberg railway station.[30] Reverberations in Paris were immediate. While a Polish exile newspaper lamented the fighting in Teschen, "where [our] brothers' blood has been shed," the minister of foreign affairs and prime minister of Poland, Ignacy Paderewski, warned the secretary of the Quai d'Orsay, Philippe Berthelot, of the risk that an even more "deadly war" would break out if the "annexationist appetites of the Czechs" were not restrained.[31] As Polish troops withdrew to the Białka River, Czech units captured and occupied the town of Teschen, and they controlled the railway station of Oderberg by January 27. The Prague government justified the invasions by stating that the country had to protect itself against bolshevism spreading in Poland.[32] Polish reinforcements arrived in the area only between January 29 and 31. In the end, the fighting at the Polish-Czechoslovak border claimed the lives of about two hundred people, 80 percent of them Polish.[33]

Though nominally launched at the behest of the Allied powers, the attack on January 23 was initiated by a group of naturalized Czechoslovak officers:

Lieutenant Colonel Josef Šnejdárek, who had served in the French army; Lieutenant Colonel Voska, who had served in the US army; and Major Rozeda, who had been a member of the Italian forces.[34] Indeed, as a fact-finding mission by American and British officers from Warsaw quickly pointed out in their statement: "None of the officers of the Entente serving in the Czech Army had received permission from his government to assume the title of the head of the Inter-Allied Commission [IAC] or to speak on behalf of the Allied powers."[35] France was also keen to dispel the false notion of having supported the Czech initiative.[36] But after a communiqué was published on February 7 denying any official participation of the French military forces, Polish leaflets still proclaimed that "the Czechoslovakian attack . . . was launched with the Allies' consent."[37]

While it is wrong to allege that the Allies supported the operation, it is nevertheless true that numerous civil and military members of the inter-Allied missions sided with one or the other camp in the Teschen quarrel. In particular, French liaison-officers, sent to the theater of war in Silesia, saw themselves as fighting for freedom against authoritarian empires and were often eager to support either the Czech or Polish cause, depending on which nationalist group they had been assigned to in the first place. Their interventions resulted from what could be described as a transmission of nationalist allegiances. The prominent journalist Louise Weiss, who was traveling through central and eastern Europe at the end of the war, commented on their tendency to identify with the nationality they had been assigned to. Though not immune to the contagion herself (she defended the Czechoslovak cause), she explained how "our generals were now driven to act as brothers at war. General Maurice Pellé [in Prague] and General Prosper Henrys, who was in command in Warsaw, hence continued to cross swords. They could no longer stand each other because the Czechs and the Poles detested each other."[38]

The attack of January 23 brought significant political fallout for France's role in central Europe. Humiliated by the victorious Czech campaign, the political fate of Paderewski's government in Warsaw was at stake. Seen from the Quai d'Orsay, the most pressing issue was to save the Polish government and secure its role as an important ally. On January 31, the peacemakers in Paris decided to draw a new demarcation line and establish a military occupation zone under international control.[39] An IAC headed by French ambassador Fernand Grenard was sent to Teschen. Its tasks were to guarantee the provisional border and gather information about the conditions for partitioning the disputed territories between Czechoslovakia and Poland. The deadline for the Allied Supreme Council to decide on a new border was set for September 10, 1919. In the short term, and seen from a narrow vantage point, the attack of January 23 cost Czech leaders a good amount of sympathy and confidence on the part of the Big Four who, while discussing the articles of the peace treaty with Germany, now had to deal also with the Polish-Czech conflict. British and French delegates did little to hide their irritation that the negotiations at the peace conference were being disrupted.[40] And the United States began to favor a division of the former duchy along ethnographic lines without special consideration for the Czechoslovak economy.[41] All the same,

Czechoslovakia was able to place the fate of Teschen on the agenda of the peace-makers and convince the victorious powers that this was not merely an internal affair pertaining to the successor states. Its gamble would eventually pay off.

After he arrived in Teschen, Ambassador Grenard immediately encountered great difficulties in enforcing the new settlement, especially as it demanded the withdrawal of Czech troops and a mutual demobilization. While the Prague government tried to avoid the removal of any troops, the Polish forces, in turn, launched a counterattack as early as January 31.[42] Conditions soon deteriorated further. When General Albert-Henri Niessel, another French emissary, arrived on the scene at the end of February, the three-week-old settlement was in rags.[43] After taking over from Grenard, who left for Paris with undisguised relief, Niessel tried to enforce the implementation of the agreement.[44] Yet skirmishes, confrontations, and wild rumors seemed unstoppable.[45] On the Czechoslovak side, the local authorities were complaining about growing revolutionary agitation and unrest among the Polish population in Silesia. This impression was influenced both by the general political turmoil as well as by a strike that had started in Lublin in February 1919.[46] On the Polish side, rumors were spreading about Czech "cruelty" unleashed against the Polish citizens of the Frýdek district.[47]

At the peace conference, in the meantime, the French diplomat Jules Cambon chaired no fewer than twenty joint sessions of the Czechoslovak and Polish border delegations between March 31 and November 11, 1919, to discuss Teschen, Spisz, and Orava.[48] All through the summer, as the September deadline drew nearer, tensions increased. Polish miners threatened to launch a general strike, while on August 28—twelve days before the decision of the Supreme Council in Paris was due—Czech activists took the Warsaw-Paris train hostage, asking for Teschen as ransom.[49] In this situation, the French proposal for a plebiscite in the Teschen district as well as the Spiš and Orava zones was accepted and ratified by the Supreme Council on September 27.[50] Czech foreign minister Edvard Beneš and the Polish representative at the Paris Peace conference, Roman Dmowski, had agreed beforehand to accept any terms set by the Allies, in particular that the votes were to be organized by municipality and that compensation for the territorial acquisitions would be negotiated.[51]

It is important to note that at this point both nations were in favor of a plebiscite. Given the composition of the Silesian population, the Poles supported the decision because they believed that it would ensure their supremacy. The Czechs, on the other hand, realized that alternative proposals put forward in Paris in late August would in any event result in an unfavorable partition of the industrial basin, especially since the British were beginning to accept ethnographic arguments more advantageous to the Polish side.[52] Beneš was convinced that the Slonzaks and the Germans would vote for the Czech side, and thus was willing to risk a plebiscite over a top-down decision in Paris. The Slonzaks were eager to preserve the unity of the industrial basin and were indeed rather pro–Czech because of their traditional economic relations with the Bohemian hinterland. As for the Germans of Teschen, they also leaned toward the Danubian basin and had already demanded the formation of a Greater Silesia federally linked to Austria as early as November 1918.[53] Finally, Beneš hoped to obtain a good share of the Polish votes due to the economic difficulties and the unstable military situation of Poland.[54] As both Czech and Polish delegates were optimistic about the outcome, the decision to have a referendum did much to generate a sense of peace and stability in the region after months of anxiousness and disorder. Local authorities even agreed on a neutral zone before the arrival of the official plebiscite commission.[55]

## The Organization of the Plebiscite (September 1919–March 1920)

As the August plan of the Supreme Council to divide the territory became increasingly unrealistic and impossible to enforce, the decision to hold a plebiscite seemed the only workable solution for the immediate future. The proposal for the referendum thus did not result from an assessment of the local situation in the first place but rather from the impotence of the authorities in charge—both the Supreme Council and the Allied military authorities in Teschen.

The holding of a plebiscite was—and this point must be emphasized—a decision that rested on France's approval. The Quai d'Orsay had been particularly eager to keep the economic structures of the coal basin intact and had sought to avoid any solution that would divide Teschen along ethnographic lines. The French diplomats, moreover, had severe doubts about the Polish pledge to honor any compensation agreements coupled to such a scenario.[56] France's central role emerges clearly in an official statement by Stephen Pichon, France's minister for foreign affairs: "It is the French delegation which ensured that the line of August 20 was pushed back and which, having tried in vain to make the Czechs accept a more advantageous line, decided that the Supreme Council would adhere to the plebiscite."[57] As for the British, once they had accepted the ethnic argument, they agreed to the plebiscite as a solution that ensured stability, especially since the Czech and Polish delegations promised to respect it.[58] And since the British had urged for plebiscites in Masuria and Upper Silesia as well, it would have been difficult to reject a similar procedure for Teschen.[59] The same was true for the Americans, who also had supported the plebiscite in Upper Silesia.[60] The exception were the Italians, who were extremely hostile to any plebiscite but did not have any means to influence the decision-making.[61]

In the end, the Council of Heads of Delegations who convened in Paris beyond the Versailles Treaty committed themselves militarily and diplomatically to the organization of the plebiscite in Teschen. Taking into account the different military missions and commissions, France was the key player in this endeavor, with about ten thousand troops on the ground, compared to forty-three hundred British, two thousand Italian, and only a handful of American soldiers.[62] The IAC was chaired by a French officer as well, Gustave de Manneville.[63] Compared to the Le Rond Commission of Upper Silesia, this committee under Manneville worked without major conflict or dissent, mostly because no German interests were at stake.[64]

After the plebiscite was announced on September 27, deciding on how a peaceful vote could be ensured became a challenge for all parties involved. Plans for an international plebiscite commission had to be worked out in Paris. In the meantime, Allied troops in Teschen had to deal not only with local inhabitants unsettled about their future citizenship but also with nationalist firebrands and the machinations of the governments in Prague and Warsaw.[65] Any unrest in Teschen weakened the peacemakers' authority.

The nationalist fervor in both Poland and Czechoslovakia forced the hand of both governments as no one wanted to appear to be a half-hearted patriot. Beneš claimed that "the politics of central Europe and of eastern Europe will, one day, revolve around this question [of Teschen]."[66] The Polish Sejm engaged in increasingly frenzied rhetoric; motions proposing to aid the Poles in Silesia by whatever means necessary reaped unanimous votes. Both governments found themselves in a political situation that barred them from accepting any compromise. In this precarious state of affairs, the plebiscite seemed to relieve them of any responsibility for the future of Teschen. Czech and Polish leaders were glad that they needed only to refer to the popular referendum. However, while the anticipation of the plebiscite lessened the pressure on the governments, this was an uneasy interlude at best. Rarely a night passed without the exchange of gunfire across the border. The genie was a long way from returning to the bottle.

By the autumn of 1919, the excitement over national independence in Czechoslovakia was tempered by the anxious wait for the last legionnaires returning from Siberia, the mourning over the war victims, and the search for meaning to their sacrifice. Poland was still at war with the Bolshevists. The situation in both Czechoslovakia and Poland was thus unstable; the public mood in each country remained extremely apprehensive. And in Teschen itself, the organization of the referendum revived earlier propaganda campaigns. Both sides were trying to seduce, intimidate, and even frighten the undecided populations—namely, the Germans and the Slonzaks. Czech posters highlighted the impoverishment of the Slonzaks in the case of a Polish victory, whereas the Polish posters emphasized the false promises of the Czechs.[67]

Concerned that several of its borders were under scrutiny, Poland even asked for donations to finance its campaign in the plebiscites. The four referenda (Warmia and Masuria, Spisz and Orava, Teschen Silesia, Upper-Silesia) were deemed a single struggle to defend its borders by the Polish nation—rendered in the slogan "the will of the people accomplishes miracles."[68] The propagandistic furor sometimes made waves on the other side of the Atlantic, as demonstrated by a *New York Times* article on May 27, 1920: "The Poles were accusing the Czechs and the Czechs were accusing the Poles of responsibility for the repeated riots and multiplication of crimes in the Teschen districts, as well as discrimination against their respective nationals."[69] Skirmishes among the Polish and Czech communities in Teschen continued as electoral offices were established. As both sides denounced the other of spreading terror and committing atrocities, propaganda stereotypes forged during the Great War were picked up again and recontextualized. The Polish newspapers were particularly prone to run articles stirring up hatred. *L'Indépendance polonaise* published allegedly true "statements from victims or eye witnesses" that described Czechs mutilating Poles—shattering hands, breaking teeth with rifle butts, and stripping and starving prisoners.[70] In spite of the demonstration ban issued by the Commission of Teschen, a general strike broke out on the Czech side on March 10 to protest changes made to the administrative commissions in the Karviná coal basin.[71] The strike immediately spread to the Polish side, which demanded the withdrawal of Czech police forces. Before long, more than twenty thousand workers were on strike, according to a report of the IAC.[72] Manneville spoke of a civil war situation, with passions whipped up on either side by nationalistic agitators.[73]

## The Practical Limits of the Right to Self-Determination (March–July 1920)

Organizing the plebiscite commission envisaged by the peacemakers took time, and this delay led some people to assume that the dispute over the border would inevitably be resolved by force. article 4 of the agreement of September 27 stipulated that the plebiscite had to be held within three months. To speed things up, each nation represented on the commission was assigned a particular task. France was in charge of the political aspects and the general coordination, Italy organized the supplies, Great Britain was responsible for commercial considerations, and the Japanese were in charge of justice and education. French troops occupied the most vulnerable locations of the railway network, the industrial basin, and the city of Teschen.[74]

The delegates on the commission also had to draw up the rules for the plebiscite, which the Czech and Polish governments were permitted to comment on. However, they were unable to reach an agreement, especially on the crucial subject of who had the right to vote. A first decision on the terms and conditions of eligibility was made on March 23, 1920. Admitted to the vote were men and women who had reached twenty years of age by August 1, 1919, and who had possessed indigenous status on August 1, 1914.[75] This last point raised some concerns and the commission had to take a stand on who actually held indigenous status. The Czechs suggested that only persons who had obtained the right of residence (*Heimatsberechtigung*) in the region prior to August 1, 1914, should be allowed to vote. The problem was that a large number of residents never had officially acquired this right—among them the mayor of Teschen. The Poles, therefore, proposed to extend the period of residence to be taken into account. According to both sides, around eighty-five thousand inhabitants would be affected by a strict definition of the right of residence. In the end, on May 26, 1920, the rules were finally published for a vote expected to take place on July 12.[76] All authorities involved believed a swift enactment of the plebiscite was of utmost importance.[77] In reality, however, each side was silently preparing for a postponement due to the considerable unrest in the area.[78] Georges Mellier, the French commanding officer in charge of the occupying forces, spoke of a dangerous situation as it proved increasingly difficult to control an agitated population.[79]

In view of this deteriorating situation, even the Polish and Czechoslovakian governments called for Allied military reinforcements.[80] From May onward, the demonstrations became more and more violent, fanned by the drop in the Polish mark and the slight rise of the Czech crown, which economically weakened all Polish workers in the Czech zone. Manneville noted that ninety municipalities had still not produced their formal electoral registers and that the situation was moving toward not a plebiscite but a war.[81] Marshal Ferdinand Foch rejected his request for backup because he saw France to be legally bound by the decision of the Council of Four to send a headcount of only seven hundred soldiers. A number of incidents—the word *terrorism* appeared in reports—harmed France's image profoundly. In this climate of civil war, the commission even prohibited any demonstration or assembly in public places.[82] In an attempt to end fighting and unrest, the Czechoslovakian and Polish governments called on their citizens to remain calm and on France to resolve the stalemate for which it was, in their perception, "responsible more than any other power."[83]

The local conditions were therefore less and less conducive to a plebiscite. Soon all involved were convinced of the need to cancel it. France and Great Britain wanted to swiftly put an end to the escalating conflict; Poland and Czechoslovakia were waiting for a decision dictated by the Entente.[84] Meanwhile, more modern and powerful weapons were arriving in Silesia, following the demobilization of the western European armies. When a Czech stationmaster's house in the west of the region exploded, Ernest Wilton, British delegate to the plebiscite commission, wrote to Lord George Curzon that "the force of the explosion showed that the bomb was indeed very different from the hand grenades which had been thrown during the incidents in March."[85] Wilton believed Polish POWs returned from Upper Silesia had organized an underground network.[86] And he felt that the Poles were seeking to have the plebiscite canceled in order to gain time. In June 1920, Foch finally sent a battalion of riflemen from the Saarland to Karviná. Amid two uprisings, accusations flew in both directions with the supervisory authorities condemning local actions while faced with protests over unjustified arrests. During the summer of 1920, while the Poles found themselves deprived of the wagons of coal that they were supposed to receive from the Karviná basin under provisional Czech authority (two thousand tons of coal and five hundred tons of coke), the Czechs were complaining about not getting the tankers of mineral oil that the Poles had agreed to deliver. The French diplomats in Prague and Warsaw confessed to having difficulty in distinguishing between which incidents were blown out of proportion and which merited intervention.[87]

In the Czechoslovakian and Polish chanceries, too, enthusiasm for the plebiscite was waning. At the time of the decision to hold a plebiscite, each of the two governments was convinced that the plebiscite would be to its advantage. A few months later, the disenchantment was palpable. While continuing to pronounce certain victory, the Czechoslovakian government was at the same time more and more open to a bilateral agreement with Poland, if Poland were to grant the Karviná basin and the Teschen-Jablunkau railway line. Beneš hinted to the French representative in Prague that such an agreement would deliver a basis for future reconciliation.[88] The president of the Czechoslovakian Council was clearly pushing, with the chief of the French mission as intermediary, to have the plebiscite canceled in favor of a compromise. He even suggested financing the construction of new mines in the part of the basin that would remain Polish.[89] Beneš's speech to the French authorities thus pulled in two directions: he continued to maintain that the plebiscite would deliver a favorable majority for the Czechs, but since voting by municipality would result in a very complex canvas, complicated transactions rather than a swift reconciliation would be the logical result. The row over the coal basin stemming from the plebiscite, Beneš warned with blackmailing rhetoric, would make it impossible for Czechoslovakia to supply Vienna and Budapest. Thereupon, "the Entente would be able to count . . . only on Poland. As Poland is likely to experience some disappointment in Upper Silesia, it will take advantage of this to dodge its commitments."[90]

For its part, Warsaw undertook a similar volte-face. The Poles were convinced that the Inter-Allied Plebiscite Commission was against them. They believed that the plebiscite commission's insufficient means, in particular with regard to the occupying forces, were creating a situation harmful to Poland. Students in Warsaw demonstrated against the commission.[91] Indeed, the number of Polish supporters seemed to be declining, arguably a combined result of weak administration in the zones entrusted to Poland and the difficult war against the Red Army. In April, General Henrys stated that "certain circles in Poland are starting to view the result of the plebiscite with less confidence."[92] Paderewski's departure allowed Poland to renege on the plebiscite since his successor as foreign minister, Stanisław Patek, never committed himself to it. In short, both sides were tacitly going back to the initially envisioned solution to the border conflict: a resolute decision enforced by the great powers that both Poland and Czechoslovakia hoped would fall in their favor.

On May 22, 1920, Patek declared that the Polish population would not take part in the plebiscite. He underlined the responsibility of the IAC for "the state of anarchy, expanding into Silesia from Cieszyn."[93] On July 2, the Polish authorities ratified the decision to end all preparations for the plebiscite and demanded a return to the arrangements taken after the Czechoslovak attack in January 1919.[94] In a similar vein, the Czech population of Teschen approved the following declaration in a town meeting on May 30: "We accuse the inter-allied plebiscite commission, which was unable to make impartiality and justice prevail in Tešín, and which is responsible for the innocent blood spilled."[95] That a similar feeling of powerlessness dominated on both sides, can be observed by the joint declaration of Beneš and Polish prime minister Władysław Grabski on July 10, 1920.[96] They admitted their failure to create a situation peaceful enough to ensure a successful referendum or a direct agreement, underlining that even though the right to self-determination was a noble cause, it did not stand above each and every course of action: "This struggle, dictated, it is true, by patriotic sentiments on either side, has often led to the employment of regrettable methods. Violence has been committed, accusations have been made, threats have been uttered." Both politicians agreed that at this point, it would be easier to accept a decision dictated by the Entente than to face public opinion and take responsibility for the plebiscite's outcome. Grabski resigned himself to any agreement suggested by the great powers: "The Polish government accepts: . . . to recognize the decision of the Supreme Council regarding . . . the future of the Teschen question."[97] This was nothing less than a blank check.

The Polish-Soviet War, too, was making a territorial division a matter of emergency. At the end of July 1920, the great powers, who had gathered in Spa to discuss the question of reparations, learned very disturbing news from the eastern front: the Red Army was approaching Warsaw and the fall of the Polish capital seemed imminent. From then on, the top priority in the Western camp was to protect the Teschen coal mines. Their hand thus forced by circumstances, the Allies improvised a solution, and on July 28, 1920, the French and the British, in the presence of Beneš, drew a demarcation line.[98] Given their motivations to act at this time, the border was, unsurprisingly, completely to the advantage of Czechoslovakia. The Czechs obtained two-thirds of the old duchy, including the coal mines, the major part of the industrial basin, and the railway junction of Oderberg; the Polish regained the largest area of the city of Teschen, which was renamed Cieszyn (east of the Olza), whereas on the other side of the bridge began Český Těšín (Czech Teschen).[99] The Czechoslovakian part counted about 148,000 Polish inhabitants, while on the other side of the border there were only 84,000. A compensation agreement was added on September 27, 1920, providing for an exchange of Czech coal against Polish petroleum. As Manneville, who still headed the IAC on Teschen, observed: "A plebiscite with the worst possible outcome for Poland would have given it better borders."[100]

## Conclusion

From the very outset, the decision to hold a plebiscite was less a conscious choice than a stopgap solution in response to impotence. After the great powers failed to divide the territory and direct negotiations between Poland and Czechoslovakia broke down, the plebiscite emerged a compromise. It was not a policy propelled by ideals of national self-determination. Moreover, the stipulations for its implementation were contested from the beginning, with the IAC reluctant to intervene in a situation of overheated nationalism. By trying to impose formal rules and a consultation procedure, the great powers hoped to take some heat out of the debate and transform a question of territoriality into a legal and administrative issue.[101] Yet the conflict quickly got out of hand. Neither Masaryk, nor Beneš, nor Paderewski or his successors were able to control events in Teschen; all their attempts to impose their political authority resulted in a weakened international position.

The case of Teschen thus provides a rich case study of the numerous paradoxes that characterized the interwar order in Europe. At its heart, the idea of a plebiscite implied a democratic process and the search for a fair border drawing. But as in other cases, be they in Klagenfurt or Upper Silesia, the claim to resolve a territorial dispute by popular referendum was not a benevolent gesture.[102] Rather, the decision to resort—or not to resort—to the people in the context of border drawings rested solely on political considerations by the great powers. They alone could decide on every step of the process: the demarcation of the territory, the interpretation of the results, and the final drawing of the border. The governments in Prague and Warsaw, for their part, were not much inclined to favor democratic procedures either. For a brief moment, the plebiscite was a seemingly convenient way for them to further their respective territorial objectives, at least as long as both sides thought that they would win the vote. Perhaps unsurprisingly, Poland and Czechoslovakia rejected the idea of a plebiscite as soon as the outcome proved uncertain. As both nations struggled with internal strife, neither wanted to risk alienating local nationalists and supporters.

The abandoned referendum of Teschen demonstrates how much all parties were making use of, and dependent on, circumstances and considerations unrelated to the will of the people. Political power and opportunities staked out the ground for how the right to self-determination would play out, turning the promise of a democratic process into a manifestation of realpolitik. The greatest indication of the triumph of power politics over ideals of self-determination was that Poland ultimately lost Teschen to the Bolshevik threat.

Still, the genie would not go back into the bottle. The claim to self-determination continued to haunt the new states in central and eastern Europe and beyond. Certainly, the relative unimportance of the Teschen case and its low strategic significance played a role in the Paris peacemakers' wavering commitment. Then again, the great powers did stay engaged. They continued to argue for new solutions and to mediate the dispute over Teschen, thus demonstrating that a conflict that had acquired international attention could not simply be passed back to the two rival nations. But their negotiation between January 1919 and July 1920 show that the so-called Wilsonian principles were at the service of the great powers rather than the other way around. That the plebiscite did not take place was less a function of the violence on the ground than the lack of will on the part of the peacemakers.[103] The great powers of 1919–20, as well as Poland and Czechoslovakia, accepted the plebiscite only as long as they felt in a position of power: rather than embracing the "idealistic" vision of the international system, they maintained reflexes that were "realistic," goaded by the playbook of power politics.

## Notes

1. Isabelle Davion, *Mon voisin, cet ennemi* (Brussels: Peter Lang, 2009).

2. Piotr S. Wandycz, *France and Her Eastern Allies 1919–1925: French-Czechoslovak-Polish Relations from the Paris Peace Conference to Locarno* (Minneapolis: University of Minnesota Press, 1962), 22. The letter of Stephen Pichon from June 29, 1918, is printed in Edvard Beneš, *Světová válka a naše revoluce*, vol. 2 (Prague: Orbis, 1927), 229.

3. Another dividing line was religion, with the census revealing one-third Protestants and two-thirds Catholics (Lucien Gallois, "Le plébiscite de Teschen," *Annales de Géographie* 30, no. 163 [1921], 176–78).

4. Isabelle Davion, "Les relations polono-tchécoslovaques dans la politique de sécurité française entre les deux guerres" (PhD diss., Paris-Sorbonne, 2004), 1:35–50.

5. Wandycz, *France and Her Eastern Allies*, 6–16.

6. Archives of the French Ministry of Defense (SHD), 7N1449: Attaché militaire en Pologne 1914–1919, Bulletin périodique de la presse polonaise no. 62 du 17 au 31 décembre 1918.

7. Peter Jackson, *Beyond the Balance of Power: France and the Politics of National Security in the Era of the First World War* (Cambridge: Cambridge University Press, 2013), 47–78.

8. Bibliothèque de Documentation Internationale Contemporaine (BDIC), *Recueil des Actes de la Conférence de la Paix*, partie 4, *Commissions de la conférence*, vol. C3, *Commissions relatives aux affaires de Teschen, Spisz et Orava* (Paris: Imprimerie Nationale, 1929).

9. Ross Kennedy, ed., *A Companion to Woodrow Wilson* (Oxford: Wiley-Blackwell, 2013), 443–527.

10. Carol Fink, "The Problem of Minority Rights and Democracy in Eastern Europe from the Paris Peace Conference to the Fall of the Soviet Empire: The International Dimension," in *L'Europe au XXe siècle: Éléments pour un bilan*, ed. Tomasz Shramm (Poznań: Instytut Historii Uniwersytet im Adama Mickiewicza, 2000), 333–46.

11. Wandycz, *France and Her Eastern Allies*; Peggy Croydon, "The Problem of Teschen at Paris Peace Conference with Special Emphasis on British Policy" (PhD diss., McGill University, 1967); Thomazena Cejka-Magnusson, "The Teschen Question at the Paris Peace Conference" (PhD diss., North Texas University, 1971).

12. Paul W. Schroeder, *The Transformation of European Politics 1763–1848* (Oxford: Oxford University Press, 1994); Peter Krüger, *Das europäische Staatensystem im Wandel* (Munich: Oldenbourg, 1996); Bruno Arcidiacono, *Cinq types de paix. Une histoire des plans de pacification perpétuelle (XVIIe–XXe siècles)* (Paris: Presses Universitaires de France, 2011); Éric Bussière, Isabelle Davion, and Stanislas Jeannesson, eds., *Penser le système international XIXe–XXIe siècles. Autour de l'œuvre de Georges-Henri Soutou* (Paris: Presses de l'Université Paris-Sorbonne, 2013).

13. Stanislas Jeannesson, *Jacques Seydoux (1870–1929). Un diplomate européen* (Paris: Presses de l'Université Paris-Sorbonne, 2012).

14. On the difficulties of ending the conflict, especially on the reintegration of veterans, see Julia Eichenberg and John Paul Newman, eds., *The Great War and Veterans' Internationalism* (London: Palgrave Macmillan, 2013); Mark Cornwall and John Paul Newman, eds., *Sacrifice and Rebirth: The Legacy of the Last Habsburg War*, Austrian and Habsburg Studies, vol. 18 (New York; Oxford: Berghahn, 2016); Lucie Kostrbová, Jana Malínská, and Lucie Merhautová, eds., *1918. Model komplexního transformačního procesu?* (Prague: Masarykův ústav a Archiv AV ČR, 2010).

15. Wandycz, *France and Her Eastern Allies*, 23–56.

16. Daniel Beauvois, *La Pologne. Histoire, société, culture* (Paris: Éditions de La Martinière, 2004), 310–13.

17. In his memoirs, David Lloyd George also hinted at his preferences for Czechoslovakia (David Lloyd George, *The Truth about the Peace Treaties* [London: Victor Gollancz, 1938], 2:942).

18. Croydon, "Problem of Teschen," 56; Lloyd George, *Truth*, 2:292. See also the recollections of Harold Nicolson, *Peacemaking 1919* (New York: Grosset & Dunlap, 1933).

19. Lloyd George, *Truth*, 1:311.

20. Alan Sharp, *The Versailles Settlement: Peacemaking in Paris, 1919* (Houndmills, UK: Macmillan, 1991). Klaus Schwabe, "Negotiating Peace Terms for Germany," in Kennedy, *Companion to Woodrow Wilson*, 461.

21. Michael R. Cude, "Wilsonian National Self-Determination and the Slovak Question during the Founding of Czechoslovakia, 1918–1921," *Diplomatic History* (2014): 158–59.

22. Lubomír Kubík, *Těšínský konflikt.Dramatické okamžiky česko-polských vztahů* (Olomouc: Votobia, 2001), 81–82.

23. French diplomats were wary of the Italian attempts, however (Jules Laroche, "La question de Teschen devant la Conférence de la Paix 1919–1920," *Revue d'histoire diplomatique* [January–June 1948], 8–27).

24. Henri Grappin, *Polonais et Tchèques: La Silésie de Teschen* (Paris: Imprimerie Flinikowski, 1919), 36; Croydon, "Problem of Teschen," 30.

25. Archives du Ministère des Affaires étrangères (AMAE), Tchécoslovaquie, vol. 50, f. 1: Appel du clergé évangélique réformé de Teschen, 3 décembre 1918.

26. Report of the American delegate of the Teschen Commission, Wilton to Curzon, May 15, 1919, quoted in Croydon, "Problem of Teschen," 163.

27. The archives contain no trace of any instruction from the central governments in this matter (Wandycz, *France and Her Eastern Allies*, 78–79; Davion, *Mon voisin*, 70).

28. AMAE, Tchécoslovaquie, vol. 50, f. 56: letter no. 277 from Stephen Pichon, January 14, 1919. For the request of an Allied intervention, see Davion, *Mon voisin*, 85–87.

29. AMAE, Czechoslovakia, vol. 50, f. 42: letter no. 5353 from the Quai d'Orsay, December 31, 1918, and f. 127: letter no. 933 from Marshal Foch, January 31, 1919.

30. AMAE, Czechoslovakia, vol. 50, f. 81: telegram of January 23, 1919.

31. "Polonais et Tchèques," *L'Indépendance polonaise* no. 2, February 8, 1919, 2–3. Paderewski's warning is in AMAE, Czechoslovakia, vol. 50, f. 81: telegram of January 23, 1919.

32. AMAE, Czechoslovakia, vol. 50, f. 91: conversations between Jules Laroche and Edvard Beneš, January 26, 1919.

33. These numbers were calculated by a Czech historian in 2001 (Kubík, *Těšínský konflikt*, 57).

34. Grappin, *Polonais et Tchèques*, 55.

35. Ibid., 57.

36. AMAE, Tchécoslovaquie, vol. 50, f. 106: communiqué, February 7, 1919.

37. AMAE, Czechoslovakia, vol. 12, f. 2: report 18242 by agent 601-A, February 16, 1919.

38. Louise Weiss, *Mémoires d'une Européenne*, vol. 2, *Combats pour l'Europe 1919–1934* (Paris: Payot, 1969), 23. On Weiss's support for the Czechoslovak cause, see Bernard Michel's chapter "La mémoire slovaque" in his book *La mémoire de Prague: Conscience nationale et intelligentsia dans l'histoire tchèque et slovaque* (Paris: Perrin, 1986), 124–54.

39. AMAE, Czechoslovakia, vol. 50, f. 124: Agreement of January 31, 1919, on the Teschen district, between the Czechoslovaks and the Poles, mediated by the great powers.

40. House of Commons (London), *Debates*, Fifth Series, vol. 114: columns 2938–39, April 16, 1919, quoted in Croydon, "Problem of Teschen," 61.

41. US Department of State, *Papers Relating to the Foreign Relations of the United States: The Paris Peace Conference, 1919*, vol. 3 (Washington, DC: US Government Printing Office, 1942–47), 821.

42. AMAE, Czechoslovakia, vol. 51, f. 56: report by M. Grenard to Minister Pichon, March 9, 1919.

43. AMAE, Czechoslovakia, vol. 50, f. 200: Memorandum of the Warsaw commission for the Teschen commission, February 22, 1919.

44. Niessel's initiative caused Pellé's complaints: AMAE, Czechoslovakia, vol. 50, f. 207: letter no. 11 from General Pellé to Clemenceau, February 26, 1919.

45. Ibid.

46. Beauvois, *La Pologne*, 310–12.

47. *L'Indépendance polonaise,* March 22, 1919, 6–7. See also the reports No. 583 and 788 of the Polish Military Charge d'Affaires in Vienna, reproduced by Grappin, *Polonais et Tchèques,* 58.

48. Antoine Marès, *Edvard Beneš. Un drame entre Hitler et Staline* (Paris: Perrin, 2015), 148.

49. AMAE, Czechoslovakia, vol. 53, f. 111: report presented under the presidency of Jules Cambon, September 10, 1919.

50. AMAE, Czechoslovakia, vol. 53, f. 119: telegram no. 300, September 11, 1919. In March 1919, French delegates in Teschen had suggested a plebiscite for partitioning the disputed territories (AMAE, Czechoslovakia, vol. 51, f. 82: letter of March 15, 1919). Most likely, this was a maneuver to gain time in hope of finding a compromise.

51. SHD, Land Forces, 7N3003, "La question polono-tchèque de Teschen," July 1920.

52. On the Czechoslovak position, see BDIC, *Recueil,* 51–57. On the British position, see Foreign Office, *Documents on British Foreign Policy 1919–1939* (*DBFP*), First Series, vol. 6, *Central Europe and the Far East, June 1919–January 1920* (London: HM Stationery Office, 1956), 165.

53. Croydon, "Problem of Teschen," 35, 88–91.

54. For comparison, two hundred thousand Poles, or one-third of the Polish population, would later vote for Germany in the plebiscite of Upper Silesia (Hunt Tooley, "The Internal Dynamics of Changing Frontiers: The Plebiscites on Germany's Borders, 1919–1921," in *L'établissement des frontières en Europe après les deux guerres mondiales,* ed. Christian Baechler and Carole Fink [Berne: Peter Lang, 1996], 149–65).

55. Davion, *Mon voisin,* 101–2.

56. AMAE, Czechoslovakia, vol. 53, f. no. 111: report presented under the presidency of J. Cambon, September 10, 1919.

57. AMAE, Czechoslovakia, vol. 53, f. no. 119: telegram no. 300, September 11, 1919.

58. *DBFP,* 682–85: Report presented at the Supreme Council by the Commission on Polish Affairs and the Commission on Czechoslovakian Affairs, united on the Teschen Question, September 10, 1919.

59. Lloyd George, *Truth,* 2:929; Croydon, "Problem of Teschen," 56.

60. BDIC, *Recueil,* 381.

61. Marès, *Edvard Beneš,* 148.

62. Alan Sharp and Glyn Stone, eds., *Anglo-French Relations in the Twentieth Century: Rivalry and Cooperation* (London: Routledge, 2000), 125.

63. See Doc. no.101, General Le Rond to Alexandre de Manneville, president of the peace conference, February 11, 1920, in Ministère des Affaires étrangères, *Documents Diplomatiques Français, 1920–1932* (DDF), vol. 1, *10 janvier–18 mai 1920* (Paris: Imprimerie nationale, 1999), 159.

64. Convinced of the pro-Polish bias of the French representatives at the plebiscite commission, the British would go as far as demanding the resignation of the delegate Le Rond (*DBFP,* doc. n°10, Lord Curzon to M. Henderson, first secretary of the British Embassy in Paris, August 31, 1920, 46–47). See also Frédéric Dessberg, "Enjeux et rivalités politiques franco-britanniques: le plébiscite de haute Silésie (1921)," *Revue historique des armées* 254 (2009), 53–66.

65. AMAE, Czechoslovakia, vol. 12, f. no. 21: report by Captain Louradour on his journey to Prague, December 6, 1919.

66. AMAE, Czechoslovakia, vol. 53, f. no. 5: letter from E. Beneš to G. Clemenceau, August 5, 1919.

67. Two examples of posters can be found on the website of the Archives of the Europa-Universität Viadrina Frankfurt (Oder), accessed February 28, 2018, http://archive.is/16zvr.

68. Witold Sienkiewicz, *Illustrowana encyklopedia dziejów Polski* (Warsaw: Książnica, 2011), 175; "Wola ludu dokona cudu." One of the posters is published at Hunt Tooley's blog, professor of History at the Austin College, accessed February 28, 2018, http://paris peace1919.blogspot.fr/2009/10/border-issues-and-paris-peace-ninety.html.

69. "Fear Czech-Polish Break," *New York Times*, May 27, 1920, 18. Several articles about the situation were published between May 23 and May 28. Articles made available online by the Archives of the New York Times, accessed February 28, 2018, spiderbites.nytimes .com/1920/articles_1920_05_00000.html

70. "Les Tchèques en Silésie," *L'Indépendance polonaise*, no.9, March 22, 1919, 6.

71. AMAE (ADN), vol. 119, f. no. 12: letter no. 4, February 23, 1920.

72. AMAE (ADN), vol. 119, f. no. 12: note no. 5, March 10, 1920.

73. Czech workers claimed to live under a regime of terror established by the Poles. For their part, the Poles denounced the forced expulsions practiced by the Czechs at workplaces (Davion, *Mon voisin*, 103–6).

74. Croydon, "Problem of Teschen," 1967; Cejka-Magnusson, "Teschen Question," 143.

75. AMAE (ADN), vol. 118, f. no. 3, letter no. 5, April 14, 1920.

76. The initial date of 1914 is finally set despite Polish complaints. See Stanislas Raubal, La fixation de la frontière entre la Pologne et la Tchécoslovaquie" (PhD diss., Université de Paris, 1928), 89.

77. Beneš himself highlighted to the French government: "The agreement will not be able to succeed unless the Great Powers act quickly and without delay" (AMAE, Czechoslovakia, vol. 12, f. no. 30: handwritten letter from General Pellé, March 31, 1920).

78. AMAE, series: League of Nations (SDN), sub-series: Secretariat General, vol. 2159, f. no. 52: report by Gustave de Manneville, February 10, 1920.

79. AMAE, Czechoslovakia, vol. 54, f. no. 47: report by head of battalion Mellier to Gustave de Manneville, February 27, 1920.

80. AMAE, Czechoslovakia, vol. 54, f. no. 71: telegram of March 13, 1920.

81. AMAE, Czechoslovakia, vol. 55, f. no. 34: report no. 18, May 19, 1920.

82. Wandycz, *France and Her Eastern Allies*, 149.

83. AMAE, SDN, Secretariat General, vol. 2159, f. no. 55: report by Gustave de Manneville, May 19, 1920.

84. Laroche, "La question de Teschen," 8–24.

85. National Archives (London), Foreign Office records, 404/1, doc. 66 p. 126: report no. 32 by E. Wilton, May 15, 1920.

86. Foreign Office, 404/1, annex to doc. 66 p. 128: report by delegate C. R. Flowers: "Of the Occurrences in Orlau and Poremba on May 7, 1920."

87. AMAE, Poland, vol. 30, f. no. 269: summary report from June 10 to July 10, 1920.

88. AMAE, Czechoslovakia, vol. 8, f. no. 187: letter from General Pellé, January 11, 1920.

89. AMAE, Czechoslovakia, vol. 12, f. no. 30: handwritten letter from General Pellé, March 31, 1920.

90. Ibid.

91. AMAE, Poland, vol. 30, f. no. 45: summary of intelligence from April 10 to May 10, 1920.

92. AMAE, Czechoslovakia, vol. 54, f. no. 144: letter no. 562 to Minister of War André Lefèvre and to Marshal Foch, April 9, 1920.

93. AMAE, Czechoslovakia, vol. 55, f. no. 75: letter from Patek to H. de Panafieu, May 22, 1920.

94. AMAE (ADN), Representation of France, vol. 119, dossier no. 12: note no. 14 from July 3, 1920.

95. AMAE, Czechoslovakia, vol. 55, f. no. 124, note no. 105 from Clément-Simon, June 4, 1920.

96. AMAE, SDN, Secretariat General, vol. 290, f. no. 6: Declaration of the Polish and Czech delegates on the Teschen Silesia Question on July 10, 1920.

97. AMAE, Poland, vol. 79, f.no. 94: engagement signed by W. Grabski on July 10, 1920.

98. AMAE, Czechoslovakia, vol. 56, f. no. 247: convention on Teschen, July 28, 1920.

99. Gallois, "Le plebiscite," 176–78.

100. AMAE, Czechoslovakia, vol. 57, f. no. 25: report no. 60, August 2, 1920.

101. The League of Nations operated on a similar logic regarding the filing of complaints, provided by the Minority Protection Treaty of 1919 (Marie-Renée Mouton, "La SDN et la protection des minorités nationales en Europe," *Relations Internationales* 75 [1993], 315–28).

102. Kai Struve and Philipp Ther, eds. *Die Grenzen der Nationen. Identitätenwandel in Oberschlesien in der Neuzeit* (Marburg: Herder-Institut, 2002).

103. In the case of Upper Silesia, the British government offered the commission any help to ensure that the plebiscite could take place; see doc. no. 138, Étienne Peretti de la Rocca to General Le Rond, February 21, 1921, in DDF, vol. 2, May 19 to September 23, 236.

# Bibliography

Arcidiacono, Bruno. *Cinq types de paix. Une histoire des plans de pacification perpétuelle (XVIIe–XXe siècles).* Paris: Presses Universitaires de France, 2011.

Beauvois, Daniel. *La Pologne. Histoire, société, culture.* Paris: Éditions de La Martinière, 2004.

Beneš, Edvard. *Světová válka a naše revoluce.*Vol. 2. Prague: Orbis, 1927.

Bibliothèque de Documentation Internationale Contemporaine (BDIC). *Recueil des Actes de la Conférence de la Paix.*Partie 4, *Commissions de la conférence.*Vol. C3, *Commissions relatives aux affaires de Teschen, Spisz et Orava.* Paris: Imprimerie Nationale, 1929.

Bussière, Éric, Isabelle Davion, and Stanislas Jeannesson, eds. *Penser le système international XIXᵉ–XXIᵉ siècles. Autour de l'œuvre de Georges-Henri Soutou.* Paris: Presses de l'Université Paris-Sorbonne, 2013.

Cornwall, Mark, and John Paul Newman, eds. *Sacrifice and Rebirth. The Legacy of the Last Habsburg War.* Austrian and Habsburg Studies. Vol. 18. New York: Berghahn, 2016

Croydon, Peggy. "The Problem of Teschen at Paris Peace Conference with Special Emphasis on British Policy." PhD diss., McGill University, 1967.

Cude, Michael R. "Wilsonian National Self-Determination and the Slovak Question during the Founding of Czechoslovakia, 1918–1921." *Diplomatic History* vol. 40, n. 1 (2016) 155–180.

Cejka-Magnusson, Thomazena. "The Teschen Question at the Paris Peace Conference." PhD diss., North Texas University, 1971.

Davion, Isabelle. "Les relations polono-tchécoslovaques dans la politique de sécurité française entre les deux guerres." PhD diss., Paris-Sorbonne, 2004.

———.*Mon voisin, cet ennemi.* Brussels: Peter Lang, 2009.

Dessberg, Frédéric. "Enjeux et rivalités politiques franco-britanniques: le plébiscite de haute Silésie (1921)." *Revue historique des armées* 254 (2009): 53–66.

Eichenberg, Julia, and John Paul Newman, eds. *The Great War and Veterans' Internationalism.* London: Palgrave Macmillan, 2013.

Fink, Carol. "The Problem of Minority Rights and Democracy in Eastern Europe from the Paris Peace Conference to the Fall of the Soviet Empire: The International Dimension." In *L'Europe au XXe siècle: Éléments pour un bilan,* edited by Tomasz Shramm, 333–46. Poznań: Instytut Historii Uniwersytet im Adama Mickiewicza, 2000.

Foreign Office. *Documents on British Foreign Policy 1919–1939.* First Series, vol. 6, *Central Europe and the Far East, June 1919–January 1920.* London: Her Majesty Stationery Office, 1956.

Gallois, Lucien. "Le plébiscite de Teschen." *Annales de Géographie* 30, no 163 (1921), 76–78.

Grappin, Henri. *Polonais et Tchèque: La Silésie de Teschen.*Paris: Imprimerie Flinikowski, 1919.

Jackson, Peter. *Beyond the Balance of Power: France and the Politics of National Security in the Era of the First World War.* Cambridge: Cambridge University Press, 2013.

Jeannesson, Stanislas. *Jacques Seydoux (1870–1929). Un diplomate européen.* Paris: Presses de l'Université Paris-Sorbonne, 2012.

Kennedy, Ross, ed. *A Companion to Woodrow Wilson.* Oxford: Wiley-Blackwell, 2013.

Kostrbová, Lucie, Jana Malínská, and Lucie Merhautová, eds. *1918. Model komplexního transformačního procesu?* Prague: Masarykův ústav a Archiv AV ČR, 2010.

Krüger, Peter. *Das europäische Staatensystem im Wandel.* Munich: Oldenbourg, 1996.

Kubík, Lubomír. *Těšínský konflikt. Dramatické okamžiky česko-polských vztahů.* Olomouc: Votobia, 2001.

Laroche, Jules. "La question de Teschen devant la Conférence de la Paix 1919–1920." *Revue d'histoire diplomatique* (January–June 1948), 8–27.

Lloyd George, David. *The Truth about the Peace Treaties.* 2 vols. London: Victor Gollancz, 1938.

Marès, Antoine. *Edvard Beneš. Un drame entre Hitler et Staline.* Paris: Perrin, 2015.

Michel, Bernard. *La mémoire de Prague: Conscience nationale et intelligentsia dans l'histoire tchèque et slovaque.* Paris: Perrin, 1986.

Ministère des Affaires étrangères. *Documents diplomatiques français, 1920–1932.* Vol. 1, *10 janvier–18 mai 1920*; vol. 2, *19 mai–23 septembre.* Paris: Imprimerie Nationale, 1997; 1999.

Marie-Renée Mouton, "La SDN et la protection des minorités nationales en Europe," *Relations Internationales* 75 [1993], 315–28.

Nicolson, Harold. *Peacemaking 1919.* New York: Grosset & Dunlap, 1933.

Raubal, Stanislas. "La fixation de la frontière entre la Pologne et la Tchécoslovaquie. Thèse." PhD diss., Université de Paris, Paris, 1928.

Schwabe, Klaus. "Negotiating Peace Terms for Germany." In *A Companion to Woodrow Wilson,* edited by Ross Kennedy, 445–66. Oxford: Wiley-Blackwell, 2013.

Schroeder, Paul W. *The Transformation of European Politics 1763–1848.* Oxford: Oxford University Press, 1994.

Sharp, Alan. *The Versailles Settlement: Peacemaking in Paris, 1919.* Houndmills: Macmillan, 1991.

Sharp, Alan, and Glyn Stone, eds. *Anglo-French Relations in the Twentieth Century: Rivalry and Cooperation*. London: Routledge, 2000.

Sienkiewicz, Witold. *Illustrowana encyklopedia dziejów Polski*. Warsaw: Książnica, 2011.

Struve, Kai, and Philipp Ther, eds. *Die Grenzen der Nationen. Identitätenwandel in Oberschlesien in der Neuzeit*. Marburg: Herder-Institut, 2002.

Tooley, Hunt. "The Internal Dynamics of Changings Frontiers: The Plebiscites on Germany's Borders, 1919–1921," 149–55. In *L'établissement des frontières en Europe après les deux guerres mondiales*, edited by Christian Baechler and Carole Fink, 149–55. Berne: Peter Lang, 1996.

US Department of State. *Papers Relating to the Foreign Relations of the United States: The Paris Peace Conference, 1919*. Vol. 3. Washington, DC: US Government Printing Office, 1942–47.

Wandycz, Piotr S. *France and Her Eastern Allies 1919–1925: French-Czechoslovak-Polish Relations from the Paris Peace Conference to Locarno*. Minneapolis: University of Minnesota Press, 1962.

Weiss, Louise. *Mémoires d'une Européenne*. Vol. 2, *Combats pour l'Europe 1919–1934*. Paris: Payot, 1969.

ISABELLE DAVION is Associate Professor of Contemporary History at Sorbonne-University in Paris. She is author of *Mon voisin, cet ennemi. La politique de sécurité française face aux relations polono-tchécoslovaques entre 1919 et 1939*.

# 3    National Self-Determination and Political Legitimacy after Versailles

*Leon Wasilewski and the German-Polish Borderlands, 1919–39*

Jesse Kauffman

Scholars seeking the origins of German brutality in Poland and elsewhere in eastern Europe during the Second World War have identified as one of its sources a poisonous *völkisch* political ideology that festered in Germany for decades before erupting into the viciousness of the Nazis' war of racial annihilation—a mere prelude, perhaps, to the still greater horrors promised by the Generalplan Ost. This völkisch ideology and its proponents aggressively laid claim to all territory that could be claimed as ethnically or culturally "German," regardless of the state within which, by virtue of historical accident, this territory happened to be located. The period after the Great War was especially propitious for the nurturing and radicalization of this ideology, and historians such as Gregor Thum have argued that German political discourse and foreign policy underwent a völkisch turn in the era of the Weimar Republic, with scholars and publicists claiming as German large swaths of European territory that extended well beyond the pre-1914 borders of the Prusso-German Empire. "An internal connection of the German people from the Rhine to the Volga," writes Thum, the most forceful and eloquent proponent of the völkisch turn reading of the period, "was propagated by this ethnocentric research and its popularization in the years between the World Wars." Thus the stage was set for the Nazis, who accelerated this drive toward radical ethnocentric expansionism at the same time that they stripped away much of the vagueness of the word *Volk* by rooting it in biological ideas of race. The ideological and political inertia generated by Weimar's völkisch turn drove Germany implacably, if not inevitably, toward the "turn's" ultimate consummation in the Nazis' murderous reign in Europe, especially in the East.[1]

Thum and others have convincingly illustrated and fortified their claims, and there is much to recommend their idea of a völkisch turn. However, there are other ways to interpret this ideology that make it less uniquely German and, at the same time, provide an expanded explanation for why it flourished in the years after the First World War. For while the völkisch turn certainly represented a continuation and expansion of prewar German nationalist thought, it was also a reflection of a much broader, more general turn after the Great War—the turn toward national self-determination, with its radical fusion of nationalism, territorial sovereignty, and the modern bureaucratic state. While self-determination, with its implicit promise of democracy and liberation from oppressive overlords, generally has positive connotations, scholars such as Eric Weitz have begun to trace the destructive effects of its implementation as a political practice. Ethnic cleansing, for example, can be interpreted as a logical, if not inevitable, outcome of the creation of sovereign states based on national self-determination, which both creates the category of national minorities and suggests, even if not explicitly, that they do not belong. In this vein, the völkisch turn, like ethnic cleansing, can be seen as a product of, rather than a deviation from, the Paris system—the European political order after the First World War based on nation-states that linked national self-determination with sovereignty.[2]

A central problem of the Paris system is that it demands a precise alignment of states, territories, and peoples in ways alien to political orders created in earlier eras. In twentieth-century Europe, this alignment had to be created, oftentimes by force—by border wars, for example, as well as by ethnic cleansing and population transfers. Somewhat less obviously, national self-determination, the system's ideological foundation, rejects the boundaries created by state-centered political identities. The territorial claims of the state based on self-determination are bounded only by the extent to which the nation can be delimited.[3] The expansiveness of the claims encouraged by this norm was reflected not only in postwar German nationalism but in the political ambitions of the Polish political elite who re-created a Polish state in Europe from the political wreckage of the Great War. "I saw M. Dmowski and M. Paderewski in Washington," Woodrow Wilson told his European counterparts in Paris during the peace conference, "and I asked them to define Poland for me, as they understood it, and they presented me with a map in which they claimed a large part of the earth."[4] This is not to impute any particularly unique avarice to Roman Dmowski or Ignacy Paderewski. Rather, it merely shows the way that the language of national self-determination dissolved the formal and informal restraints of earlier eras and encouraged wide-ranging claims—which is precisely, as scholars such as Thum have noted, what made the völkisch turn so destructive.

In spite of the profound impact it had on the European society of states and the people who inhabited that society, national self-determination in this period was less a fully fledged and clearly articulated political program than a nebulous but powerful language of legitimacy—that mysterious force that cloaks the demands made by power and renders them acceptable. Legitimacy is, in turn, always linked to and derived from a broader political culture—those values and ideas that determine, usually tacitly and informally (and even unconsciously) the specific forms that claims to legitimacy may take. Legitimacy and political culture play roles in both domestic and foreign politics; and in the world after the Great

War, national self-determination became the ne plus ultra of political legitimacy at home and abroad.[5] Consequently, it drew on the cultural raw material from which such claims to legitimacy might plausibly be formed and, conversely, channeled the attention of political elites toward the places where such materials might be found. In other words, certain intellectual disciplines—for example, history or linguistics—lent themselves well to the articulation of political claims based on self-determination and so found themselves both contributing to, and being shaped by, the political disputes of the era. While a great many languages of legitimacy have existed over time, the fact that states and political movements *all over the world* claimed after 1918 to speak for "the people," both at home and in their interactions with other states, strongly suggests that these other languages (of law, or dynastic right, or religion, or tradition, for example) had lost their power to legitimate with stunning rapidity. Whether motivated by the deepest sincerity or the emptiest cynicism, states after the First World War positioned themselves at home and abroad as vehicles for the interests and aspirations of their people— their Volk.[6] (The fact that *Volk* and *völkisch* are usually left untranslated in English-language monographs has helped to obscure the family resemblance between Germany's postwar ethnopolitical claims and those of other countries.) [7]

One way to illustrate the broader cultural context within which Germany's völkisch claims to territory were formulated is to examine the way that Polish claims to the same territory were advanced. As will be shown below using the case of the scholar, diplomat, and political activist Leon Wasilewski (1870–1936) and his activities related to the Polish-German border dispute after the First World War, such a comparison reveals a great deal of linguistic and ideological overlap between Polish and German political rhetoric in this period. While these similarities have been noted by other historians, comparative analyses of the two have tended to focus on the question of whether this suggests an essential unity between Nazi and Polish conceptions of race, nation, and state.[8] However, even if such a unity exists, this simply demands an explanation of *why* it exists. One answer is that the process of translating the vague notion of "national self-determination" into a specific set of claims about territory and the nature of the people living on it was responsible for the radicalization of ethnonational claims to land in central Europe in both Poland and Germany. Drawing on a nineteenth-century intellectual inheritance, Germany's völkisch turn, which animated Germany's claims to territory ruled by Poland after 1919, was both a product and an accelerator of this process, as was Poland's embrace of similar rhetoric in its disputes with Germany over where Poland ended and Germany began. In a world in which national self-determination had risen to normative supremacy, there were few, if any, other ways of articulating legitimate claims to territory.[9]

## *Ostforschung* and *Myśl Zachodnia*: Nineteenth-Century Sources

As the Polish-German border dispute smoldered in the years after Versailles, both parties articulated their arguments by drawing on political ideologies that stretched back into the century or so preceding the outbreak of the war. In these early formative years, the competing ideologies, for all their differences, already bore many similarities. In Poland, the ideology from which its postwar rhetoric would be fashioned was "westernism" (*myśl zachodnia*), an amorphous current of nineteenth-century thought that claimed as rightfully Polish the mixed German-Polish areas in the eastern territories of the German empire, including parts or all of Silesia, Pomerania, West Prussia, Posen, and East Prussia. The formation of westernism was connected with the rise of National Democracy in partitioned Poland, which sought a westward-focused Polish state—in contrast to the nationalism of the Polish Socialist Party, which focused on the eastern reaches of the former Polish-Lithuanian Commonwealth. Scholars from a variety of disciplines contributed to the articulation of westernism's intellectual contours, though history, geography, and archaeology played particularly important roles. The last discipline lent itself especially well to the conflict over the original ethnic composition of the territory in dispute (that is, the attempt to determine who the region's "true" autochthons were)—a key point of contention in the Polish-German border disputes. This was due in part to methodological principles in the field, associated most prominently with the German philologist and antiquarian Gustaf Kossinna, which held that the ethnic identity of ancient and long-vanished peoples could be ascertained by a careful study of the material culture they left behind. Archaeology was also well suited to anachronistic political debates because its "silent sources" could be made, in capable hands, to say many different things. Thus Kossinna and his German disciples argued that archaeological evidence clearly indicated that the earliest settlements in the Oder-Vistula region were German. Any Slavs living there were therefore descended from intruders who arrived at some later date.[10] In 1914, a Polish student of Kossinna's, Józef Kostrzewski, examined the same evidence and concluded that the land between the Oder and Vistula Rivers was the ancient ancestral homeland of Slavs. Any Germans who happened to be living there in 1914 must, therefore, be descended from outsiders who arrived at some later date.

Polish geographers also played a prominent role in the culture wars over the borderlands. A notable example of this is the atlas produced in 1914 by a geographer at Lwów University, Eugeniusz Romer. In it, "Poland" was portrayed as encompassing broad stretches of territory, including Silesia, that were under German sovereignty at that time. The Austrians tried to suppress the book during the war, since the question of what might become of Poland after it was over presented the Austro-German alliance with a formidable challenge; neither wanted to see the other's influence increased in Polish Europe, but each had a significant Polish population that could be drawn into the influence of any newly created Polish polity carved from the ruins of the Russian Empire.[11] After the Central powers' defeat, Romer's atlas surfaced in Paris, where it was consulted by those redrawing the map of Europe.[12] Historians also joined the fray, creating and promoting a master narrative of Polish history that buttressed Poland's claims to Imperial Germany's eastern borderlands. According to this narrative, the Piast dynasty, the founders and rulers of Poland from the ninth to the fourteenth centuries, had created an illustrious, mighty state, whose history, interests, and ambitions oriented it toward the west (according to tradition, the dynasty founded Poland in the city of Gniezno, which was under German rule by the nineteenth century). Then, owing to a series of political miscalculations in the twelfth century, the kingdom began to weaken, with the result that aggressive German predators began an invasion that had continued, unceasing, until the present day. The end result was that the German state was built atop a massive "Slavic cemetery." And if there were people in the erstwhile Polish lands who believed themselves to be German, they were either invaders or Poles who had been brutally forced to assimilate to Germanic culture and had forgotten their true, essential identity.[13]

A similar process occurred in Germany, where scholars and publicists articulated claims to legitimate German rule in supposedly more backward central Europe, including the German-Polish borderlands, claims that became part of the political vocabulary of that country's post-Versailles hostility toward Poland. The idea that first Prussia and then, after 1871, Germany had the right to rule over the inferior Slavs of central Europe dates back at least to the eighteenth-century partitions of the Polish Republic, when Prussia, Russia, and Austria annexed and divided up the large but weak state. The Prussians justified their rule over their new Polish subjects in part by claiming that the Poles had proven themselves incapable of self-governance. *Polnische Wirtschaft*, literally "Polish economy" but perhaps more loosely but accurately translated as a "Polish state of affairs," became synonymous with indolence, chaos, inefficiency, dirt, and backwardness. German rule and culture were therefore necessary to bring order, discipline, and prosperity to the unfortunate lands of the Poles. In the nineteenth century, these condescending attitudes were propagated by numerous intellectual figures, including the writer Gustav Freytag. In his novel *Soll und Haben*, hardworking Germans bring the blessings of civilization to the shabby Slavic town of Rosmin, where they settle and sell high-quality goods to the ignorant Slavic farmers and build impressive, sturdy buildings to replace their primitive dwellings.[14] Several factors, including an increase in aggressive German nationalism along with fears that the Germans in the Prussian east were going to be demographically overwhelmed by the Polish population, encouraged the development and spread of these ideas. One of their most prominent (and virulent) advocates was the eminent historian Heinrich von Treitschke. Treitschke looked back to the medieval invasion and settlement of central Europe by the Teutonic Knights as a great moment in the history of European progress. The knights had brought the light of German order and culture to the dark heart of Slavic Europe and had served as a bulwark against the encroachments of eastern barbarism. In 1862, Treitschke singled out the "northward and eastward rush of the German spirit and the formidable activities of our people as conqueror . . . teacher, discipliner of its neighbors" as the "most stupendous and fruitful occurrence of the later Middle Ages."[15] Later in the nineteenth century, the sociologist Max Weber warned that the Germans and their civilization in the East were in danger of being drowned in a flood of Polish chaos. The Poles, he told his audience at an address in Freiburg in 1895, were well suited to life in the East, where their primitive state allowed them to thrive and multiply in harsh places where the more advanced Germans could live only with great difficulty.[16] A related phenomenon, connected to both anti-Polish chauvinism and increased popular nationalism, was the widespread interest among scholars and political activists in the late nineteenth century in settlements of ethnic Germans outside of Germany, particularly in the East.[17]

In both Poland and Germany, the outbreak of the First World War gave renewed life and energy to these ideas, although neither German nor Polish ideas about how political and ethnic space in central Europe should be arranged made much of an impact on events during the war.[18] In the bitter disputes of the postwar years, the unmistakable family resemblances between German and Polish ethnonational political rhetoric, already visible in their nineteenth-century adolescence, came into sharper relief when they were mustered in support of their respective states' postwar claims.

## Theory to Practice

The postwar period, from the convening of the peace conference until well after the signing of the Treaty of Versailles, marked the period within which the competing ethnonational claims to the German-Polish borderlands came to full maturity. This was due to the complex array of historical forces and processes which, though essentially discrete, intertwined and reinforced each other within the world of postwar central Europe. One process, which formed the broad historical background within which Germany and Poland argued over the location of their new border, was the realignment of territory and the creation of new polities in central Europe after 1918. While this process is frequently seen as the beginning of a new era, it helps explain the fraught nature of the process when we bear in mind that it was also the end of another. Beginning in 1917 with the Russian Revolution and continuing into the years after the war ended, the political order established in central Europe after the Napoleonic Wars completely collapsed. After that earlier conflict, sovereignty in central Europe, including authority over the Polish vassal state created by Napoleon, had been returned to the Kingdom of Prussia and the Austrian and Russian Empires. This arrangement generally held firm for the century between the Congress of Vienna and the outbreak of the Great War, though it was repeatedly challenged from within. Serious upheaval for most of the nineteenth century was limited primarily to Russia's Polish territories, but by the late nineteenth century, a host of social and political movements sought either the modification or the overthrow of this order. While the imperial states (including, after 1871, Imperial Germany) were perhaps more resilient than it may seem in retrospect and could have adapted to these challenges, they were nonetheless unable to cope with the strains of total war. First Russia and then, a year later, Austria collapsed (as did, somewhat less completely, Germany) and disintegrated, inaugurating a protracted, bloody struggle to determine what would fill the void.[19]

From this struggle emerged a reborn Polish state: the Second Republic. The last sovereign Polish state had been absorbed by its more powerful neighbors in the eighteenth century, and the varieties of Polish nationalism that had developed over the next hundred years held differing ideas about where, exactly, "Poland" was. Partly for this reason, and partly due to the simultaneous establishment of other new states in central Europe that likewise lacked a way clearly to determine where their borders should be, the new Polish state was immediately embroiled in a series of border disputes with its neighbors, disputes that festered throughout the postwar period. One of the most intractable was its border dispute with Germany, which was the result of the acquisition by Poland, with the support of the victorious powers gathered in Paris, of territory that had been under German sovereignty before the war (namely Posen, West Prussia, and, later, parts of Silesia) but to which the Polish state now laid claim. For numerous reasons, including the presence of a substantial German minority in these territories, Germany refused to accept this loss, resulting in a state of unresolved German-Polish tension that endured for decades.

Finally, acting as an accelerant on this combustible material was the establishment at the Paris Peace Conference of national self-determination as the universal norm for legitimating domestic and foreign political claims. The conference and its resulting treaties and agreements marked the moment at which self-determination became fused with nationalism. This was partially the result of the western Allies' wartime decision to support the demands of the European nationalities of the Austro-Hungarian Empire (and postrevolutionary Russian Empire) for self-government. At the same time, Woodrow Wilson began to proclaim that self-determination would have to be the foundation on which a just and stable postwar world was built (even if neither he, nor anyone else, knew quite what was meant by the term or how it might be used to create political structures).[20] The fusion of the two—national liberation and self-determination—resulted in the drive to align peoples, borders, and states in Europe that was, next to the desire to punish Germany, the animating force of the peace conference and the resulting Paris system. This inaugurated a border dispute in the heart of Europe, any solution of which would have to take into account, or appear to take into account, "the people."

Defining, locating, counting, and sorting "the people," as well as documenting their connection to a given piece of territory, thus became matters of political urgency and a key feature of the Paris system.[21] This led to another salient characteristic of the Paris system—the newly prominent role technocratic and scholarly experts played in shaping international affairs. While such experts had played a role in creating policies, laws, and institutions within states for centuries, in 1919 they emerged as a powerful force in directing relations between them, a force that endured after the conference was over.[22] Thus scholars in both Poland and Germany played an active role in supporting their respective nations' claims in the disputed territories, just as they had in the nineteenth century, but now with greater prominence and influence.

While international boundaries may have been reinforced in this period, boundaries between intellectual disciplines certainly were not: as in the nineteenth century, linguists, geographers, historians, economists, and anthropologists readily joined forces to do intellectual combat with their ideological opponents across the border. At conferences and meetings and within the pages of pamphlets, books, and learned journals, these academics and propagandists denounced with outrage the claims of the other side and advanced, with all the trappings of serious scholarly inquiry, their own. The other side was carefully watched, and activity on one side could provoke (relatively) swift countermeasures by the other. The 1930 publication in Germany of a book entitled *Ostpreußen. 700 Jahre deutsches Land* (East Prussia: 700 years a German land), for example, led directly to a Polish work meant to refute and discredit it, *Prusy Wschodnie. Przeszłość i teraźniejszość* (East Prussia: Past and present), which was issued in 1932. The work of those active in this transnational argument was supported, codified, and disseminated by a variety of institutions. A prominent center of westernism after the war was Poznań University. Its Western Slavic Institute in particular, led by Mikołaj Rudnicki, played an important role in gathering historical ammunition for Polish diplomats and politicians to use against Germany. The institute's focus was the ancient history of the region, and its scholars collected evidence that they believed established primordial Slavic claims to the borderlands.[23]

Another institution advancing the cause of Polish westernism was the Baltic Institute, founded for the express purpose of disputing German claims to the borderlands.[24] The institute supported, for example, the work of geographers who sought to establish proof of deep cultural and economic links between Pomerania and the rest of Poland. Prominent affiliates of the institute included Stanisław Pawłowski, head of the Geographical Institute at Poznań University, whose work sought to portray Pomerania as an "ancient . . . Slavic region on the Baltic." (His German opponents, meanwhile, included N. Creutzberg, his counterpart at Danzig Polytechnic University, who laid claim to the same territory as a "German cultural landscape in north-eastern Europe.")[25] A 1930 Polish appeal to the League of Nations illustrates how such seemingly vacuous and arcane disputes could trigger international tensions as well as how these arguments could filter down to other levels of society. As part of a lengthy protest of what the Polish state insisted was the shabby treatment of Poles in Danzig, strenuous objections were raised to what the protest referred to as the "unseemly and tendentious propaganda" served up to schoolchildren in Danzig. One particular cause for outrage was a book entitled *Mein Vaterland. Lesebuch für das 5. bis 8. Schuljahr* (My Fatherland. A primer for the fifth to eighth school year), which informed students that "even when Jesus walked the earth, Germans lived in our country on the banks of the Vistula."[26] Thus in the age of national self-determination did arguments over ancient history reach down into the lives of children and up into the highest spheres of international politics.

The work of Wasilewski illustrates in greater detail the way that Polish propagandists countered such German claims and how they articulated specifically Polish demands within the general cultural framework of national self-determination. Wasilewski was a veteran activist with the nationalist wing of the Polish Socialist Party, a member of the party's executive committee, and a close confederate of Józef Piłsudski. He briefly served as foreign minister of the re-created Polish state after the war, before traveling to Paris to serve as part of the Polish delegation at the peace conference. Whatever his political qualifications for such a post may have been, his intellectual background made him superbly equipped to do ideological battle amid the cacophony of conflicting national demands that beset the key figures at the conference; Wasilewski was, in addition to his work as a political activist, an amateur ethnographer and historian. Before 1918, he had published books on Silesia, on Jews in Poland, on Poland's eastern marches (*Kresy*), and on nationalities in the Russian Empire. There was no better preparation for the international political arena after the First World War. In the years after the peace settlement was concluded, Wasilewski continued his scholarly work, heading the Institute for Research on Recent Polish History as well as the Institute for the Study of Ethnic Affairs.[27] He also continued to contribute to the ongoing international argument over the legitimacy of the new Polish state's territorial claims in its borderlands.

## Polish and Völkisch: Wasilewski's *Nationalities in Pomerania*

Among Wasilewski's publications in this era was a 1934 pamphlet, *Nationalities in Pomerania*, published as part of the Baltic Institute's "Baltic Pocket Library" series. Wasilewski's arguments in the pamphlet are valuable in that they reveal how a Polish scholar and politician translated the vague language of national self-determination into specific claims to disputed territory. In addition, since the pamphlet, published in English, was intended for wide consumption, it illustrates the kinds of arguments that Wasilewski believed would carry weight in the international community—a community whose mores and norms Wasilewski was intimately familiar with. Wasilewski's propaganda is also valuable in that, as a member of the Polish Socialist Party, his ideological focus should have been on the eastern, rather than the western border, and he should have been sympathetic to civic-cultural definitions of the "nation." Yet in his broadsides against German claims in Poland's border areas, Wasilewski defends Polish rights there using the language of völkisch-nativist ethnonationalism with a vehemence and a fluency that was equal to that of any National Democrat or German völkisch ideologue. This shows the way that international disputes conducted in the language of self-determination encouraged the spread and strengthening of völkisch ideology throughout Europe. Far from being a uniquely German pathology, it was the vernacular in which political arguments were conducted.

Wasilewski's pamphlet musters this language specifically to defend Polish claims to the voivodeship of Pomerania—the so-called Polish corridor, formed from the erstwhile Prussian province of West Prussia. Wasilewski summarily rejects the idea that purely political or utilitarian considerations were behind the incorporation of the voivodeship into the new Polish state. Seeking to clothe this territorial shift in moral draperies tailored to the sensibilities of the post-Versailles world, Wasilewski argues that it represented the correction of a terrible historical injustice, since Polish land was merely being returned to its rightful sovereigns from whom it had been so brutally seized. To defend this position, Wasilewski, much like the scholars of the previous century had, weaves together a narrative that blends together ancient rule of the region by Polish kings with the supposed long-standing residence there of ethnic Poles, both of whom were, over the centuries, harassed by waves of aggressive Teutonic invaders. Mustering evidence such as place names, medieval chronicles, registers of family names, and population statistics, *Nationalities in Pomerania* represents an attempt to link together nation, territory, and state and then to project the resulting fusion back in time.

Wasilewski's pamphlet demonstrates several of the ways in which the bond between people and territory could be ideologically established in the postwar world, as well as the way they drew on the arguments and methods established in the nineteenth century. One tactic was to show that a given people inhabited a piece of land "first"—that is, to claim the status of autochthons for one's own ethnic group. Hence the emphasis on the ancient history of the Polish-German borderlands in both sides' propaganda. "In the earliest historical information we have about Pomerania, dating from the 9th century," Wasilewski writes, "we are told that it is a Slav country." These ancient Slavic inhabitants—ancestors of the Kashubes—were ethnic cousins of other primeval tribes, the Polanians and the Mazovians, which, when taken together, formed an ethnic whole, the Lechites, the putative ancestral ethnic mass from which twentieth-century Poles emerged.[28] Similar counterarguments were mounted by German scholars, who also plumbed the depths of the ancient past in order to claim right of original tenancy for the Germans. Wolfgang LaBaume, for example, wrote in 1926 that Germany had the right to territory in the East on the basis of ancient habitation, since "the whole of eastern Germany up to the Oder in the West and the greater part of the present Republic of Poland . . . is, as the germanic character of the finds enables us to recognize, germanic, and in particular eastern germanic territory," and had been since centuries before the birth of Christ.[29]

Continuous habitation by an ethnic group was thus one way that the link between people and territory was asserted after Versailles. This was not, however, enough to justify the Polish Republic's claim to sovereign rule in the region, since political loyalties there had long been constructed out of dynastic, legal, and religious raw materials. Did not a Polish-speaking subject of the Prussian crown owe his loyalty to that crown and hence to the German republic that succeeded it? Wasilewski dispenses with such objections by locating the origins of the modern Polish state in the consolidation of the Piast Kingdom under Mieszko I. While this was, and remains, a staple of the master narrative of Polish national history, in Wasilewski's treatment the organic, primeval ethnonational (or völkisch) link between the dynasty and the Polish people is emphasized.[30] The Piasts, he writes, evolved from the Polanian branch of the Lechite people, and as their power grew, they inevitably turned their attention to the Pomeranians and their territory—not because the Piasts were expansionist, but because they "regarded the Pomeranians as a group so closely related to themselves from the ethnic point of view that the incorporation of Pomerania into the general organization of the State appeared to be unquestionably right and just."[31] It was ultimately Mieszko I who, like some ancient Bismarck, was able to overcome regional and religious divisions (the Pomeranians were, according to Wasilewski, pagans) and remedy this unnatural and unjust state of affairs by uniting the Polish people into their own state. "The first ruler of Poland known to history," Wasilewski writes, "Mieszko I (962–992), realized even in his time that the Pomeranians were but just one of the Lechite tribes, like many others of which his young state was made up[,] and he persevered untiringly in his efforts to annex Pomerania and finally included the whole of it, from Stettin to Danzig, into Poland." Thus was the first Polish state created on the basis of national self-determination.[32]

With Polish rule firmly established by Mieszko, successive rulers of Pomerania presided over the fortification of its original Polish character in both ethnic and cultural terms: as large numbers of Polish settlers arrived, they brought with them Polish elite culture, in particular the Polish language. This wholly natural and just process was rudely interrupted by the Teutonic Knights, who invaded and violently forced an alien ethno-cultural character on the region. (In Danzig, according to Wasilewski, the Polish character of the city was eradicated in a genocidal slaughter.) The knights were followed by other German intruders until, in 1466, the order was finally defeated. Pomerania was returned to the Polish crown and acquired the name of Royal Prussia.[33]

Wasilewski's argument that the spread of the Polish language reinforced the Polish character of the region and, in turn, the right of a Polish state to rule it, illustrates another connection between the ideologues on either side of the Polish-German border in this period. One seemingly—but deceptively—simple way to translate national self-determination from theory to practice is to award disputed territories to a claimant state based on the nationality of the majority of the population living in said territory. Therefore, Wasilewski, like the armies of politicians, scholars, and activists trying to reconstruct the political world after the First World War, pressed Poland's claims to Pomerania using numerical data, including in his pamphlet population statistics of suspicious precision, constructed around categories of dubious clarity (claiming, for example, that in 1931, 89.9 percent of Pomerania was "Polish"). However, in Poland, Germany, and beyond, feuding national factions did not rely on sheer numbers (or history) alone. After all, this meant that population shifts could easily tip the balance of the population to the side of a rival—if a region's population changed, for example, from 49 percent Polish and 51 percent German to 51 percent Polish and 49 percent German, then the Poles could potentially claim the land as theirs based on national self-determination. Thus, Polish and German ideologues, like nineteenth-century archaeologists, advanced the idea that a region could bear the *cultural* stamp of its rightful inhabitants, even if, in sheer numerical terms, most of these inhabitants had faded away, or were simply outnumbered by intruders from other nationalities. While the specific contours of the cultural imprint left by a nation varied, propagandists tended to focus on markers such as architecture, agricultural practices, and language. In Germany, this cultural imprint became known as a *Kulturboden*—a cultural landscape, in contrast to a *Volksboden*, a place inhabited by a distinct group of people. Geographers such as Albrecht Penck, for example, argued that Germans could rightfully claim territory in the East wherever a distinct German Kulturboden could be discerned. To Penck, this meant places distinctively marked and shaped by German order and hard work, particularly in the cultivation of the land. He compared this with the Polish Kulturboden, which was distinguished by its ramshackle, poor villages and inefficient, poorly managed fields. Much like the attempted fusion of state with population, the fusion of state with cultural landscapes is radical because it is potentially limitless: wherever a Kulturboden can be established, there the state can extend its reach.[34] It is bounded only by the limits of technology, the will and ability of others states to resist, and the extent to which a state can demonstrate, with at least a modicum of credibility, the existence of such a zone of distinctive national culture.

According to Wasilewski, the defeat of the order allowed the ethnic and cultural Polonization of the region—that is, the reinforcement of its Volks- and Kulturboden—to continue, like a river temporarily and artificially diverted from its course being allowed to return to the path along which nature intended it to flow.[35] Sadly, however, this marked merely an interlude before the next, and more consequential phase of the region's deformation at the hands of its avaricious Teutonic neighbors. To Wasilewski, the period of the partitions marked the start of a concerted, carefully orchestrated attempt by the Germans to establish both a Kulturboden and a Volksboden in Pomerania by means of settling colonists. The results of this policy were the lingering traces of German culture *and* the German people still living there. Both were artificial, unwelcome intruders that had been deployed in a zero-sum struggle to deprive the Poles of their natural and rightful place.[36] Therefore, according to Wasilewski "the flight of the German element from Pomerania (as well as from all Polish territories after the War)" represented no injustice or misfortune but rather a "circumstance which brought about in great measure the restoration to these territories of their original ethnical character."[37] The seemingly radical upheavals of the postwar era had represented no more than a restoration of the ancient and just fusion of state, territory, and nation in Poland.

## Conclusion

Wasilewski's use of völkisch rhetoric to support Poland's claims to Pomerania illustrates several important characteristics of political culture in post-Versailles Europe. First, it shows that the body of ideas and rhetoric embraced by German cultural and political elites in the period was not unique to that country. Instead, it was a reflection of the attempt—informed by pre-existing cultural patterns and traditions—to give meaningful content to the vague slogan of "national self-determination." Second, it shows how knowledge and ideas that were later implemented in barbarous ways were created by these forces. Michael Burleigh has noted that Nazi racial policy depended for its implementation on information created by those who, in Germany, drove the völkisch turn—that is, by scholars who sought to analyze, sort, classify, define, and locate, all in an attempt to determine, with maximum clarity, who people were, where they lived, and where they *should* live.[38] While this is true, the example of Wasilewski shows that there was nothing uniquely German about the quest for this kind of knowledge in this period. There is little difference between Wasilewski and his völkisch antagonists in Germany and the army of cartographers, geographers, and other experts who descended on Paris and elsewhere in 1919 to draw borders, evaluate disputed claims, and assign people to one "nation" or another. Like Wasilewski, they all tried to figure out how to define a collective "self" and decide where it might legitimately pursue its determination. It is true that the Nazis carried this ideology to a terrible extreme due to its solution to the ambiguities of "self": stripping away all cultural-juridical elements of the definition and reducing it to a purely biological category. However, this possibility is always inherent in self-determination since its application requires a clarity that reality stubbornly refuses (hence the powerful appeal of a simplistic solution like "race"). In Eric Weitz's elegant formulation, "the searing problem of 'the people' remains."[39] In addition, the competition to establish the claims of one nation against another can fuel the radicalization of the potentially destructive aspects inherent in national self-determination, even without the addition of crude biological racism. The division of a population into invaders and natives, for example, which stems from the attempt to link people and territory, can very easily lead to violence since behavior toward invaders is regulated by different norms and rules than behavior toward rightful inhabitants. Wasilewski's argument that in the "earliest times . . . representatives of various Teutonic races invaded Pomerania"—invaders who were followed by German colonizers from "all parts not only of Germany but also from Austria and Russia"—is rife with latent menace.[40] Indeed, the potential for violence, repression and upheaval linked to the implementation of national self-determination was on full display after the Great War—in, for example, the population exchanges between Greece and Turkey.[41]

In the end, however, it is difficult to see how Wasilewski—or the scholars of the völkisch turn—could have made their arguments in any other way. The demands of national self-determination require just the sort of information and ideas that they muster. And it is perhaps the most intriguing and unsettling aspect of the triumph of this vague ideal that, after thousands of years in which power had been legitimated in a host of ways, national self-determination so thoroughly and rapidly annihilated all competition and ascended to the status of supreme norm for the organization of politics both domestic and foreign.

# Notes

1. Gregor Thum, "Mythische Landschaften. Das Bild vom 'deutschen Osten' und die Zäsuren des 20. Jahrhunderts," in *Traumland Osten. Deutsche Bilder vom Östlichen Europa im 20. Jahrhundert*, ed. Gregor Thum (Göttingen: Vandenhoeck & Ruprecht, 2006), quote from p. 191. For more examples, see David Blackbourn, "Germans Abroad and Auslandsdeutsche: Places, Networks and Experiences from the Sixteenth to the Twentieth Century," *Geschichte und Gesellschaft* 41 (2015): 321–46, especially pp. 344–45, and Annemarie H. Sammartino, *The Impossible Border: Germany and the East, 1914–1922* (Ithaca, NY: Cornell University Press, 2010), especially pp. 118–19. For a critique, see Winson Chu, *The German Minority in Interwar Poland* (Cambridge: Cambridge University Press, 2012), 26–27.

2. Eric D. Weitz, "From the Vienna to the Paris System: International Politics and the Entangled Histories of Human Rights, Forced Deportations, and Civilizing Missions," *American Historical Review* 113, no. 5 (2008); Eric D. Weitz, "Self-Determination: How a German Enlightenment Idea Became the Slogan of National Liberation and a Human Right," *American Historical Review* 120, no. 2 (2015).

3. Robert H. Jackson, *Sovereignty: Evolution of an Idea* (Cambridge: Polity, 2007), 97–104.

4. Paul Mantoux, *The Deliberations of the Council of Four (March 24–June 28, 1919)*, ed. and trans. Arthur Stanley Link (Princeton, NJ: Princeton University Press, 1992), 108.

5. Mlada Bukovansky, *Legitimacy and Power Politics: The American and French Revolutions in International Political Culture* (Princeton, NJ: Princeton University Press, 2002), 112.

6. Erez Manela, *The Wilsonian Moment: Self-determination and the International Origins of Anticolonial Nationalism* (Oxford: Oxford University Press, 2007).

7. Studies of the nationalization of the state system in Europe after the war, particularly in the German-Polish borderlands, have tended to focus on the way individuals embraced, rejected, or otherwise came to grips with the new identities and loyalties demanded of them. Exemplary in this respect is James Bjork's *Neither German nor Pole: Catholicism and National Indifference in a Central European Borderland* (Ann Arbor: University of Michigan Press, 2008), with its exploration of Catholics in Upper Silesia. However, the focus of this article is less on how individuals found their place in this changed world and more on the broader forces that made their decisions necessary. Perhaps many people in central Europe were indifferent to nationalism, but nation-states and their leaders, and even trans- and international institutions, were not indifferent to them.

8. John J. Kulczycki has recently highlighted the similarities in his *Belonging to the Nation: Inclusion and Exclusion in the Polish-German Borderlands* (Cambridge, MA: Harvard University Press, 2016); see especially pp. 300–308. See also Gernot Briesewitz, *Raum und Nation in der polnischen Westforschung 1918–1948* (Osnabrück: fibre, 2014), 15–16, for a contrasting view.

9. Thum, "Mythische Landschaften," 34–35.

10. Zofia Kurnatowska and Stanisław Kurnatowski, "Der Einfluss nationalistischer Ideen auf die mitteleuropäische Urgeschichtsforschung," in *Deutsche Ostforschung und polnische Westforschung im Spannungsfeld von Wissenschaft und Politik*, ed. Jan Piskorski, Jörg Hackmann, and Rudolf Jaworski (Osnabrück: fibre, 2002), 97–99; Briesewitz, *Raum und Nation*, 16–21; on archaeology and national politics more generally, as well as how archaeology was linked to a different German border dispute, see J. Laurence Hare,

*Excavating Nations: Archaeology, Museums, and the German-Danish Borderlands* (Toronto: University of Toronto Press, 2015).

11. For more on Austro-German tensions over Poland during the war, see Gary Shanafelt, *The Secret Enemy: Austria-Hungary and the German Alliance, 1914–1918* (New York: Columbia University Press, 1985); Werner Conze, *Polnische Nation und deutsche Politik im Ersten Weltkrieg* (Cologne: Böhlau, 1958); Bogdan Graf von Hutten-Czapski, *Sechzig Jahre Politik und Gesellschaft*, vol. 2 (Berlin: E. S. Mittler, 1936); and Kauffman, *Elusive Alliance*.

12. Kulczycki, *Belonging*, 21–22.

13. Roland Gehrke, *Der polnische Westgedanke bis zur Wiedererrichtung des polnischen Staates nach Ende des Ersten Weltkrieges* (Marburg: Herder-Institut, 2001), 133–36.

14. Michael Burleigh, *Germany Turns Eastwards: A Study of Ostforschung in the Third Reich* (Cambridge: Cambridge University Press, 1988), 3–5. Key works on this topic include, in addition to Burleigh's foundational book, Kristin Kopp, *Germany's Wild East: Constructing Poland as Colonial Space* (Ann Arbor: University of Michigan Press, 2012), and Vejas Liulevicius, *The German Myth of the East: 1800 to the Present* (Oxford: Oxford University Press, 2009).

15. Burleigh, *Germany Turns Eastwards*, 5–6.

16. Max Weber, "The Nation-State and Economic Policy (Inaugural Lecture)," in *Weber: Political Writings*, ed. Peter Lassman and Ronald Speirs (Cambridge: Cambridge University Press, 1994); quoted in Kauffman, *Elusive Alliance*, 18.

17. Kulczycki, *Belonging*, 19. It is important to note, however, that scholars have questioned how far these ideas took root beyond rather narrowly defined sociocultural milieus. See, for example, Thomas Serrier, *Provinz Posen, Ostmark, Wielkopolska: Eine Grenzregion zwischen Deutschtum und Polen, 1848–1914* (Marburg: Herder-Institut, 2005).

18. See, in addition to Kauffman, *Elusive Alliance*, Arkadiusz Stempin, *Próba "moralnego podboju" Polski przez Cesarstwo Niemieckie w latach I Wojny Światowej* (Warsaw: Neriton, 2013), and Janusz Pajewski, *Odbudowa państwa polskiego 1914–1918* (Warsaw: Państwowe Wydawnictwo Naukowe, 1978).

19. An excellent guide to this period is Alexander Prusin, *The Lands Between: Conflict in the East European Borderlands, 1870–1992* (Oxford: Oxford University Press, 2010).

20. Alfred Cobban, *The Nation State and National Self-Determination* (London: Collins, 1969), 18–19.

21. Weitz, "From the Vienna to the Paris System," 1314. However, Weitz's assertion that the Paris system was less concerned with "clearly defined borders" than post-Napoleonic Europe is belied by the excruciating detail with which the German-Polish border is delimited in part 2, article 27 of the Treaty of Versailles.

22. For the need to draw on expert opinion to meet complex political needs within expanding states, see Ulrike Jureit, *Das Ordnen von Räumen: Territorium und Lebensraum im 19. und 20. Jahrhundert* (Hamburg: Hamburger Edition, 2012); on 1919 as the key moment at which such experts arrived on the international scene, see Dimitri Kitsakis, *Le Rôle des Experts à la Conférence de la Paix* (Ottawa: Éditions de l'Université d'Ottawa, 1972), 5–7.

23. Kulczycki, *Belonging*, 23.

24. Bernard Piotrowski, *W służbie nauki i narodu: Instytut Bałtycki w latach 1925–1939* (Poznań: Uniwersytet im. Adama Mickiewicza w Poznaniu, 1991), 35–36.

25. Piotrowski, *W służbie nauki i narodu*, 105–7.

26.  *Collection of Documents Relating to the Dispute between the Free City of Danzig and the Polish Republic Regarding Article 33 of the Treaty Between Danzig and Poland of November 9th, 1920: "Protection of Minorities"* (Gdańsk: A. Schroth, 1931), 29.

27.  "Wasilewski, Leon," https://zapytaj.onet.pl/encyklopedia/9437,,,,wasilewski _leon,haslo.html, last accessed February 28, 2018. See also Barbara Stoczewska, *Litwa, Białoruś, Ukraina w myśli politycznej Leona Wasilewskiego* (Krakow: Księgarnia Akademicka, 1998).

28.  Leon Wasilewski, *Nationalities in Pomerania* (Toruń, Poland: Baltic Institute, 1934), 8–12.

29.  Quoted in Burleigh, *Germany Turns Eastwards*, 30.

30.  This, too, was an idea that had surfaced in nineteenth-century Polish historical writing, when the Piast dynasty's supposed connection with the peasants, the "true" Poles, rather than the nobility, had been emphasized; Gehrke, *Der polnische Westgedanke*, 128–29.

31.  Wasilewski, *Nationalities in Pomerania*, 11–12.

32.  Ibid., 13.

33.  Ibid., 13–19.

34.  Burleigh, *Germany Turns Eastwards*, 25–26.

35.  Wasilewski, *Nationalities in Pomerania*, 20–22.

36.  Ibid., 24–31, quote from 25.

37.  Ibid., 36.

38.  Burleigh, *Germany Turns Eastwards*, 10.

39.  Weitz, "Self-Determination," 496.

40.  Wasilewski, *Nationalities in Pomerania*, 45.

41.  Weitz, "Self-Determination," 487–88.

# Bibliography

Bjork, James. *Neither German nor Pole: Catholicism and National Indifference in a Central European Borderland*. Ann Arbor: University of Michigan Press, 2008.

Blackbourn, David. "Germans Abroad and Auslandsdeutsche; Places, Networks and Experiences from the Sixteenth to the Twentieth Century." *Geschichte und Gesellschaft* 41 (2015): 321–46.

Briesewitz, Gernot. *Raum und Nation in der polnischen Westforschung 1918–1948*. Osnabrück: fibre, 2014.

Bukovansky, Mlada. *Legitimacy and Power Politics: The American and French Revolutions in International Political Culture*. Princeton, NJ: Princeton University Press, 2002.

Burleigh, Michael. *Germany Turns Eastwards: A Study of Ostforschung in the Third Reich*. Cambridge: Cambridge University Press, 1988.

Chu, Winson. *The German Minority in Interwar Poland*. Cambridge: Cambridge University Press, 2012.

Cobban, Alfred. *The Nation State and National Self-Determination*. London: Collins, 1969.

*Collection of Documents Relating to the Dispute between the Free City of Danzig and the Polish Republic Regarding Article 33 of the Treaty Between Danzig and Poland of November 9th, 1920: "Protection of Minorities."* Gdańsk: A. Schroth, 1931.

Conze, Werner. *Polnische Nation und deutsche Politik im Ersten Weltkrieg*. Cologne: Böhlau, 1958.

Gehrke, Roland. *Der polnische Westgedanke bis zur Wiedererrichtung des polnischen Staates nach Ende des Ersten Weltkrieges.* Marburg, Germany: Herder-Institut, 2001.

Hare, J. Laurence. *Excavating Nations: Archaeology, Museums, and the German-Danish Borderlands.* Toronto: University of Toronto Press, 2015.

Hutten-Czapski, Bogdan Graf von. *Sechzig Jahre Politik und Gesellschaft.* Vol. 2. Berlin: E. S. Mittler, 1936.

Jackson, Robert H. *Sovereignty: Evolution of an Idea.* Cambridge: Polity, 2007.

Jureit, Ulrike. *Das Ordnen von Räumen: Territorium und Lebensraum im 19. und 20. Jahrhundert.* Hamburg: Hamburger Edition, 2012.

Kauffman, Jesse. *Elusive Alliance: The German Occupation of Poland in World War I.* Cambridge, MA: Harvard University Press, 2015.

Kitsakis, Dimitri. *Le Rôle des Experts à la Conférence de la Paix.* Ottawa: Éditions de l'Université d'Ottawa, 1972.

Kopp, Kristin. *Germany's Wild East: Constructing Poland as Colonial Space.* Ann Arbor: University of Michigan Press, 2012

Kulczycki, John J. *Belonging to the Nation: Inclusion and Exclusion in the Polish-German Borderlands.* Cambridge, MA: Harvard University Press, 2016.

Kurnatowska, Zofia, and Stanisław Kurnatowski. "Der Einfluss nationalistischer Ideen auf die mitteleuropäische Urgeschichtsforschung." In *Deutsche Ostforschung und polnische Westforschung im Spannungsfeld von Wissenschaft und Politik,* edited by Jan Piskorski, Jörg Hackmann, and Rudolf Jaworski, 93–103. Osnabrück: fibre, 2002.

Liulevicius, Vejas. *The German Myth of the East: 1800 to the Present.* Oxford: Oxford University Press, 2009.

Manela, Erez. *The Wilsonian Moment: Self-Determination and the International Origins of Anticolonial Nationalism.* Oxford: Oxford University Press, 2007.

Mantoux, Paul. *The Deliberations of the Council of Four (March 24–June 28, 1919).* Edited and translated by Arthur Stanley Link. Princeton, NJ: Princeton University Press, 1992.

Pajewski, Janusz. *Odbudowa państwa polskiego 1914–1918.* Warsaw: Państwowe Wydawnictwo Naukowe, 1978.

Piotrowski, Bernard. *W służbie nauki i narodu: Instytut Bałtycki w latach 1925–1939.* Poznań: Uniwersytet im. Adama Mickiewicza w Poznaniu, 1991.

Prusin, Alexander. *The Lands Between: Conflict in the East European Borderlands, 1870–1992.* Oxford: Oxford University Press, 2010.

Sammartino, Annemarie H. *The Impossible Border: Germany and the East, 1914–1922.* Ithaca, NY: Cornell University Press, 2010.

Serrier, Thomas. *Provinz Posen, Ostmark, Wielkopolska: Eine Grenzregion zwischen Deutschtum und Polen, 1848–1914.* Marburg, Germany: Herder-Institut, 2005.

Shanafelt, Gary. *The Secret Enemy: Austria-Hungary and the German Alliance, 1914–1918.* New York: Columbia University Press, 1985.

Stempin, Arkadiusz. *Próba "moralnego podboju" Polski przez Cesarstwo Niemieckie w latach I Wojny Światowej.* Warsaw: Neriton, 2013.

Stoczewska, Barbara. *Litwa, Białoruś, Ukraina w myśli politycznej Leona Wasilewskiego.* Krakow: Księgarnia Akademicka, 1998.

Thum, Gregor. "Mythische Landschaften. Das Bild vom 'deutschen Osten' und die Zäsuren des 20. Jahrhunderts." In *Traumland Osten. Deutsche Bilder vom Östlichen Europa im 20. Jahrhundert,* edited by Gregor Thum, 181–211. Göttingen: Vandenhoeck & Ruprecht, 2006.

Wasilewski, Leon. *Nationalities in Pomerania.* Toruń, Poland: Baltic Institute, 1934.

Weitz, Eric D. "From the Vienna to the Paris System: International Politics and the Entangled Histories of Human Rights, Forced Deportations, and Civilizing Missions." *American Historical Review* 113, no. 5 (2008): 1313–43.

———. "Self-Determination: How a German Enlightenment Idea Became the Slogan of National Liberation and a Human Right." *American Historical Review* 120, no. 2 (2015): 462–96.

JESSE KAUFFMAN is Associate Professor of History at Eastern Michigan University and author of *Elusive Alliance: The German Occupation of Poland in World War I.*

# 4 The End of Egypt's Occupation

*Ottoman Sovereignty and the British Declaration of Protection*

Aimee Genell

On December 14, 1914, the Foreign Office formally incorporated Egypt into the British Empire as a protectorate. Egypt had been administered under British military occupation since 1882 but remained under the sovereignty of the Ottoman sultan. British foreign secretary Edward Grey noted that Egypt's peculiar international position became untenable in the early days of the Great War: "Technically Egyptians became enemy subjects after the entry of Turkey intothe war against us. Something had to be done to prevent legal complications."[1] The Ottoman entry into the First World War in November provided Britain with the opportunity to resolve Egypt's anomalous international legal status as a *de jure* Ottoman territory under *de facto* British control. The protectorate severed the legal bond between the Ottoman Empire and Egypt and ended nearly four hundred years of Ottoman sovereignty in the province.

Yet terminating Ottoman sovereignty in Egypt would not be an easy sell in Cairo or in international politics. Britain could depend only on France and Russia to recognize the new order of things and even then only if European privileges in Egypt were maintained. When British troops arrived in Egypt in 1882, Ottoman institutions were preserved, among them the Capitulations, which were treaties that exempted European residents from Ottoman-Egyptian law and taxation. More important, Egypt was one of a number of Ottoman privileged or autonomous provinces (*eyalet-i mümtaze*). Egypt had gained autonomy in 1840–41 and had a special status within both the Ottoman constitutional order by imperial firman and international law by treaty.[2] As one British foreign secretary put it, from 1841 Egypt was "recognized as lying outside the sphere of European warfare and international jealousies."[3] The 1914 British declaration of protection unilaterally abolished the treaties and imperial firmans that guaranteed Egypt's status as an autonomous province in international law since the mid-nineteenth century.

From the declaration of protection through the interwar years, legal and political commentators, colonial administrators, and bureaucrats, as well as Ottomans and Egyptians, wrote about the meaning of the end of Ottoman sovereignty in Egypt.[4] Even though there was extensive commentary about the British declaration of protection in Egypt at the time, for the most part the transfer from Ottoman to British sovereignty does not make up a significant part of the historiographical debate. With few exceptions, Egypt's wartime story has generally been bracketed from the events of the Ottoman First World War. But Egypt's legal status mattered in international politics in 1914 as much as it had since 1840. It threatened to bring the Ottomans into the war against Britain long before the Ottoman state was prepared for battle. Both Germany and Britain used Egypt to incentivize the Ottomans for their own ends early in the war. More significantly, Egypt was the first of the European territorial claims to Ottoman Arab lands.

British internal debates on the future of Egypt prior to the declaration of a protectorate anticipated discussions in 1918 and 1919 about what would happen to Ottoman territories under British military occupation—all those territories that would soon become "class A" mandates under the League of Nations. This chapter argues that Egypt provided a model for thinking about British imperial control in the Middle East after the war. British internal debates on the virtues of annexation versus protection, as well as the protectorate experiment, were an important testing ground for thinking about controlling the postwar Middle East. By the end of the war, most figures in the British Foreign Office viewed the protectorate as a deviation from British policy in Egypt since 1882 and a mistake that had antagonized Egyptians. While Egypt was never part of the mandates system, it was nevertheless the crucial arena for British thinking about the location of formal sovereignty in relationship to imperial control.

## To Annex or to Protect? Pan-Islam and the Problem of Egypt in British Imperial thought in 1914

In 1914, Britain's position in Egypt was strong from a military and administrative perspective. From a legal perspective, however, it remained weak. The ambiguity of Egypt's international position as an autonomous Ottoman province under British military administration became increasingly awkward in the context of the European political crisis in 1914. War provided Whitehall with an opening to "regularize" the relationship between the British Empire and Egypt. At the same, war between the British and Ottoman Empires posed a serious danger—all Egyptians were legally Ottoman subjects and in the event of war, the entire population would become enemies of the British Empire. Compounding Britain's legal dilemma in Egypt was the fear that war against the Ottoman sultan would incite rebellion among Britain's Muslim subjects because the sultan acted also as caliph, that is, as leader of the Muslim community.[5]

In the fall of 1914, a debate emerged between the acting consul general in Cairo and the Foreign Office in London about the future of Egypt. The Foreign Office oscillated between two possibilities: annexation or protection.[6] For many in the Foreign Office, there was little substantive difference between annexation and protection. But whichever policy Britain pursued, there were two significant obstacles to end the occupation and terminate Ottoman sovereignty in Egypt. The first and most persistent problem was Egyptian support. In order to legitimize breaking with the Ottomans, the British required public backing especially from Egyptian ministers. The second impediment to ending Ottoman sovereignty in Egypt was the European powers. While France and Russia might be counted on with the right inducements to recognize changes in Egypt's political status, the Central powers would not. Germany and the Habsburg Empire formally reiterated their recognition of Egypt as an Ottoman province in September 1914. Moreover, if Germany were to win the war, the Ottoman claim to Egypt would be significantly bolstered—a concern that the Foreign Office and members of the Egyptian government shared.

There were a number of practical and political considerations related to bringing Egyptians and the other European powers on board with British plans to sever Ottoman ties to Egypt. Changing Egypt's political status produced a range of questions about the future of Ottoman institutions in Egypt, including the khedivate, the Capitulations, the Egyptian tribute to Istanbul, the firmans, and the international legal instruments that had guaranteed Egyptian autonomy within the Ottoman Empire—questions that would not be resolved until Egyptian "independence" in 1922 and the Treaty of Lausanne in 1923. The underlying tension in British internal debates was the dilemma of what would replace Ottoman sovereignty in Egypt and how the British-Egyptian relationship would be defined in legal terms. The Egyptian question in 1914 foreshadowed internal debates at the end of the war about the future of former Ottoman provinces under British control at the time of the armistice—particularly in terms of following a policy of annexation or protection.

Between August and December 1914, when Britain finally issued the declaration of protection, Foreign Office officials in Cairo and London searched for the right theory to support terminating Ottoman sovereignty in Egypt. At the outset, Horatio Herbert Kitchener, the counsel general in Egypt, and to a large degree Egyptian ministers, led the drive to end Ottoman sovereignty in Egypt with a declaration of protectorate, while London urged caution and delay. Once the Ottoman and British Empires were at war, these positions would be reversed. British officials in Cairo first seriously considered the protectorate option in mid-August, following the rumored sale of German warships to the Ottoman Empire, which had raised some alarm in London that the Ottomans might end neutrality and join the war on the side of the Central powers. Cairo charged ahead with substantive plans despite the fact that Foreign Secretary Grey did not think that the sale indicated that the Ottomans would abandon neutrality or that Egypt was at risk from an Ottoman attack.[7]

Milne Cheetham, acting consul general in Cairo, reported that rumors of war with the Ottoman Empire had greatly agitated Egyptian ministers.[8] Complicating matters was the fact that the khedive, Abbas Hilmi II, was visiting Istanbul when the war broke out and Husayn Rushdi Pasha, the president of the Egyptian

Council of Ministers, was acting as regent in his absence. Rushdi and Adli Pasha (Yagen), who at the time was Egypt's foreign minister, were the two key Egyptian figures with whom British agents in Cairo attempted to strike a bargain for the protectorate, along with Prince Husayn Kamil Paşa, the khedive's uncle. Cheetham was a step ahead of the Foreign Office in London and suggested that Egypt might be legally separated from the Ottoman Empire via a policy of protection if the British could provide an incentive for Egyptian ministers to support the policy. His proposals were animated by discussions with Rushdi, who argued that the ministers could not stay in office in the case of war with the "suzerain power." Rushdi proposed that Egyptian ministers might support a protectorate if it were "accompanied by the announcement of arrangement with His Majesty's Government granting to Egypt a measure of self-government in local matters compatible with general control by Great Britain."[9]

While officials in London looked for a solution that would not limit their hold, British administrators and advisors in Cairo supported relinquishing some amount of internal administrative control for tighter British external control of Egypt. Cheetham proposed a scheme that would provide Egypt with more internal autonomy. He noted that "if the fiction of Ottoman suzerainty were then maintained, Egyptians, and above all Egyptian officials would be placed in a position of divided allegiance, and their cooperation with us would be thus seriously affected." The only plausible solution was to sunder the legal ties between Istanbul and Cairo and, in exchange, provide Egyptian elites with more administrative control for their support. Cheetham continued: "If it were considered possible to accompany the declaration of protectorate by a statement to the effect that the progress of Egypt towards internal self-governance would not be retarded, but rather accelerated, by such a protectorate, I am firmly convinced that the majority of enlightened Egyptians would receive the declaration not only with acquiescence, but even with favour."[10] Cheetham insisted that even as Egyptians would secure the full status and advantages of British subjects under a protectorate, "the principle of an Egyptian national entity" should be fostered.[11]

In late August, Ronald Storrs, oriental secretary in Cairo, reported on public opinion in Egypt and contended that though there was some support for Germany in Egypt, it emanated from the "Turks, Circassians, lawyers, students and extremist journalists," who represented Germany "as having befriended Islam without acquiring one acre of Muslim territory."[12] This faction circulated rumors stating that if Germany should win the war, Britain would be expelled from Egypt and the province returned to regular Ottoman administration. But Storrs argued, too, that providing Egyptians with some form of greater autonomy or quasi-independence could mitigate the problem of Ottoman loyalty in Egypt.

> Unmistakable hints have been received from the most responsible circles, that a formal change of regime, leaving the position of the occupation unimpaired without wounding Egyptian *amour-propre* and "sense of nationality" would be far from unwelcome. It is pointed out that a transference of the temporal suzerainty from the Sultan to His Majesty the King, accompanied by guaranteed "autonomy"

(for England must not show herself less generous than the Turks) or "independence" with subsequent abolition of the Capitulations, would go far towards disembarrassing the conscientious from the incubus of Ottoman loyalty, localizing aspirations, and diminishing almost to a vanishing point the attraction and influence of Pan-Islam.[13]

In other words, Storrs believed that it would be possible to transfer sovereignty from the sultan to the British king and maintain the status quo of the occupation, so long as some measure of autonomy could be promised to Egyptian ministers and elites in Cairo.[14] At this stage, when the British did not know about the German-Ottoman secret treaty of alliance, the main concern of officials in Cairo was how to acquire and maintain support from Egyptian ministers and notables in order to maintain civil government.

Throughout August and early September, Rushdi continued to offer Egyptian support for a protectorate in exchange for greater autonomy. In conveying these messages to the Foreign Office, Cheetham did not offer anything that would jeopardize the benefits and "progress" of the occupation but, at the same time, pushed officials in London to recognize the importance of gaining Egyptian support for ending Ottoman sovereignty in Egypt. Referring to Rushdi's proposal, Cheetham reported:

This proposition, as put before me, was equivalent to a plea for autonomy of a nature to endanger the progress which had been made in Egypt, and I have been very careful not to give the slightest encouragement to it. I should however, take the opportunity to state, for your information, that it is now apparent that a certain section of the politicians have been discussing possibilities of the kind described among themselves, though no allusion has been made to the subject in the press. It is clear that a large number of prominent Egyptians would look with complacency on a severance of the connection with the Ottoman Empire, though they would desire at the same time some satisfaction of moderate nationalist aspirations.[15]

Cheetham was less concerned with defining the terms of Egyptian autonomy and how to satisfy "modest nationalist aspirations," as he was with inducing Egyptian elites to break with the Ottoman state. Like Storrs, he viewed Ottoman loyalty as a serious impediment to changing the legal status of Egypt in the event of war with the Ottoman Empire.

By the middle of September, the Foreign Office's initial call for calm and caution in Cairo had shifted toward urgency to change Egypt's political status. Cheetham drafted a proclamation of protection for Egypt but without articulating what would happen to Ottoman sovereignty in Egypt. Was it to be forfeited by breaking neutrality or was it to be merely suspended? The draft proclamation simply stated that due to war between the British and Ottoman Empires, the British would protect Egypt and the khedival dynasty because "Egypt is liable to attack no less than British territory, and rights of autonomy won on the battlefield by [the] founder of the Khedival dynasty, as well as the reforms of the last thirty years are in danger."[16] Cheetham's appeal to Mehmed Ali Paşa, the first hereditary governor of Ottoman Egypt, was an attempt to satisfy local opinion and was in line with earlier advice to the Foreign Office—any declaration of protection had to be accompanied by a statement ensuring "the progress of Egypt towards internal self-government." But he did not define the meaning and content of the "rights of autonomy won on the battle field." Mehmed Ali and subsequent khedive's rights of autonomy were derived precisely from the international guarantees of 1840 and subsequent firmans, which granted the family of Mehmed Ali hereditary "administration of the Pashalic of Egypt." The logic of appealing to these rights was clear from a British perspective—they were administrative rights, not sovereign rights. But by avoiding the question of who would possess sovereignty in Egypt, while at the same time appealing to the rights won by Mehmed Ali, Cheetham underscored the legal precariousness of the British position in Egypt.[17] Grey provisionally supported Cheetham's draft declaration but emphasized that the status quo in Egypt should be maintained until the Ottomans broke definitively with the Entente Powers. Grey pointed out that the Capitulations and other privileges would have to be preserved to satisfy European opinion.

By late September, the Foreign Office proceeded under the assumption that war with the Ottomans would entail the simultaneous announcement of a declaration of war and a declaration of protection that would "terminate Turkish suzerainty." Grey proposed that Prince Husayn Kamil should assume the khedivate.[18] Along with the declaration of protection, Cheetham drafted a document that would become the blueprint for the protectorate. It explained the British decision for the protectorate and how it would function, noting first that Husayn had been selected "to occupy the Khedival throne free from all the rights of suzerainty or other rights heretofore claimed by the Sultan or by his Government."[19]

On the eve of the Ottoman entry into the war, Rushdi met with Cheetham to discuss administration under protection. Rushdi argued that the British would win support for the protectorate if it included an explicit statement promising "a larger measure of self-government for Egypt." He threatened to resign from office without such a statement, claiming he would be unable to control the reaction in Cairo. Cheetham wrote to the Foreign Office that Rushdi feared "religious feeling in favour of Turkey would create a situation in which it would be impossible to control without a promise of increased rights of self-government."[20] Cheetham proposed that they add the phrase: "the clearer definition of Great Britain's position in the country will accelerate progress towards self-government." Prince Husayn, like Rushdi, drew on British anxieties about the appeal of pan-Islam, by arguing that a promise of self-government for Egyptians would trump an ostensibly more obvious allegiance to the Ottoman sultan-caliph.

When the Ottoman Empire attacked Russia in the Black Sea in late October, Grey proposed Britain issue a proclamation of protectorate within two days, pending Prince Husayn's willingness to assume the khedivate. Cheetham, somewhat distraught, wrote that due to religious feeling in Egypt, agitated by the prospect of war against the caliph, Prince Husayn was inclined to refuse the position. Drawing on British fears of pan-Islamic rebellion in Egypt and the empire,

Prince Husayn argued that he "could not accept the Khedivate without a grant or promise of autonomy to Egypt under British suzerainty." Cheetham did not think that Rushdi and Prince Husayn were acting in concert but rather that both possessed "the idea of necessity of some form of compensation to Egypt to break with Turkey."[21] Cheetham suggested that the declaration of protection be delayed given Prince Husayn's unwillingness to assume office. Grey agreed, noting, "You will of course postpone the declaration of protectorate until rupture with Turkey is complete, for this would alter status of Egypt, but there is no reason for postponing martial law."[22]

When Britain declared war on the Ottoman Empire on November 5, 1914, the general commanding officer in Egypt, John Maxwell, announced the state of war in Cairo, and proclaimed that Great Britain would take responsibility for Egypt's defense. He went further, stating, "Great Britain is now fighting both to protect the rights and liberties of Egypt which were originally won upon the battlefield by Mohammad Ali and to secure to her the continuation of peace and prosperity, which she has enjoyed during thirty years of British occupation." The text was almost exactly Cheetham's original draft declaration of protection from September, with a subtle shift in language and meaning. The "rights of autonomy won on the battlefield" by Mehmed Ali was changed to "the rights and liberties" of Egypt.[23] Autonomy in an Ottoman, and especially in an Egyptian, context had a specific administrative meaning with particular privileges attached. Though "rights and liberties" were far more ambiguous than autonomy, at the outset of the war, the reference to Mehmed Ali made it appear that Britain had committed itself to protect Egypt's autonomy and special international legal status. For the British, it was a risky bargain to thwart Egyptian allegiance to the Ottoman Empire. The compromise appeared to secure Egypt in 1914, but when the British defaulted on the promise to uphold rights derived from Mehmed Ali in 1919, Egypt would explode in protest, as I will show later in this chapter.

On the same day that Maxwell issued his statement, Enver Paşa, the Ottoman minister of war, declared the Ottoman Empire would protect all Muslims and that it was obliged to put an end to the disorders in Egypt and bring the territory back under the caliph rule. He attacked the British idea of liberating nationalities as a war aim and added that if Britain stood by its rhetoric it should at long last release Egypt from British control. Egyptian nationalists would use Maxwell's language at the end of the war when making clams for independence in Cairo and Paris, especially the "rights of Mehmed Ali."[24] What is more striking is that Enver mobilized Islam as war propaganda even before the Ottoman declaration of Jihad on November 11.[25]

After the declaration of war and martial law, British officials in Cairo worked to find ways to bring Prince Husayn on board with the protectorate. For Cheetham and Storrs the problem was balancing Foreign Office objectives with Egyptian public opinion. Grey worried about yielding too much and prejudicing the future administration of Egypt, whereas Husayn demanded concessions for risking a break with Istanbul and the caliphate. It was in this context that the decision was made to exchange the title of khedive with that of sultan, meaning ruler or sovereign.[26] Storrs proposed the change based on Husayn's professed desire to transform Egypt into a kingdom, analogous to those in the Balkans, with an Egyptian monarch.[27] He argued that the title's benefit lay in its elasticity. The title "sultan of Egypt and the Sudan" would satisfy Egyptian public opinion but would also emphasize Egypt's preeminence among the Muslim powers of North Africa, a clear asset in the war against the Ottoman Empire.[28] Such influence would balance "the political effect of possible French acquisitions in Syria" and "any subsequent creation of rival potentates by hostile powers." Most importantly, he wrote, "The honour would cost Great Britain nothing whatever. But I venture to assert that its possible effect in the near future of the Eastern Mediterranean might be beneficial and far-reaching."[29] In short, British policy in Egypt focused on the postwar, not just in Egypt, but also in the wider region.

While Storrs and Cheetham worked to bring Husayn around, the Ottoman declaration of jihad on November 11 caused the Foreign Office to radically shift its approach in Egypt. London suddenly switched course and insisted instead on annexation and the direct incorporation of Egypt into the British Empire as a colony. Grey wrote that the British government believed that "the most effective step would be to declare annexation of Egypt, thus getting rid of all of the difficulties about succession to Khedive, and giving Egyptians at once the status of British subjects."[30] Grey mandated again that the Capitulations and mixed courts remain unchanged in order to appease the other European powers, above all France. He sent a draft annexation order to Cairo on November 17—a few days after the declaration of jihad in Istanbul. The Order in Council justified the policy of annexation on the grounds that the British military occupation, which itself had been implemented for the security and good governance of Egypt, was now under threat due to war between the British and Ottoman Empires. To preserve the progress and order of the occupation, Britain declared it "necessary that the suzerainty of His Imperial Majesty the Sultan of Turkey over Egypt should be annulled, and that Egypt should cease to form a part of the Ottoman Dominions. . . . From and after the date hereof, Egypt is annexed to and forms part of His Majesty's Dominions."[31]

British officials in Cairo were stunned by the Foreign Office's new plan. Annexation was out of sync with the situation on the ground. Cheetham understood that annexation would dismantle the entire apparatus of occupation and argued that Britain would lose all the benefits of the system in place since 1882. However, Grey argued that the plan for the protectorate had been worked out before the Ottomans and British were actually at war. Now that the two empires were belligerent, he thought the protectorate would in fact make things more ambiguous. In the first place, Prince Husayn would not accept the khedivate while the yet to be deposed khedive Abbas resided in an enemy capital. "Egyptian subjects would cease to be Ottoman subjects, i.e. subjects of a large Moslem empire, and would be relegated the ambiguous position as protected subjects in a relatively small country. Our other Moslem subjects in other parts of the world would also probably consider that we had placed the Egyptians on a footing inferior to that which they had occupied under Turkish suzerainty."[32] London worried, too, that the uncertainty of the situation helped support Ottoman designs on Egypt. Grey emphasized that from the perspective of international relations it mattered little whether Egypt were annexed or under protection, particularly as the Capitulations and Mixed Tribunals would remain in place until further discussion with France.

The fact that Grey did not see a world of difference between annexation and protection prompted Cheetham to outline in rather stark terms the benefits of the system of occupation, which he argued could be maintained to a greater degree under protection rather than if Egypt were incorporated into the empire as a Crown colony. Moreover, Rushdi and the ministers were in discussion with Prince Husayn about "an arrangement with us for inclusion in the British Empire without the loss of Egyptian individuality." Cheetham noted that Cairo was calm following the declaration of martial law and that Maxwell's statement "in reference to the preservation of rights won by Mehmed Ali" did much to appease the Egyptians, even the nationalists and "extremists." Annexation would disturb the relative calm that prevailed in Cairo and the ministers would almost certainly resign. Cheetham again argued that the ministers were the only force in Cairo who could control the so-called "religious element." He implored Grey to consider the effect of annexation "as contrasted with creation of Mahommedan nation under our protection, on Mohammedan feeling generally, and especially in the Arab world." Beyond the effect of the annexation on Muslims, the real problem with annexation was that it would mean more accountability for the British while creating greater dissatisfaction among Egyptians. Cheetham continued:

> I would add that the existing system of governing through native hands is not the most efficient form of government, but it is understood here and provides an excuse for administrative shortcomings which would disappear with annexation. Annexation must involve a more direct responsibility for Great Britain, for a higher standard of government, and for stricter protection of foreign interests. This would ultimately be attained, but only by free displacement of native officials. Although increased efficiency might be appreciated, an influential class of malcontents would be created.[33]

Alongside the concerns of officials in Cairo, France also worried that the British annexation of Egypt would backfire in various ways and places. The minister of foreign affairs, Théophile Declassé, thought that annexation would give the impression that Britain was already enjoying the territorial spoils of war— particularly after the annexation of Cyprus on November 2. Declassé argued that the Ottomans and Germans would use it against the Entente and that it would alienate public opinion in France and the empire. He insisted that all territorial questions should be deferred until the end of the war and argued "that a protectorate is better suited than annexation to preservation of the internal situation of Egypt."[34]

Arguments emanating from Cairo, along with Kitchener's support for protection over annexation, brought Foreign Office opinion around. Grey was prepared to accept the protectorate if it would preserve the "internal situation" in Egypt. He authorized the policy with the understanding that Cheetham ask Husayn to accept the khedivate, "intimating that if he refuses the alternative is annexation."[35] Until the declaration of protection, Grey emphasized repeatedly that nothing should be done that would limit British control of Egypt later. Accordingly, he was especially concerned with the wording of texts ending Ottoman sovereignty and creating the Egyptian sultanate. He wished to "guard against words which might be quoted afterwards to imply that the new Sultan was to be in practice the independent ruler and Governor of Egypt."[36] Grey was troubled that the British were giving away too much to appease Egyptian opinion and that these compromises were getting in the way of achieving British aims in Egypt: "We are afraid the cumulative effect of all the concessions wanted by Prince Hussein [Husayn] will be to prejudice British control and make it less than heretofore; whereas our object is to substitute a British protectorate for Turkish suzerainty, retaining the British control exercised before."[37] Though there were outstanding questions related to succession and nationality, Grey approved a draft declaration of protection that in one blow terminated Ottoman sovereignty, deposed khedive Abbas Hilmi, and appointed Husayn as the sultan of Egypt.

Husayn finally accepted the sultanate but with the reservation that the protectorate approved by Grey be disaggregated into three separate statements: the termination of Ottoman sovereignty and the establishment of British protection, the deposition of Abbas Hilmi II with Husayn's appointment as sultan, and finally a statement explaining the terms of the protectorate. Cheetham noted the order in which Britain severed the link between the Ottoman Empire and Egypt was of profound significance "because the feeling that the Sultan of Turkey still represents the legal authority remains strong, whereas once that authority is declared null and void Hussain would be justified in recognizing a new situation."[38] In other words, Husayn could not accept the sultanate without first changing the legal status of Egypt. Lastly, Cheetham assured Grey that Husayn, the regent, and ministers were all in favor of the protectorate, "which they anticipate and understand would tighten our control of administration, while giving them, as they have had hitherto, a reasonable voice in local affairs."[39]

On December 18, Britain proclaimed the protectorate in Egypt, and terminated Ottoman sovereignty in the province.[40] The next day, Abbas Hilmi II, the last khedive, was deposed, and Husayn Kamil was offered the title of sultan as the "eldest living Prince of the family of Mohammad Ali." The offer of the sultanate to Husayn was accompanied by a text addressed as a letter to Prince Husayn that justified the protectorate and the transfer from Ottoman "suzerainty" in Egypt to Britain under protection.[41] From a legal perspective, the statement provided very little in terms of explaining what would replace the system of occupation in Egypt. "The future form of government" remained to be worked out, but it would be "freed from all rights of suzerainty or other rights heretofore claimed by the Ottoman Government." The document did not cancel the firmans—it would have been difficult to justify such a move since the family of Mehmed Ali derived their administrative and hereditary rights from these imperial commands—but it did lift some restrictions imposed by them, including the size of the Egyptian army and the ability of the now sultan to issue honors in his name. Elements from Cheetham's draft declaration of protection from September were reproduced in the statement to Husayn, including the argument that clarifying Britain's position in Egypt would "accelerate progress towards self-government" and that Britain would continue to "associate the governed in the task of Government" as during the occupation. The only explicit statement on governance under protection concerned foreign relations, which would now explicitly be conducted through the new British high commissioner of Egypt, a new post that replaced the consul general.[42] For Europe, as promised, the Capitulations would remain in place until the end of the war. Finally, the letter concluded by noting that though the protectorate meant that Egypt was free from obedience to Istanbul, Britain was not motivated by hostility toward the caliphate and that loyalty to the caliph was completely independent of political ties between Egypt and the Ottoman Empire.

The British legal advisor in Egypt, Malcolm McIlwraith, summarized the legal revolution in Egypt succinctly: "Such were the brief announcements which, by a stroke of the pen, put an end to the complicated international status of Egypt, built up—as between the Porte and Europe—by a long succession of treaties in the course of the last five centuries, and—as between the Porte and Egypt—by a series of diplomatic conventions and Imperial firmans from 1840 onwards."[43] Though they tried, the Foreign Office protectorate could not "with the stroke a pen" undo all the international treaties and imperial edicts guaranteeing Egypt's international status. Claims, especially by Egyptians, would continue to be made based on Egypt's legal status well after the conclusion of the war, and Cairo would explode in revolution against the "illegal protectorate" in 1919.

## From the "Illegal Protectorate" to Independence

In the aftermath of the annexation-protectorate debate, Egypt played a significant role in wartime British planning about the new Middle East. Between Cairo and London, various plans were made and remade, but most imagined Egypt at the center of Britain's "new Middle East Empire." The 1914 annexation-protection debate between London and Cairo was revived in the spring of 1917, with the illness and death of Sultan Husayn. In a reversal, it was the Foreign Office that maintained the position that annexation would not secure anything more for the British, while General Reginald Wingate, the British high commissioner in Cairo, argued that Britain's position in Egypt needed to be placed on more secure footing, advocating Egypt's annexation as a colony. At this stage in the war, it was the Ottoman Empire that troubled British officials in London and Cairo rather than rising nationalist sentiment in Egypt, which was ascribed to a small but vocal "Turkish clique." Wingate noted:

> It seems to me that a great deal will depend on the future of Turkey. If this Ottoman Empire is still to continue in more or less independent position in the world

with a Sultan at its head who will be the Caliph of Islam, and if that re-established Ottoman Empire is not to be allied heart and soul with the British Empire, then I foresee considerable difficulties ahead for Egypt. No one knows better than yourself how intimately connected Egypt and Turkey are, especially amongst the higher classes, by race and religion, and the latter of course bulks more largely than the former and is the mainstay of the influence of the classes over the masses in this country. There is as you know, no *vox populi* in Egypt and it is a case throughout of "the tail wagging the dog"; in other words it is the small and noisy Turkish pasha clique, who are largely imbued with Nationalistic ideas, who can generally secure the adhesion of the Fellaheen to their views through the influence of religion.[44]

The idea that the Ottomans posed a greater threat than Egyptian nationalism to British efforts to secure imperial interests in Egypt and the Middle East shaped British thinking until the end of the war. The Ottomans and later Turkish Republicans did indeed continue to pose legal problems to the new British Empire until the Treaty of Lausanne in 1923, but it was the extent of Egyptian mobilization against the British protectorate that most threatened British control over Egypt.

Two days after the armistice, a group of prominent Egyptians met with General Wingate to request permission to send an Egyptian delegation to Paris. Led by Sa'd Zaghlul, the *Wafd*, the "Delegation," stated that Egypt wanted "full independence."[45] The British government refused Zaghlul's "programme of complete autonomy," but at that stage, the Foreign Office did not yet think that the Egyptians saw themselves as one of the "liberated countries" that had been one of the rationales for the war. Rather, London was focused on keeping Egyptian questions out of the Paris Peace Conference, particularly any discussion of Egypt's legal status, and insisted that Egypt was "an imperial and not an international question." The Foreign Office argued that as long as the Ottomans were weakened politically, it would be possible to manage Egyptian demands for autonomy that had been promised in 1914. Yet as the Paris Peace Conference approached, Egyptian demands for independence only increased. The "illegal protectorate" was widely denounced and members of the Wafd began appealing directly to Woodrow Wilson and Georges Clemenceau to attend the peace conference.

On January 20, 1919, Zaghlul sent Clemenceau a memorandum on "Egyptian National Claims."[46] In addition to appealing to Wilson and national self-determination, he argued that British legal claims to Egypt were unjustified on the basis of Egypt's guaranteed international status. Much like Ottoman lawyers and diplomats throughout the occupation, Zaghlul invoked Egypt's status as an autonomous province guaranteed in international law by treaty. He did so to argue that Ottoman sovereignty could only be transferred to the Egyptians. He refuted Great Britain's title to Egypt by recapitulating the history of the "Egyptian question" in international relations from Mehmed Ali through the protectorate:

Before the events of 1882 led to the English occupation, Egypt was a country under the Ottoman suzerainty, but possessing under the Government of the Khedives, who succeeded to the throne according to dynastic order of succession, complete autonomy. The Turkish suzerainty came to nothing more than the payment of an annual tribute, some limitation on the military establishment, and the observance of any treaties signed by the Sublime Porte. This complete autonomy was obtained by the Egyptians on the field of battle, and at the price of their blood. It needed nothing less than the intervention of Europe to stop the victorious march of Mohammed Aly, and to compel him to accept autonomy in place of the independence which was the aim pursued. The Convention of London of the 15th of July, 1840, followed by the Hatte Cherif of the 13th February, 1841, constituted the Charter of Egypt. Thus the recognition of the rights of the latter was not by Turkey alone, but also by the Great Powers, whose intervention guaranteed this complete deliverance. Is it conceivable that the rights thus acquired can be lost because interior troubles, exaggerated at will, had for a moment caused anxiety to a few European residents?[47]

In addition to invoking the treaties and firmans, Zaghlul drew directly on General Maxwell's language in 1914 that Britain was fighting to protect the rights of Egypt "won upon the battlefield by Mohammad Ali." Zaghlul cast doubt on the legality of the occupation itself, noting that the juridical meaning of "occupation" was itself unclear and that "the public law even omits to mention it as being a means or regulating the relations that may exist between two countries."[48] He denounced the 1904 Entente Cordiale between Britain and France as nothing more than an agreement between two countries, noting that the agreement could not intrude on "the rights of Egyptians" or on their recognized "autonomy."[49] Zaghlul underlined the fact that the protectorate was a wartime measure and the mechanism alone could not negate Egypt's acknowledged political status. He claimed Egyptian independence was already recognized on the basis of Wilsonian principles as the "natural indefeasible right of nations" and because Egypt was now free of "Turkish suzerainty," it could finally proclaim "full sovereignty justified by her moral and material conditions."[50] Criticizing Prince Faysal's presence at Paris, he argued, too, that it was not possible to treat Hejaz or other parts of Arabia differently from Egypt: "It seems to us that when Europe considers that the Hedjaz, which was but yesterday a Turkish province, has a right to independence, she cannot but treat Egypt, infinitely more developed and, in addition, autonomous, on the same footing of equality."[51] Finally, in keeping with his legalist arguments, Zaghlul pledged that Egypt would continue to recognize the rights of foreigners and to pay its debt.

These themes—the rights of Mehmed Ali and the civilizational superiority of Egypt over Hejaz and other Ottoman provinces—were repeated in a number of other letters and petitions sent by the Wafd around Paris, London, and Cairo. For instance, following riots and strikes against the protectorate, General Edmund Allenby replaced Wingate as high commissioner of Egypt. The Wafd sent him a letter that stated that Egypt had a stronger to claim to independence than any other part of the Ottoman Empire. on the basis of its internationally guaranteed legal status, its civilization, and the fact that Egypt had supported Britain during the war: "During the time the Egyptians were reading with astonishment the news concerning the Delegations of other countries: the Hedjaz, Armenia, Syria, and the Lebanon etc., which yesterday still Turkish provinces, were for the most part in war against the allies, while Egypt richer, more civilized, and enjoying already an autonomy guaranteed by international treaty, had aided in the conquest of these same countries."[52]

On March 7, 1919, Zaghlul and key members of the Wafd were arrested for their activities against the British protectorate and deported to Malta. Massive protests and a general strike in Cairo followed almost immediately. Wingate was recalled to London and replaced by General Allenby at the end of March. Nationalist pressure in Egypt was felt in Paris too.

Since 1914, international recognition of Britain's protectorate in Egypt had been protracted and incomplete at best. The United States never recognized the protectorate and Russia's acceptance of Egypt's changed legal status no longer mattered as the Bolsheviks were outside of European diplomacy at the start of the Paris Peace Conference. While Britain managed to avoid discussion of Egypt's legal status with Europe and the United States, events in Egypt forced Britain to deal with recognition of the protectorate. Allenby pressured the Foreign Office to obtain wide international recognition of the protectorate especially from the United States. On April 4, 1919, Allenby wrote to Arthur Balfour, the British foreign secretary, "I would reiterate the great importance of obtaining an early announcement that our protectorate is recognized by the Powers."[53] After years of Foreign Office pressure, the United States responded to Allenby's request against growing unrest in Egypt, which was a massive blow to the Wafd. In the end, all of the treaties imposed by the Allies on Germany, Austria, Hungary, and Bulgaria included provisions to recognize the British Protectorate in Egypt and to renounce their Capitulatory rights there. The first and second Ottoman/Republic of Turkey treaties (Sèvres and Lausanne) were slightly different from the other European treaties and forced the Ottomans, and later the Republicans, to relinquish all rights and titles over Egypt and the Sudan and to surrender all claims on the Egyptian tribute.

Recognition of Britain's protectorate in Egypt did not quell the revolution in Egypt. In May 1919, the British government announced that a special mission headed by Lord Alfred Milner, British secretary of state for the colonies, would be sent to Egypt to "inquire into the causes of the late disorders in Egypt and to report on the current situation in the country and the form of constitution which under the protectorate would be best to promote peace, the progressive development of self-governing institutions, and protection of foreign interests." The Milner Mission consisted of a group of British colonial experts, and the principal legal advisor at the Foreign Office, Sir Cecil Hurst.[54] The mission arrived in December 1919 and returned to London in March 1920.[55] The Wafd boycotted the mission, which was also met with another waves of strikes.

The Milner Mission's internal discussions revolved around the meaning of the protectorate and what it had done for British interests in Egypt. The members of the mission discussed the meaning of the term "protectorate" at length. Rennell Rodd argued that it was the word itself that had offended Egyptians, as the same word was used in Arabic to "indicate the protection accorded under traditional usage by western Powers to subjects of the old Turkish Empire." He noted that the word "thus implies a diminution of sovereignty to Egyptians and has an unwelcome suggestiveness for them, as implying foreign intervention."[56] Similarly, General Owen Thomas interviewed local elites and reported that the Arabic word for protectorate, *himaye*, was the same word applied to protected foreign subjects in Egypt.[57] He concluded that the "complete independence" that Egyptians demanded could be "satisfied with a little more than a shadow of independence with but very little substance."[58] For Milner, the mission should not bother with terms but identify "how much authority" Britain should exercise in Egypt and that meant thinking clearly about what to control versus what could be left alone. Secondly, he thought it was important to decide if the British could come to an agreement with Egyptians or if Britain should be "obliged simply to arrogate to ourselves such powers as we may deem necessary without their consent." He explained:

> The 'veiled protectorate' had defiantly come to an end. It was perhaps the best system possible. But it was necessarily temporary—the wonder is that it lasted so long—the veil could not be maintained for forever and the veil has gone. Something has to be substituted for it, having a more definite and open character. I do not ignore the fact that, whatever the formal relations between Great Britain and Egypt, the reality will always be something different. But we cannot very well go on any longer without any formal relations at all, beyond the phrase 'Protectorate.'

Milner argued that when possible, Britain should exercise control, in whatever branch of administration. Without "assuming executive authority," he noted, "the indirect method of effecting our object by guidance and advice is preferable to the direct method of doing all of the work ourselves or by direct orders."[59] He thought that too much had been made of the word *protectorate* but that it could not be abandoned all together because it excluded all foreign influence from Egypt and at the same time was recognized in the peace treaties. He noted: "It is quite possible that what we mean by 'Protectorate' is not really incompatible with what they mean by 'independence." He argued that the protectorate could remain in place, but that Britain could work out a bilateral arrangement with Fuad, who had become sultan of Egypt in 1917, following the death of Husayn:

> My own idea of the form . . . is that of a contract (I will not call it a treaty) by which we should undertake to guarantee an agreed constitution for Egypt against foreign intervention and internal disorder, and Egypt, in return for this guarantee, would acknowledge our right to keep an army of occupation and to retain certain posts in the administration, and the control of the Sudan. All these could be based on obligations we should be undertaking for the defense of Egypt and for the maintenance of the constitution, including any provisions it might contain for the protection of foreigners. I do not see why it should not be possible to have such an understanding with the Egyptians without abandoning the Protectorate, which we have so far only defined as implying the control of Egypt's foreign relations, which control would be explicitly recognized in this contract. As between us and the rest of the world our position would rest on the declaration of 1914, and its acknowledgement by the

Great Powers, and the Peace Treaties. But as between us and the Egyptians it would rest on a bi-lateral agreement, not inconsistent with but *in foro demestico*,[60] taking the place of these various sets. I conceive that it is not beyond the skill of the draftsmen, who have invented in the last twelve months—"Mandates" and such like—to construct a document which would embody these ideas.[61]

Milner's plan for what would replace the so-called veiled protectorate, his expression for the British occupation of Egypt, was an idealized version of the occupation.[62] Lord Cromer, the British counsel general in Egypt between 1883 and 1907, and others, including Milner in the 1890s, had long argued against "internationalism" in Egypt. For much of the occupation, British Foreign Office officials complained that European and Ottoman interference in Egypt had obstructed British efforts at reform. For Milner, a form of "independence" could be found to satisfy Egyptians while maximizing British interests and limiting European interference in British administrative practices. Upon returning to London, he recommended full sovereignty for Egypt over its internal government, including the right to conclude treaties with foreign nations. In return, Egypt should acknowledge the right of Great Britain to maintain capitulatory rights with some modifications. He argued that Britain should have rights to military bases to prevent "foreign intervention" in Egypt. Milner also thought Britain should negotiate with Zaghlul and the Wafd.

The British cabinet found Milner's suggestions unacceptable. Britain had finally obtained Egypt, and now Milner wished Britain to relinquish any sovereign claims to the territory. Subsequent negotiations between Egypt and Britain failed to produce a treaty that was satisfactory to nationalists. After a long stalemate, Allenby, without cabinet support, unilaterally declared Egyptian independence on February 28, 1922. Egypt was proclaimed a sovereign and independent state but subject to four reservations. Britain would control the security of communications and defense. Minorities and foreign interests would be protected, including the preservation of the Capitulations. Finally, Sudan would not be affected by the declaration of independence and would remain jointly under British and Egyptian control. Britain's short-lived "sultan" became a king with the establishment of the constitutional monarchy and new constitution promulgated in April 1923. Egyptian independence looked rather like Milner's idealized version of occupation, especially since Britain's permanent military presence would continue as a "veiled protectorate."

## Conclusion

The occupation of Egypt had a lasting effect on British imperial policy in the Middle East after the First World War. William Roger Lewis has in fact argued that the British Empire as a whole was revived and reinvented in the Middle East after the First World War.[63] Yet the reinvention of the empire that Lewis posits began in Egypt prior to the outbreak of the war. British officials in the Foreign Office had learned much from the occupation and over time developed a model of rule that was distinct from formal political control. Sovereignty could reside elsewhere, preferably in a local monarch, as long as an army of British advisors controlled foreign and economic policy. The British-Ottoman diplomatic relationship, but also the consolidation of positivist international law and the global territorialization of sovereignty between the 1880s and the end of the First World War, had a decisive influence on that model. The practice of ruling through Ottoman institutions, along with justifications for the occupation that highlighted international stability and the development of self-government, offered a distinct model of imperial administration that the British employed in the form of League of Nations mandates in the territories seized from the Ottoman Empire after the First World War.

During the protectorate experiment in Egypt, the Foreign Office learned something very important about formal sovereignty. The protectorate lasted briefly, but debates about it continued in London and Cairo from 1914 through the mid-1920s. During the war, these debates led to rather frank discussions concerning the past and future of British power in Egypt and the Middle East. The protectorate was a wartime exigency and one that deviated from the Foreign Office's usual anti-annexationist position in Ottoman territories—preferring a range of options to manage Ottoman weakness, from creating "autonomous" provinces to permanent military occupation. By the end of the war, many officials viewed the protectorate as a misstep, particularly as Egyptian nationalists, in demanding independence, continued to appeal to Egypt's special status in international law. Independence in 1922 was in many ways a return to the occupation, where formal sovereignty could reside in Egypt, as it had in the Ottoman sultan during the occupation, while Britain administered core functions of the state.

## Notes

1. Viscount Grey of Fallodon, *Twenty-Five Years*, vol. 2 (New York: Frederick A. Stokes, 1925), 176–77.

2. Başbakanlık Osmanlı Arşivi (hereafter BOA)/MMM, defter 15[1256/1841] Firman of investiture conferring hereditary rights on Mehmed Ali Paşa; "Convention for the Pacification of the Levant, 1840," in *The Map of Europe by Treaty*, vol. 2, ed. Edward Hertslet (London, 1875), 1021–23; government of Egypt, *Recueil de firmans impériaux ottomans addressés aux valis et aux khedives d'Égypte* (Cairo: L'institut Français d'archéologie orientale du Caire, 1934); Gabriel Noradounghian, *Recueil d'actes internationaux de l'Empire ottoman*, vol. 3 (Paris, F. Pichon, 1897–1903), 261. This is the subject of my current manuscript project, "Empire by Law: The Ottoman Origins of the Mandates System in the Middle East, 1840–1923," forthcoming.

3. Lord Granville, National Archives, UK (hereafter NA)/FO/78/3454, Turkey (Egypt), Lord Dufferin's Special Mission, Dufferin to Granville, November 11, 1882.

4. For example, George Louis Beer's book on the peace conference contains a large section on Egypt and legal work necessary for the protectorate in Egypt. He also drafted the articles related to recognition of the British protectorate in Egypt for all of the peace

treaties concluding the First World War. George Louis Beer, *African Questions at the Paris Peace Conference, with Papers on Egypt, Mesopotamia, and the Colonial Settlement* (New York: Macmillan, 1923); Vernon O'Rourke, *The Juristic Status of Egypt and the Sudan* (Baltimore: Johns Hopkins Press, 1935); Malcolm McIlwraith, "The Declaration of a Protectorate in Egypt and Its Legal Effects," *Journal of the Society of Comparative Legislation* 17, no. 1/2 (1917): 238–59; Malcolm McIlwraith, "Legal War Work in Egypt," *Problems of the War* 3 (1917): 71–90; Valentine Chirol, *The Egyptian Problem* (London: Macmillan, 1920). The 1914 protectorate appears as a major issue in many if not most postwar memoirs of British officials stationed in Cairo during and after the war. For instance, Ronald Storrs, *Orientations* (London: Nicholson & Watson, 1937); George Lloyd, *Egypt since Cromer* (London: Macmillan, 1933–34). On the Ottoman side see Rağib Raif and Ahmed Rauf, *Mısır Meselesi* (Istanbul: Bab-ı Ali, Hariciye Nezareti, 1334 [1915]); Süleyman Kani Irtem, *Osmanlı Devleti'nin Mısır Yemen Hicaz Meselesi* (Istanbul: Temel Yayınları, 1999). Though the 1919 revolution in Egypt was framed in different ways at the time and since, one of the most important arguments emanating from Cairo and Paris was that the British established an "illegal protectorate"; see *Egyptian Delegation to the Peace Conference, Collection of Official Correspondence from November 11, 1918, to July 14, 1919* (Paris: Delegation, 1919).

5. Ottoman sultans obtained the title "caliph"—literally "successor" to the Prophet Muhammad—with the conquest of Egypt in 1517. The title "caliph" was one of many to which the Ottoman sultans laid claim, including "khan" and the "Caesar of Rome." In the late nineteenth century, Sultan Abdülhamid II emphasized his role as caliph and the Commander of the Faithful (*Emir ül-Müminin*) in his dealings with European empires, who by the late nineteenth century ruled over more Muslims than the Ottoman Sultan. The institutions of the sultanate and caliphate were tied together until the Grand National Assembly in Ankara separated them on November 1, 1922. The new Turkish Republic abolished the Ottoman caliphate in 1924. See Cemil Aydın, *The Idea of the Muslim World: A Global Intellectual History* (Cambridge, MA: Harvard University Press, 2017) and Selim Deringil, *The Well Protected Domains: Ideology and Legitimization of Power in the Ottoman Empire 1876-1909* (London: I.B. Tauris, 1998). For the historical significance of the Ottoman sultan as caliph and other legitimacy practices for the sultanate see Hakan T. Karateke, ed. *Legitimizing the Order: The Ottoman Rhetoric of State Power* (Leiden: Brill, 2005).

6. Ronald Storrs argued later: "Neither Turkey nor the rest of the World could imagine that the Occupying Power, if attacked by the Suzerain, would any longer tolerate suzerainty that had been but a figure of speech for the past half century. The only question was, what form of government should replace the forfeited suzerainty. The uncertainty of Occupation, with its remote hopes and hypothetical fears, must obviously be abolished." But this was not a legal argument and was a position that would be difficult to sustain after the war. See Storrs, *Orientations*, 150.

7. NA/FO/800/48/229 Sir Edward Grey Papers, Grey to Cheetham, August 12, 1914.

8. Cheetham was acting consul general serving in Kitchener's place. Kitchener was on leave in London when the war broke out and was appointed as the secretary of state of war—though he planned to return to Cairo in his capacity as consul general. Cheetham's ideas followed Kitchener's very closely.

9. NA/FO/407/183, Cheetham to Grey, August 14, 1914.

10. Sudan Archives, Durham (hereafter SAD)/164/6/95–97, Wingate Papers, No. 139, Cheetham to Grey, September 10, 1914, from document "Notes on Egyptian Protection."

11. NA/FO/407/183, No. 7, Cheetham to Grey, September 1, 1914.

12. NA/FO/407/183, Enclosure, Ronald Storrs, Oriental Secretary, "Note respecting the state of public opinion in Egypt," August 31, 1914. The quotes around the expression and words "sense of nationality," "autonomy," and "independence" were Storrs's. Storrs reproduced his note on public opinion in his memoir after the war to show that Britain was concerned about the effect of war between the British and Ottoman Empires on the Muslim subjects of the British Empire: "I have said that our major preoccupation was the threat of Turkey on the Canal; less for its military effect than for the repercussion upon a Moslem Egypt" (Storrs, *Orientations*, 145).

13. NA/FO/407/183, Enclosure.

14. Storrs did not elaborate on the content of "independence" or "autonomy," nor did he link these words to their Arabic or Ottoman counterparts (*idara al-hukm al-dhati* and *muhtariyet*, *ötonomie*, respectively), but by this stage, officials in Cairo, particularly those around Kitchener, were well away of Arab demands for autonomy within the Ottoman Empire, especially in Syria, as well autonomy as an actual administrative category of province within the Ottoman Empire. See Rashid Khalidi, *British Policy towards Syria & Palestine, 1906–1914* (London: Ithaca Press, 1980).

15. NA/FO/407/183, No. 8, Cheetham to Grey, September 7, 1914.

16. NA/FO/407/183, No. 5, Cheetham to Grey, September 10, 1914.

17. As will be seen below, Sa'd Zaghlul and the Wafd would later argue that ending Ottoman sovereignty in Egypt could only mean that it reverted to Egypt. This is one of the key arguments that the Wafd presented in Paris.

18. SAD/164/6/95-97, Wingate Papers, "Notes on the question of succession," no. 226, Grey to Cheetham, September 26, 1914 "Appointment of Prince Hussain as Khedive approved." NA/FO/407/183, no. 11, Grey to Cheetham, September 27, 1914.

19. NA/FO/407/183, no. 17, Cheetham to Grey, October 12, 1914.

20. NA/FO/407/183, no. 29, Cheetham to Grey, October 30, 1914.

21. Ibid.

22. NA/FO/407/183, no. 36, Grey to Cheetham, November 1, 1914. Martial law was proclaimed on November 2, 1914.

23. Mehmed Ali's name is rendered as "Mehmet Ali" or "Mehmed Ali" in Turkish and Ottoman. Whereas in Arabic, his name is rendered as "Muhammad Ali."

24. BOA/HR.SYS./2404/14, November 5, 1914.

25. Mustafa Aksakal, "'Holy War Made in Germany'? Ottoman Origins of the 1914 Jihad," *War in History* (April 2011): 184–99.

26. Noradounghian. *Recueil d'actes internationaux de l'Empire ottoman*, 261; See government of Egypt, *Recueil de firmans impériaux ottomans*, 301, no. 936, 5 Sefer 1284 (June 8, 1867); Edward Dicey, *The Story of the Khedivate* (London: Rivingtons, 1902).

27. "Prince Husayn has, at more than one interview, reiterated his opinion that Egypt should be transformed into a Kingdom under an Egyptian King. He has compared the extent and wealth of this country with that of the Balkan Kingdoms, and laid stress upon the very great satisfaction which such a transformation would give to Egyptians of all classes." Middle East Center, St. Antony's College, Oxford/GB165-0055/ File 4, Cheetham papers, Cheetham to Tyrrell, November 10, 1914, enclosure note by Ronald Storrs.

28. "*Sultan Misr wa al-Sudan*" MEC/GB165-0055/4. Grey eventually approved of the title "sultan," but instructed Cheetham to exclude any reference to Sudan.

29. MEC/GB165-0055/4.

30. SAD/164/6/95-97, Wingate papers, no. 334, Grey to Cheetham, November 13, 1914, in "Notes on the question of succession."

31. NA/FO/407/183, no. 45, Grey to Cheetham, November 17, 1914.

32. SAD/164/6/95-97, Wingate papers, no. 350, Grey to Bertie, November 17, 1914, in "Notes on the question of succession."

33. SAD/164/6/95-97, Wingate papers, no. 274, Cheetham to Grey, November 18, 1914, in "Notes on the question of succession."

34. NA/FO/407/183, no. 52, Bertie to Grey, November 19, 1914. NA/FO/407/183, no 16, Cheetham to Grey, October 12, 1914; William Renzi, "Great Britain, Russia, and the Straits, 1914–1915," *Journal of Modern History* 42, no. 1(March 1970): 1–20; see especially p. 6.

35. NA/FO/800/48/259, Grey papers, Grey to Cheetham and Wingate, November 18, 1914.

36. NA/FO/407/183, no. 59, Grey to Cheetham, November 25, 1914.

37. NA/FO/407/183, no. 65, Grey to Cheetham, December 1, 1914.

38. SAD/164/6/95-97, Wingate papers, no. 306, Cheetham to Grey, December 8, 1914.

39. Ibid.

40. *Journal Official du Gouvernement Égyptien*, December 18 and 19, 1914; George Lloyd, *Egypt since Cromer*, 376–79; NA/FO/407/183, no. 86 Cheetham to Grey, December 21, 1914, three enclosures.

41. The main justification for terminating Ottoman sovereignty in Egypt was that the government abandoned neutrality and attacked Russia ports and that Ottoman armed bands crossed into Egyptian territory.

42. The Foreign Office appointed Sir Henry McMahon as first high commissioner for Egypt, where he remained through the end of 1916. Reginald Wingate, who previously held the post of Sidar in Sudan, later replaced him.

43. McIlwraith, "Declaration of a Protectorate."

44. SAD/164/7/32-42 Wingate to Graham, May 28, 1917.

45. The Wafd was named for the desired Egyptian delegation to be sent to Paris to press Egyptian claims. The exchange between Zaghlul, Ali Sharawi, Abd al-Aziz and Wingate has been reproduced in numerous places. All of the sources indicate that Zaghlul asked for "complete independence," but in some versions of the event, Zaghlul is reported to have discussed a "program of complete autonomy." While there may not be a titanic difference between independence and autonomy, both the Foreign Office and Egyptian lawyers like Zaghlul would have understood "autonomy" in its Ottoman context as well. Complicating matters is the fact that autonomy is rendered in modern Arabic as *hukm dhati*, which can also mean "self-determination" or "self-governance." See also John D. McIntyre, *The Boycott of the Milner Mission: A Study in Egyptian Nationalism* (New York: Peter Lang, 1985).

46. *The Egyptian National Claims: A Memorandum Presented to the Peace Conference by the Egyptian Delegation Charged with the Defense of Egyptian Independence*, (Paris: Imprimerie artistique Lux, 1919).

47. Ibid., 10.

48. Ibid., 12.

49. Ibid., 13.

50. Ibid., 20–21.

51. Ibid., 20.

52. "Report presented in Arabic, with a French Translation to the British High Commissioner on March 30, 1919," in *Egyptian Delegation to the Peace Conference*, 35. Like members of the Wafd argued in Paris, Egyptian nationalists who were willing to meet with the Milner Mission continued to insist that Egyptian autonomy was won by Mehmed Ali. Rennell Rodd met with a Mahmoud Pasha Soliman at Luxor, who maintained, "Egypt must have complete independence. The people of Egypt had won it by arms in 1841. There

remained only a shadow nexus with Turkey but that had had no importance in their eyes." Rodd replied that he "was not prepared to admit that Turkish sovereignty was a mere fiction as he seemed to imply and that Egypt had ever since been independent in the accepted sense of the word. The question was what he meant by independence. He said he meant just the same conditions that were enjoyed by Serbia and Greece and other such countries. Egypt was in a higher state of civilization than these countries and once she also had her independence she would go ahead as rapidly as Japan had done in recent years" (NA/FO848/8, visit of Sir Rennell Rodd to Mahmoud Pasha Soliman at Luxor, 144).

53. NA/FO608/213 Allenby to Balfour, April 4, 1919.

54. Rennell Rodd, John Maxwell, Sir Cecil Hurst, John Spender, Sir Owen Thomas and A.T. Loyd.

55. McIntyre, *Boycott of the Milner Mission*, 35.

56. NA/FO/848/8, Milner Mission, "Note on the Arabic translation of the word protectorate," Rennell Rodd, October 21, 1919.

57. NA/FO 848/3, Milner Mission, "Record of conversations held with various people of authority in Egypt," conversation between Brigadier General Sir Owen Thomas and Delabor Bey and Saddik Sahmy.

58. Ibid.

59. NA/FO/848/8, Milner Mission, "The Veiled Protectorate."

60. *In foro demestico* is a legal expression meaning "in a domestic court" versus a foreign court. Emphasis in original.

61. NA/FO/848/8, Milner Mission, "The Veiled Protectorate."

62. Lord Milner, *England in Egypt* (London: Edward Arnold, 1909).

63. See Wm. Roger Lewis, *Ends of British Imperialism: The Scramble for Empire, Suez and Decolonization* (London: I. B. Tauris, 2006) and Matthew A. Fitzsimons, *Empire by Treaty: Britain and the Middle East in the Twentieth Century* (Notre Dame, IN: University of Notre Dame Press, 1964).

# Bibliography

Aksakal, Mustafa. "'Holy War Made in Germany'? Ottoman Origins of the 1914 Jihad." *War in History* 18, no. 2 (April 2011): 184–99.

Aydın, Cemil. *The Idea of the Muslim World: A Global Intellectual History*. Cambridge, MA: Harvard University Press, 2017.

Beer, George Louis. *African Questions at the Paris Peace Conference, with Papers on Egypt, Mesopotamia, and the Colonial Settlement*. New York: Macmillan, 1923.

Chirol, Valentine. *The Egyptian Problem*. London: Macmillan, 1920.

Deringil, Selim. *The Well Protected Domains: Ideology and Legitimization of Power in the Ottoman Empire 1876-1909*. London: I.B. Tauris, 1998.

Dicey, Edward. *The Story of the Khedivate*. London: Rivingtons, 1902.

*Egyptian Delegation to the Peace Conference, Collection of Official Correspondence from November 11, 1918, to July 14, 1919*. Paris: Delegation, 1919.

Fallodon, Viscount Grey. *Twenty-Five Years*, 2 vols. New York: Frederick A. Stokes, 1925.

Fitzsimons, Matthew A. *Empire by Treaty: Britain and the Middle East in the Twentieth Century*. Notre Dame, IN: University of Notre Dame Press, 1964.

Genell, Aimee. "Empire by Law: The Ottoman Origins of the Mandates System in the Middle East, 1840–1923." Forthcoming.

Government of Egypt. *Recueil de firmans impériaux ottomans addressés aux valis et aux khedives d'Égypte*. Cairo: L'institut Français d'archéologie orientale du Caire, 1934.

Hertslet, Edward, ed. *The Map of Europe by Treaty*. Vol. 2. London: Butterworth, 1875.

Irtem, Süleyman Kani. *Osmanlı Devleti'nin Mısır Yemen Hicaz Meselesi*. Istanbul: Temel Yayınları, 1999.

*Journal Official du Gouvernement Égyptien*, December 18 and 19, 1914.

Karateke, Hakan T., ed. *Legitimizing the Order: the Ottoman Rhetoric of State Power*. Leiden: Brill, 2005.

Khalidi, Rashid. *British Policy towards Syria & Palestine, 1906–1914*. London: Ithaca Press, 1980.

Lewis, Wm. Roger. *Ends of British Imperialism: The Scramble for Empire, Suez and Decolonization*. London: I. B. Tauris, 2006.

Lloyd, George. *Egypt since Cromer*. London: Macmillan, 1933–34.

Milner, Alfred. *England in Egypt*. London: Edward Arnold, 1909.

McIlwraith, Malcolm. "Legal War Work in Egypt." *Problems of the War* 3 (1917): 71–90.

———. "The Declaration of a Protectorate in Egypt and Its Legal Effects." *Journal of the Society of Comparative Legislation* 17, no. 1–2 (1917): 238–59.

McIntyre, John D. *The Boycott of the Milner Mission: A Study in Egyptian Nationalism*. New York: Peter Lang, 1985.

Noradounghian, Gabriel. *Recueil d'actes internationaux de l'Empire ottoman.*. Paris: F. Pichon, 1897–1903.

O'Rourke, Vernon. *The Juristic Status of Egypt and the Sudan*. Baltimore: Johns Hopkins Press, 1935.

Raif, Rağib, and Ahmed Rauf. *Mısır Meselesi*. Istanbul: Bab-ı Ali, Hariciye Nezareti, 1334 [1915].

Renzi, William. "Great Britain, Russia, and the Straits, 1914–1915." *Journal of Modern History* 42, no. 1(March 1970): 1–20.

Storrs, Ronald. *Orientations*. London: Nicholson & Watson, 1937.

*The Egyptian National Claims: A Memorandum Presented to the Peace Conference by the Egyptian Delegation Charged with the Defense of Egyptian Independence*. Paris: Imprimerie artistique Lux, 1919.

AIMEE GENELL is Assistant Professor of Middle East History at the University of West Georgia.

# 5  Ordering the "Land of Paradox"

## *The Fashioning of Nationality, Religion, and Political Loyalty in Colonial Egypt*

### Jeffrey Culang

Reflecting on his rule and the art of governance in colonial Egypt, former consul general Lord Cromer posed ethnic, racial, and national difference as a problem:

> It might naturally be supposed that, as we are dealing with the country called Egypt, the inhabitants . . . would be Egyptians. Any one who is inclined to rush to this conclusion should remember that Egypt . . . is the Land of Paradox. If any one walks down one of the principal streets of London, Paris, or Berlin, nine out of ten of the people with whom he meets bear on their faces evidence . . . that they are Englishmen, Frenchmen, or Germans. But let any one who has a general acquaintance with the appearance and physiognomy of the principal Eastern races try if he can give a fair ethnological description of the first ten people he meets in one of the streets of Cairo. . . He will find it no easy matter.[1]

Cromer's remarks reflect the centrality of population to the political rationalities of what David Scott, expanding on Michel Foucault's Europe-centered theorization, calls colonial governmentality, a modern form of power "concerned above all with disabling old forms of life by systematically breaking down their conditions, and with constructing in their place new conditions so as to enable—indeed, so as to *oblige*—new forms of life to come into being."[2] In nineteenth- and early twentieth-century Egypt, colonial governmentality actively sought to dismantle a complex, interconnected web of distinct, largely autonomous communities, each with its own memories, practices, and horizons of expectation. As in other colonial contexts, this form of governmentality engendered new structures that sought to produce easily governable subjects within a homogenous polity demanding discipline and, in a national context, also unassailable loyalty. For Cromer, Egypt was a "Land of Paradox" in contrast to Europe's then–homogenizing nation-states. The political community he idealized would become normative globally, including in Egypt, where by the interwar period nationality was becoming a primary category of identification and belonging. Unlike earlier such categories, nationality, in the words of one Egyptian jurist from the 1930s, had "simple, singular meanings that do not tolerate mixing or overlapping."[3]

This chapter draws on periodicals, legal sources, and British and Egyptian archival records to provide a genealogy of the "Egyptian national." It traces how the "Egyptian" (*misri*) became a legal category and, eventually, was understood to denote a nationality.[4] The British-dominated colonial state initially established a legal definition of the "Egyptian" in its efforts to govern Egypt; then, in the crucible of colonial politics, this definition was transformed further. When the category of the Egyptian national was first articulated in the 1920s, it both reflected prior definitions of Egyptian subjecthood and was shaped heavily by what historian Eric Weitz, referring to the Paris peace settlement of 1919–23, calls "the Paris system," in which populations, conceived as racially, ethnically, or nationally homogenous units, became central to governance and sovereignty.[5] After the British unilaterally granted Egypt limited independence in 1922, Egyptian legislators and British advisers adapted earlier colonial definitions of the Egyptian to an emergent global system of bounded national territories. Through the case of Egypt, a country that was not beholden to the settlement's treaties but was heavily influenced by its central concepts, this chapter points to the global scope of Paris's capillaries.

In laying out this genealogy, the chapter focuses on the relationship between the Paris system and religion. Scholarship on the late Ottoman Empire and its successor states has analyzed both the emergence of sectarianism and the ways in which secular governance exacerbated rather than resolved religious discord and inequality.[6] This study explores how the international order that emerged after the First World War reconfigured religion in the "Middle East," a then novel geopolitical concept that was just being consolidated in the minds of international policymakers.[7] Animated by the colonial civilizing mission, this new order lent religion particular salience in Middle Eastern contexts.[8] In Egypt, the ideas that undergirded the Paris peace treaties, which were disseminated and engaged with well beyond the realm of law and legislation, meshed with local concerns. In the process, categories inherent to the nation-state (i.e., majority and minority) were grafted onto established communities and, in many cases, tethered these communities to their "rightful" nations in formation elsewhere. Rogers Brubaker has argued that nationality, as an "instrument and object of social closure" critical to the rise and sustenance of bounded nation-states, allowed for legal and social distinctions to be made between "insiders," "outsiders," and those in between.[9] Yet in post-Ottoman contexts, thinking along national lines untangled interconnected communal formations toward homogenous polities; it also rearranged how these groups remembered their collective past, lived their lives as a group, and envisioned their future. The drafting of nationality laws constructed the past of the nation and state (often before historians did so), delineated its character, and situated it along a historical path of progress. In engaging with national categories in unpredictable ways, subjects in turn precipitated changes in how the nation was defined. Through this ongoing looping effect, the boundaries of the nation, insider and outsider, remain ever in flux.[10]

## An "Internationalist Nationality":
## The Egyptian Local Subject

Egyptian nationalism saw itself as a repudiation of Egypt's Ottoman past. Yet the country's first implemented nationality law of 1929 laid overtop the Ottoman Nationality Law of 1869, which remained in effect in Egypt into the 1920s. The two laws involved complex processes of translation and, when viewed together, reveal important linguistic transformations. For the French term *nationalité*, the 1869 Ottoman nationality law used the Arabic/Ottoman Turkish word *tabʿiya/tabiiyet*, related to the noun *tabiʿ/tabii*, which means "follower," and in an imperial legal context referred to a subject of the sultan or state. Use of this word, which coexisted with the term *raʿaya/raya*, meaning "subjects" (again, of the sultan or state), particularly non-Muslims, arguably reflected a transfiguration of Ottoman political community defined in part by the vertical relationship between sultan and subject into a form of citizenship.[11] The 1869 law was one of a number of Ottoman reforms concerned with state centralization and bureaucratization in the face of the interconnected problems of imperial intervention and incipient nationalism. It was the product of a new ideology of Ottoman constitutionalism in which undifferentiated citizenship would supersede religious and/or ethnic difference, though in its implementation Islam continued to be the basis of state identity and a factor in naturalization.[12] Among the Ottoman state's immediate aims in devising this law was to prevent loss of subjects to foreign powers that could offer them privileges sanctioned by long-standing Capitulatory agreements (e.g., exemption from local courts, taxes, and conscription). The 1869 law presumed everyone on its territory to be Ottoman unless demonstrated otherwise and was relatively flexible in its requirements for naturalization.[13] Thus, while it produced a new category of governance—the Ottoman imperial citizen—this category's terms of inclusion/exclusion had less to do with the perceived character of populations than with geopolitics.

The Arabic term for "nationality" used in later Egyptian codes and common today, *jinsiyya*, has a very different connotation. This word was likely a neologism of the nineteenth century deriving from the word *jins*, itself an Arabization of the Greek *genus* that eventually became the Arabic trilateral root *janasa*, meaning "to make homogenous" or "classify." Over time, *jins* has taken numerous meanings such as "kind," "species," "category," "sex" (male, female), "gender" (in grammar), and, more recently, "race" and "nation."[14] In the mid-nineteenth century, *jinsiyya* referred to "common origin," a meaning with the flexibility to absorb various associations.[15] By the turn of the twentieth century, it still carried this meaning, but was overlaid with ethnicity.[16] When the Egyptian colonial state sought to articulate a distinct political category of "Egyptian local subjects" in 1900 (see later in the chapter), the word *jinsiyya* was chosen over *tabʿiya*, perhaps for the element of binding that it connoted.

The shift from Ottoman *tabʿiya* to Egyptian *jinsiyya* was largely precipitated by the British occupation of Egypt starting in 1882, which brought a shift of suzerainty over the province even as a veneer of Ottoman control and links between

Egypt and the empire remained.[17] Colonial governance in Egypt involved in part the reconstruction of Egypt's legal system through the establishment of the National Courts in 1883.[18] This new institution was accompanied by a matrix of governing structures and legal codes that yielded the legal category of the Egyptian local subject. Announced in the Egyptian government's official journal, the 1883 Organic Law replaced what had been the Council of Notables, established under Khedive Isma'il, with a new, quasi-representative Legislative Council and General Assembly based on models from India.[19] These bodies had a largely advisory role and little authority. According to then British ambassador Lord Dufferin, who first proposed them, their purpose was to "erect some sort of barrier, however feeble, against the intolerable tyranny of the Turks."[20] The British also viewed them as pedagogical tools for self-governance, though British authorities refrained from conferring real authority on them until doing so became politically expedient right before the First World War.

The deputies who were to fill these new governing structures would be elected according to the Electoral Law. Announced on the same day as the Organic Law, this new law stated that eligible voters were limited to "Egyptian local subjects," a new category that included male Ottoman subjects in Egypt at least twenty years of age, certain "undesirables" aside.[21] In reality, the articulation of the Egyptian local subject was less about establishing a right than about a colonial effort to render Egypt governable by defining its territory and population, without appearing to upset the idea of Ottoman suzerainty, threaten Capitulatory powers, or disrupt the international balance of power. The inclusiveness of the category—excepting gender—is indicative of the modus operandi of the Egyptian colonial state to append all subjects within the territory of Egypt to itself.[22] Lord Cromer echoed this objective in his assertion that Egypt's assorted peoples should be fused into what he paradoxically termed an "internationalist nationality," an idea that must have had greater appeal to him amid incipient Egyptian nationalism than "Egyptian nationality."[23]

In the 1890s, this first articulation of the Egyptian local subject would be followed by others delineating eligibility for service in government posts and the National Courts. These decrees introduced a new condition excluding male Ottoman subjects who had lived in Egypt for less than fifteen years.[24] The exclusion of newcomers was likely intended to assuage local outrage over British favoritism toward "Syrians," who received a disproportionate number of high government positions.[25] This largely Christian group from Ottoman Syria was one of many Ottoman and non-Ottoman groups to arrive in Egypt in the second half of the nineteenth century for economic opportunities and/or refuge from state repression, and some Syrians came to play important roles in Egyptian society. As the category of the Egyptian local subject expanded from the electoral domain to other arenas of eligibility, subjects began to claim and adapt it, widening the new divisions it had introduced. One example involves a group of six Syrian Effendis (middle-class professionals) residing in Egypt who in 1898 applied to the Cairo Governorate (*muhafizat misr*) to register their names on the electoral roll. On June 2, 1898, the head of the National Court of Appeals in Cairo,

Ahmad 'Afifi, and two judges considered their application in court. The Syrians based their claim to Egyptian local subjecthood on not only their continued residence in Egypt, but also their payment of taxes to the Egyptian government and their subjection to local Egyptian law and courts. Further, it was clear to them that the Egyptian government defined the term (*lafza*) "Egyptian local subject" in the Electoral Law so as to include all Ottomans residing in Egypt.[26]

'Afifi, who was clearly influenced by ideas of nationalism, refuted the Syrians' claims by arguing that residence, payment of taxes, and subjection to law and courts each represents its own legal domain independent of Egyptian local subjecthood, which he viewed as an operative nationality that was critical to public law. Further, he maintained that Egypt, though still under the suzerainty of the Ottoman Empire to which it paid tribute, was independent in its internal affairs. This independence, he argued, was initially achieved in 1841 by Egypt's rebellious viceroy Muhammad 'Ali, who extracted a firman from the Ottoman sultan granting him and his male bloodline right of rule over Egypt. Because any independent nation must have its own nationality, 'Afifi reasoned, Egyptian nationality, even if absent in law, held valid legal standing. In the context of local communal competition under colonial governance, 'Afifi defined Egyptian nationality by drawing on earlier definitions of the Egyptian local subject, though he included only residents of Egypt since 1841.[27] He thereby established an origin point for the birth of the modern Egyptian nation and inscribed Muhammad 'Ali as its "father," well before Egyptian royalist historians did so in the 1920s.[28]

Interestingly, despite advocating Egyptian nationality, in his ruling 'Afifi used the term *lafza* rather than *kalima* in association with the word *misri* (Egyptian). Though *lafza* and *kalima* both mean "word," the former specifically evokes the spoken word, and so 'Afifi's use of this term indicates *misri*'s continued oral character and undefined quality.[29] As we have seen, 'Afifi's own ruling contributed to stabilizing the word's meaning, at least in the legal realm. Moreover, in defining this subject, 'Afifi contributed to a distinction between "native" Egyptians (*al-ahali al-asliyyin*) and "non-native" ones. For him, the Egyptian included "the Orthodox, the Jew (*isra'ili*), the Catholic, and the Protestant . . . because the Egyptian is not confined to the native Egyptian but includes others who . . . became linked to [the Egyptians] in the period of the late Muhammad 'Ali Pasha" (though not after 1841).[30] This binary would become increasingly operative in law and beyond in the years ahead.

Likely responding to contestation over how to define the Egyptian local subject, the colonial government issued a new Electoral Law on June 29, 1900. The new law's preamble stated that it was concerned with attribution of "Egyptian nationality" to diverse categories of persons. Although this was the first law to invoke Egyptian nationality, its clauses were confined to voter eligibility, and it in no way replaced Ottoman nationality. Egyptian voters now included Ottoman subjects settled and habitually residing in Egypt since 1848 (chosen because it was the year of the first countrywide census, illustrating the importance of the census to nation-building even in the minds of nation builders themselves),[31] those born in Egypt whose parents settled and resided there, those who performed military service or paid the exemption tax, and orphans with unknown parents. The eligibility of Ottoman subjects who had resided in Egypt for at least fifteen years now depended on their declaring a desire for Egyptian local subjecthood to local officials and having completed military service.[32] This decree law was followed by myriad others, each defining the "Egyptian local subject" according to the exigencies of its issuing office. In short, this category had no singular definition and focused on eligibility, without reference to any kind of national characteristic.[33]

In a final iteration of the Egyptian local subject, Herbert Kitchener, a successor to Lord Cromer as consul general, issued a new Organic Law and Electoral Law in July 1913 in an attempt to enhance the authority of Egypt's legislative bodies to appease Egyptian nationalists and check the power of then khedive 'Abbas Hilmi II. The Organic Law replaced the Legislative Council and General Assembly with the Legislative Assembly, comprising the Council of Ministers (itself part of the executive branch), sixty-six elected members, and seventeen government-nominated members. The Electoral Law determined election procedures and voter eligibility, this time making no mention of Egyptian nationality. Voters were limited to Egyptian local subjects as defined by the 1900 decree law, a tiny minority of whom would actually vote.[34] Meanwhile, the seventeen government-nominated members had to be, according to the Organic Law, from underrepresented social and professional groups, including Bedouins, doctors, engineers, and educational and municipal employees, along with one religious community, the Copts.[35]

The inclusion of Copts, but no other religious group, partially relates to the emergence of Coptic minority politics several years earlier.[36] Often considered by the British and themselves to be the "original Egyptians," the Copts were Egypt's only potential minority that could not be associated with a nation or ethnicity elsewhere. In Europe, this association was the best protection minorities had from majority rule when the League of Nations proved inept at enforcing minority protection treaties, and thus groups that nowhere formed a majority, such as Jews, were vulnerable to being made into refugees and/or stateless people.[37] In Egypt, where the nation-state took form under the shadow of colonial rule, the inverse was true. As we shall see, during and after the First World War, Christians from Ottoman Syria and others became linked to new nation-states carved out of the Ottoman Empire, largely excluding them from Egyptian nationality, whereas the status of Armenians (whose numbers were relatively small) and Jews would remain as nebulous as that of the Armenian and Jewish national projects.[38]

## Protected Nationals, Foreign Ottomans

Britain's announcement of a protectorate over Egypt in November 1914, after the Ottoman entrance into the First World War, formalized Egypt's separation from the Ottoman Empire, raising thorny legal questions around sovereignty, jurisdiction, and nationality, as explored in the previous chapter by Aimee Genell. Egypt's "independence" initiated a terminological shift within legal and political discourse from "Egyptian local subjects" to "Egyptians." Within the jurisdiction of what was now a distinct national territory, the protectorate state considered all inhabitants—men, women, and children—Egyptian nationals unless demonstrated otherwise. Ironically, however, until Egyptian nationality laws could be written and effectuated, the 1869 Ottoman law remained in use.[39] The split between "Egyptians" and "Ottomans" in the political-legal realm would soon become axiomatic more broadly, shaping the boundaries of national community.

In theory, Egypt's national formation meant that "Ottomans" could be classified as foreigners or, given the war's battle lines, enemy foreigners. The question of who was an Ottoman remained open, and the category became available to subjects to claim or disclaim. Legal debates during the war focused on whether the Mixed Courts, historically reserved for disputes between litigants of different nationalities, were now competent in cases between Egyptians and Ottomans. In a February 22, 1916 Mixed Courts case, a judge ruled in the affirmative because "Egypt, being independent now, is no longer part of Turkey, and, in consequence, there is a difference in nationality between an Ottoman subject and a local subject."[40] In 1917, when a man named Georges Farah demanded a sum of money from a certain Wahid al-Fahakni, who self-servingly denied the Mixed Courts were competent in the case because "my adversary, like my humble self, has the honor of being a local subject," a different judge made an opposite ruling. According to reports, Farah responded indignantly that he was a Greek subject and could prove it. Moreover, he claimed that if the evidence he had presented should be deemed insufficient, he had originally been an Ottoman subject, making him a foreigner in Egypt since the announcement of the protectorate. The court rejected his claim and refused to classify him or other "Ottomans" as foreigners.[41] Ultimately, however, such subjects, though remaining under the jurisdiction of the National Courts, would become foreigners by law and could claim or disclaim their new status. Thus, similar to Farah, who declared himself a foreigner, in 1917 a group of Syrian Jews in Egypt petitioned the British to treat them as "friendly aliens," a new category that appeared in wartime Egypt.[42]

With the start of the protectorate, the British Office of the Judicial Advisor in Egypt's Ministry of Justice set out to draft a law establishing the Egyptian subject/national as an internationally recognized legal subject, producing at least four draft decrees during the war. The task was critical not only to confirming Egypt's "independent" status and thus forcing foreign powers to recognize the protectorate, but also to ordering a nationally heterogeneous population along a grid of "friend" and "foe." In fact, the two drafts on which I focus here reflect a gradual shift toward a concern with loyalty, a concept that would be central to the postwar Paris project to expand the nation-state system globally. The first, stamped November 25, 1914, was by British judicial advisor William E. Brunyate, who would have a major hand in postwar Egyptian legal reform. Although the draft was titled "Draft Law Defining Those Who Are Entitled to Egyptian Status" (rather than Egyptian nationality), it acknowledged in its first line the formal end of Ottoman suzerainty. On a copy of it in the British National Archives, the last two words of the title are crossed out in pencil and replaced with "Egyptian Nationality."[43] British legal experts and administrators were hesitant to call this a "nationality law," exposing the paradox of establishing an independent nation-state under a protectorate.

In a similar vein, Brunyate's draft preserved the language of subjecthood used in prewar decrees, invoking the "Egyptian subject" rather than the "Egyptian national." Its definition of this subject mirrored earlier definitions of the Egyptian local subject in its inclusivity. Brunyate's "Egyptian subject" included Ottomans previously recognized as Egyptian local subjects or domiciled in Egypt and maintaining residency. However, for the first time Egyptian status now implied "allegiance to the khedive" (and soon, the British-installed sultan Husayn Kamil). Unlike the Ottoman Nationality Law, Brunyate's proposal also explicitly limited the transmission of nationality to men, contributing to a shift toward the notion that national community, though it could be represented as a woman, was essentially bequeathed by its male subjects.[44] The draft was eventually sent to the Egyptian Council of Ministers, which continued to be authorized to review new legislation under the protectorate. On receiving the proposal, the council rejected it. This group of Egyptian nationalists, lawyers, and landowners reportedly opposed granting Egyptian nationality to "Syrians and other Ottomans" in Egypt, whom they viewed as competitors.[45]

The second draft was released by the Office of the Judicial Advisor on December 29, 1918. After the Sykes-Picot Agreement, the British felt new urgency to define Egyptian nationality so as to mitigate ambiguities over national status after the pending breakup of the Ottoman Empire into new states. Apparently based on suggestions by Arthur Balfour, best known for the 1917 Balfour Declaration, the draft was the first to refer to the "Egyptian" in a national sense, opposite to the "alien."[46] It regarded all Ottoman subjects residing in Egypt on December 5, 1914, the date when the protectorate was declared, as Egyptian. But unlike prior decrees and draft laws, this one stipulated that Ottoman subjects who repudiated Egyptian nationality would be forced to leave Egyptian territory within an unspecified period. This innovation was consistent with the logic of collective plebiscites and individual options emerging out of the concurrent negotiations at Paris, which would reorder the populations of central and eastern Europe along lines of national loyalty. According to then high commissioner Edmund Allenby, who would later be involved in drafting the Egyptian constitution, the new provision was directed at those in Egypt with strong Ottoman sympathies, "whose presence . . . might be politically embarrassing."[47] Among this group were members of the family of 'Abbas Hilmi II, the former khedive whom the British deposed while he was in Istanbul and banned from returning to Egypt.[48]

The British also wished to avoid the presence of permanent "foreign" residents, particularly Syrians and Armenians, on Egyptian soil. As George Lloyd, Allenby's eventual successor as high commissioner, pointed out: "Our object is to set up an independent Syria and Armenia and not independent Syrians or Armenians elsewhere. If Syrians or Armenians in Egypt want to adopt the nationality of their mother country, should they not be required to leave and qualify by residence?"[49] Lloyd's use of the phrase "mother country" when a Syrian nation-state had yet to be formally established and the Armenian nation-state had only just emerged, reflects how indigenous communities speaking a different language and following different customs than the majority were deemed to naturally belong to foreign polities. Along similar lines, Brunyate, the author of the 1914 draft law, would state in 1919: "My impression . . . is that an Armenian will always regard himself as an Armenian, although habitually resident in Egypt, and that if an Armenian state is erected he would desire Armenian subjection. So, too, to a certain extent with the Syrian."[50] By the end of 1918, British administrators no longer saw Armenians and Syrians as part of a patchwork that would congeal into modern Egypt, viewing them instead as outsiders who inherently belonged to nation-states in formation elsewhere. This shift of perception was reflected in the 1917 census, the first to introduce national categories, all of which were deemed "foreign."[51]

Yet the understanding of peoples as sovereign did not necessarily preclude "non-Egyptians" from becoming Egyptian. After all, the 1918 draft presumed Ottomans to be Egyptians in the first instance. This was partly attributable to the persistence of the colonial tactic of sponsorship. Thus, one British official suggested that Christian Syrians who became Egyptians could "exercise a moderating influence, and as they will be able to continue to enter Government Service as at present, they will by their superior intelligence and hard work play a very important role and will . . . secretly favour Great Britain as against the more extreme and antiforeign Egyptian Moslems with whom they can never really coalesce."[52] Similar ideas were held about "semi-European" Jews.[53] But some held more optimistic views of assimilation. Despite his assertions about the national sympathies of Armenians and Syrians in Egypt, Brunyate maintained his earlier position that Ottomans residing in Egypt should be Egyptian, for "in any case, a change will come in the next generation."[54] At issue was not whether homogeneity was desirable but how it should be achieved.

British officials suspected that, as with the 1915 proposal, Egyptian ministers would likely view the 1918 draft, or a slightly revised version of it that was produced in 1919, as "too liberal to Syrians and other Ottoman Christians whose immigration and competition is feared."[55] In frustration, George Lloyd wrote, "We cannot create Egyptian subjects and then refuse to admit bona fide residents of non-Egyptian birth."[56] To allay these fears, Allenby suggested inclusion of a caveat that attribution of Egyptian nationality to Ottomans did not confer political rights absent certain conditions, an idea that reappeared in the eventual Egyptian nationality law.[57] The draft law granted the state the ability to deny some "Egyptians" nationality. Those born in Egypt who were living abroad on the law's date of publication would have a year to return and acquire nationality, but only with the approval of the Egyptian government.[58] The state would have the power to include or exclude based on perceived loyalty to its nation.

The revised draft was put to the Consultative Committee for Legislation made up of British administrators in Egypt, which reviewed the text in April 1920 and made further revisions, including the specification that anyone who renounces the nationality of a new state must leave within six months.[59] Swept aside by postwar treaties and events as well as the specter of Egyptian independence, the draft never became law, but it foreshadowed how international postwar treaties, law, and institutions would shape Egyptian nationality.

## Sovereignty, Imperial Politics, and the Paris System

The British unilaterally declared Egyptian independence in 1922 but retained authority over "foreign interests" and the "protection of minorities," among other domains. As a result, the question of sovereignty was central in Egypt, and "foreigners" and "minorities" were thrust into the heart of it. As the nation-state model gained traction globally after the First World War, so too did the aspiration to gain national sovereignty. National sovereignty, like other so-called universal concepts, carried "intimations of pre-existing histories that were singular and unique, histories that belonged to the multiple pasts of Europe," and was in turn reconfigured by specific conditions of translation and local "pre-existing concepts, categories, institutions, and practices."[60] In the colonial world, the translation of sovereignty held allure for it promised to invert unequal power relations, but, as Shaden Tageldin points out, achieving liberation in the very idiom of empire often reinscribed colonial domination. "Egyptian sovereignty, not British," she contends, "stutters in the balance of translation."[61]

The drafting of Egypt's first constitution provides an instructive case in point in the realm of law. When the Constitutional Committee of 1923 took up this task, it debated how to translate *souverain/souveraineté* from French, an especially pressing question because Egypt's sovereignty was to be affirmed in article 1. In an early draft, the committee used the adjective *sayyida*, defining Egypt as "an independent, free, and sovereign country (*dawla sayyida*)." However, one committee member, drawing on al-Jurjani's fourteenth-century *Kitab al-Ta'rifat* (Book of Definitions), objected to this translation on the basis that the historical meaning of *sayyida*— "one who exercises authority over the great majority" (*alladhi yamlak tadbir al-sawwad al-'azm*)—inadequately captured the collective active will and capacity (*qudra*) associated with the French original. He argued that the word *al-qudra*, as defined in *Kitab al-Ta'rifat*, possessed the capacity of will contained in *souveraineté*, even as he preferred the word *wilaya* (a country, province, or town, or governed territory generally, and eventually another word for "sovereignty"), as in Egypt is a country with paramount sovereignty over itself (*misr dawla liha al-wilaya al-'uzma 'ala nafsiha*).[62] Another committee member, the former grand mufti al-Shaykh Muhammad Bakhit al-Muti'i, agreed, adding that the word *sayyida* had a second meaning of "honorable" (*sharif*) that may sow confusion. Incidentally, *sayyida* is also an honorific title for women (i.e., lady, Mrs.), and the nation's natural companion—sovereignty—likely had to be expressed in masculine terms. Al-Shaykh Bakhit al-Muti'i preferred the phrasing *tamat al-qudra*, as in, Egypt has "complete sovereignty." But a consensus could not be reached. "We spent much time searching for a word that indicates the meaning Souvrainté and we did not find its equivalent. Perhaps the word is unfamiliar [to us Egyptians]," argued al-Shaykh Bakhit al-Muti'i's colleague Mahmud Abu al-Nasr. Favoring the original term, *sayyida*, he contended that "there is adequate time to mitigate its peculiarity to the mind" and that its other meanings (e.g., honorable) would not interfere.[63]

Uneasy about *sayyida*'s multireferential quality, al-Shaykh Bakhit al-Muti'i implored the committee to find a word that "bears no resemblance" to any other word, that would have an unmistakably clear meaning. He proposed *al-siyada*, from the same trilateral root as *sayyida* but with two meanings that could not be confused: *su'dud* (dominion, rule) and *nifadh al-qawl* (correctness of speech). "I request its adoption" he argued, "because we want to write a constitution [whose meaning] every person understands." This word had in fact already come up at a prior point when the committee had considered adopting the phrase *misr balad dhat siyada* (Egypt is a country possessing sovereignty), but it dispensed with this formulation because it seemed to fall short of expressing "complete sovereignty," reflecting how Egypt's political status hovered over the act of translation. Responding to al-Shaykh Bakhit al-Muti'i, another one of his colleagues, 'Abd al-Latif al-Mikbati, proposed a compromise that would account for Abu al-Nasr's preference for *sayyida*, al-Shaykh Bakhit al-Muti'i's desire for clarity, and the perceived gap (*naqs*) in the phrase *misr balad dhat siyada*. He suggested adopting *al-siyada*, as a relative of *sayyida* with clearer meaning, but modifying it with the word *tama* (complete)—*tamat al-siyada* (complete of sovereignty)—for emphasis. Yet, inversely to the phrase *misr balad dhat siyada*, this new wording may have been seen as incongruent with Egypt's actual status, thereby highlighting the gap in sovereignty even more. Although the committee eventually agreed upon 'Abd al-Latif al-Mikbati's suggestion, it was the more circumspect phrasing that ultimately made it into the constitution. Egypt was a country possessing sovereignty, but how much was debatable.[64]

For Egyptian nationalists, addressing the sovereignty gap meant addressing continued British authority in Egypt, including over components of Egypt's population. It was therefore a matter that touched on nationality. But well before Egyptian legislators turned to drafting an Egyptian nationality law, the Paris system had already begun reordering populations along national lines. On August 10, 1920, the Allies and the defeated Ottoman Empire signed the Treaty of Sèvres, which partitioned large parts of the empire into separate states. Although the Turkish nationalist leader Mustafa Kemal later rejected the treaty, forcing the Allies back to the negotiating table, it would have important effects on nationality in Ottoman successor states. In terms of Egypt, the Ottoman Empire had formally recognized the protectorate and renounced all rights over Egyptian territory effective November 5, 1914. It also abandoned claims to Ottoman subjects habitually residing in Egypt on December 18, 1914, while those who came to habitually reside in Egypt after that date and remained there until the signing of the treaty could opt for Egyptian nationality, with the caveat that Egypt could lawfully reject their option presumably based on questions of loyalty. European legal experts viewed the right of option as a complement to the plebiscite that granted individual subjects the ability to choose between nationalities. But in doing so, it adhered to the Paris ideal of homogeneity by discouraging the constitution of minority populations. Thus, the Treaty of Sèvres stated that only former

Ottoman subjects not belonging to the "majority race" where they lived could opt for another Ottoman successor state, but on the condition that they were part of that state's "majority race."[65] As we will see, this clause would soon be adapted by Egyptian legislators.

The Treaty of Lausanne replaced the Treaty of Sèvres in 1923, establishing the Republic of Turkey, but it dealt with the nationality question in similar ways as its predecessor. The treaty did not apply to Egypt, which was already independent, but as one legal observer noted, Egypt could not ignore it.[66] The right of option forced Ottoman successor states to settle the status of some subjects on their territories cooperatively. Already by the start of the First World War, Egypt had come to terms with France and Greece over the national status of subjects from French Tunisia and Greece. Between 1923 and 1927, Egypt reached a settlement with Italy over subjects from Cyrenaica and Tripolitania and with France over subjects from Morocco and Mandate Syria and Lebanon (though Syrians and Lebanese established in Egypt prior to the treaty's signing were left out). It also negotiated with the British over "Iraqis," "Palestinians," and "Transjordanians." Each settlement was different, but in all cases foreign consulates in Egypt were expected to compile lists of subjects they claimed, which the Egyptian government and subjects themselves could approve or challenge, usually based on aspects of the individual's past.[67] Egypt campaigned, often successfully, to prevent subjects appearing on these lists from enjoying Capitulatory privileges.

The status of now former Ottomans not covered in these arrangements could not be determined until Egypt pronounced a nationality law. In the meantime, subjects began to adapt new national categories operative in international legal treaties. On February 22, 1924, the satirical weekly *al-Kashkul* (Scrapbook) ran two articles describing separately the nationality status of "Syrians" and "Lebanese" in Egypt. In the first article, the author divided Syrians in Egypt into four categories: merchants and capitalists who want to be French for Capitulatory privileges; bank and shop employees who generally want to be Egyptian, except for some who seek "status as well as moral and material benefits" linked to French nationality; government employees, who generally wish to be Egyptian, except for a minority who desire French nationality if afforded the "rights of foreigners"; and youth, who "refuse everything but to be Egyptian."[68] The second article, written by a self-identified "Egyptianized Lebanese" (*lubnani mutamassari*) named Farid Hubayshi, suggested that most like him—"Lebanese" born or having long lived in Egypt—desire Egyptian nationality "if the Egyptian nation makes up its mind to absorb the Egyptianized [Lebanese] *mutamassarin* and to treat them as brothers."[69]

As the new international order began to congeal, and in an effort to fit into it, Egyptian legislators turned to the task of drafting a nationality law. In the words of one parliamentarian, defining the Egyptian in law would "show to other countries that we are an independent country and have our own sovereignty [*siyada*]."[70] Equally important, it provided an initial basis for Egypt to fashion a more governable population by excluding subjects who remained exempt from its law by virtue of extraterritorial privileges. When the constitution was passed in

1923, it stated only that "the law defines Egyptian nationality."[71] On July 31, 1925, the Egyptian government formed a committee under the leadership of Minister of Justice Saʻid Dhu al-Fiqar to draft a law. This committee was composed largely of French-educated jurists and legislators who generally shared an inclusive view of citizenship articulated by the likes of the liberal Egyptian intellectual Ahmad Lutfi al-Sayyid. It also included a British "advisor" who communicated British interests.[72] In fact, a copy of a draft of the law in the British National Archives is replete with cross outs and revisions for the committee's attention, though in many cases this "advice" was unheeded.[73] The new law was pronounced by royal decree on May 26, 1926.[74]

Based largely on the 1920 British draft, the 1926 law was the first legislation to define the Egyptian national. However, as the jurist Paul Ghali pointed out, the law's priority, reflected in the order of its articles, was to determine the status of Ottomans whose loyalties were thought to lie outside Egypt.[75] In this sense it was a product of Paris thinking. Different from prior British draft laws, which were intended to create Egyptian nationals out of a population presumed to be Ottoman, this law assumed a priori the existence of "original Egyptians," while introducing a new category of people—"Ottoman nationals"—whom it subjected to special legislation.

The law's first article defined "Ottoman nationals" as all (non-Egyptian) nationals of the former Ottoman Empire before the Treaty of Lausanne came into effect, meaning that only Tunisians, Libyans, and others subject to bilateral nationality agreements concluded prior to July 24, 1923, were excluded. Among the rest, those habitually residing in Egypt on November 5, 1914, who maintained their residency until the date of the decree law were deemed Egyptian, while those who did not could apply to the Interior Ministry within a year. Those who came to habitually reside in Egypt after November 5, 1914 and preserved their residency until the date of the decree law were also Egyptian. Meanwhile, any Ottoman born, or whose father was born, in territory that had been incorporated into an Ottoman successor state could opt for that state's nationality within one year, after which he or she would be required to leave Egypt within six months. If that person failed to leave Egypt or returned within five years, the option would be canceled, and he or she would automatically become Egyptian. Ottoman nationals filling none of these conditions had a year to make Egypt their place of habitual residence and could then apply for Egyptian nationality after five years. In general, the law presumed everyone on Egyptian territory to be Egyptian until his or her nationality was established. Yet absent the latter, political rights were disallowed, leaving many as neither full citizens nor foreigners with access to the Mixed Courts.[76]

Similar to the 1920 British draft, the 1926 law's definition of the Egyptian favored jus sanguinis through the father's line. The Egyptian included anyone born in Egypt or abroad to an Egyptian father, unknown parents, or a foreign father also born in Egypt. Importantly, however, this law specified that the foreign father had to belong "in his ethnicity" (bi-jinsihi) to a country with an Arabic-speaking or Muslim majority.[77] In fact, echoing the rationality of the Treaty of

Sèvres and other Paris treaties, the 1926 law's main innovation was the insertion of Arabic and Islam as terms of inclusion. For example, it stipulated that those wanting to be naturalized needed not only ten years of residency in Egypt, good behavior, and the ability to earn a living, but also knowledge of Arabic.[78]

The 1926 law was only partially enacted. After Sa'd Zaghlul's Wafd Party dominated the 1924 parliamentary elections and British governor general of the Sudan Lee Stack was assassinated, King Fu'ad disbanded parliament. Having no opportunity to review the law, it deemed it unconstitutional.[79] In consequence, the Interior Ministry, which then handled issues of nationality, never systematized naturalization. Still, the law was referred to in the courts and used as a basis for resolving interstate disputes over nationality. It also elicited strong reaction among former Ottomans. In the pages of *Le Reveil*, a Lebanese lawyer in Egypt named Bishara Tabbah, who had recently opted for French protection, expressed dismay at being forced to leave Egypt. He made a powerful plea for Egypt to allow optants of other countries to remain in its territory.[80] Others sought Egyptian nationality. Likely unaware that applications were not being processed, Egypt's chief rabbi Haim Nahum tried to convince his Sephardic Jewish community to submit applications to the Interior Ministry, part of an effort to emphasize his and his community's loyalty to the Egyptian nation. Unlike many of his coreligionists, the chief rabbi naturalized immediately after the 1926 law was replaced by its successor law.[81]

## The Egyptian National

This successor law appeared in 1929 as the brainchild of 'Abd al-Hamid Badawi, a graduate of the Khedival Law School who later studied in France and had a long career in Egyptian and international law.[82] Though generally similar to the previous law, this one introduced several changes to address parliament's concerns. Most notably, it prioritized the definition of the "Egyptian," which the committee felt should constitute the first clause (in place of the status of "Ottomans"). The "Egyptian" included first and foremost members of the royal family, a new insertion likely intended to ensure that certain relatives of King Fu'ad would qualify for Egyptian nationality. It also included Egyptian local subjects according to article 1 of the 1900 decree law (though not the more lenient article 2), meaning residents of Egypt since January 1, 1848, their offspring, and those with military recruitment certificates. Legislators chose the 1900 decree as a basis for Egyptian nationality rather than prior Ottoman law out of national pride. Despite the decree's colonial origins, they saw it as a national past for Egyptian nationality.[83] Members of the committee who supported an exclusive definition of Egyptian nationality even saw those meeting the first article's criteria as "true Egyptians" (*al-misriyin al-samimin*).[84]

Parliament was split over how to deal with "Ottomans" and "foreigners." The committee had a relatively inclusive view of Egyptian nationality based generally on the French model. It favored including those for whom assimilation (*indimaj*) was possible, and thus sought to preserve the 1926 law's clause rendering naturalization of former Ottomans available only to those from a country with an Arabic-speaking or Muslim majority. As the parliamentarian ʿAbd al-Salam Fahmy Muhammad put it, "there is no debate that we complain about the large number of groups (*tawaʾif*) that are minorities (*aqliyyat*), but there are groups that are not minorities, so why don't we permit the integration of those into the Egyptian nation so it is not said in the future that they are minorities that require protection."[85] (Note how the minority is outsider.) Opposing the committee's recommendation was another group of parliamentarians led by, among others, future prime minister Ismaʿil Sidqi. In this group's view, such an approach would "open the flood gates to naturalization" in a country with an already large and growing population. Moreover, it would render it too easy for those who "live a sectarian life" to naturalize, and their inability to integrate would cause them to become "another Balkans." Decrying Egypt's openness in prior centuries, one parliamentarian argued: "Enough of what was inflicted upon us due to the generosity that we are known for and that makes us proud—that generosity which was the reason for granting the Capitulations that we are still unable to get rid of."[86]

Ultimately, the 1929 law accepted the principle of assimilation, maintaining its predecessor's preference for jus sanguinis and its construction of a "majority ethnicity." The law considered as Egyptian former Ottoman nationals who had habitually resided in Egypt since November 5, 1914, and maintained residency until the publication of the 1929 law. Perhaps due to outside pressure, it dropped the requirement that optants for Ottoman successor states must depart Egypt, though the Interior Ministry maintained the ability to lawfully expel them and, in any case, opting periods for most subjects had already expired. For former Ottomans wishing to become Egyptian, conditions became more difficult. Those who fixed their habitual residence in Egypt after November 5, 1914, or who had done so prior to that date but did not maintain it, were no longer automatically Egyptian; they had to request nationality within one year from the Interior Ministry.[87] Despite such restrictions, some considered the law too lenient. In *al-Siyasa,* one writer with the penname "true Egyptian" (*misri samim*)—which echoed the language of the committee that drafted the 1926 nationality law—complained that the new law rendered Egyptian nationality wide open. In his view, its effect would be to create new minorities out of subjects of the old Ottoman Empire who, unlike the "true minority" (*aqliyya samima*) (i.e., Egyptian) of the Copts, have no loyalty to Egypt—and this at a time when minorities in general came to be viewed as a complicated international problem.[88] In this writer's view, Copts were unquestionably Egyptian, but other minorities should depart for their majority states; their loyalty was questionable, and their ability to claim "minority rights" would sow division. The "true Egyptian" associated difference with suspicion.

By the time the 1936 Anglo-Egyptian Treaty afforded greater sovereignty to Egypt (the last British soldiers left Egypt only in 1956), inspiring attempts to gradually "Egyptianize" (*tamsir*) Egypt's public and private sectors, the "true Egyptian" had become synonymous with the "Egyptian," ironically excluding already "Egyptianized" (*mutamassir*) subjects. Thus, when the Suez Canal

Company and the Egyptian government agreed in 1937 to gradually Egyptianize the company's staff, it was "true Egyptians" (as understood by some of the committee members who wrote the 1929 nationality law) who were the intended beneficiaries.[89] When it was discovered that a certain employee of the Suez Canal Company was born in Egypt to a father born in Lebanon, he was forced out of his position and was unable to regain it through legal avenues. Though his father had worked for the Egyptian government since 1915, been confirmed as a local subject by the Egyptian government after demonstrating more than fifteen years of residence in Egypt, been excused from army service due to his employment with the state, been issued an Egyptian passport to travel to France for law school, been eligible to vote and made head of the election council in the *mudiriyya* of Aswan, and even been appointed by the Ministry of Justice to the Mixed Courts in an attempt to increase Egyptian representation in its halls, he was Egyptian only by residence.[90] The 1929 legal construction of the Egyptian national had come to shape definitions of the Egyptian in other domains.

## Conclusion

Unlike its predecessor from 1926, the 1929 law was actually put into effect, and it remained in place until 1950 when it was replaced with a more restrictive law. Nevertheless, the Interior Ministry, under whose authority matters of nationality now fell, processed few naturalizations during the 1930s and 1940s.[91] As late as 1951, the United Nations could report that "a considerable number of former Ottoman subjects, through neglect, ignorance or for other reasons, lost their opportunity of becoming Egyptian nationals through option, and many of them are to-day still legally stateless and can become Egyptian only through the more difficult, time-consuming and costly process of naturalization." Those able and willing to undergo this process encountered an Egyptian state that was at best apathetic about facilitating it.[92]

With the rise of radical politics in Egypt during the 1930s, the Egyptian state was arguably more concerned with denaturalizing nationals. It had stipulated conditions of denaturalization in article 13 of the 1929 law, which stated that any Egyptian who serves in a foreign army or works for a foreign government without the prior permission of the Egyptian state can be stripped of nationality.[93] A 1931 addendum to this article widened its scope. It stated that Egyptian nationality can also be stripped from any Egyptian abroad who partakes in "revolutionary activity" against the Egyptian social, political, or economic order.[94] The addendum was a substantial marker of political loyalty's increasing centrality to conceptions of belonging in Egypt. It was no great conceptual leap, therefore, when in November 1956, on the heels of the Suez Crisis and for the "protection of the national community," Egypt's government led by President Jamal 'Abd al-Nasir announced a new nationality law introducing "Zionism," "[dis]loyalty," and "treason" (*khiyana*) as undefined disqualifying conditions for Egyptian nationality, and establishing "state security" as a rationale for stripping it.[95] Clearly, the legal construction of the "Egyptian national" beginning under the protectorate, and heavily shaped by the Paris system, was integral to the conceptual architecture that framed the politics of exclusion from the late 1940s through the 1960s.

## Notes

1. Evelyn Baring, *Modern Egypt* (New York: Macmillan, 1908), 2:126.
2. David Scott, "Colonial Governmentality," in *Anthropologies of Modernity: Foucault, Governmentality, and Life Politics*, ed. Jonathan Xavier Inda (Malden, MA: Blackwell, 2005), 25. Emphasis in the original. For Foucault's original theorization, see Michel Foucault, "Governmentality," in *The Foucault Effect: Studies in Governmentality with Two Lections by and an Interview with Michel Foucault*, ed. Graham Burchell, Colin Gordon, and Peter Miller (Chicago: University of Chicago Press, 1991), 87–104.
3. *Al-Muhama'*, March 16, 1935, issue 1, 12.
4. For prior studies of Egyptian nationality, see Shimon Shamir, "The Evolution of the Egyptian Nationality Laws and Their Application to the Jews in the Monarchy Period," in *The Jews of Egypt: A Mediterranean Society in Modern Times*, ed. Shimon Shamir (Boulder, CO: Westview Press, 1987), 33–67; Mahmud Muhammad Sulayman, *al-Ajanib fi Misr: Dirasa fi Ta'rikh Misr al-Ijtima'i* (Alexandria: al-Hay'a al-'Amma li-Maktabat al-Iskandariya, 1996); Frédéric Abécassis and Anne Le Gall-Kazazian, "L'identité au miroir du droit, le statut des personnes en Egypte (fin XIXe–début XXE siècle), *Egypte–Monde Arabe* (CEDEJC) (1992): 11–38; and Will Hanley, *Identifying with Nationality: Europeans, Ottomans, and Egyptians in Alexandria* (New York: Columbia University Press, 2017). For studies on nationality in other Ottoman and post-Ottoman contexts, see Zainab Saleh, "On Iraqi Nationality: Law, Citizenship, and Exclusion," *Arab Studies Journal* 21 (2013): 48–78; and Lale Can, "The Protection Question: Central Asians and Extraterritoriality in the Late Ottoman Empire," *International Journal of Middle East Studies* 48 (2016): 679–99.
5. Eric D. Weitz, "From the Vienna to the Paris System: International Politics and the Entangled Histories of Human Rights, Forced Deportations, and Civilizing Missions," *American Historical Review* 113 (2008): 1313–43.
6. On sectarianism, see, among others, Ussama Makdisi, *The Culture of Sectarianism: Community, History, and Violence in Nineteenth-Century Ottoman Lebanon* (Berkeley: University of California Press, 2000); and Max Weiss, *In the Shadow of Sectarianism: Law, Shi'ism, and the Making of Modern Lebanon* (Cambridge, MA: Harvard University Press, 2010). On secularism, see Saba Mahmood, *Religious Difference in a Secular Age: A Minority Report* (Princeton: Princeton University Press, 2015).
7. On religion and internationalism broadly, see Nathaniel Berman, "'The Sacred Conspiracy': Religion, Nationalism, and the Crisis of Internationalism," *Leiden Journal of International Law* 25 (2012): 9–54.
8. On international law's colonial origins, see Antony Anghie, *Imperialism, Sovereignty and the Making of International Law* (Cambridge: Cambridge University Press, 2005).
9. Rogers Brubaker, *Citizenship and Nationhood in France and Germany* (Cambridge, MA: Harvard University Press, 1992), 75. However, Patrick Weil has shown that Brubaker's contrast between an open French model of citizenship based on jus soli and an exclusive German model based on jus sanguinis is misleading. French nationality law actually favored jus sanguinis from 1804 to 1889, when it shifted to jus soli to naturalize large numbers of immigrants. Prussian and then German legislation followed the French

example (Patrick Weil, *How to Be French: Nationality in the Making since 1789* [Durham, NC: Duke University Press, 2008]).

10. On the looping effect, see Ian Hacking, "The Looping Effects of Human Kinds," in *Causal Cognition: A Multidisciplinary Debate*, ed. Dan Sperberet, David Premack, and Ann James Premack (Oxford: Oxford University Press, 1996), 351–61.

11. Whereas Arabic dictionaries from the early 1860s do not seem to include the word *tab'iyya* (e.g., E. W. Lane's *An Arabic and English Lexicon* [London: Williams & Norgate, 1863]), later dictionaries define it as "nationality" (e.g., J. G. Hava, *Arabic-English Dictionary for the Use of Students* [Beirut: Catholic Press, 1899], 54). I accessed these dictionaries via ejtaal.net. On this terminology, see also Will Hanley, "When Did Egyptians Stop Being Ottomans?: An Imperial Citizenship Case Study," in *Multilevel Citizenship*, ed. Willem Maas (Philadelphia: University of Pennsylvania Press, 2013), 93; and Hanley, *Identifying with Nationality*, 57–58.

12. Selim Derengil, *Conversion and Apostasy in the Late Ottoman Empire* (Cambridge: Cambridge University Press, 2012), 195. See also Karen Kern, *Imperial Citizen: Marriage and Citizenship in the Ottoman Frontier Provinces of Iraq* (Syracuse: Syracuse University Press, 2011), 89–90.

13. Dar al-Watha'iq al-Qawmiyya (Egyptian National Archives) (DW), *Majlis al-Wuzara'* (Council of Ministers) 0075-018651, "Loi Sur La Nationalité Ottomane," Le Caire Imprimerie Nationale, 1887.

14. I draw on Samia Mehrez's discussion of the word in *Egypt's Culture Wars: Politics and Practice* (Cairo: American University in Cairo Press, 2008), 109.

15. See, for example, Jamal al-Din al-Afghani's usage in an 1879 speech in Alexandria in which he refers to the *jinsiyya* of "Eastern peoples" as a shared civilizational origin. (The speech was transcribed in *Misr* as "Hakim al-Sharq," 24 May 1879). See also Nikki Keddie, *Sayyid Jamāl ad-Dīn "al-Afghāni": A Political Biography* (Berkeley: University of California Press, 1972), 108–9.

16. Indicatively, J. G. Hava's 1899 *Arabic-English Dictionary*, also accessed via ejtaal. net, defines it as "common race, origin." See p. 96. During this period, Egyptians began to engage with discourses on ethnicity and race from Europe in complex ways (see Eve M. Troutt Powell, *A Different Shade of Colonialism: Egypt, Great Britain, and the Mastery of the Sudan* [Berkeley: University of California Press, 2003], 86–89).

17. Frédéric Abécassis and Anne Le Gall-Kazazian suggest that it was Khedive Isma'il who, in forming a new Council of Ministers under Sharif Pasha, established an initial demarcation between "natives" and other subjects of the Ottoman Empire by using the phrase "Egyptian elements" in an official document for the first time. However, it should be noted this was not a legal category (see Abécassis and Le Gall-Kazazian, "L'identité au miroir du droit," 5).

18. On colonialism and law in Egypt, see Samera Esmeir, *Juridical Humanity: A Colonial History* (Stanford: Stanford University Press, 2012).

19. Jacob Landau, *Parliaments and Parties in Egypt* (Tel Aviv: Israel Publishing House, 1953), 41–42; 'Abd al-Rahman al-Raf 'i, *Misr wa-l-Sudan fi Awa'il 'Ahd al-Ihtilal, al-Tab'a al-Rab'a* (Cairo: Dar al-Ma'arif, 1983), 53–55.

20. Quoted by Evelyn Baring in *Modern Egypt*, 2:274.

21. See *al-Waqa'i' al-Misriyya*, May 1, 1883. The laws are reproduced in Mahmud Hasan al-Fariq, *al-Qanun al-Dusturi al-Misri wa-Tatawwur Nizam al-Dawla al-Misriyya Ibtida' min al-Fath al-'Uthmani ila al-Waqt al-Hadir* (al-Matba'a al-Tijariyya al-Kubra, n.d., c. 1924), 150–82. The equivalent French and Arabic terms for "Egyptian local subjects" are *égyptiens, sujets locaux* and *al-misriyin min ra'ayat al-hukuma al-mahaliyya*, respectively.

22. On the inclusivity of the colonial project in Egypt, see Esmeir, *Juridical Humanity*.

23. The phrase "internationalist nationality" was attributed to him by Ahmad Lutfi al-Sayyid in *al-Jarida*, 13 April 1907, quoted in Charles Wendell, *The Evolution of the Egyptian National Image: From Its Origins to Ahmad Lutfi al-Sayyid* (Berkeley: University of California Press, 1972), 301.

24. Iskandar Assabghy Bey, *La nationalité Égyptienne: Etude historique et critique* (Paris: Société Orientale de Publicité, 1950), 4. They can also be found in *al-Waqa'i' al-Misriyya*.

25. Although "local" (*mahalli*), as Will Hanley points out, was a spatial administrative term and not in use as an identity category in late nineteenth- and early twentieth-century Egypt, I use it to refer to residents of Egypt who were not "foreign" (by which I mean possessing a nationality other than Ottoman or, in some cases, extraterritorial privileges) in the period prior to World War I both for convenience and because it is more indicative of Egypt's political status at the time than the anachronistic term "Egyptian" (Hanley, *Identifying with Nationality*, 262-63). In terms of "Syrians," this largely Christian population of Greek Catholics, Greek Orthodox, and Maronites originating from Ottoman Syria was often referred to as a composite whole in Egypt, whether with the descriptor "Syrians" or, in the case of the nationalist Mustafa Kamil, with pejorative terms such as *dukhala'* (intruders). Neither of these descriptors should be understood in a territorial nationalist sense. These groups remained largely within their respective communal frames, and the unity they may have come to feel was an outcome of their interactions with others in Egypt. For simplicity, I refer to them as "Syrians"; Thomas Philipp, *The Syrians in Egypt, 1725–1975* (London: Steiner, 1985), 149–52.

26. For details of the case, I draw on the court ruling, which was in 'Afifi's voice. The ruling appeared in *Al-Ahram*, June 16, 1898. For another take on the case, see Hanley, *Identifying with Nationality*, 256-57. I thank Will Hanley for directing me to this source. Reference to the case is also made in Pierre Arminjon, *Étrangers et protégés dans l'Empire ottoman* (Paris: A. Chevalier-Marescq, 1926), 181–82.

27. *Al-Ahram*, June 16, 1898.

28. On Egyptian royalist historians, See Yoav Di Capua, *Gatekeepers of the Arab Past: Historians and History Writing in Twentieth-Century Egypt* (Berkeley: University of California Press, 2009).

29. Will Hanley notes that use of the word *misri* remained limited in the realm of identification and protection during the late nineteenth century (Hanley, *Identifying with Nationality*, 263).

30. *Al-Ahram*, June 16, 1898.

31. *Al-Muhama'*, issue 1, 1935–36, 15. On this census and later censuses in Egypt, see Kenneth M. Cuno and Michael J. Reimer, "The Census Registers of Nineteenth-Century Egypt: A New Source for Social Historians," *British Journal of Middle Eastern Studies* 24 (1997): 193–216. On the census and the nation-state, see Benedict Anderson, *Imagined Communities*, 2nd ed. (London: Verso, 2006), ch. 10.

32. For the 1900 law, see *al-Waqa'i' al-Misriyya*, July 4, 1900.

33. These included a civil employment law in 1901, a conscription law in 1902, and a penal code in 1904.

34. The law also used the term *misriyin* (Egyptians), but one jurist of the 1920s explains that its authors understood this term as commensurate with "Egyptian local subjects." For the laws, see J.-A. Wathelet and R.-G. Brunton, *Codes égyptiens et lois usuelles en vigeur en Égypte* (Brussels: Veueve F. Larcier, 1919–20), 371–89, and *al-Waqa'i' al-Misriyya*, June 1, 1913. On terminology, see 'Ali al-Zayni, *al-Qanun al-Dawli al-Khass al-Misri wa-l-Muqarin, al-Juz' al-Awwal* (Cairo: al-Matba'a al-Rahmaniyya bi-Misr, 1930), 232. On the voter

count, see The National Archives of the UK (TNA) Foreign Office (FO) 78/3555, "Etat Général des Electeurs dans la Basse et la Haute Egypte," n.d.

35. Landau, *Parliaments and Parties*, 55–57. The inclusion of Bedouin is notable but beyond the scope of this chapter.

36. Seteney Shami and Saba Mahmood have argued that the Arabic word for "minority," *aqliyya*, was not used in the Egyptian press until the early 1920s, in the context of debates over whether the 1923 constitution should guarantee minority rights (which it did not). However, in the lead up to the 1911 Coptic Congress in Assuit, Coptic lay leaders deployed the term *aqliyya* in their appeal for proportional representation in parliament, before deciding to abandon it; *Tidhkar al-Mu'tamir al-Qibti al-Awwal: Majmu'at Risa'il Musawwira* (Cairo: Matba'at al-Akhbar bi-Misr, 1911); Seteney Shami, "*Aqalliyya*/Minority in Modern Egypt Discourse," in *Words in Motion: Towards a Global Lexicon*, ed. Carol Gluck and Anna Lowenhaupt Tsing (Durham, NC: Duke University Press, 2009), 153; Mahmood, *Religious Difference*, 69–70, 70n11. For further discussion of the Coptic Congress and early debates over minority rights among other secular concepts in Egypt, see Jeffrey Culang, "Liberal Translations: Secular Concepts, Law, and Religion in Colonial Egypt," (PhD diss., Graduate Center, City University of New York, 2017). See also C. A. Bayly, "Representing Copts and Muhammadans: Empire, Nation, and Community in Egypt and India, 1880–1914," in *Modernity & Culture: From the Mediterranean to the Indian Ocean*, ed. Leila Tarazi Fawaz and C. A. Bayly (New York: Columbia University Press, 2002), 158–203; and Tariq al-Bishri, *al-Muslimun wa-l-Aqbat fi Atar al-Jama'a al-Wataniyya* (Cairo: Dar al-Shuruq, 1982).

37. Hannah Arendt, *The Origins of Totalitarianism* (Orlando, FL: Harcourt Brace, 1979), 289.

38. According to the 1917 census, there were 12,854 Armenians and 59,581 Jews in Egypt at the time (Ministry of Finance, *The Census of Egypt Taken in 1917* [Cairo: Government Press, 1920–21]).

39. This point is reflected in a range of Mixed Courts cases ('Abd al-Hamid Abu al-Hayf Bek, *al-Qanun al-Dawli al-Khass fi Uruba wa fi Misr, al-Majmu' al-Awwal* [Cairo: Matba'a al-Sa'ada, 1927], 110–11). For details of the cases, see al-Zayni, *al-Qanun al-Dawli al-Khass al-Misri*, 226.

40. *Gazette de Tribunaux Mixtes d'Egypte*, November 10, 1916, 3.

41. "Chronique Judiciare: de la Situation Juridique des Sujets Ottomans," *La Bourse Égyptienne*, May 30, 1917. A number of similar cases occurred between 1914 and 1926, when Egypt pronounced its first nationality law, with most concluding there was no legal distinction between local subjects and Ottomans.

42. TNA FO 141/530/2, "Foreign Office to High Commissioner for Egypt," August 30, 1917. The British never declared Ottomans to be enemies under martial law, as they had Austro-Hungarians and Germans, for whom special courts were set up. They instead saw them as "harmless subjects of a technically enemy state."

43. TNA FO 141/552/3, "Projet du Loi définissant les personnes qui ont droit aux status d'Égyptien," c. November 25, 1914.

44. Ibid; Beth Baron, *Egypt as a Woman: Nationalism, Gender, and Politics* (Berkeley: University of California Press, 2007).

45. TNA FO 141/552/3, "Viscount Grey of Fallodon K.G. to the Residency," August 21, 1916.

46. TNA FO 608/212/12, "Draft Nationality Law: 3rd Draft," December 29, 1918.

47. TNA FO 608/212/12, "Decypher of Telegram from Field-Marshal Allenby, Bacoaramreh, Addressed to Astoria and Repeated to Foreign Office, No. 1239," August 15, 1919.

48. 'Abbas Hilmi II lived the rest of his life abroad, dying in Switzerland. However, the Egyptian government never allowed him to naturalize elsewhere (DW, 'Abdin Files [0069-025328], "Nationality of the Ex-Khedive").

49. TNA FO 608/246/5, "Copy of Minutes from Paper No. 1555/W/16: Nationality of Ottoman Subjects Resident in Egypt," January 4, 1919.

50. TNA FO 141/552/II, "Brunyate to Hurst," June 15, 1919.

51. See *Census of Egypt Taken in 1917.*

52. TNA FO 141/552/2, "Greg to Furness," February 24, 1921.

53. The idea was to grant them British nationality but have them form a colony in Egypt through which the British could continue to exert influence (TNA FO 141/552/2, "Note to High Commissioner," January 23, 1921).

54. TNA FO 141/552/2, "Brunyate to Hurst," June 15, 1919.

55. TNA FO 608/212/12, "Decypher of Telegram from Field-Marshal Allenby, Bacoaramreh, Addressed to Astoria and Repeated to Foreign Office, No. 1239," August 15, 1919.

56. TNA FO 608/246/5, "Copy of Minutes from Paper No. 1555/W/16: Nationality of Ottoman Subjects Resident in Egypt," January 4, 1919.

57. TNA FO 608/212/12, "Decypher of Telegram from Field-Marshal Allenby, Bacoaramreh, Addressed to Astoria and Repeated to Foreign Office, No. 1239," August 15, 1919.

58. TNA FO 141/552, "Draft Nationality Law," August 12, 1919.

59. TNA FO 141/552, "Projet de Loi sur la nationalité," April or May 1920.

60. Dipesh Chakbraberty, *Provincializing Europe: Postcolonial Thought and Historical Difference,* reissue, with a new preface by the author (Princeton: Princeton University Press, 2008 [2000]), xxii–xxiii.

61. Shaden M. Tageldin, *Empire and the Seductions of Translation in Egypt* (Berkeley: University of California Press, 2011), 196–97.

62. *Lajnat al-Dustur: Majmu'a Muhadir al-Lajna al-'Amma* (Cairo: al-Matba'a al-Amiriyya, 1924), 124.

63. Ibid. Indicatively, nineteenth-century Arabic-English dictionaries defined *siyada* not as "sovereignty" but as "chiefdom," "lordship," "mastery," etc. See, e.g., Lane, *Arabic-English Lexicon,* 1461.

64. *Lajnat al-Dustur,* 124. The phrase is also used in Egypt's latest constitution pronounced in 2014.

65. "The Treaty of Sèvres," World War I Document Archive, last accessed February 28, 2018, https://wwi.lib.byu.edu/index.php/Section_I,_Articles_1_-_260.

66. Paul Ghali, *Les nationalités détachées de l'Empire ottoman à la suite de la guerre* (Paris: Les Éditions Domat-Montchrestien, 1934), 125–27.

67. See Assabghy, *La nationalité Égyptienne,* 9–24.

68. "Al-Curiyú la-l-Jinsiyya," *al-Kashkul,* February 22, 1924, 2.

69. "Al-Lubnaniyun fi Misr wa-l-Jinsiyya," *al-Kashkul,* February 22, 1924, 15.

70. *Majmu'at Mudabit al-In'iqad al-'Adi al-Thalith,* vol. 2 (Cairo: al-Matba'a al-Amiriyya, 1928), 1154.

71. Yusuf Qazmakhuri, *Al-Dasatir fi al-'Alim al-'Arabi: Nusus wa-Ta'dilat, 1839–1987* (Beirut: Dar al-Hamra', 1989), 539.

72. See, for example, TNA FO 141/552/368/104, "Judicial Advisor to Hartopp," May 25, 1926.

73. TNA FO 141/552, "Decret-Loi sur la la nationalité égyptienne," May 5, 1926.

74. *Al-Waqa'i' al-Misriyya,* May 26, 1926.

75. Ghali, *Les nationalités détachées,* 126–27.

76. *Al-Waqa'i' al-Misriyya,* May 26, 1926.

77. The term *jins* used in the Arabic version of the law can mean "race," but here more likely refers to an ethnic/national affiliation. In English versions of the law, and in some of the English-language literature on Egyptian nationality, the word is translated as "race."

78. Ibid.

79. See a discussion of the law in Ghali, *Les nationalités détachées*, 127–34.

80. *Le Revéil*, May 28, 1926. The critique was reproduced in Maurice De Wée, *La nationalité Égyptienne: Commentaire de la Loi du 26 Mai 1926* (Alexandria: Whitehead Morris Limited, 1926), 26–28.

81. TNA FO 371/13149, "Memorandum," June 7, 1928. See also Gudrun Krämer, *The Jews in Modern Egypt, 1914–1952* (London: I. B. Tauris, 1989), 170. The rabbi gained Egyptian nationality in 1929 via article 11 of the 1929 Nationality Law, according to which foreign heads of Egyptian religious groups were automatically eligible for Egyptian nationality. His naturalization was announced in *al-Waqa'i' al-Misriyya*, December 2, 1929.

82. *Gazette de Tribunaux Mixtes d'Égypte*, March 1929, 113.

83. Some members understood it had not been a nationality law (*Majlis al-Nuwwab: Majmu'a Mudabitat al-In'iqad al-'Adi al-Thalith* [Cairo: al-Matba'a al-Amiriyya, 1924], 1138; see also p. 1156).

84. Muhammad 'Abd al-Mun'im Riyad, *Mabadi' al-Qanun al-Dawli al-Khass* (Cairo: Matba'a Misr al-Hurra, 1933), 110. See also Shamir, "Evolution," 46–48.

85. *Majlis al-Nuwwab: Majmu'a Mudabitat al-In'iqad al-'Adi al-Thalith*, 1156.

86. Ibid., 1155.

87. *Al-Waqa'i' al-Misriyya*, February 27, 1929.

88. "Qanun al-Jinsiyya: Ra'i Fard 'Anuh," *al-Siyasa*, April 22, 1929.

89. The agreement was confirmed by parliament and became law (*Majmu'at al-Mabadi' al-Qanuniyya Allati Qarraratha Mahkamat al-Qada' al-Idari fi Khamsat 'Ashar 'Amman, 1946-1961* [Cairo: al-Maktab al-Fanni, 1961], November 10, 1956, 46).

90. Ibid., 44, 46.

91. The August 24, 1929, issue of *al-Ahram* reports that the Interior Ministry still had not explained to the public how to address questions of nationality they invariably faced. By 1930, the names of those who managed to naturalize were being published in *al-Waqa'i'a al-Misriyya* each month, though their numbers gradually decreased.

92. Jacques Vernant, *The Refugee in the Post-war World: Preliminary Report of a Survey of the Refugee Problem* (Geneva: United Nations, 1951), 123–25. See also Muhammad Rif'at al-Imam, *al-Arman fi Misr, 1896–1961* (Cairo: Tab'a bi-Dar Nubar li-l-Taba'a, 2003), 252–68; and Shamir, "Evolution," 54–59. On subjects from the territory that became Turkey, see DW, 0069-002735, "Mudhakkira 'an Mashru'a Mu'hadatay al-Jinsiyya wa-l-Iqama Ma'a Turkiya Sanat 1935."

93. *Al-Waqa'i' al-Misriyya*, February 27, 1929.

94. "Marsum bi-Qanun Raqam 92 for the Year 1931," *al-Waqa'i' al-Misriyya*, June 18, 1931.

95. See *Journal officiel du gouvernement égyptien*, November 20, 1956.

# Bibliography

'Abd al-Mun'im Riyad, Muhammad. *Mabadi' al-Qanun al-Dawli al-Khass*. Cairo: Matba'a Misr al-Hurra, 1933.

Abécassis, Frédéric, and Anne Le Gall-Kazazian. "L'identité au miroir du droit, le statut des personnes en Egypte (fin XIXe–début XXE siècle)." *Egypte–Monde Arabe (CEDEJC)* (1992): 11–38.

Anderson, Benedict. *Imagined Communities*. 2nd ed. London: Verso, 2006.

Anghie, Antony. *Imperialism, Sovereignty and the Making of International Law*. Cambridge: Cambridge University Press, 2005.

Arendt, Hannah. *The Origins of Totalitarianism*. Orlando, FL: Harcourt Brace, 1979.

Arminjon, Pierre. *Étrangers et protégés dans l'Empire ottoman*. Paris: A. Chevalier-Marescq, 1926.

Assabghy Bey, Iskandar. *La nationalite Égyptienne: Etude historique et critique*. Paris: Société Orientale de Publicité, 1950.

Baring, Evelyn. *Modern Egypt*. Vol. 2. New York: Macmillan, 1908.

Baron, Beth. *Egypt as a Woman: Nationalism, Gender, and Politics*. Berkeley: University of California Press, 2007.

Bayly, C. A. "Representing Copts and Muhammadans: Empire, Nation, and Community in Egypt and India, 1880–1914." In *Modernity & Culture: From the Mediterranean to the Indian Ocean*, edited by Leila Tarazi Fawaz, and C. A. Bayly, 158–203. New York: Columbia University Press, 2002.

Berman, Nathaniel. "'The Sacred Conspiracy': Religion, Nationalism, and the Crisis of Internationalism." *Leiden Journal of International Law* 25 (2012): 9–54.

al-Bishri, Tariq. *Al-Muslimun wa-l-Aqbat fi Atar al-Jama'a al-Wataniyya*. Cairo: Dar al-Shuruq, 1982.

Can, Lale. "The Protection Question: Central Asians and Extraterritoriality in the Late Ottoman Empire." *International Journal of Middle East Studies* 48 (2016): 679–99.

Chakbraberty, Dipesh. *Provincializing Europe: Postcolonial Thought and Historical Difference*. Reissue with a new preface by the author. Princeton: Princeton University Press, 2008 [2000].

Culang, Jeffrey. "Liberal Translations: Secular Concepts, Law, and Religion in Colonial Egypt." PhD diss., Graduate Center, City University of New York, 2017.

Cuno, Kenneth M., and Michael J. Reimer. "The Census Registers of Nineteenth-Century Egypt: A New Source for Social Historians." *British Journal of Middle Eastern Studies* 24 (1997): 193–216.

De Wée, Maurice. *La nationalité Égyptienne: Commentaire de la Loi du 26 Mai 1926*. Alexandria: Whitehead Morris Limited, 1926.

Derengil, Selim. *Conversion and Apostasy in the Late Ottoman Empire*. Cambridge: Cambridge University Press, 2012.

Di Capua, Yoav. *Gatekeepers of the Arab Past: Historians and History Writing in Twentieth-Century Egypt*. Berkeley: University of California Press, 2009.

Esmeir, Samera. *Juridical Humanity: A Colonial History*. Stanford, CA: Stanford University Press, 2012.

al-Fariq, Mahmud Hasan. *Al-Qanun al-Dusturi al-Misri wa-Tatawwur Nizam al-Dawla al-Misriyya Ibtida' min al-Fath al-'Uthmani ila al-Waqt al-Hadir*. Al-Matba'a al-Tijariyya al-Kubra, n.d., c. 1924.

Foucault, Michel. "Governmentality." In *The Foucault Effect: Studies in Governmentality with Two Lections by and an Interview with Michel Foucault*, edited by Graham Burchell, Colin Gordon, and Peter Miller, 87–104. Chicago: University of Chicago Press, 1991.

Ghali, Paul. *Les nationalités détachées de l'Empire ottoman à la suite de la guerre*. Paris: Les Éditions Domat-Montchrestien, 1934.

Hacking, Ian. "The Looping Effects of Human Kinds." In *Causal Cognition: A Multidisciplinary Debate*, edited by Dan Sperberet, David Premack, and Ann James Premack, 351–61. Oxford: Oxford University Press, 1995.

Hanley, Will. *Identifying with Nationality: Europeans, Ottomans, and Egyptians in Alexandria*. New York: Columbia University Press, 2017.

———. "When Did Egyptians Stop Being Ottomans? An Imperial Citizenship Case Study." In *Multilevel Citizenship*, edited by Willem Maas, 89–109. Philadelphia: University of Pennsylvania Press, 2013.

Hava, J. G. *Arabic-English Dictionary for the Use of Students*. Beirut: Catholic Press, 1899.

al-Hayf Bek, ʿAbd al-Hamid Abu. *Al-Qanun al-Dawli al-Khass fi Uruba wa fi Misr, al-Majmuʿ al-Awwal*. Cairo: Matbaʿa al-Saʿada, 1927).

al-Imam, Muhammad Rifʿat. *Al-Arman fi Misr, 1896–1961*. Cairo: Tabʿa bi-Dar Nubar lil-Tabaʿa, 2003.

Keddie, Nikki. *Sayyid Jamāl ad-Dīn "al-Afghāni": A Political Biography*. Berkeley: University of California Press, 1972.

Kern, Karen. *Imperial Citizen: Marriage and Citizenship in the Ottoman Frontier Provinces of Iraq*. Syracuse: Syracuse University Press, 2011.

Krämer, Gudrun. *The Jews in Modern Egypt, 1914–1952*. London: I. B. Tauris, 1989.

*Lajnat al-Dustur: Majmuʿa Muhadir al-Lajna al-ʿAmma*. Cairo: al-Matbaʿa al-Amiriyya, 1924.

Landau, Jacob. *Parliaments and Parties in Egypt*. Tel Aviv: Israel Publishing House, 1953.

Lane, E. W. *An Arabic and English Lexicon*. London: Williams & Norgate, 1863.

Mahmood, Saba. *Religious Difference in a Secular Age: A Minority Report*. Princeton: Princeton University Press, 2015.

*Majlis al-Nuwwab: Majmuʿa Mudabitat al-Inʿiqad al-ʿAdi al-Thalith*. Cairo: al-Matbaʿa al-Amiriyya, 1924.

*Majmuʿat Mudabit al-Inʿiqad al-ʿAdi al-Thalith*. Vol. 2. Cairo: al-Matbaʿa al-Amiriyya, 1928.

Makdisi, Ussama. *The Culture of Sectarianism: Community, History, and Violence in Nineteenth-Century Ottoman Lebanon*. Berkeley: University of California Press, 2000.

Masuzawa, Tomoko. *The Invention of World Religion*. Chicago: University of Chicago Press, 2005.

Mehrez, Samia. *Egypt's Culture Wars: Politics and Practice*. Cairo: American University in Cairo Press, 2008.

Ministry of Finance. *The Census of Egypt Taken in 1917*. Cairo: Government Press, 1920–21.

Philipp, Thomas. *The Syrians in Egypt, 1725–1975*. London: Steiner, 1985.

Qazmakhuri, Yusuf. *Al-Dasatir fi al-ʿAlim al-ʿArabi: Nusus wa-Taʿdilat, 1839-1987*. Beirut: Dar al-Hamraʾ, 1989.

al-Raf ʿi, ʿAbd al-Rahman. *Misr wa-l-Sudan fi Awaʾil ʿAhd al-Ihtilal, al-Tabʿa al-Rabʿa*. Cairo: Dar al-Maʿarif, 1983.

Rogers, Brubaker. *Citizenship and Nationhood in France and Germany*. Cambridge, MA: Harvard University Press, 1992.

Saleh, Zainab. "On Iraqi Nationality: Law, Citizenship, and Exclusion." *Arab Studies Journal* 21 (2013): 48–78.

Scott, David. "Colonial Governmentality." In *Anthropologies of Modernity: Foucault, Governmentality, and Life Politics*, edited by Jonathan Xavier Inda, 23–49. Malden, MA: Blackwell, 2005.

Shami, Seteney. "*Aqalliyya*/Minority in Modern Egypt Discourse." In *Words in Motion: Towards a Global Lexicon*, edited by Carol Gluck and Anna Lowenhaupt Tsing, 151–73. Durham, NC: Duke University Press, 2009.

Shamir, Shimon. "The Evolution of the Egyptian Nationality Laws and Their Application to the Jews in the Monarchy Period." In *The Jews of Egypt: A Mediterranean Society in Modern Times*, edited by Shimon Shamir. Boulder, CO: Westview Press, 1987.

Sulayman, Mahmud Muhammad. *Al-Ajanib fi Misr: Dirasa fi Ta'rikh Misr al-Ijtima'i.* Alexandria: al-Hay'a al-'Amma li-Maktabat al-Iskandariya, 1996.

Tageldin, Shaden M. *Empire and the Seductions of Translation in Egypt.* Berkeley: University of California Press, 2011.

*Tidhkar al-Mu'tamir al-Qibti al-Awwal: Majmu'at Risa'il Musawwira.* Cairo: Matba'at al-Akhbar bi-Misr, 1911.

Troutt Powell, Eve M. *A Different Shade of Colonialism: Egypt, Great Britain, and the Mastery of the Sudan.* Berkeley: University of California Press, 2003.

Vernant, Jacques. *The Refugee in the Post-war World: Preliminary Report of a Survey of the Refugee Problem.* Geneva: United Nations, 1951.

Wathelet, J.-A., and R.-G. Brunton, *Codes égyptiens et lois usuelles en vigeur en Égypte.* Brussels: Veueve F. Larcier, 1919–20.

Weil, Patrick. *How to Be French: Nationality in the Making since 1789.* Durham, NC: Duke University Press, 2008.

Weiss, Max. *In the Shadow of Sectarinism: Law, Shi'ism, and the Making of Modern Lebanon.* Cambridge, MA: Harvard University Press, 2010.

Weitz, Eric D. "From the Vienna to the Paris System: International Politics and the Entangled Histories of Human Rights, Forced Deportations, and Civilizing Missions." *American Historical Review* 113 (2008): 1313–43.

Wendell, Charles. *The Evolution of the Egyptian National Image: From Its Origins to Ahmad Lutfi al-Sayyid.* Berkeley: University of California Press, 1972.

al-Zayni, 'Ali. *Al-Qanun al-Dawli al-Khass al-Misri wa-l-Muqarin, al-Juz' al-Awwal.* Cairo: al-Matba'a al-Rahmaniyya bi-Misr, 1930.

JEFFREY CULANG is a postdoctoral fellow at the Institute for Historical Studies at the University of Texas at Austin.

# 6 Fashioning the Rest

## National Ascription in Austria after the First World War

### John Deak

In late 1918, the Habsburg Empire crumbled as politicians and political parties from its constituent crownlands formed committees and formally broke with the regime. Kaiser Karl hoped to save his family's empire with his imperial manifesto of October 16, 1918, which proclaimed, "Austria should, according to the will of its peoples, become a federated state [*Bundesstaat*], in which each nation [*Volksstamm*] determines, in its own territory, its own governmental polity."[1] By late October 1918, however, the territories of the Habsburg Monarchy, whose dynastic and institutional history stretched back into the High Middle Ages, were joining other independent states or splitting themselves off from the Monarchy to create their own.

The crumbling of the Habsburg Empire, however, was not total. Many institutions and offices remained standing in place, possibly held together by the sheer speed of that which was crumbling around them. On October 21, 208 German-speaking members of the Austrian Imperial Parliament met in the building that normally housed the Lower-Austrian Diet and proclaimed that they formed the National Assembly of German-Austria. The legislators believed that their actions would be accompanied by other national councils that represented the Southern Slavs (Illyria), Czechs, and Ruthenians.[2] But these German-speaking representatives were alone in their commitment to continue the multinational Austrian state on a national-federal basis. In the last days of October 1918, the other parts of the monarchy had seceded or proclaimed independence. Some of these crownlands would merge to form the newly constituted state of Czechoslovakia. Austrian Galicia joined the emerging Polish state, which had already been constituted during the Central powers' policies toward the end of the war. Other provinces were drawn into the orbit of other states: Italy claimed parts of Tyrol, the Austrian Littoral, the Istrian Peninsula, and the city of Trieste. The political leadership of Slovene, Croatian, and Serbian-speaking areas agreed to form a union of Serbs, Croats, and Slovenes. The Austrian province of Bukovina and the

Hungarian counties in Transylvania and the Banat fell to Romania as a result of secret treaties, the votes of local Romanian national councils, and—importantly—Romania's willingness to send in its military to enforce its claims. The territorial claims of the old and new states were enforced with militias and armies. Material chaos accompanied random acts of violence and organized military clashes.[3]

Eric D. Weitz has cogently written about the transition from a Vienna to the Paris system that came to dominate international relations in the twentieth century. The Vienna system, which emerged out of the settlements following the French Revolutionary and Napoleonic Wars, sought peace by promoting stability based on traditional diplomacy and the principle of state sovereignty. The Paris system, a phrase Weitz coined, marked a "shift from traditional diplomacy to population politics," in which entire populations were defined according to varying combinations of "ethnicity, nationality, or race" and became the object of diplomatic discourse. This shift, importantly, led the international system away from "the acceptance and promotion of multi-ethnic and multi-confessional societies"—empires like the Habsburg Monarchy—"to a system in which the state was the presumed representative of one nation."[4] The transformation from one system to the other, from a diplomacy based on dynasties and states to one based on peoples, drew on shifts of understanding of sovereignty and the emergence of group rights underway already in the nineteenth century. But as the Wilsonian principle of national self-determination exercised the imagination of political thinkers and statesmen across Habsburg central Europe, it created moments of great chaos as the empire, along with the Vienna system, fell. The Paris system that emerged granted legitimacy based on the idea of ethnic populations. New states that were forged out of this system had to reimagine themselves and reconstitute themselves based on this principle.

This chapter aims to take the founding of the Austrian republic and the creation of republican institutions and dissect it as a moment not only when republican institutions were created, but as *the moment* when Austria discarded ideas and institutions of supranationality. Between the establishment of German-Austria in October/November 1918 and the Treaty of Saint-Germain-en-Laye of September 10, 1919, Austria went through the eye of the needle, shedding not only its role as the center of an empire but also ideas of multinationalism and equal rights under the law that had anchored that empire. Such a process of de-imperialization was well underway, even finished, by the time Austria's politicians went to Paris in 1919.

To a great degree, the birth narratives of the Habsburg successor states have followed constitutional developments, the creation of constitutional republics, and the descent into dictatorships. These are stories that take the national state as a given. The story of Austria is in many ways no exception. Such histories begin with a national-state framework that was cemented by the Paris Peace Conferences, without questioning that framework. Moreover, they leave out of the story the violence and chaos that accompanied the birth of these national states. Such stories remind us that the nation-state was not a given but had to be forged with hammers and anvils and with laws and economic deprivations.[5]

Austrian historiography has tended to elide the moment when it became a nation-state into a larger history of constitutional change and the development of the Austrian national idea. But such historiographic frameworks emphasize the post-1945 present of Austria and miss much of the important framing moments of the establishment of the republic. These moments included the tortured founding of a new, democratic state based on national principles and national self-determination. National self-determination and the Paris system had their own logics of justification, based on the idea that sovereign states grounded their sovereignty in the nation. As German-Austria was proclaimed from the steps of Vienna's erstwhile imperial parliament, its politicians searched for ways to make Austria a nation-state among nation-states. They articulated Austria's reason for being in direct distinction to its multinational past. Such reasoning found parallels in many of Austria's neighbors.

Following the groundbreaking work in recent years on the process of nationalization and its conflict with national indifference in Habsburg central Europe, this chapter seeks to disrupt the birth narratives of nation-states and instead emphasize their shared inheritance and experiences at their inception.[6] In the crucial months between October 1918 and the Paris Peace Conference of the following spring and summer, politicians and officials in central Europe made both difficult and conscious decisions to forge new regimes based on varying codes of national identities as they sought to transfer public authority and power from the multinational Habsburg Empire to new national states. Even before the Paris peacemakers sat down to remake the world, central Europeans sought to anticipate the postwar order and organize their states based on ideas of national self-determination. But such a high concept was instrumentalized from the very beginning. Ironically, just as the territories of the Habsburg Empire were pulling apart to create or join nation-states, they underwent a process together. This process entailed a nationalization of institutions, norms, and discourses that were once multinational. Moreover, this nationalization process was completely intertwined with the consolidation of power and public authority, as well as the legitimation of that authority. It certainly was neither natural nor already present but contingent, contested, and improvised throughout central Europe.

We can therefore view what was happening in Austria at the moment of the fall of the Habsburg Empire as a way of exploring this simultaneity of interconnectedness and division in central Europe. As a window into Austria's nationalization process, this chapter looks at how the German-Austrian Republic created its civil service and determined who was eligible to serve and draw a pension from the new German-Austrian state. Within this process of hiring, firing, and pensioning was also entangled the confused yet fundamental questions of national belonging (and the criteria for determining such belonging) and citizenship. Moreover, German-Austria's politicians and policy-makers were not able to create a civil service corps out of the existing corps it inherited from the Habsburg Monarchy according to abstract, objective categories; they instead had to assemble one as part of a larger process of negotiating borders and determining citizenship along with its new neighbors, including Yugoslavia, Italy, Czechoslovakia, Poland, and Romania.

Thus, the process of creating a civil service can highlight the complex processes at work in 1918–19, including the creation of new forms of national citizenship, the delineation of space and people, and—importantly—the reconfiguration of the relationship of former Habsburg citizens to their recent (Habsburg) past. In the end, the fall of the Habsburg Empire and the creation of new national and nationalizing states in the center of Europe should not be seen as two discrete events in which the first ends one story and the latter begins another but as one in the same event. The chaos of the fall of the empire was the context for the contingencies and chaos of the national states' founding. It provided the fire in which the steel was forged.

What if historians treated Austria as a nationalizing state among other nationalizing states? For instance, what if we look at how existing state institutions—in this case, positions and offices inherited from the Habsburg Empire—are given national content? Rogers Brubaker defines "nationalizing states" as "states that are conceived by their dominant élites as nation-states, as the states of and for particular nations, yet as 'incomplete' or 'unrealized' nation-states, as insufficiently 'national' in a variety of senses."[7] If we see Austria as a nationalizing state, not as a state with a ready-made nation in 1918, what do we see? We see that (1) Austria and its institutions had to undergo a process of transforming from the core and central provinces of a multinational empire to a nation-state; (2) internationally, it had to adapt its institutions and create a discourse of itself as belonging to a system of nation-states; (3) as it was transformed into a small, republican and parliamentary democracy, this transformation was accompanied by a new articulation of the state-citizen relation and revealed that national belonging and national exclusion accompanied building a democratic state; and (4) finally, despite all these developments, legacies of a multinational identity—left over from Habsburg practice—remained awkwardly in place alongside new, emerging national conceptions.

The Habsburg Empire's fall was not a moment of complete rebirth, a moment when the slate of European history was wiped clean. The postwar order was forged in moments of uncertainty. The National Assembly met for the second time on October 30, 1918—nearly two weeks before proclaiming the Republic of German-Austria—and agreed on a provisional constitution that established the framework for the exercise of legislative and executive authority in the fledgling state.[8] This document—though a new republic would not be proclaimed for another thirteen days—in reality founded the new state. It proclaimed that the National Assembly would exercise the legislative authority. Executive authority would be exercised by a state council—the Staatsrat—which would be elected by the National Assembly from its own membership.[9] Moreover, it did two important things for the establishment of its own authority and the legitimation of that authority: it established new ministries—which it named state offices—and it established a constitutional and legal continuity between the monarchy and the new republic. Article 16 of this document stated that "laws and institutions, which existed in the kingdoms and lands represented in the Reichsrat, in so far as they are not abolished or changed by this document, for the time being remain in effect until further notice."[10]

Outside the halls of central Europe's parliaments, however, the new territories desperately needed the order that the political parties were trying to call into being with their pronouncements. Firstly, the borders of central Europe were not fixed, and the disintegration of Austria-Hungary was accompanied by the disintegration of the army on the Italian front. The government of German-Austria issued a statement, not to ameliorate feelings of uncertainty, but to confirm such fears. "The Land is in Danger[!]," it proclaimed, informing the populace that "the army is dissolving into disarray." The disorderly demobilization would add to the people's misery, it claimed, in the form of more mouths to feed and hands to employ or, worse, the plundering of the countryside. All the while, Italian, Russian, and Serbian prisoners of war were flooding into the countryside as their guards no longer maintained the camps. The proclamation called for soldiers to voluntarily report for service in a new German-Austrian army.[11]

## Forging a New State

In the midst of these moments of real anxiety, the new German-Austrian Republic inherited the core territories of a multinational empire and the supranational bureaucracy that came with them. The three presidents of the state council of the German-Austrian Republic met with the last prime minister of the Austrian half of the empire, Heinrich Lammasch, on October 31, 1918. In what signaled the changing of the guard and the passing of monarchy to republic, Lammasch gave his assent to the "complete transfer of the administration" from the imperial Austrian to the German-Austrian government.[12] This transfer was followed up by the German-Austrian National Assembly with the law of November 12, 1918 (StGBl. No. 5), titled "Form of the State and the Government of German-Austria." That law sought to create a stable foundation on which to build a new administration. It abolished the special laws and privileges of the emperor and the imperial house in one article and released the imperial bureaucracy from its oath of loyalty to the emperor in the next.[13]

The Habsburg imperial bureaucracy had been a melting pot for the empire. It was multilingual, diverse, and mobile.[14] The draw of the center of power brought thousands of officials from the crownlands to Vienna, the capital of this multinational empire. Moreover, just as the central ministries of the Habsburg Empire reflected the diversity of the empire itself, the bureaucracy had cultivated a supranational identity.[15] Bureaucratic families married into one another, were promoted sometimes on the basis of multilingualism, and generally sought to transcend national conflict. There were, of course, exceptions to this rule, but national activism was generally muted in the civil service because it could be harshly disciplined with removal from a post, demotion, and financial penalties. On top of this supranational ethos existed a cultural Germanophilia, an outlook that saw the German language as a key to social mobility and higher cultural status.[16]

Thus, when German-Austria was declared on the steps of parliament, it inherited not only the buildings at the center of the imperial government but also the multinational workforce in them. This would prove to be inconvenient and too expensive for the new republic. When State Chancellor Karl Renner addressed the bureaucrats of the central ministries of the new German-Austrian Republic in November 1918, he admitted, "German-Austria will be a poor state and will not be able to afford a larger bureaucratic apparatus." But the crisis and its solutions were increasingly put in national terms. Renner added that, despite the financial hardship, there would be every effort given "to take up all the German public servants and employees into the new state."[17]

Taking care of Germans in the chaos of the fall of the empire took on a moral obligation in a world where everyone cared only for their own. Indeed, the state did take over all the officials who happened to find themselves in German-Austria at the beginning of November 1918—but it did not want them all.[18] And it differentiated between who was an "Austrian" and who was a "German." Since these terms had different meanings in 1918 than they do now, we should dwell on them for a moment. An Austrian was a former citizen of the non-Hungarian parts of the Habsburg Empire. What a German was, however, was given a more nebulous definition that relied on cultural, ethnic, and linguistic markers. The German-Austrian state, closely paying attention to the nationalization efforts of its neighbors, would work to define who belonged. What its policy-makers, including the State Chancellery, increasingly labeled as the German-Austrian nation was a group that existed at the confluence between "Austrian" and "German."

Even before peacemakers assembled at Paris, the states of central Europe anticipated the world order that they would create based on the idea of the sovereign nation-state. For instance, in late November 1918, the State Chancellery's Office, in what amounted to a national purge, ordered the "divestiture" (*Enthebung*) of all "non-German" state employees.[19] This action was paralleled by activities in the other successor states. In fact, an international conference involving representatives of Poland, Czechoslovakia, Ukraine, Yugoslavia, and Romania followed on November 29, 1918, to handle these aspects of the disentangling of the bonds of the Habsburg Monarchy. But despite these agreements and mutual assurances, the national purging of the bureaucracies of the successor states—the removal of officials who had belonged only months before to the same institution—took on a haphazard and almost punitive character. In Austria, all civil servants and state employees, "formerly Austrian citizens," were to be released from service and given a severance package (they were to be paid their salary, which their adopted homeland was to cover) and were expected to leave. The authorities were to collect the names, the last position held, and the national identity of the governmental employees who were to be forced out of office and given a severance payment.[20] By January 1919, German-Austria was still negotiating with Romania, Yugoslavia, and Czechoslovakia to take up the severance packages of purged state employees, while Poland had already taken over directly covering the costs of Polish civil servants living in German-Austria who had been purged on account of their nationality.[21]

In the six months following the collapse of the monarchy—well before the peace treaties were signed at Paris—the Austrian government and the free press both articulated the necessity of a "German" civil service and sought to refine who was German enough to work for the government. *Der Staatsbeamte*, the official publication of the Civil Servants League in Vienna, wrote in its lead article on December 1, 1918, that the dissolution of Austria-Hungary has made way for a new order, and that order would be a national one. "The centuries-long ideas of belonging together," the paper wrote, "along with the shared burdens and joys have been dropped and in place of an imperial unity, a series of national states have appeared." As the bureaucrats' paper lamented the collapse of the old, multinational era, they simultaneously committed themselves to a national future—however uncertain that future was. The relationships between the national successor states, and how they would treat their national minorities, remained a mystery. The editorial staff of *Der Staatsbeamte*, however, did not expect Germans living outside of German-Austria to be treated well. And however they felt before the fall of the monarchy, they now identified with them. "With the formation of independent national states in the territory of the former Austrian Empire, the imperial bureaucracy has fallen prey to a sharp nationalization and with regards to that must be subject to a special purification." German-Austria, too, had to undergo such purification for the sake of its people—German-Austrians. *Der Staatsbeamte* sought to articulate this in terms that it had never had to use before: "In the same measure, just as German officials are said to be ruthlessly besieged, so must our enemies be treated, it would therefore be the surest path if the German-Austrian state would only take Germans as its employees."[22]

There are at least two observations that can be made at this point. First, state employees became a central component of the nationalization process for the Austrian republic, to be handled like "national property" even before the peace negotiations at Paris.[23] Second, fear of the new national politics of central Europe led Austria's officials to believe that it would be up to German-Austria to protect Germans—both within and outside the new borders of the German-Austrian Republic. The solution to the question of how to disentangle Austria's multinational administrative inheritance turned out to be a sticky one. The state secretary for justice informed the Cabinet Council in November that non-German civil servants could be dismissed from the employment in German-Austria on the bases of their "membership in another nationality"—that is, they could be laid off with pay.[32] This, however, was no solution to a republic that was burdened with maintaining the large, multinational, central apparatus of the old monarchy. Austrian officials, therefore, sought to purge the civil service of non-Germans and to make the other successor states pay for their severance packages. German-Austrian officials at the same time feared that the other successor states would do the same, prompting a massive influx of German-speaking bureaucrats forced to enter Austria from posts far and wide in the lands of the former monarchy. German-Austria's fiscal fears and nationalizing goals motivated Austria's central government and its ministries to embark on a national purge, even rooting out civil servants who wanted to remain. At the very least, it would clear the payrolls and allow for German-Austria to take Germans into its governmental ministries from the other successor states.

## Germans and Non-Germans in 1918–19

As the German-Austrian government turned its attention to the nationalization of its civil service, it ordered the Cabinet Council to draw up a series of "guidelines" for the adjudication of admittance into the German-Austrian civil service. These guidelines, produced in a meeting of the council on November 23, 1918, differentiated civil service employees according to national identity. It provided for handling civil servants who were former "Austrian" citizens and (a) of German nationality living in the territory of German-Austria; (b) of German nationality living outside the territory of German-Austria; or (c) of non-German nationality living in the territory of German-Austria. In all cases, the guidelines stipulated that only "employees who belong to the German nation" may swear the oath to take up service for the German-Austrian state. Moreover, the state authorities reserved the right to determine who may swear the oath in cases that needed adjudication. To do this, the Cabinet Council established a committee of high-level officials from the new State Offices for Justice, Finance, Trade, Education, and the Interior and called it the Intergovernmental Committee. This committee took on the responsibility of guiding the transfer of the administration from Reich to republic. As part of its work, the committee drew up further norms for the admission into the Austrian republic's civil service.[24]

The Intergovernmental Committee essentially had to find ways to cut down the civil service while also making sure that it would be loyal to a new German-Austrian state. The guidelines stipulated age and service qualifications. Civil servants who were over the age of sixty were to be cashiered, as well as civil servants—regardless of their national group—who had served less than five years. For non-Germans who served in the Austrian civil service before 1918, a final resolution to their employment would be negotiated between the various successor states.[25] The guidelines also produced norms for accepting Germans from the other successor states into the German-Austrian administration. In this case, the uncertainties of the immediate postwar moment—especially concerning the relationship of the various national successor states to each other—meant that the committee anticipated that other states would be cashiering Germans who found themselves in office in the other successor states. Thus, expectations of national purges in all of Habsburg central Europe were made an integral part of policy.

The Intergovernmental Committee met no less than sixty times between November 1918 and September 1919. Its meeting minutes provide a wealth of information about how the Austrian government began to transverse the chasm between multinational empire and nation-state. They also reveal that it deliberated in cases in which non-Germans wanted to remain in service to the German-Austrian state, widows living outside German-Austria who wanted their pensions to be paid by German-Austria, and matters relating to German civil servants living outside of the borders of German-Austria who were removed from their post.

Questions of citizenship and ethnicity were therefore immediately combined with questions of existence. Employment meant payment of salary. Recognition of service meant the payment of pensions. But Germanness, whatever that was, did not automatically make one a citizen. More importantly, non-Germanness did not exclude one from citizenship in German-Austria either. Citizenship in German-Austria was not based on ethnicity; it was based on residence. In fact, the Law Concerning German-Austrian State Citizenship of December 5, 1918 (StGBl. Nr. 91/1918) explicitly stated in its first article that "German-Austrian citizens include all persons who at the time of this law's proclamation can claim right of residence [heimatberechtigt] in a municipality of the German-Austrian Republic." In essence, the new republic took over the old supranational citizenship law of the Habsburg Empire, Heimatrecht, which had grounded imperial citizenship in local citizenship.[26] Thus, this residential form of citizenship clashed with the expectations of admission to state service, which was being formulated in terms of ethnic belonging. Potentially, one could be a citizen of German-Austria without being a German, but non-German citizens did not necessarily have the same rights as Germans. What the rights of "national minorities" would be had to await final articulation in the text of the Treaty of Saint-Germain-en-Laye, which was not signed until September 1919. But as the German-Austrian state improvised its entry into the world of nation-states, it did as the other states did, and created the category of national minority—something that had been unknown to the legal world of the Habsburg Empire.

The Intergovernmental Committee was empowered to draw a line around German-Austria and what it meant to belong there. The process implied divorcing the new state from its multinational heritage and drawing lines between former Austrian citizens. The criteria used to draw these new boundaries between people varied between territorial citizenship and personal, social, and ethnic categories. As the Intergovernmental Committee debated the internal process of creating a German-Austrian civil service out of a multinational Austrian one, they simultaneously had to improvise a relationship to the past. We can see traces of the breakup of the Habsburg Empire, and the pains with which the offices tried to justify and articulate the nationalization of a formerly multinational bureaucracy in the various ministries.

Who could claim a government job or a pension in German-Austria? The first set of clear cases dealt with former Austrian citizens who did not claim to be members of the German nation and who did not live in German territory. The Intergovernmental Committee dealt with numerous requests from the former periphery of the empire, from provinces now in Italy, Poland, Romania, the Czech Republic, and Yugoslavia to be taken up into the Austrian state. These were flatly denied. They also dealt with lingering loyalties to the old empire and to its supranational concepts among former Austrian civil servants and their families. An Armenian from the Bukovina did not want to be in the employment of Poland. He hoped that the multinational sentiment that once reigned in Vienna was still present. His application was denied. One widow of a postal official in Italy complained that they had been Austrian (in the sense of imperial Austrian) patriots and therefore feared persecution from the Italian authorities who had moved into South Tyrol. The Intergovernmental Committee reported that the request for any payment must be denied because the former employee lived in a territory that was not part of the German-Austrian Republic, and as a member of an "alien nationality" (they were deemed to be Italians), the former official was not eligible for support by German-Austria.[27]

As German-Austria sought to pare down its civil service, the Intergovernmental Committee received reports that the other successor states were likewise purging Germans. German officials from Trieste had been dismissed and not given severance monies. The Slovenian authorities of Yugoslavia had begun the process of dismissing German civil servants and confiscating their apartments. In fact, the committee was notified that schoolmaster, *Oberlehrer*, and retired colonel Eduard Löser, living in Ljubljana, was issued an eviction notice by the city magistrate's office. He had one month to remove his belongings and leave voluntarily. He was barred from appealing the decision or from contesting the eviction. The committee turned over the matter to the Ministry of Foreign Affairs.[28]

As German-Austria's Intergovernmental Committee weighed how to decide who belonged and who did not, they did not fully endorse ethnic models of nation or territorial models of citizenship, which often could be unclear. The committee approved payments to Germans outside of German-Austria's sovereign territory who were expelled from their posts and their apartments. And yet, as the state moved toward ethnic ideas of belonging, the German nation could still be a choice. But it had to be an active choice, a choice grounded in taking an oath of loyalty to the state that simultaneously proclaimed that one was a member of the German nation. In two cases before the Intergovernmental Committee, the committee was perplexed by Jews who refused to swear an oath to German-Austria because the oath of office required that they declared themselves to belong to the German nation. The committee admitted that if they swore the oath, they could be admitted to the service. But instead, they declared themselves to be of a non-German nationality. In the first case, a "Zionist" in the State Office of Transportation complained that he could not swear the oath because, as a "member of the Jewish People," he was not a German. He requested that another oath, one that did not require him to declare himself a German, be administered. His request was denied. In the other case, Anna Muschl, an assistant in the State Vocational School in Vienna, declared herself to be a member of the Jewish nation. But to the consternation of her superiors and to the Intergovernmental Committee, she met all the normal requirements for being a "German" according to the guidelines: she was born in Vienna and had right of residence there; she attended German schools and listed her language of daily use as German in the 1910 census. The State Office for Public Works asked the committee if she could swear the oath anyway. The committee replied that according to the Cabinet Council's own guidelines, only those who "expressly declare themselves members of the German nation" could take the oath of office. Accordingly,

Muschl had to be immediately dismissed from employment for failure to swear the oath.[29]

The German-Austrian state, as it sought to nationalize itself and divest itself of its multinational and supranational origins, had to define what it meant to be German on a legal basis. In many ways, such policy-making contradicted the policy-making and policy research that had occurred within the Habsburg Monarchy itself. Fifty years before, as the international statistical community sought to make language and nationality rubrics in the census, officials from Austria argued for the exclusion of such rubrics. Austrian officials and statisticians argued that the linkage between language and ethnicity or national belonging was not a measurable, objective category.[30] Now, German-Austrian officials had to argue the opposite, while creating standards for evidence and discernment. Moreover, there were good, existential reasons for people to not play by the rules. If one had right of residence within the borders of German-Austria, and a job with the government, one was compelled by circumstances to declare oneself a German.

The Intergovernmental Committee thus discussed additional guidelines and procedures for dealing with so-called dubious cases. In such cases, the person's entry on the 1910 census was to be used as a definitive account of the person's nationality. But even in such cases as these, the committee opined, the census may not be definitive. It imagined cases in which Germans declared themselves to be of another national group. Such cases warranted further investigation and, possibly, a decision that went against what the person wrote in the 1910 census. Here was a tacit recognition of the complex, multinational past of old Austria's nationality politics, even as the Intergovernmental Committee tried to erase that past.[31]

Dubious cases abounded, of course. Especially in the Finance Ministry, we witness a particular form these cases took: lower-ranking civil servants, clerks, and staff members who wished to keep their current jobs and a ministry that struggled to understand the old categories of bilingualism and national indifference in a new system that did not recognize, or mistrusted, such things. George Cihlař, an assistant clerk in the accounting section of the Finance Ministry, listed on his application to be taken into service in the German-Austrian Republic that he was "German." But in his case, it was determined that not only was he born in lands that had become part of Czechoslovakia but also, more importantly, he had listed Czech as his "language of idiomatic use" on the 1910 census. He was dismissed. His colleague Johann Krysa likewise tried to pass as a German in 1919—but he was labeled as a Pole and also dismissed.[32]

The committee and the various ministerial officials had difficulty rendering judgments in ambiguous cases—as in the case of a "Slavic" doorman who had married a German-speaker and raised his children as Germans.[33] Given his "Germanic disposition," he was accepted into the employment of the new republic.[34] In another case, Franz Lavička had declared in the 1910 census that his language of idiomatic use was German. But his file contained conflicting information: he was born in Příbram and his parents were "both Czech" according to the personnel file, but he identified as a German and was active in German associational life. The file noted, for instance, that he was a member of the German

*Turnverein* and Christian-Social Trade Union. The head of department labeled Lavička as a "Germanized Czech." He was accepted into German-Austrian state employment and allowed to take the oath of service.[35]

As the committee weighed the personal choices made by civil servants to be Germans, it also opened the door to questioning the authenticity of those choices. The "national membership" of Dr. Rudolf Sajovic was brought into jeopardy precisely because the choices of individuals conflicted with the idea that the nation was an objective category. Dr. Sajovic, Oberfinanzrat, had to prove his Germanness after it came to light that his brother lived in Ljubljana/Laibach and worked as a lawyer, while his sister had allegedly married a leading Slovenian national activist. Sajovic was forced to write a definitive declaration of his belonging to the German nation. That declaration, dated July 4, 1919, carefully addressed the points of the Intergovernmental Committee's guidelines for determining the national belonging of doubtful cases. Firstly, he declared, "I am of German nationality" and indicated that he listed German as his language of daily use in the 1910 census. Second, he maintained that he was educated in German schools. Third, he listed the clubs and organizations to which he belonged and was careful to point out the Slovenian alternative clubs that he did not belong to. Fourth, he excused the fact that he never belonged to a purely German political association because as a civil servant, such behavior had been frowned upon. He worked for understanding and cooperation between Germans and Slovenians—such behavior was expected of the Austrian civil service. "With regards to my ethnic heritage [*Abstammung*], I must admit that I have mixed Slovenian and German blood." But gradually, Sajovic declared, through his education and socialization, he had lost the ability to speak and write Slovene.[36] He had turned his back on the Slovenian nationality. That was good enough for the Finance Ministry. It wrote to Sajovic on August 13, 1919, that he met all the qualifications for inclusion in the German nation. He could keep his job.

Personal choices and feelings, however, could only take one so far. In the case of Hilfsunterdirektionsadjunkt Johann Kokesch/Kokeš, the state could contest the protestations of the supplicant. Kokesch and Kokeš are the German and Czech spellings of his name, representing the possibilities of citizenship: German-Austrian or Czechoslovak. But tellingly, both the German-Austrian state and Johann Kokesch/Kokeš himself used them both—though by the end of the paper trail they had settled on the Czech spelling. Kokeš contested the decision by the State Office for Finances that declared him to be a member of an alien nation and thereby dismissed him from service.[37] Kokesch/Kokeš was born in Moravia in 1867—he was in his early fifties in 1918. He was educated in a dual-language school in Austerlitz/Slavkov u Brna. He was also a product of *Kindertausch*—he was sent by his parents to live with a German family before they sent him to a Vienna Realschule for his secondary education. Kokesch/Kokeš claimed that he had served in the Austrian military before entering the civil service and had been granted residence status in Vienna twenty-seven years before. He declared his allegiance to the German-Austrian state and indicated that he could not just pick up his things and become a Czechoslovak. For Kokesch/Kokeš, it was also a matter of existence: his nineteen years of working in a German-speaking office made it impossible for him to work in Czechoslovakia.

As the presidium of the State Office for Finances considered Kokesch/Kokeš's case, it denied his right to determine his own national belonging and reinterpreted the supposedly objective factors that the applicant used to bolster his case. The Finance Office instead focused on Kokesch/Kokeš's indications that he could be Czech. Kokesch/Kokeš admitted that he came from Czech parents, that the "Bohemian language" (i.e., Czech) was his mother tongue, and that on the 1910 census he had listed both German and Czech as his language of daily use. Moreover, the Finance Ministry noted that his colleagues saw him as a Czech. The office saw no reason to overturn its decision to terminate his employment and found no grounds for the decision to be reviewed by the State Chancellery.

Kokesch/Kokeš appealed the decision, which reached the Supreme Administrative Court. This court had undergone the same procedures only months before, removing not only its non-German staff but also its non-German judges and clerks. The court refused to hear the case and issued its reasoning in June 1919. The court found determinative that no right existed for the transfer from employment in the empire to the new republic. The right of the new republic to determine whom it employed was paramount, and therefore, Kokesch/Kokeš had no case.[38]

Kokesch/Kokeš did not give up; he directed another request to the State Ministry of Finances and sought the personal intervention of the minister himself. Kokesch/Kokeš this time made arguments based on subjective factors, hoping to appeal to the new standards of the age. Though he sought special merciful circumstances for his employment, *im Gnadenwege*, as he put it, he did not admit that he posed any exception to the rules. "For my entire life," he wrote, "I have only ever felt myself to be a German." He had attended German schools, lived in Vienna since 1900, and married a German woman. "I entered the civil service at the young age of twenty-eight and dedicated my entire strength and energy, my best years [to service]. . . . If the officials of the former Finance Ministry have no right to transfer of employment into the German-Austrian civil service, I still believe that I, through my life's work and my first-rate qualifications, born through years of service, have earned a moral right to not go into ruin in my autumn years."[39]

The State Office for Finances contested the idea that Kokesch/Kokeš "always had felt himself to be German" and stated that his transfer to the German-Austrian civil service had nothing to do with his qualifications or his many years of service. Rather, the decision to not offer him a place in the German-Austrian Office of Finance was rendered as it had to be: "based on his own admissions and according to the results of the official investigations into his belonging to the German nation." The absolute "minimum" prerequisite for consideration for admission to the German-Austrian civil service was the declaration of German on the 1910 census. This minimum, in the case of Kokesch/Kokeš, was not met. But their decision was based on something else as well. Kokesch/Kokeš, as the marginalia in one of his case files noted, "had two irons in the fire." He had also applied to work in the civil service of the Czechoslovak government.

Kokesch/Kokeš reminds us of the slipperiness of national belonging and of the multinational past of Habsburg central Europe. But also that, for all the talk of minority rights in the Paris peace treaties, the rights of minorities did not trump the rights of states to hire whomever they considered their own. Moreover, Kokesch/Kokeš sought to make his way in two different nationalizing states at the same time. The difference was—probably because he was nationally indifferent or nationally opportunistic—that after November 1918, neither state would have him. In the postwar reconfiguration of Habsburg central Europe, Kokesch/Kokeš was caught between the mechanisms and their movements to create national states. As a resident of Vienna, he was guaranteed Austrian citizenship, but as he was from Moravia and at one time spoke Czech on a regular basis, the Austria state tried to paint him as a foreigner and therefore unwanted as a civil servant. The State Ministry of Finance in reviewing his case made the determination that Kokesch/Kokeš, if he were not accepted into the Czechoslovakian civil service, would be eligible for a pension from Czechoslovakia. In the draft of the final decision of their case, they initially wrote to him that "you are free to request retirement in the case that your transfer into the state service of the Czechoslovak Republic is not permitted or in the case that the request is unsuccessful." This was then crossed out and presumably omitted from the final draft.[40] They decided not to leave any door open for him and let him find his own path into the unknown.

## Conclusion

One month after Kokesch/Kokeš's case was decided, an Austrian delegation was in Paris to sign the Treaty of Saint-Germaine-en-Laye. That treaty contained eight articles that sought to protect the rights of minorities. Minority rights, as defined by the treaty, applied to the expenditure of public funds, the ability to use other languages than German in public, and the right of minority populations to be schooled in their own language. It said nothing about public employment. Austria had, from the moment of its inception, decided that it would be a state that was run by Germans. This was, in essence, a moment of self-determination. The Austrian state reserved the right to employ only "Germans" and created commissions to determine who was German in the first place. Language, social factors, and—tellingly—the subjective views of one's colleagues all mattered in these determinations. In the process, Austria had created two types of citizenship: those who could be employed by the state and those who could not.

Austria had fashioned itself into an uncertain nation-state. In cases such as these, the old, monarchical, nonnationalist conception of "Austrian" as a disposition and state of mind could still find resonance, as in the cases of Sajovic or Lavička, even as central Europe divided itself into nationalizing states. And yet, the nationalist notion of race and of persons belonging to one national community could exist among these various rulings by the Intergovernmental Committee at the same time. By mid-1919, the German-Austrian government had begun to backtrack on its rhetoric, realizing that among the civil servants whom they were pushing out of office were many long-standing bureaucrats whose expertise would be essential for establishing the new state. These reprieves were for high- and mid-level servants, not the lowly clerks or doormen who depended on state employment for their daily bread. We can see in their applications a wish to be accepted into the "rest"—a leftover state that still carried with it the baggage of national ambiguity, code-switching, and bilingualism. But, at least on paper, that state was gone.

In a sense, the multinational setting, the idea of national self-determination, underscored the belief that Austria had to become a nation-state. And while the national narratives of many of the successor states of the Habsburg Empire view these moments as moments of building—building new states that reflected the cultural, institutional, and democratic aspirations of their people—it is difficult with these cases of national purges, forced retirements, and material deprivation to see this as a progressive moment. It was also a moment of destruction and of unmaking a state: the unmaking of multinational—or even nationally indifferent—possibilities for European history.

## Notes

The author wishes to thank the Nanovic Institute for European Studies at the University of Notre Dame for generous support of travel and research for the preparation of this article. The author also wishes to thank Dr. Miha Šimac for timely assistance and help reading texts in Slovenian. The author is responsible for all translations.

1. For Kaiser Karl's Manifesto, see Walter Goldinger and Dieter A. Binder, *Geschichte der Republik Österreich 1918–1938* (Vienna: Verlag für Geschichte und Politik, 1992), 13.

2. For the establishment of the National Assembly, see Wilhelm Brauneder, *Deutsch-Österreich 1918: Die Republik entsteht* (Vienna: Amalthea, 2000), 32–45.

3. Recent work has highlighted the idea that the First World War and deprivation did not end when the war on the western front came to a close. See the articles collected in Robert Gerwarth and John Horne, eds., *War in Peace: Paramilitary Violence in Europe after the Great War* (Oxford: Oxford University Press, 2012).

4. Eric D. Weitz, "From the Vienna to the Paris System: International Politics and the Entangled Histories of Human Rights, Forced Deportations, and Civilizing Missions," *American Historical Review* 113, no. 5 (2008): 1314.

5. The historiography of the successor states of the Habsburg Empire share a focus on the long antecedents of statehood on the one hand and the political histories of democratic development and constitutional history once they had achieved statehood. For Yugoslavia, see Sabrina P. Ramet, *The Three Yugoslavias: State-Building and Legitimation, 1918–2005* (Washington, DC: Woodrow Wilson Center Press, 2006); Dejan Djokić, *Elusive Compromise: A History of Interwar Yugoslavia* (New York: Columbia University Press, 2007). The history of Czechoslovakia has, in contrast, also focused on the immediate establishment of the state and the quest to draw and secure its borders. See, for instance, Jörg K. Hoensch, *Geschichte der Tschechoslowakei*, 3rd ed. (Stuttgart: Kohlhammer, 1992),

ch. 2; Dagmar Perman, *The Shaping of the Czechoslovak State: Diplomatic History of the Boundaries of Czechoslovakia, 1914–1920* (Leiden: Brill, 1962).

6. Rogers Brubaker, *Nationalism Reframed: Nationhood and the National Question in the New Europe* (Cambridge: Cambridge University Press, 1996); Pieter M. Judson, *Guardians of the Nation: Activists on the Language Frontiers of Imperial Austria* (Cambridge, MA: Harvard University Press, 2006); Jeremy King, *Budweisers into Czechs and Germans: A Local History of Bohemian Politics, 1848–1948* (Princeton, NJ: Princeton University Press, 2002); Tara Zahra, *Kidnapped Souls: National Indifference and the Battle for Children in the Bohemian Lands, 1900–1948* (Ithaca, NY: Cornell University Press, 2008).

7. Rogers Brubaker, "Nationalizing States in the Old 'New Europe'—and the New," *Ethnic and Racial Studies* 19, no. 2 (1996): 412.

8. This appeared as the "Der Beschluß der Provisorischen Nationalversammlung für Deutschösterreich vom 30. Oktober 1918 über die grundlegenden Einrichtungen der Staatsgewalt" (StGBl. No. 1/ 1918). "German-Austria" or *Deutschösterreich* was the name the Provisional National Assembly gave to the fledgling state. It would be barred from using this name—since it indicated that Austria eventually would be incorporated into the German Reich—by the victorious Entente countries in the Treaty of St. Germain in September 1919. The position of the victorious powers toward the Anschluss question at the Paris Peace Conference is described in detail in Lajos Kerekes, *Von St. Germain bis Genf: Österreich und seine Nachbarn, 1918–1922*, trans. Johanna Till (Vienna: Herman Böhlaus Nachfolger, 1979), 41–44. The republic was renamed according to the Treaty of St. Germain by the "Law on the Form of the State" on October 21, 1919 (StGBl. No. 174/ 1919).

9. The *Staatsrat* consisted of the three presidents of the assembly—each of whom represented one of the major political blocks: the Social Democrats (Karl Seitz), the Christian Socials (Johann Hauser), and the German Nationals (Franz Dinghofer).

10. Tellingly, on October 28, 1918, the National Council of Czechoslovakia similarly pronounced that "all previous Provincial and Imperial laws and ordinances remain provisionally in force" (Malbone W. Graham, *New Governments of Central Europe* [New York: Henry Holt, 1924; reprint, Fite Press, 2007], 607–8; original in *Sbírka zákonů a nařízení státu československého*, No. 11).

11. *Neue Freie Presse*, No. 19466 (November 3, 1918), page 1.

12. Gottfried Köfner, "Eine oder wieviele Revolutionen? Das Verhältnis zwischen Staat und Ländern in Deutschösterreich im Oktober und November 1918," *Jahrbuch für Zeitgeschichte* 2 (1979): 138.

13. *Gesetz vom 12. November 1918 über die Staats- und Regierungsform von Deutschösterreich*, in *Staatsgesetzblatt für den Staat Deutschösterreich*, Nr. 5/ 1918, articles 5 and 6.

14. For the social history of the late imperial Austrian bureaucracy, see Waltraud Heindl, *Josephinische Mandarine: Bürokratie und Beamte in Österreich. Bd. 2, 1848–1914* (Vienna: Böhlau, 2013); Karl Megner, *Beamtenmetropole Wien 1500–1938: Bausteine zu einer Sozialgeschichte vorwiegend im neuzeitlichen Wien* (Vienna: Österreich, 2010).

15. The literature on "national indifference" in the Habsburg Empire has been instrumental in revising our understanding of the nationalist activism and nationalist politics in central Europe. For a key text in this field, see Tara Zahra, "Imagined Noncommunities: National Indifference as a Category of Analysis," *Slavic Review* 69, no. 1 (2010): 93–119.

16. Enlightening in this regard is Gerald Stourzh's analysis of his own great-grandfather's education and civil service career in the nineteenth century: Gerald Stourzh, "'Aus der Mappe meines Urgroßvaters': Eine mährische Juristenlaufbahn im 19. Jahrhundert," in *Der Umfang der österreichischen Geschichte: Ausgewählte Studien 1990–2010*, Studien zu Politik und Verwaltung 99 (Vienna: Böhlau, 2011), 126–37.

17. *Der Staatsbeamte*, No. 491 (December 1, 1918), 70.

18. Herta Hafner, "Der sozio-ökonomische Wandel der österreichischen Staatsang-estellten," (PhD. diss., University of Vienna, 1990), 217–18.

19. The memorandum was given the number Pr.Z. 1387/St.K. The copy I viewed was in the Archiv des Österrreichischen Verwaltungsgerichtshofs (hereafter VwGh), Präsidium, 1919, Z. 4.

20. Memorandum of the Deutschösterreichisches Staatsamt für Finanzen to the State Chancellery and all Ministries, (November 30, 1918, org. Z.4389) in VwGh, 1919, Z. 10.

21. Staatsamt der Finanzen to all the D-Ö Ministeries, December 30, 1918, org. Z. 10.173 in VwGh, Präsidium 1919, Z. 12.

22. *Der Staatsbeamte*, No. 494 (March 1919), 1.

23. For the rhetoric of National Property in the nineteenth-century context, see Pieter M. Judson, "'Not Another Square Foot!' German Liberalism and the Rhetoric of National Ownership in Nineteenth-Century Austria," *Austrian History Yearbook* 26 (1995): 83–97.

32. Kabinettsprotokoll Nr. 7. (November 10, 1918), in Austrian State Archives/Archive of the Republic (hereafter AT-OeStA/AdR) Bundeskanzleramt (hereafter BKA) Kabinett-sratsprotokolle, 1 Rep., K 5.

24. See chapter 4 of Hafner, "Der sozio-ökonomische Wandel," which followed the im-mediate social transformation in the Austrian Imperial bureaucracy after the foundation civil service law, or "Dienstpragmatik," of 1914. Hers was one of the first scholarly works (if not *the* first) to use the files of the Intergovernmental Committee, which oversaw the national purge of the Austrian civil service. She provides a thorough orientation of much of the source material and I am indebted to her work for being able to find my way quickly through the material.

25. The guidelines were published in *Wiener Zeitung*, No. 272 (November 24, 1918), 1. They are also available in the minutes of the Intergovernmental Committee in AT-OeStA/ Archiv der Republik [hereafter AdR] Bundeskanzleramt [herafter BKA] Staatskanzlei / Bundeskanzleramt alt [herafter Stk/BKA alt] Karton [hereafter K] 246.

26. See the excellent article on citizenship in Habsburg central Europe and the suc-cessor states: Ulrike von Hirschhausen, "From Imperial Inclusion to National Exclusion: Citizenship in the Habsburg Monarchy and in Austria 1867–1923," *European Review of History: Revue Européenne d'Histoire* 16, no. 4 (2009): 551–73, especially, 559–61.

27. For instance, see the meeting minutes of the Intergovernmental Committee, Nrs. 12, pt. 2 and pt. 10 (January 9, 1919) in AT-OeStA/AdR BKA Stk/Bka Alt Marterien-Sonderlegung [hereafter MSL] K 246.

28. See the meeting minutes of the Intergovernmental Committee, Nr. 20 pts. 2, 4 & 5 (Trieste) and Nr. 20, pt. 9 and Nr. 23, pt. 2 (Yugoslavia/Ljubljana) in AT-OeStA/AdR BKA Stk/Bka Alt MSL K246.

29. For these two cases, see meeting minutes of the Intergovernmental Committee, Nr. 20 pt. 3 and Nr. 24, pt. 5 in AT-OeStA/AdR BKA Stk/Bka Alt MSL K246.

30. For an enlightening discussion of the censuses and the statistical community in the Habsburg Empire, see, above all, Wolfgang Göderle, *Zensus und Ethnizität: Zur Herstel-lung von Wissen über soziale Wirklichkeiten im Habsburgerreich zwischen 1848 und 1910* (Göttingen: Wallstein, 2016).

31. For the guidelines surround dubious cases, see the minutes to the Intergovernmen-tal Committee Nr. 21 (February 3, 1919) pt. 1 in AT-OeStA/AdR BKA Stk/Bka Alt MSL Karton 246.

32. AT-OeStA/AdR Bundesministerium für Finanzen [hereafter BMF] 1. Rep. Präsidium 1919 Z. 73, "Erhebungen bezüglich der nationalen Zugehörigkeit einiger Aushilfsdiener."

33. Brauneder, *Deutsch-Österreich 1918*, 64–68; Hafner, "Der sozio-ökonomische Wandel," 234.

34. Hafner, "Der sozio-ökonomische Wandel," 235.

35. This is just a short list of cases that fill the files of the finance ministry. These cases can be found in OeStA-AdR, BMF 1. Rep. Präsidium 1919 Z. 73.

36. Sojovic's declaration is in BMF 1. Rep. Präsidium 1919 Z. 1216.

37. The case of Kokesch/Kokeš is reconstructed from the following files: AT-OeSta/AdR BMF 1. Rep. Präsidium Z. 244, 664, and 1131.

38. Z. 3388 ex 1919/VwGH, likewise in Z. 244, AT-OeStA/AdR BMF 1. Rep. Präsidium 1919.

39. Kokesch/Kokeš's letter, dated July 1, 1919, is in AT-OeStA/Adr BMF (1. Rep.) Präsidium 1919 Z. 1131.

40. See the draft of the letter from the D.ö. Staatsamt für Finanzen to Johann Kokesch, dated August 8, 1919, in AT-OeStA/Adr BMF 1. Rep. Präsidium Z. 1131.

# Bibliography

Brauneder, Wilhelm. *Deutsch-Österreich 1918: Die Republik entsteht.* Vienna: Amalthea, 2000.

Brubaker, Rogers. *Nationalism Reframed: Nationhood and the National Question in the New Europe.* Cambridge: Cambridge University Press, 1996.

———. "Nationalizing States in the Old 'New Europe'—and the New." *Ethnic and Racial Studies* 19, no. 2 (1996): 411–37.

Djokić, Dejan. *Elusive Compromise: A History of Interwar Yugoslavia.* New York: Columbia University Press, 2007.

Gerwarth, Robert, and John Horne, eds. *War in Peace: Paramilitary Violence in Europe after the Great War.* Oxford: Oxford University Press, 2012.

Göderle, Wolfgang. *Zensus und Ethnizität: Zur Herstellung von Wissen über soziale Wirklichkeiten im Habsburgerreich zwischen 1848 und 1910.* Göttingen: Wallstein Verlag, 2016.

Goldinger, Walter, and Dieter A. Binder. *Geschichte der Republik Österreich 1918–1938.* Vienna: Verlag für Geschichte und Politik, 1992.

Graham, Malbone W. *New Governments of Central Europe.* American Political Science Series. New York: Henry Holt, 1924; reprint, Fite Press, 2007.

Hafner, Herta. "Der sozio-ökonomische Wandel der österreichischen Staatsangestellten." PhD diss., University of Vienna, 1990.

Heindl, Waltraud. *Josephinische Mandarine: Bürokratie und Beamte in Österreich. Bd. 2, 1848–1914.* Vienna: Böhlau, 2013.

Hirschhausen, Ulrike von. "From Imperial Inclusion to National Exclusion: Citizenship in the Habsburg Monarchy and in Austria 1867–1923." *European Review of History: Revue Européenne d'Histoire* 16, no. 4 (2009): 551–73.

Hoensch, Jörg K. *Geschichte der Tschechoslowakei.* 3rd ed. Stuttgart: Kohlhammer, 1992.

Judson, Pieter M. *Guardians of the Nation: Activists on the Language Frontiers of Imperial Austria.* Cambridge, MA: Harvard University Press, 2006.

———. "'Not Another Square Foot!' German Liberalism and the Rhetoric of National Ownership in Nineteenth-Century Austria." *Austrian History Yearbook* 26 (1995): 83–97.

Kerekes, Lajos. *Von St. Germain bis Genf: Österreich und seine Nachbarn, 1918–1922.* Translated by Johanna Till. Vienna: Herman Böhlaus Nachfolger, 1979.

King, Jeremy. *Budweisers into Czechs and Germans: A Local History of Bohemian Politics, 1848–1948*. Princeton, NJ: Princeton University Press, 2002.

Köfner, Gottfried. "Eine oder wieviele Revolutionen? Das Verhältnis zwischen Staat und Ländern in Deutschösterreich im Oktober und November 1918." *Jahrbuch für Zeitgeschichte* 2 (1979): 131–67.

Megner, Karl. *Beamtenmetropole Wien 1500–1938: Bausteine zu einer Sozialgeschichte vorwiegend im neuzeitlichen Wien*. Vienna: Verlag Österreich, 2010.

Perman, Dagmar. *The Shaping of the Czechoslovak State: Diplomatic History of the Boundaries of Czechoslovakia, 1914–1920*. Studies in East European History 7. Leiden: Brill, 1962.

Ramet, Sabrina P. *The Three Yugoslavias: State-Building and Legitimation, 1918–2005*. Washington, DC: Woodrow Wilson Center Press, 2006.

Stourzh, Gerald. "'Aus der Mappe meines Urgroßvaters': Eine mährische Juristenlaufbahn im 19. Jahrhundert." In *Der Umfang der österreichischen Geschichte: Ausgewählte Studien 1990–2010*, 126–37. Studien zu Politik und Verwaltung 99. Vienna: Böhlau, 2011.

Weitz, Eric D. "From the Vienna to the Paris System: International Politics and the Entangled Histories of Human Rights, Forced Deportations, and Civilizing Missions." *American Historical Review* 113, no. 5 (2008): 1313–43.

Zahra, Tara. "Imagined Noncommunities: National Indifference as a Category of Analysis." *Slavic Review* 69, no. 1 (2010): 93–119.

———. *Kidnapped Souls: National Indifference and the Battle for Children in the Bohemian Lands, 1900–1948*. Ithaca, NY: Cornell University Press, 2008.

JOHN DEAK is Associate Professor of History at the University of Notre Dame. He is author of *Forging a Multinational State: State Making in Imperial Austria from the Enlightenment to the First World War.*

# 7    National Claims and the Rights of Others

## Italy and Its Newly Found Territories after the First World War

Roberta Pergher

### The Claims of Others across Nation and Empire

When the Italians in 1911 invaded the Ottoman provinces of Tripolitania and Cyrenaica in North Africa, they expected quick victory over a failing
empire and easy rule over an acquiescent native population.[1] However, while an
ambiguous peace agreement with the Ottomans ended hostilities between the
two powers, the indigenous population fought on.[2] The Italians were determined
to retain hold of "their" colonies, but once they entered the Great War and had to
concentrate their forces in the struggle against Austria-Hungary, they lost control of all but some enclaves along the coast.[3] By 1918, both the Italians and the
indigenous forces were war-weary and eager to reach a peace accord, though the
two sides' expectations of what the peace terms and future relations might look
like were very different.

True, the year 1917 had already seen a first treaty between the Italians and the
local leadership of Cyrenaica.[4] Brokered by the British, who occupied neighboring Egypt, the Acroma Accord was, however, simply a truce recognizing the status quo: the Italians controlled enclaves along the coast, while the Sanusiyya, a
Muslim political-religious order, dominated the vast majority of the territory.[5]
The situation in Cyrenaica could not satisfy Italy in the longer term, nor were
the Italians willing to put up with developments in Tripolitania, where a faction of local leaders proclaimed a republic in November 1918 and sent a delegation to Paris to defend its legitimacy on the world stage.[6] When talks between
the Italians and the Tripolitanians finally took place in April 1919, the Italians
believed themselves sovereign masters over a colony, while indigenous leaders
approached the negotiating table as representatives of an independent nation.
The latter maintained that "after having waged a bloody war for independence"

against Italy, Tripolitania wanted to be "left to govern itself." Embracing the notion of self-determination, the people of Tripolitania invoked their "natural right" as a people to form their own state. Italy's "colonizing intentions," they averred, were by now an "anachronism" that was "bringing the dead back to life" and "pretending to ignore the natural progress toward new principles unfolding the world over."[7] Clearly, Tripolitanian leaders were aware they were not alone in their anticolonial struggle. Their resolve to secure their political independence was strengthened by the ongoing peace negotiations in Paris and concurrent discussions of colonial emancipation.[8] Even Italian commentators conceded that the political battle that the Tripolitanians were waging was "the logical consequence of a veritable transformation in ideas."[9]

Local resistance to foreign, imperial rule was nothing new; new rather was the international context as well as the language of rights and sense of entitlement that accompanied these challenges. The "veritable transformation in ideas"—of self-determination, colonial emancipation, and minority rights—took the world stage while the war was still raging and became common currency during the Paris peace negotiations where a new world order was to be forged. As the sentiments expressed above indicate, the authority and appeal of such ideas shaped the ways in which native populations conceptualized their political status and justified their demands. They also influenced dominant powers, molding the ways in which they legitimated their rule over diverse populations. The Italians, for instance, in 1919 entered into a remarkable agreement with the people of Tripolitania and Cyrenaica, so marking a new kind of relation between colonizer and colonized.

Against this backcloth, this chapter explores the place of "others" in the Italy that emerged victorious from the world conflict but continued to struggle to cement its place in the new, postwar world order. It discusses Italy's efforts to strengthen hitherto uncertain colonial possessions in Tripolitania and Cyrenaica (which together with the desert colony Fezzan, also wrested from Ottoman control in 1911, make up present-day Libya). But the chapter also looks at how Italy sought to incorporate into the nation the multiethnic territories Italy acquired from the defunct Habsburg Empire in the north—the southern part of Tyrol, including the Trentino and South Tyrol, and the former Austrian Littoral, including parts of the Venezia Giulia, Trieste, and Istria. The peace conference in Paris may have dashed Italian hopes for further colonies, but victory in the Great War did bring new national territories. The Libyans were thus not the only conquered populations with whom the Italians were seeking an understanding in 1919 and beyond. As negotiations were underway with the local leadership in Italy's North African colonies, the Italians were also debating the line to take toward the new, non-Italian subjects at the northern fringes of the nation. In both these areas, Italy's sovereignty felt tenuous. Native populations were pining for independence or at the very least autonomy, often backed by powerful players abroad. Both realms were profoundly affected by a new postwar order that changed the terms of what it meant to be a nation, what it meant to be an empire, and what the place of others could be.

After briefly discussing the approach taken by Italy's liberal governments, the chapter focuses on Fascist efforts to determine what status the others held inside the polity. What rights should they enjoy? Could they be deemed Italian? These questions and the Fascists' answers to them took shape in an international context that prized homogenous nation-states but at the same time promised protection to others—be it national minorities or colonized populations. As Nathaniel Berman has convincingly argued, the stability of the post-Versailles order in fact hinged on two sets of balancing acts, one between national sovereignty, minority rights, and further demands for self-determination, the other between colonial overlordship, the civilizing mission, and the promise of colonial emancipation. From the moment they came to power in 1922, the Fascists faced these contradictory pressures. Unwilling to compromise between ideals that often pulled in different directions, they were constantly at odds with the postwar order. In the first place, they elevated national homogeneity to prime principle, at the expense of minority rights. At the same time, because they believed the national claim to sovereignty was more enduring than the imperial one, they extended the principle of nation onto colonial territories, which of course brought more others into the nation. What would the place of those others be in the enlarged nation? The answer would be a new understanding of national rule and citizenship that, to use Berman's words, "transformed the original meaning of the Versailles principles, at times to the extent of reversal."[10]

## Italy and Its Others under Liberal Rule

Exhausted by a long and costly war against the Central powers, Italy's liberal government responded to the challenges to Italian colonial rule in Tripolitania and Cyrenaica with agreements that were path-breaking with regard to colonial governance. The statutes issued by the Italian state in June 1919 for Tripolitania gave the indigenous population a high degree of self-rule, allowing for an autonomous regional parliament, with officials appointed by the Italian governor from a list of previously elected representatives.[11] Italy thus still retained a strong say in the selection of local leadership. However, the statutes' most remarkable concession pertained to the status of the indigenous population—Arabs, Jews, and other ethnic groups living in Tripolitania. They were all granted Italian citizenship, on par with the Italian metropolitan citizens living in the colony. If they traveled to the Italian mainland, however, they forfeited their political rights. Most remarkably, citizenship did not require the local population to rescind its religious laws. In other words, the statutes permitted a separate jurisprudence from Italian law for matters inscribed in Islamic and Jewish religious code. The new citizens moreover were guaranteed schooling in their native languages, in a manner that would not violate their religious teachings. The statutes further granted the right to bear arms but guaranteed freedom from mandatory military service. They also warranted that all collected taxes would be spent in the colony. Finally, the implementation of the 1919 accords would have placed many local leaders on the Italian payroll—a policy that has been interpreted as an attempt to bribe the country into submission.[12] In October 1919, the same statutes were extended to the colony of Cyrenaica.[13]

It is of course relevant that the Italians entered such agreements out of weakness rather than conviction; in fact, the statutes were hardly implemented and ultimately failed. But such recognition should not blind us to their innovative character. They marked a new type of relationship between colonizer and colonized, in significant ways eroding the classic distinction between the two.[14] The question in fact arises of whether the statutes were some form of "progressive" imperialism, giving indigenous populations rights and local parliaments, thereby corresponding to the mandate system overseen by the League of Nations, which sought to create a more "humane" colonialism that would lend rule over others a new legitimacy.[15] Or were they a form of "proto-national" integration of the colonies into the Italian nation, in that citizenship rights on Libyan territory were the same for Libyans and Italians, thus foreshadowing an expansion of the Italian nation and a new understanding of citizenship based not on ethnic or racial principles of homogeneity (so extolled at the Paris Peace Conference) but on participation in a political community?

Foreign observers read the statutes as a new form of colonial rule, and they did not like what they saw. Both French and British observers were anxious about how their own colonial subjects in nearby Egypt, Tunisia, and Algeria might view the Italian-Libyan agreement and deemed the Italian concessions a serious mistake.[16] Yet the statutes should not have alarmed them. After all, what the Italians set up was similar to a protectorate, which afforded some level of "native sovereignty" over internal affairs while ensuring European control over external ones. Great Britain and France were each overseeing arrangements in Egypt and Morocco that, with the exception of the citizenship provisions, were not all that different.[17] Given that empires by definition allow for a variety of political and administrative arrangements with their subjects, the statutes could be viewed not as pathbreaking but as more of the same.[18] But what the reactions of the British and French also show is how conflicted they themselves were and how much of their own mandate thinking, in the context of the Paris peace treaties, was just lip service precisely to that kind of trusteeship. They wanted to maintain imperial rule, and they saw the Italian-Libyan agreement as undermining it.

It is not easy to ascertain what the Italians were thinking—whether they saw the statutes as a temporary concession, a foretaste of colonial emancipation, or a step toward Libyan inclusion into an expanded Italian nation. This last notion of Libyan incorporation into a greater Italy was in keeping with the myth of a "Roman return" to Africa.[19] The myth of Rome extolled Libya as "a continuation of the native land," not unlike the island of Sicily, which since 1861 was part and parcel of the Italian kingdom.[20] Indeed, by the 1930s, the Italians came to celebrate Libya as a "fourth shore" that complemented the other three shores of the peninsula.[21] But what would such metaphors and understandings of the territory as part of Italy proper portend for the native populations? The 1919 statutes seemed to suggest that the North African people of Tripolitania and Cyrenaica were indeed Italian, warranting their inclusion in the nation on equal terms—or almost, given that their political rights were curtailed once they traveled from the Libyan shore to the Italian mainland.

The statutes not only integrated the population into the nation but also granted a high degree of self-government. In some respect, they seemed to be inspired by the Paris principle of "minority rights," which sought to integrate others into the nation while affording autonomy and protecting language, religion, and custom. Quite a few aspects of the 1919 statutes would indeed have looked appealing to the European peoples who found themselves forcefully annexed to Italy. With the crumbling of Austria-Hungary, Italy was awarded territories it deemed to be genuinely Italian, yet these territories were inhabited not only by Italian speakers but also by German, Slovene, Croat, and Ladin speakers. Some five hundred thousand so-called *allogeni*, "foreign natives," would now reside inside Italy's borders. The concept of the allogeni is itself is a telling construction, as it designates native populations as "foreign" to the nation that forcefully incorporated them. Many of them longed to be part of different states in the making, and their demands were backed these very states. The Kingdom of Serbs, Croats, and Slovenes argued at the Paris Peace Conference that the majority of the people of Istria, Trieste, and Goriška (or what had been the Austrian Littoral under Habsburg rule) were "ethnically" not Italian and decried their incorporation into the Italian nation as an "absurdity."[22] In a similar fashion, the German speakers of the occupied South Tyrol wrote a letter to US president Woodrow Wilson pleading that their homeland not be awarded to Italy. They highlighted their sacrifice in the war against Italy, presented Italian occupation as a "foreign domination," and portrayed their fate as "undeserved" and "unjustifiable." They made a fierce cultural, linguistic, and ethnic argument against their incorporation into the Italian nation, which they claimed was inimical to their soul, tradition, language, blood, custom, and history.[23] A new language of rights and new expectations about popular will and political power emboldened native populations and those speaking on their behalf.

In this case, the allogeni's call for national self-determination remained unheard. As Brendan Karch outlines in chapter 1, the Wilsonian principle was in fact rarely applied in border disputes and never when a victorious nation was involved, as in the case of the Italian-occupied former Habsburg territories. Given the geography of mixed-population areas across central and eastern Europe, it was clear to the peacemakers that "minorities" would have to live inside states dominated by a different national community. While Paris extolled the homogenous nation as the legitimate unit of statehood, the new legal concept of minority rights conceded that not every state would be inhabited by a single nationality. The concession of minority rights became a way to manage situations where national self-determination was not granted and to divert popular expectations into forms that could be contained within different sovereign nations.[24] Tellingly, the various treaties that included such concessions did not recognize minorities as national communities but simply as "groups" with different languages, religions, and customs that deserved protection.[25]

In the case of the non-Italian populations residing inside Italy, however, minority rights were not granted in writing. As a victor nation, Italy did not have to commit to minority rights in the peace agreements with the successor states of the vanquished Habsburg Empire. Nevertheless, King Victor Emmanuel III, Prime Minister Francesco Saverio Nitti, and even an emergent right-wing rabble rouser, Benito Mussolini, promised to respect minority rights in schooling, language, and indigenous traditions, in line with the Paris tenor.[26] They ensured protection of language and customs—in Mussolini's case, for no other reason than to hinder the minority populations from developing irredentist aspirations of their own. Across the Italian political spectrum, however, these assurances sat side by side with a strong desire to Italianize the allogeni and a conviction that eventually they would be persuaded to turn Italian, lured by the nation's great civilization.[27]

As the Libyan statutes demonstrated, the Italian state in fact was not unwilling to make the type of concessions that minority rights could encompass: protection of language, religion, and customs, including instruction in the minority language; autonomous status with local parliaments and local taxation; exemption from mandatory military service; and so forth. But while granting these rights was thinkable for the Italian government in the *colonial* context, such concessions were hard to countenance on *national* territory, governed on the principle of national uniformity. In the annexed regions within the nation, the government gave full citizenship to its new subjects, but it did not give autonomy. True, the Italian government initially created a special division, the *Ufficio speciale per le nuove province* (Special Office for the New Provinces), to coordinate the integration of the new provinces. Italian leaders, however, found it difficult to accept the idea that the newly unified Italy should be diluted or differentiated by the newly acquired minorities. Formally recognizing their special status meant fundamentally altering the self-perception and character of the Italian nation-state. Thus, there was considerable uncertainty as to how much special treatment the new provinces and their inhabitants should be granted, and how far they should be subject to central control and aligned with the other provinces.

From the Italian perspective, the native populations in the annexed northern provinces, who in some areas were in the majority, represented a threat to the legitimacy of Italian sovereignty by dint of their different languages, cultures, and traditions, as well as their demands for self-determination or autonomy. This was all the more true because the Italians claimed to have "redeemed" these territories from foreign rule. Now they found their claim contested not only by the allogeni but also by governments and powerful interest groups across the border. Italian nationalists in general, and the Fascists in particular, thus saw the "redeemed" provinces as places where Italy had to make a stand. As Mussolini explained in 1920, two years before ascending to power, "in these lands the task of the Fascists is more delicate, more sacred, more difficult, more necessary. Here Fascism has its reason for being; here Fascism finds its natural terrain for development."[28] Indeed, "border fascism" (*fascismo di confine*) became a recognized slogan for radical nationalist action against alleged enemies of the nation.[29]

Though Libya was not initially hailed by Mussolini as "natural terrain" for Fascist action, it, too, would become a crucial testbed for new ways to assert Italian rule. In Libya, just as in the northern provinces, Italy's liberal governments failed to resolve the dispute with the non-Italians, in spite of concessions that seemed to the Italians all too generous. Just as in the northern provinces, the indigenous populations of Tripolitania and Cyrenaica pined for independence, in this case resorting to violence to end Italian rule over their homeland. By the late 1920s, the Fascists would find themselves waging a near genocidal campaign against tribal armies once dismissed contemptuously by Mussolini as "a handful of Arabs rebelling in Libya."[30] But in the wake of that bloody war, the Fascists would end up seeking subtler and more lasting means to assert sovereignty, acting, just as in the northern territories, in part with and in part against the grain of the Paris system.

## Italy and Its Others under Fascism

When the Fascists came to power in 1922, they inherited a highly unstable situation in Libya, and in the newly annexed provinces, there was great uncertainty about the integration of the native populations and the implementation of Italian law. In Libya, Mussolini's regime took to the challenge with utmost violence, embroiling itself in a drawn-out military conflict resolved only through the mass incarceration of the civilian population in concentration camps in the early 1930s.[31] In 1927, it reneged on the earlier liberal statutes, and its new administrative arrangement removed equal citizenship and any form of local government. It was a return to the crudest forms of colonial rule. In the annexed provinces, the Fascists chose to assert Italian sovereignty by denying minority rights, carrying out massive centralization, forcing assimilation, and promoting the settlement of Italians from other provinces in order to alter the ethnic makeup.

In both areas, then, the regime turned its back on the rights of others promised by the new world order that emerged from the Paris peace treaties. They denied minority rights to the non-Italian citizens inside the nation and rejected the mandate system's implicit promise to colonial subjects of future independence. While assimilation seemed to be the solution in one realm, differentiation, segregation, and even annihilation was the answer in the other. Yet for all the differences in policies adopted toward colony and annexed territories, there were also strong parallels and connections between them. A 1928 exchange between a German journalist and Mussolini gives us a first sense of how the rights and expectations created by the new postwar principles influenced perceptions regarding both colonized populations and national minorities. The journalist explained that he had just returned from Tripoli, where he observed Arabs enjoying their own schools and the young speaking their native tongue. "Why," he asked Il Duce, "[did] Italy not concede this elemental right to its new citizens in the Alto Adige?"[32] The journalist was referring to the German speakers of South Tyrol (Alto Adige in Italian), who, like their Slovene and Croat counterparts in the annexed provinces farther east, were granted citizenship but denied native language instruction in public schools. In reality, the premise of the question was flawed—or perhaps the interviewer was being disingenuous. The situation in Tripoli was nothing like as rosy as implied. There was hardly any schooling for local children, and although the defeat of the native resistance had secured Italian rule in Tripolitania, war continued in Cyrenaica.[33] But the question is nevertheless illuminating. On the one hand, it betrayed classical imperialist assumptions about hierarchies of entitlement—if the Libyans had been granted the "elemental right" of language use, how much more did the German speakers inside Italy proper deserve protection and autonomy? But on the other, it showed how the postwar concepts of colonial emancipation and minority rights were muddling expectations of the state's claims on and responsibilities toward its subjects.

Aware of an international audience, Mussolini assuaged his interlocutor by noting that there were German schools and German newspapers in South Tyrol. This response was at least as disingenuous as the question. It is true that use of the German language was still permitted in the ecclesiastical schools and that a German-language newspaper directed by the Fascist Party was in circulation, but Mussolini's response hardly painted the situation in the northern borderlands accurately. All public schooling, which the vast majority of children attended, was exclusively in Italian, and most non-Italian cultural and social organizations had been banned. There was a massive denationalization effort underway, underscored by a strong belief in assimilation. The Fascists fully embraced the Paris conception that the nation-state's natural bedrock of legitimacy was the tightly knit linguistic and cultural community. But the corollary for the Fascists was not minority rights for non-Italians but their transformation into Italians or else their removal.

In juxtaposing Arabs in Libya and German speakers in South Tyrol, the journalist conveyed how closely related minority rights and colonial emancipation were in theory. Colonial emancipation promised increasing roles in administration for locals and respect for indigenous ways—this is what the journalist claimed to have observed in Libya (though by 1928, the opposite was true, and the Italians had moved a long way from the 1919 statutes). Minority rights promised similar gains for minorities inside the nation. Granting minority rights could be seen as importing imperial differentiation into the heart of the European nation, though "difference" here was understood not as a form of subjugation but as a right granted to the minority group. It is noteworthy that Mussolini did not challenge the journalist's juxtaposition of colonized and minority populations, and of colonies and annexed provinces. Yet where the journalist saw Arabs and Germans as being treated differently by the Italian state, Mussolini suggested that they had similar rights. As we will see, the Fascist state did indeed move toward eliding the distinction between colonies and annexed provinces, but it did so neither by granting minority rights nor by fostering colonial emancipation. Where then did the allogeni and the Libyans stand in the Fascist imagination and what were their rights in the Fascist polity? Did the Paris principles have any effect on the how the Fascists treated colonized and minorities?

The idea of assimilating the minority was inimical to minority rights, but for individual members of the minority, it meant that they could indeed become Italians. This openness to incorporating the minority implied that there was for the Fascists no innate, and thus insurmountable, difference of character between the majority and the minority. One way of explaining the assimilability of the others was by claiming that the outsiders were not really other but in fact lost Italians. Thus when Mussolini referred to the German speakers of the South Tyrol in a speech to parliament in 1927, he called them Italians who had lost their true identity and needed to find it anew.[34] Similarly, a Fascist senator called the Croat and Slovene speakers of the Venezia Giulia, "degenerate Italians," who over the centuries had turned into Slavs and needed to be restored to their Italian origins.[35]

In these interpretations, a policy of assimilation was justified by a racialized understanding of nationality, whereby an Italian essence was still present in spite of generations of non-Italian language and customs. Hence, the regime continued to strive for transformation, believing that if the older generation proved difficult, the children could definitely be Italianized. This policy of transformation rested of course on Italians' willingness to go to the new provinces and do the work of Italianization—as teachers and administrators but increasingly also as agricultural settlers who were supposed to speed up the Italianization, create a reversal in numbers, and absorb the allogeni around them. But even this "national vanguard" needed to be "made" in some sense. Their regionalist allegiances needed to be overcome, their political leanings controlled and guided, their buccaneer instincts in these newly redeemed territories curbed.[36] In sum, while Mussolini at times paid lip service to the language of minority rights, as he did with the German correspondent, in reality his regime sought to impose national homogeneity. Fully committed to the postwar world's increasingly racial definition of national identity, the Fascists premised an Italian core inside every allogeno and assiduously worked toward their assimilation.

In the colonies of Tripolitania and Cyrenaica, the same option of assimilation was never contemplated. Though the former liberal regime had granted citizenship to the indigenous populations back in 1919, it too had never aspired to turn Libyans into Italians culturally or linguistically, hence the peculiar concession of far-reaching citizenship rights that were territorially constrained to the colony. The Fascists in any case did not accept such compromise; instead, they reimposed clear colonial status on the two territories. Only select Libyans could get partial citizenship, and only by fulfilling a number of prerequisites, including the rejection of Muslim personal statute law, a step that would have alienated them from their communities. Apparently, during the eleven years in which this legislation was in force, only three or four Libyans asked to be granted partial Italian citizenship.[37] Moreover, in the aftermath of quelling the resistance, the Fascists widened the separation between colonizers and colonized in every aspect of life. Deploying the standard repertoire of colonial rule, the Italians murdered and expelled their enemies, expropriate and seized land by ruse and force, and brought in settlers while resorting to a modicum of collaboration with some local elites.

Of course, just as in other European colonies, the lines between colonizer and colonized were never entirely clear-cut and were constantly rethought and redrawn. The Jewish case is instructive here.[38] Following the 1927 administrative overhaul, Libyan Jews, like their Muslim neighbors, no longer enjoyed Italian citizenship, nor were they integrated in the Italian community. But there were those who thought they should be. While exhibiting a striking amount of anti-semitism, colonial administrator Alberto Monastero argued in 1929 that Italy's interests in Libya called for the transformation and assimilation of the Libyan Jews. In his view, the Jews in Tripoli were "16,000 individuals for the most part beggars, filthy, ignorant, spiritually absent."[39] He saw them as very different from Jews in Italy, arguing even that they "were infinitely more distant from us than the Arabs themselves." Despite this dark assessment, Monastero wanted to turn them into Italians. Realizing that assimilation would not ensue automatically, he suggested breaking up the community in order to absorb it more easily. The Italian state had to "shake these people . . . mix them . . . Italianize them." He believed that schooling would turn them into "real and faithful Italians." Their Italianization was to occur "without them noticing it and being able to oppose it" in order to achieve "true and intimate Italianization of mentality, culture, and sentiments." Moreover, Monastero favored extending full Italian citizenship to the Jews of Libya, whose rights, like those of Muslim Libyans, were at that time heavily restricted. Only as citizens would they behave responsibly, Monastero claimed. Whoever refused citizenship, on the other hand, was to be expelled from the colony.

Interesting as Monastero's recommendation was, nothing came of it. There were plenty of Fascists who did not share his views. Unlike on the mainland, where Jews were active in the Fascist movement and served in high government positions, the Fascists would never come to embrace Jewish assimilation in the Libyan colonies.[40] In any case, attitudes were changing on the mainland too. With the passing and subsequent implementation across Italy of the 1938 racial laws targeting Jews, Jewish dissimilation became the norm.[41] After the laws, any kind of discourse of Jewish assimilation became impossible.

As for Muslim Libyans, it is hard to find any regime official suggesting the same kind of wholesale assimilation that Monastero mooted for the Jews. What we find instead is that over the course of the 1930s official rhetoric about respect and appreciation for Muslim customs—in other words, rhetoric that involved honoring difference—grew louder. This stance was in line with the pro-Islamic foreign policy taken on by the regime in an effort to undermine British and French influence in North Africa and the Middle East. But it also dovetailed with the racial laws with which the regime sought to prevent relations between Italians and Africans. After the 1935 invasion of Ethiopia and concerned about the practice of *madamato*—whereby Italian men took African women as domestic helpers and lovers, and sometimes even married them—the regime passed legislation in 1937 prohibiting intermarriage, sexual relations, and cohabitation.[42] The laws targeted the subjects of the newly created Italian East Africa, which combined the longer-standing colonies of Eritrea and Somalia with conquered Ethiopia, and all other "foreigners" belonging to populations with similar traditions and social mores.

It is not clear where this legislation left Libya, where Muslim customs meant that mixed relations were in any case a rarity. But there is no doubt that the general trend was to promote dissimilation also in the case of the populations of Libya. Even so, the boundaries of interaction and segregation continued to be debated. The same year the racial laws for East Africa were passed, for instance, Governor Italo Balbo argued with Mussolini about the strictness of racial separation. Mussolini scolded Balbo for allowing soccer matches between Arab and Italian youth; Balbo retorted that if Libyans and Italians were to fight together, they should also be permitted to play soccer together.[43] A glance at the circumstances around this seemingly trivial exchange between Mussolini and Balbo lets us know that Fascist policy in Libya was no longer merely replaying colonial policy of differentiation and segregation but was seeking a new way to secure Italian control.

In 1934, newly appointed governor Balbo had united the two colonies of Tripolitania and Cyrenaica into one and was overseeing a major territorial reconfiguration. Four years later, Libya's coastal areas would be declared part and parcel of Italy, with four provinces making up the nineteenth region of Italy. Though not without international precedent (the examples of Algeria and Ireland come to mind), this was no longer colonialism as usual. The national incorporation of the Libyan shore went hand in hand with the implementation of a mass settlement program. In 1938, Italian families from across Italy, all in all around sixteen thousand people, were settled in specially constructed agricultural villages.[44] The project foresaw the settlement of one hundred thousand Italians in the course of just five years. The ultimate goal was the relocation of half a million Italians.

What the Libyan reconfiguration shows is that the classical imperial model was no longer working for the Fascists. The native resistance had greatly unsettled the Italians, and they came to believe that the claims of nation would serve them better in securing Italian rule in Libya. This claim of nation was to be ensured by Italian settlers from the peninsula. Maurizio Rava, the Jewish general secretary of Tripolitania, maintained already in 1928 that settlement of the metropolitan population meant "absolute security forever."[45] And with the resistance finally defeated in 1932, Alessandro Lessona, then undersecretary of the Ministry for the Colonies, explained that the "secure possession of our Mediterranean colonies cannot be deemed concluded until we have embedded Italians in a sufficient enough number to constitute a national social unit."[46]

Yet in this annexation project, in contrast to the northern provinces after the Great War, there was no plan for the transformation of the nearly 830,000 native Libyans.[47] They were not be made into Italians, nor were they to be given citizenship. The Libyan children, unlike those in South Tyrol and Istria, were not to be assimilated through schooling. Unlike the young German or Slovene speakers, the Libyan children were "granted" what the former could not be, namely some schooling in their native language (though they had to learn some Italian too). Once again, though, we can see that different ideas circulated of what the "nationalization" of a territory involved and how far inclusion should and could go. In a national examination for teacher posts in Libya, for example, one candidate, Giuseppina Crapanzano, proposed to teach the young Arab children the wonders of Italian civilization and technology, turning them into "little Marconis."[48] While her essay exhibited a contemporaneous sense of superiority and condescension, her zeal in transforming the Libyans went decidedly too far for her examiners. They added a question mark in the margins and underlined in red her suggestion to educate Libyan children to resemble national hero Giuglielmo Marconi, the inventor of the radio. Clearly, Crapanzano, who envisioned her future charges "to be themselves the authors of this sublime invention," had misunderstood what national transformation meant in this context. Resistant as the Fascists were to "raising up" the native population, their pursuit of nation left their own citizens unsure of what this nationalization of the territory actually meant and to what extent Libyans would be included. There was no doubt, however, that the regime was moving toward new and stricter policies of segregation of those deemed unfit to join the national community. Thus Arabs were excluded from the nation, even though by 1939 they lived within its formal boundaries.

In the northern territories, too, the Fascists were departing from the approach to assimilation that had remained part of their nationalization policy during the 1920s and 1930s and were now willing to resort to different measures to assert Italian sovereignty. Twenty years after the annexations, assimilation was in fact far from achieved. If the territory's Italianness was to be secured once and for all, those who did not want to belong, who refused to be assimilated, and who loudly and brazenly proclaimed allegiance to a different nation, had to be silenced. That was all the more pressing if there was a foreign power willing to bolster the allogeni's irredentist claims. The Slovene and Croat speakers in the east had no such power to turn to; by 1937, Yugoslavia had entered into an agreement with Italy and was not going to openly challenge Mussolini. But a more threatening power loomed in the north. Adolf Hitler promised to reunite all Germans into the Reich, and many South Tyroleans increasingly placed their hopes in him.

Because Mussolini ultimately embraced the Paris tenet that there could be no legitimate rule where the nationality of territory and people did not align, he had to find a solution to the South Tyrolean claim to Germanness—especially once Germany, after the 1938 Anschluss, bordered directly on Italy. Mussolini feared losing the province. Yet for all his virulent pan-German stance, Hitler was not willing to risk his alliance with Il Duce in order to annex South Tyrol. The two dictators reached an agreement where the land would stay Italian and the people who felt German would move to the Reich. When put to a vote in 1939, almost 90 percent of the Germans speakers in the region opted to resettle.[49] What that meant for the Italians is that they could now settle the land with "real Italians" who would then "racially absorb" the remaining 10 percent who had decided to stay in their native homeland.[50] With real Italians on the ground, the land itself would become irrevocably Italian, and Italy's claim to sovereignty would be secured.

## Conclusion

Fascism is generally understood as a political force that rocked the liberal postwar order, challenging the very premises of the world system created in Paris after the First World War. Italy did so most obviously with the invasion of Ethiopia in 1935.[51] The assault on a fellow member of the League of Nations made Italy the first major European power blatantly to contravene the new Paris norms of national sovereignty. And the institution of an outrightly and unapologetically racist and exploitative colonialism in East Africa further flouted the principles of the mandate system and the promise of colonial emancipation.[52]

Yet in spite of its willingness to thumb its nose at the League of Nations, Mussolini's Italy did in fact respond to the new interwar principles of sovereignty and national self-determination in important, though not always coherent, ways. The Fascists whole-heartedly embraced the notion that a legitimate and stable nation-state was homogenous in ethnic terms. The eagerness and effort expanded to force the transformation of the allogeni into Italians in the territories annexed from the Habsburg Empire are evidence enough. The Fascists understood that in an era that prized national self-determination a non-Italian majority in these regions undermined Italy's claim to sovereignty.

The Fascists also understood—though this recognition might seem counterintuitive given their persistent talk of empire—that in this new era the national claim was much stronger than the imperial one. Even though the British and French Empires were larger than ever, colonial populations had started to question the imperial system, demanding "self-determination" and "national" autonomy or even independence. The Fascists understood that amid this "veritable transformation in ideas," their hold over Libya would be stronger if a large number of Italians lived there and if the nominal "fourth shore" were to become part and parcel of Italy proper.[53] The Fascist myth of reviving *imperial* Rome thus served to cement Libya as a *national* territory, inhabited and cultivated by Italians. Mussolini's empire talk was persistently suffused with notions of Italian settlement. In Libya, Rome's return would be enacted by Italian reincarnations of Roman legionaries. The conquest of Ethiopia was similarly justified with rhetoric of a Roman rebirth, engendered by industrious Italians. In his speech to the Italian people on May 9, 1936, announcing victory and proclaiming empire, Mussolini asserted that Italy was following the "tradition of Rome" and that "the Italian people" would enrich the empire through their labor.[54] Regime propaganda continually talked of an empire for the Italian people, one of settlement rather than exploitation. Indicatively, the Italians named their consolidated possessions in the Horn of Africa "*Italian* East Africa" and renamed their Ministry for the Colonies "Ministry for *Italian* Africa." By the late 1930s, there was much that pointed toward a vison for Italian East Africa that dovetailed with the national transformation unfolding in Libya.

Yet if the Fascists were children of Paris in prizing the nation even when they pursed their imperial dreams, they were in other respects very much set against the Paris principles. Above all, they felt at odds with its mandate of colonial emancipation and the protection of minorities. Their response to the crisis in sovereignty generated by minority and colonial populations was to provide more muscle, in Libya brutally so, with few concessions to local autonomy. In neither context, however, did the Fascists achieve the cohesive greater Italy to which they aspired. Instead, they found themselves diluting the nation by incorporating others as inferior subjects and not as full citizens.

Libya's place in the evolution of a new approach to the treatment of native populations in the consolidation of contested territory is particularly interesting, as it shifted from colony to administrative region. In January 1939, when the Libyan shoreline was declared a region of Italy comprising four new national provinces, Libyans were granted "Italian-Libyan citizenship."[55] The label of "citizen" was just that, a label; the designation had little to no substance. The Libyans had already been granted that same label with the administrative overhaul in 1927. A ministerial report from 1937 clarified what "Italian-Libyan citizenship" meant: it was "Italian" only insofar as the Libyans were "Italian *subjects*."[56] If the label had not changed, neither did Libyans' status in the Italian polity, where they continued to possess only limited civil liberties and no political rights. After 1939, some select Muslim Libyans could apply for "special Italian-Libyan citizenship," which did not buy them any further civil or political rights but made it possible for them to serve in the administration, hold higher ranks in the military, and participate in the Fascist associations for Arabs.

This dilution of the meaning of citizenship in newly minted national provinces in some respects matched the ways in which citizenship was becoming meaningless across Italy. With the consolidation of the Fascist dictatorship in the mid-1920s, Italians lost their political rights of democratic participation. It was clear from the beginning that the Fascists did not conceive of the nation as a community of citizens with equal formal right to determine the shape of the polity. Political participation did not mean involving the population in decision-making but rather mobilizing the nation behind decisions taken in its name. By the late 1930s, the understanding of nation had become even more segmented, with entire groups excluded from citizenship. Though Italian Jews initially were able to retain their Italian citizenship, they became de facto second-class citizens with the institution of the 1938 racial laws, which targeted them in myriad ways that made their lives in Italy impossible. There were, however, Jews who did lose their citizenship in 1938—namely, those who had received it after 1918, including the Jewish inhabitants of the territories annexed after the First World War, most notably the city of Trieste.[57]

If the idea of nation that Fascist Italy was implementing was thus one that very much veered from the Paris principles of minority rights and colonial emancipation, it also increasingly veered from the homogeneity principle. Italy's citizens were not all equal. By expanding, Italy was incorporating others and introducing them as lesser citizens. At the same time, it was stripping some citizens of their citizenship, like the Jews in the former Habsburg territories. Moreover, "race" became a marker of difference that targeted groups even when citizenship was not revoked, as in the case of all Italian Jews. The exclusion of Jews from the national community in 1938 needs to be seen in this light, as a redefinition of what the nation could be and what it tolerated within its borders.

It is true that all modern nation-states rest on differences of power and status. In the early twentieth century, for example, a constituent element of nation-states was the widespread exclusion of women from political participation. But in formal terms the nation-state's novelty as a political formation was precisely the fundamental equality of citizenship rights. Fascist Italy, however, was introducing the differentiations that we know from empires—of rights and status, of citizenship and subjecthood—into the nation.[58] The elision of nation and empire was very much in evidence in Mussolini's 1936 empire proclamation when he celebrated the "reappearance of the empire on the fated hills of Rome."[59] Mussolini was speaking of the Seven Hills of Rome whence Ancient Rome had set out to conquer the world, and which since 1871 had become the core of the Italian nation. In a speech that blurred the boundaries between nation and empire, Mussolini implicitly articulated the dilemma facing a radical nationalist power that prized homogeneity but wanted to expand—or, in other words, the challenge for aspirational "have-not" powers in the post-Versailles world. The only solid claims now were national ones. But to be a world power you needed to grow and that inevitably meant presiding over others. In an era of national self-determination and in the name of radical nationalism, the Fascists thus imported the differentiations and hierarchies of empire into the heart of the European nation. The result was the inferior citizenship for Libyans, the revoking of citizenship to the Jews of the annexed provinces, and other new forms of inequality and subjecthood created in the name of a greater Italy.

## Notes

1.  On the Italian invasion and the Turkish-Italian war, see Luca Micheletta and Andrea Ungari, eds., *The Libyan War, 1911–1912* (Newcastle upon Tyne: Cambridge Scholars Publications, 2013); Nicola Labanca, *La guerra italiana per la Libia 1911–1931* (Bologna: Il Mulino, 2011); Salvatore Bono, *Tripoli bel suol d'amore. Testimonianze sulla guerra italo-libica* (Rome: Istituto italiano per l'Africa e l'Oriente, 2005); Angelo Del Boca, *Tripoli bel suol d'amore* (Rome: Laterza, 1986); and Sergio Romano, *La quarta sponda. La guerra di Libia 1911–1912* (Milan: Bompiani, 1977). For a history of modern Libya with a particular focus on Italy's colonial rule, see Angelo Del Boca, *Dal fascismo a Gheddafi* (Rome: Laterza, 1988), and Del Boca, *Tripoli bel suol d'amore, 1860–1922*. For a good general overview, see Ali Abdullatif Ahmida, *The Making of Modern Libya: State Formation, Colonization, and Resistance, 1830–1932* (Albany: State University of New York Press, 1994).

2.  The peace of Ouchy of October 1912 ended the military conflict. The Ottomans committed to withdrawing their military officers and administrators, but the sultan retained religious authority over the Muslim population, which from an Islamic viewpoint entailed also secular authority. See John Wright, *A History of Libya* (New York: Columbia University Press, 2010), 118, and Anna Baldinetti, *The Origins of the Libyan Nation: Colonial Legacy, Exile and the Emergence of a New Nation-State* (New York: Routledge, 2010), 40.

3. For a brief but comprehensive overview of Italy's engagement in the colonies during the war, see Richard Bosworth and Giuseppe Finaldi, "The Italian Empire," in *Empires at War: 1911–1923*, ed. Robert Gerwarth and Erez Manela (New York: Oxford University Press, 2014), 34–51.

4. Wright, *History of Libya*, 123–24.

5. The Sanusiyya was a Muslim religious and political order that took on a central role in the anticolonial resistance against the Italian invader. Founded in Mecca in 1837, it relocated several times and eventually established its headquarters in the oasis of Kufra. But in the late 1800s, it expanded from Fez to Damascus and Constantinople and into India; however, the order had arguably its greatest influence in Libya. In Cyrenaica and in the southern parts of Tripolitania, the Sanusiyya became the single most powerful political force, holding almost complete territorial sovereignty. Ali Abdullatif Ahmida has termed the Sanusiyya a "de facto state." See Ali Abdullatif Ahmida, *Forgotten Voices: Power and Agency in Colonial and Postcolonial Libya* (New York: Routledge, 2005). For a different interpretation, arguing that the order positioned itself as more influential locally than it actually was, see Eileen Ryan, "Italy and the Sanusiyya: Negotiating Authority in Colonial Libya, 1911–1931" (PhD diss., Columbia University, 2012).

6. The delegation sent to Paris was not recognized by the Allies, who had already guaranteed the Italians sovereignty over Tripolitania and Cyrenaica.

7. "Note of the Tripolitanian Government regarding the principles and the indispensable foundation for avoiding war and resolving all difficulties in order to initiate a life of peace and friendship with the Italian Government," cited in Ottone Gabelli, *La Tripolitania dalla fine della guerra mondiale all'avvento del fascismo* (Tripoli: Airoldi editore, 1937), 212–13.

8. Gabelli, *Tripolitania dalla fine della guerra mondiale*, 203. Gabelli states that the Arabs were dragging their feet in the negotiations, hoping that the concurrent peace negotiations in Paris would bring some strengthening of their cause in relation to the Italians.

9. Cited in Giambattista Biasutti, "La politica indigena italiana in Libya dall'occupazione al termine del governatorato di Italo Balbo (1911–1940)" (PhD diss., University of Siena, 2004), 117.

10. Nathaniel Berman, *Passion and Ambivalence: Colonialism, Nationalism, and International Law* (Leiden: Brill, 2011), 382.

11. The decree of June 1, 1919, n. 931, approved the norms for Tripolitania.

12. Lisa Anderson, *The State and Social Transformation in Tunisia and Libya, 1830–1980* (Princeton, NJ: Princeton University Press, 1986), 208. A similar interpretation is also put forth in E. E. Evans-Pritchard, *The Sanusi of Cyrenaica* (Oxford: Clarendon Press, 1949).

13. The decree of October 31, 1919, n. 2401, approved the norms for Cyrenaica.

14. Obviously the distinction was never quite as clear-cut, but it mattered greatly for a person's economic, social, and political opportunities.

15. For an argument that views the mandate system as a new form of colonial legitimation rather than simply as a path toward independent statehood, see Susan Pedersen, *The Guardians: The League of Nations and the Crisis of Empire* (New York: Oxford University Press, 2015).

16. Anderson, *State and Social Transformation*, 207.

17. The statutes were on some level comparable to the extension of French full citizenship to the inhabitants of the Quatre Communes in Senegal since 1848 and even more so since 1916, though the statutes did not enable the Libyans to elect officials to the Italian parliament. On French empire and citizenship see Frederick Cooper, *Citizenship*

*between Empire and Nation. Remaking France and French Africa, 1945–1960* (Princeton, NJ: Princeton University Press, 2014).

18. For the British Empires as a "system" comprising different arrangements, see John Darwin, *The Empire Project. The Rise and Fall of the British World-System 1830–1970* (Cambridge: Cambridge University Press, 2009).

19. See, for instance, Massimiliano Munzi, *L'epica del ritorno. Archeologia e politica nella Tripolitania italiana* (Rome: "L'Erma" di Bretschneider, 2001).

20. Giovanni Pascoli, "La grande proletaria si è mossa," *La Tribuna*, November 27, 1911.

21. Gabriele D'Annunzio, "Canzoni delle gesta d'oltremare," in *Merope*, vol. 4 of *Laudi del cielo del mare della terra e degli eroi* (Milan: Fratelli Treves, 1912).

22. "Memoranda Presented to the Peace Conference in Paris, Concerning the Claims of the Kingdom of the Serbians, Croatians and Slovenes" (Paris, 1919).

23. "Memorandum of the South Tyroleans to President Wilson, 11 March 1919," reproduced in Richard Schober, *Die Tiroler Frage auf der Friedenskonferenz von Saint Germain* (Innsbruck: Universitätsverlag Wagner, 1982), 542.

24. Carole Fink, *Defending the Rights of Others: The Great Powers, the Jews, and International Minority Protection, 1878–1938* (Cambridge: Cambridge University Press, 2006), 273.

25. Ibid., xvi.

26. Memo of the prime minister to all ministers, July 26, 1919, n. 48, cited in Andrea Di Michele, *L'italianizzazione imperfetta. L'amministrazione pubblica dell'Alto Adige tra Italia liberale e fascismo* (Alessandria: Edizioni dell'Orso, 2003), 74; Benito Mussolini, "La soluzione 'Tardieu,'" *Il Popolo d'Italia*, no. 147, May 31, 1919, VI, reprinted in *Opera Omnia*, ed. Edoardo Susmel and Duilio Susmel (Florence: La Fenice, 1951–63), 13:162.

27. The exception were a few politicians on the left, among them Leonida Bissolati and Gaetano Salvemini. See Gaetano Salvemini, *Racial Minorities under Fascism in Italy* (Chicago: Women's International League for Peace and Freedom, 1934).

28. Benito Mussolini, "Discorso di Trieste," in *Opera Omnia*, 15:214–23.

29. For a discussion of "border fascism," see Giorgio Mezzalira and Hannes Obermair, eds., *Geschichte und Region/Storia e regione* 20, no. 1 *Faschismus an den Grenzen: Il Fascismo di Confine* (2011).

30. Ibid., 220.

31. On the brutal methods employed in defeating of the Libyan resistance, see Nicola Labanca, ed., *Un nodo. Immagini e documenti sulla repressione coloniale italiana in Libia* (Rome: Piero Lacaita Editore, 2002); Enzo Santarelli, Georgio Rochat, Romain Rainero, and Luigi Goglia, eds., *Omar al-Muktar and the Italian Reconquest of Libya* (London: Darf Publishers, 1986); and Eric Salerno, *Genocidio in Libia* (Milan: SugarCo, 1979). For a Libyan viewpoint see Ahmida, *Forgotten Voices*. Important sources of Libyan memory of the Fascist campaign are the oral histories collected by the Libyan Studies Center in Tripoli. Giorgio Rochat estimated that 100,000 Libyans were deported (see Giorgio Rochat, *Guerre italiane in Libia e in Ethiopia. Studi military 1921–1939* [Treviso: Pagus Edizioni, 1991], 84). Official Italian numbers at the time speak of 79,800 deportees (see Rochat, *Guerre italiane*, 84). Ahmida sets the number of deportees at 110,832 (see Ahmida, *Forgotten Voices*, 42).

32. Benito Mussolini, *Opera Omnia*, 23:135. Summary of the interview given in Rome to the correspondent of the "Tag di Berlino" on April 28, 1928, originally published in *Il Popolo d'Italia*, no. 102, April 29, 1928. The referred to Berlin newspaper was in all likelihood the *Berliner Tageblatt*. The journalist, however, is probably not Emil Ludwig, who

worked for the *Tageblatt* and whose conversations with Mussolini were published in 1932. In the introduction to the publication, Ludwig claims he met Mussolini for the first time in March 1929 (Benito Mussolini, *Mussolinis Gespräche mit Emil Ludwig* [Berlin: P. Zsolnay, 1932]).

33. On schooling of the non-Italian population in Libya, see Francesca Di Pasquale, "'Sentinelle avanzate della patria lontana'. Gli insegnanti in Libia in epoca coloniale (1911–1943)," in *Governare l'Oltremare. Istituzioni, funzionari e società nel colonialismo italiano*, ed. Gianni Dore et al. (Rome: Carocci, 2013), 117-130; Federico Cresti, "Per uno studio delle 'elites' politiche nella Libia indipendente: la formazione scolastica (1912–1942)," *Studi Storici* 41, no. 1 (2000): 121-158; Khalifah El-Bah, "Fascist Colonial Schooling of Libyan Muslim Arab Children (1922-1942): A Political System Analysis" (PhD diss., University of California, Los Angeles, 1985); Leonard Appleton, "The Question of Nationalism and Education in Libya under Italian Rule," *Libyan Studies. Annual Report of the Society for Libyan Studies* 10 (1979): 29-33.

34. Benito Mussolini, "Il discorso dell'Ascensione" in *Opera Omnia*, 22:360-90.

35. Giorgio Bombig, "Le condizioni demografiche della Venezia Giulia e gli allogeni," *Gerarchia* 7, no. 9 (1927): 807-19.

36. Roberta Pergher, *Mussolini's Nation-Empire: Sovereignty and Settlement in Italy's Borderlands, 1922-1943* (Cambridge: Cambridge University Press, 2018).

37. Archivio Storico Diplomatico del Ministero degli Affari Esteri (ASDMAE), Archivio Storico Ministero Africa Italiana V, Materiale recuperato al Nord, busta (b.) 7, fascicolo (f.) Lineamenti generali della nostra azione politica in Libia: Book manuscript, no author, but the last page seems to be signed "Riccardo Astuto."

38. On the Jews of Libya under Fascism, see Maurice M. Roumani, *The Jews of Libya: Coexistence, Persecution, Resettlement* (Brighton: Sussex Academic Press, 2009).

39. ASDMAE, Archivio Storico Ministero Africa Italiana III, b. 36, f. Scuole Libia 1, scuole israelite: letter October 20, 1929.

40. Several hundred Italian Jews participated in the 1922 March of Rome; by the early 1930s, nearly five thousand were in the Fascist Party. Guido Jung was finance minister between 1932 and 1935, and Maurizio Rava was vice governor of Libya (October 1930 to July 1931) and governor of Somalia (1931–34) (Giampiero Carocci, *Storia degli ebrei in Italia. Dall'emancipazione a oggi* [Rome: Newton & Compton Editori, 2005]).

41. See Marcello Flores et al., eds., *Storia della Shoah in Italia. Vicende, memorie, rappresentazioni*, 2 vols. (Turin: Einaudi, 2010); Enzo Collotti, *Il fascismo e gli ebrei. Le leggi razziali in Italia* (Rome: Laterza, 2009); Michele Sarfatti, *The Jews in Mussolini's Italy: From Equality to Persecution* (Madison: University of Wisconsin Press, 2006); Renzo De Felice, *Storia degli ebrei sotto il fascismo* (Turin: Einaudi, 1961).

42. Law (regio decreto-legge) of April 19, 1937, n. 880, published December 30, 1937, n. 2590. On colonial racism, see Giulia Barrera, "Mussolini's Colonial Race Laws and State-Settlers Relations in AOI (1935–41)," *Journal of Modern Italian Studies* 8, no. 3 (2003): 425-43; Gabriele Schneider, *Mussolini in Afrika: die faschistische Rassenpolitik in den italienischen Kolonien, 1936–41* (Cologne: SH-Verlag, 2000); Barbara Sòrgoni, *Parole e corpi: antropologia, discorso giuridico e politiche sessuali interrazziali nella colonia Eritrea: 1890-1941* (Naples: Liguori, 1998).

43. ASDMAE, ASMAI, Gabinetto archivio segreto (GAB), b. 70, f. Problemi della razza (1): Article in the newspaper "Avvenire di Tripoli" on April 11, 1937, n. 88. Minister Lessona wrote a telegram to Balbo on April 16, 1937, saying that Mussolini had read about the championship in the "Avvenire" and demanded such tournaments banned. Balbo answered the following day, on April 17, 1937, defending the championship.

44. On the settlement program specifically, see Federico Cresti, *Non desiderare la terra d'altri. La colonizzazione italiana in Libia* (Rome: Carocci, 2011), and Cresti, *Oasi di Italianità: la Libia della colonizzazione agraria tra fascismo, guerra e indipendenza (1935-1956)* (Turin: Società editrice internazionale, 1996), as well as Claudio Segrè, *Fourth Shore: The Italian Colonization of Libya* (Chicago: University of Chicago Press, 1974).

45. Maurizio Rava, "Demografia e colonizzazione. Esperienze e verità," *L'Oltremare* 2, no. 6 (1928): 214.

46. Alessandro Lessona, "Il popolamento della Libia," *La Rassegna Italiana* (1932), republished in Alessandro Lessona, *Scritti e discorsi coloniali* (Milan: Editoriale Arte e Storia, 1935), 71.

47. Consociazione Turistica Italiana, *Italia Meridionale e Insulare—Libia. Guida breve*, vol. 3 (Milan: 1940), 385.

48. Archivio Centrale dello Stato (ACS), Ministero Africa Italiana (MAI), b. 1892, f. 1: essay no. 23, Giuseppina Crapanzano.

49. For the Italo-German agreement of 1939, known as the Option, see Mauro Scroccaro, *Dall'aquila bicipite alla croce uncinata: l'Italia e le opzioni nelle nuove provincie Trentino, Sudtirolo, Val Canale, 1919-1939* (Trento: Museo storico in Trento, 2000); Rudolf Lill, *Die Option der Südtiroler 1939: Beiträge eines Neustifter Symposions* (Bozen: Athesia, 1991); Klaus Eisterer and Rolf Steininger, eds., *Die Option. Südtirol zwischen Faschismus und Nationalsozialismus* (Innsbruck: Innsbrucker Forschungen zur Zeitgeschichte 5, 1989).

50. Archivio Storico del Commissariato del Governo per la Provincia di Bolzano, 1942 XI, Ente Nazionale per le Tre Venezie: The suggestion of "racial absorption" is from a letter of investors, dated July 22, 1940, proposing a land development scheme in South Tyrol in the aftermath of the 1939 Option agreement.

51. On the reshuffling of diplomatic alliances surrounding the invasion, see G. Bruce Strang, ed., *Collision of Empires: Italy's Invasion of Ethiopia and Its International Impact* (Burlington, VT: Ashgate, 2013). For an interpretation of the Ethiopian war as a prelude to the Second World War, see Aram Mattioli, *Experimentierfeld der Gewalt. Der Abessinienkrieg und seine internationale Bedeutung 1935-1941* (Zurich: Orell Füssli, 2005).

52. Specifically on Italian military conduct during the war and the occupation, see Giulia Brogini Künzi, *Italien und der Abessinienkrieg 1935/36. Kolonialkrieg oder Totaler Krieg?* (Paderborn: Schöningh, 2006); Matteo Dominioni, *Lo sfascio dell'impero. Gli italiani in Etiopia (1936-1941)* (Rome: Laterza, 2008); and Angelo Del Boca, *La guerra di Abissinia 1935-1941* (Milan: Feltrinelli, 1966).

53. For the "veritable transformation in ideas," see note 9.

54. Mussolini, "Proclamazione dell'impero" in *Opera Omnia*, 27:268-69.

55. R.D.L January 9, 1939, n. 70 (G.U. February 3, 1939, n. 28), Aggregazione delle quattro provincie libiche al territorio del Regno d'Italia e concessione ai libici musulmani di una cittadinanza italiana speciale con statuto personale e successorio musulmano.

56. ASDMAE, ASMAI, Affari Politici 1934-55, el. 3, c. 91, f. 291: report by the Direzione Generale Africa settentrionale. My emphasis.

57. See Michele Sarfatti, *Gli ebrei nell'Italia fascista: vicende, identità, persecuzione* (Turin: Einaudi, 2000), 165. On the Jews of Trieste specifically, see Maura Hametz "Foreigners in Their Own City: Italian Fascism and the Dispersal of Trieste's Port Jews," *Jewish Culture and History* 9, nos. 2-3 (2007): 16-32; and Hametz, "Zionism, Emigration, and Antisemitism in Trieste: Central Europe's 'Gateway to Zion,' 1896-1943," *Jewish Social Studies* 13, no. 3 (2007): 103-34.

58. It was this question of internal hierarchies, of the ways in which modern states were differentiating between their subjects, that Hannah Arendt wanted to foreground

in tracing the lineage from colonialism to totalitarianism: the way in which the erosion of notions of human equality migrated from the colonies into the heart of Europe's nation-states. See Hannah Arendt, "Preface to Part Two: Imperialism," in *The Origins of Totalitarianism*, new edition with added prefaces (New York: Harcourt Brace, 1979), xxi. On imperial differentiations, see Ann Laura Stoler, "On Degrees of Imperial Sovereignty," *Public Culture* 18, no. 1 (2006): 125–46.

    59. Mussolini, "Proclamazione dell'impero." in *Opera Omnia* 27:269.

# Bibliography

Ahmida, Ali Abdullatif. *Forgotten Voices: Power and Agency in Colonial and Postcolonial Libya*. New York: Routledge, 2005.

———. *The Making of Modern Libya: State Formation, Colonization, and Resistance, 1830–1932*. Albany: State University of New York Press, 1994.

Anderson, Lisa. *The State and Social Transformation in Tunisia and Libya, 1830–1980*. Princeton, NJ: Princeton University Press, 1986.

Appleton, Leonard. "The Question of Nationalism and Education in Libya under Italian Rule." *Libyan Studies. Annual Report of the Society for Libyan Studies* 10 (1979): 29–33.

Arendt, Hannah. *The Origins of Totalitarianism*. New edition with added prefaces. New York: Harcourt Brace, 1979.

Baldinetti, Anna. *The Origins of the Libyan Nation: Colonial Legacy, Exile and the Emergence of a New Nation-State*. New York: Routledge, 2010.

Barrera, Giulia. "Mussolini's Colonial Race Laws and State-Settlers Relations in AOI (1935–41)." *Journal of Modern Italian Studies* 8, no. 3 (2003): 425–43.

Berman, Nathaniel. *Passion and Ambivalence: Colonialism, Nationalism, and International Law*. Leiden: Brill, 2011.

Biasutti, Giambattista. "La politica indigena italiana in Libia dall'occupazione al termine del governatorato di Italo Balbo (1911–1940)." PhD diss., University of Siena, 2004.

Bombig, Giorgio. "Le condizioni demografiche della Venezia Giulia e gli allogeni." *Gerarchia* 7, no. 9 (1927): 807–19.

Bono, Salvatore. *Tripoli bel suol d'amore. Testimonianze sulla guerra italo-libica*. Rome: Istituto italiano per l'Africa e l'Oriente, 2005.

Bosworth, Richard, and Giuseppe Finaldi. "The Italian Empire." In *Empires at War: 1911–1923*, edited by Robert Gerwarth, and Erez Manela, 34–51. New York: Oxford University Press, 2014.

Brogini Künzi, Giulia. *Italien und der Abessinienkrieg 1935/36. Kolonialkrieg oder Totaler Krieg?* Paderborn: Schöningh, 2006.

Carocci, Giampiero. *Storia degli ebrei in Italia. Dall'emancipazione a oggi*. Rome: Newton & Compton Editori, 2005.

Collotti, Enzo. *Il fascismo e gli ebrei. Le leggi razziali in Italia*. Rome: Laterza, 2009.

Consociazione Turistica Italiana, *Italia Meridionale e Insulare—Libia. Guida breve*. Vol. 3 Milan: Consociazione Turistica Italiana, 1940.

Cooper, Frederick. *Citizenship between Empire and Nation. Remaking France and French Africa, 1945–1960*. Princeton, NJ: Princeton University Press, 2014.

Cresti, Federico. *Non desiderare la terra d'altri. La colonizzazione italiana in Libia*. Rome: Carocci, 2011.

———. *Oasi di Italianità: la Libia della colonizzazione agraria tra fascismo, guerra e indipendenza (1935–1956)*. Turin: Società editrice internazionale, 1996.

———. "Per uno studio delle 'elites' politiche nella Libia indipendente: la formazione scolastica (1912–1942)." *Studi Storici* 41, no. 1 (2000): 121–58.

D'Annunzio, Gabriele. "Canzoni delle gesta d'oltremare." In *Merope*, vol. 4 of *Laudi del cielo del mare della terra e degli eroi*. Milan: Fratelli Treves, 1912.

Darwin, John. *The Empire Project. The Rise and Fall of the British World-System 1830–1970*. Cambridge: Cambridge University Press, 2009.

De Felice, Renzo. *Storia degli ebrei sotto il fascismo*. Turin: Einaudi, 1961.

Del Boca, Angelo. *Dal fascismo a Gheddafi*. Rome: Laterza, 1988.

———. *La guerra di Abissinia 1935–1941*. Milano: Feltrinelli, 1966.

———. *Tripoli bel suol d'amore, 1860–1922*. Rome: Laterza, 1986.

Di Michele, Andrea. *L'italianizzazione imperfetta. L'amministrazione pubblica dell'Alto Adige tra Italia liberale e fascismo*. Alessandria: Edizioni dell'Orso, 2003.

Di Pasquale, Francesca. "'Sentinelle avanzate della patria lontana.' Gli insegnanti in Libia in epoca coloniale (1911–1943)." In *Governare l'Oltremare. Istituzioni, funzionari e società nel colonialismo italiano*, edited by Gianni Dore, Chiara Giorgi, Antonio Morone, and Massimo Zaccaria, 117–130. Rome: Carocci, 2013.

Dominioni, Matteo. *Lo sfascio dell'impero. Gli italiani in Etiopia (1936–1941)*. Rome: Laterza, 2008.

Eisterer, Klaus, and Rolf Steininger, eds. Die Option. *Südtirol zwischen Faschismus und Nationalsozialismus*. Innsbruck: Innsbrucker Forschungen zur Zeitgeschichte 5, 1989.

El-Bah, Khalifah. "Fascist Colonial Schooling of Libyan Muslim Arab Children (1922–1942): A Political System Analysis." PhD diss., University of California, Los Angeles, 1985.

Fink, Carole. *Defending the Rights of Others: The Great Powers, the Jews, and International Minority Protection, 1878–1938*. Cambridge: Cambridge University Press, 2006.

Flores, Marcello, Simon Levis-Sullam, Marie-Anne Matard-Bonucci, and Enzo Traverso, eds. *Storia della Shoah in Italia. Vicende, memorie, rappresentazioni*. 2 vols. Turin: Einaudi, 2010.

Gabelli, Ottone. *La Tripolitania dalla fine della guerra mondiale all'avvento del fascismo*. Tripoli: Airoldi editore, 1937.

Hametz, Maura. "Foreigners in Their Own City: Italian Fascism and the Dispersal of Trieste's Port Jews." *Jewish Culture and History* 9, nos. 2–3 (2007): 16–32.

———. "Zionism, Emigration, and Antisemitism in Trieste: Central Europe's 'Gateway to Zion,' 1896–1943." *Jewish Social Studies* 13, no. 3 (2007): 103–34.

Labanca, Nicola. *La guerra italiana per la Libia 1911–1931*. Bologna: Il Mulino, 2011.

———, ed. *Un nodo. Immagini e documenti sulla repressione coloniale italiana in Libia*. Rome: Piero Lacaita Editore, 2002.

Lessona, Alessandro. "Il popolamento della Libia." In *Scritti e discorsi coloniali*, 69–80. Milan: Editoriale Arte e Storia, 1935.

Lill, Rudolf. *Die Option der Südtiroler 1939: Beiträge eines Neustifter Symposions*. Bozen: Athesia, 1991.

Mattioli, Aram. *Experimentierfeld der Gewalt. Der Abessinienkrieg und seine internationale Bedeutung 1935–1941*. Zurich: Orell Füssli, 2005.

"Memoranda Presented to the Peace Conference in Paris, Concerning the Claims of the Kingdom of the Serbians, Croatians and Slovenes." Paris, 1919.

Mezzalira, Giorgio, and Hannes Obermair, eds. *Geschichte und Region/Storia e regione* 20, no. 1 *Faschismus an den Grenzen: Il Fascismo di Confine* (2011).

Micheletta, Luca, and Andrea Ungari, eds. *The Libyan War, 1911–1912*. Newcastle upon Tyne: Cambridge Scholars Publications, 2013.

Munzi, Massimiliano. *L'epica del ritorno. Archeologia e politica nella Tripolitania italiana*. Rome: "L'Erma" di Bretschneider, 2001.

Mussolini, Benito. *Mussolinis Gespräche mit Emil Ludwig*. Berlin: P. Zsolnay, 1932.

———. *Opera Omnia*. 36 vols. Edited by Edoardo and Duilio Susmel. Florence: La Fenice, 1951–63.

Pedersen, Susan. *The Guardians: The League of Nations and the Crisis of Empire*. New York: Oxford University Press, 2015.

Pergher, Roberta. *Mussolini's Nation-Empire: Sovereignty and Settlement in Italy's Borderlands, 1922–1943*. Cambridge: Cambridge University Press, 2018.

Rava, Maurizio. "Demografia e colonizzazione. Esperienze e verità." *L'Oltremare* 2, no. 6 (1928): 213–216.

Rochat, Giorgio. *Guerre italiane in Libia e in Ethiopia. Studi military 1921–1939*. Treviso: Pagus Edizioni, 1991.

Romano, Sergio. *La quarta sponda. La guerra di Libia 1911–1912*. Milan: Bompiani, 1977.

Roumani, Maurice M. *The Jews of Libya: Coexistence, Persecution, Resettlement*. Brighton: Sussex Academic Press, 2009.

Ryan, Eileen. "Italy and the Sanusiyya: Negotiating Authority in Colonial Libya, 1911–1931." PhD diss., Columbia University, 2012.

Salerno, Eric. *Genocidio in Libia*. Milan: SugarCo, 1979.

Salvemini, Gaetano. *Racial Minorities under Fascism in Italy*. Chicago: Women's International League for Peace and Freedom, 1934.

Santarelli, Enzo, Georgio Rochat, Romain Rainero, and Luigi Goglia, eds. *Omar al-Muktar and the Italian Reconquest of Libya*. London: Darf Publishers, 1986.

Sarfatti, Michele. *The Jews in Mussolini's Italy: From Equality to Persecution*. Madison: University of Wisconsin Press, 2006.

Schneider, Gabriele. *Mussolini in Afrika: die faschistische Rassenpolitik in den italienischen Kolonien, 1936–41*. Cologne: SH-Verlag, 2000.

Schober, Richard. *Die Tiroler Frage auf der Friedenskonferenz von Saint Germain*. Innsbruck: Universitätsverlag Wagner, 1982.

Scroccaro, Mauro. *Dall'aquila bicipite alla croce uncinata: l'Italia e le opzioni nelle nuove provincie Trentino, Sudtirolo, Val Canale, 1919–1939*. Trento: Museo storico in Trento, 2000.

Segrè, Claudio. *Fourth Shore: The Italian Colonization of Libya*. Chicago: University of Chicago Press, 1974.

Sòrgoni, Barbara. *Parole e corpi: antropologia, discorso giuridico e politiche sessuali interraziali nella colonia Eritrea: 1890–1941*. Naples: Liguori, 1998.

Stoler, Ann Laura. "On Degrees of Imperial Sovereignty." *Public Culture* 18, no. 1 (2006): 125–46.

Strang, G. Bruce, ed. *Collision of Empires: Italy's Invasion of Ethiopia and Its International Impact*. Burlington, VT: Ashgate, 2013.

Wright, John. *A History of Libya*. New York: Columbia University Press, 2010.

ROBERTA PERGHER is Associate Professor of History at Indiana University, Bloomington. She is author of *Mussolini's Nation-Empire: Sovereignty and Settlement in Italy's Borderlands, 1922–1943*.

# 8 Between Race, Nation, and Empire

## Tensions of (Inter)-Nationalism in the Early Interwar Period, 1919–23

Caio Simões de Araújo

### Unhindered, Unthreatened, Unafraid

On January 22, 1917, Woodrow Wilson addressed the US Senate with his plan for peace. As an antidote to the causes of war, he hailed the equality of nations and rights as the guiding principle of a future world order. Only cooperation between nations—embodied in an envisioned "League for Peace"—would hinder divisive politics and secure the permanent settlement of the "vexed questions of territory or racial and national allegiance." To Wilson, this institutional reform of international relations was not the only concern raised by the war, however. Noting that governments derive their "just powers" from the "consent of the governed," the president concluded that a necessary condition for future peace was that every people be "left free to determine its own polity, its own way of development, unhindered, unthreatened, unafraid."[1] These words encapsulate the principles most commonly associated with Wilsonian liberal internationalism: the equality of nations under international law, the institutionalization of world politics, and people's rights to self-determination (mostly understood as democratic self-government and popular legitimacy).[2] A few months later, in April, the United States entered the First World War, claiming to fight in defense of freedom.

Inspired by Wilson's address to the Senate, in the same year a diverse group of scholars, journalists, and politicians met under the auspices of the American Academy of Political and Social Science to debate the role of the United States in the conflict and the prospects of "coming peace." From democracy to the use of force, from international justice to territorial questions, myriad issues were discussed, which all seemed to converge on the need for a new theory and politics of "sovereignty." Theodore Marburg, a former US diplomat in Belgium, pointed out that "sovereignty unimpaired leads to disaster." Instead, he advocated a society of nations in which sovereignty would be strongly determined by the state's ability to promote "the welfare of men organized (within them)."[3] With regard to the problem of "race conflict," Marburg deemed the solution to lie in the equality of rights and liberties to be enjoyed by "all white men in white men's countries."[4] But as Simon Nelson Patten of the University of Pennsylvania pointed out, the search for a new international code of conduct based on democracy and home rule raised the question of how sporadic violations were to be identified and intervened on. After all, he remarked, if lynching in the American South was obviously a "serious evil," it was still "less than the evils its suppression would impose."[5] A league to enforce peace would ultimately have to face the thorny question of how to protect international standards without disturbing home rule.

If these remarks sound unsettling to our contemporary ear, they expose perhaps the most remarkable shortcoming of the Wilsonian imagination: the question of racial equality. While for Marburg the equality of rights and liberties were restricted to the white man in white men's countries, for Patten the welfare and civic rights of African Americans could be sacrificed in the name of public order and international stability. I do not suggest that these were arguments Wilson supported, although his record on race relations was at best conservative and at worst complicit in racial inequality and even supportive of segregation.[6] Rather, I am engaging these texts to illustrate the both emancipatory and exclusionary potential underlying much political thought and practice on the eve of the armistice and in following years.

To contemporary observers, the Great War had exposed with violent clarity the human costs of power politics, economic and geopolitical expansionism, unrestrained state sovereignty, and autocratic rule, including some forms of imperial dominance. The Wilsonian vision for postwar reconstruction was perhaps the most influential in elaborating these concerns in a coherent diagnosis, as well as the most consequential in translating them into a practicable political project. Yet the immediate aftermath of the war saw a proliferation of debates over the terms in which the tenets of equality, self-determination, sovereignty, and internationalism were to be understood and put in motion. Wilsonian political idealism and philanthropic concerns over the welfare of colonial peoples coexisted with an imperial order, while various forms of discrimination persisted in government and public policy, including in independent nations such as the United States.[7] The concerns raised by both Marburg and Patten, therefore, point to a critical problem at the time: that of defining the new boundaries of political subjectivity or, to put it differently, the question of "who" was allowed entry into the postwar world order as a subject with rights and, as a consequence, who was not. The fractures, contradictions, and silences of this early postwar moment are embodied in a formally simple, yet politically convoluted question: "self-determination to whom?"[8]

In this chapter, I argue that the question of racial equality was a crucial part of this conundrum. Not only was the Wilsonian vision profoundly wedded to racial and civilizational hierarchies, but the peace resulting from Versailles was fundamentally constituted by—and constitutive of—a global color line.[9] The active silencing of racial equality as a valid principle at the Paris Peace Conference in

1919 was symptomatic of the exclusionary biases and political limitations under-lying the dominant strand of Anglo-American internationalism that most decid-edly came to shape the Versailles system and its most remarkable innovation, the League of Nations. That racial equality was left out of the peace settlement—an outcome Wilson had a decisive role in bringing about—did not mean the cause was lost, however.[10] Indeed, by the time the victorious powers convened, repre-sentatives of the colored cause and the champions of racial equality sought to promote their own internationalist vision of a postwar future, *both* along Wilso-nian lines and in opposition to them.[11] Perhaps the most prominent of these per-sonalities was the African American intellectual W. E. B. Du Bois, who made his way to Paris as a leading figure in the Pan-African Congress to be held at the end of February. Through his activism in Paris, in the press, or even through his par-allel diplomacy, Du Bois attempted to influence the outcomes of the negotiations while defending the black cause as a global issue.[12]

What Du Bois and other colored intellectuals teach us is that "Paris 1919" as a space-time of political articulation was much vaster than the immaculate corri-dors of "Versailles." Of course, I use both terms metaphorically, to refer to com-peting political projects and visions rather than to physical spaces. While the Royal Palace of Versailles hosted major ceremonial activities such as the sign-ing of the peace treaty that carried its name, most of the peace conference took place in Paris, in private chambers and hotel rooms or in the "Salon de la Paix" of the French Ministry of Foreign Affairs, in the Quai d'Orsay.[13] Likewise, for a few months in 1919 Paris was much vaster than itself, for the presence of innumerable actors and pressure groups—including but not limited to colored intellectuals—connected, with varying degrees of success and persuasion, the high politics of peace negotiations to the struggles being staged elsewhere, from the United States to the colonial world. In this chapter, I use Versailles as a metaphor for the dominant form of internationalism being discussed by the great powers and leading to the Versailles Treaty and, eventually, to what is commonly known as Paris system. To this, I contend, we must oppose the various other internation-alist agendas circulating at the time, many of which sent their spokespersons or representatives to Paris in early 1919. I draw this distinction to stress that the peace treaty and the international architecture it established for the postwar era involved a gesture of political closure and did not necessarily translate the plu-rality of projects and aspirations voiced in Paris in 1919. As it will become clear bellow, with all its limitations and challenges, the internationalist imaginings ad-vocated by Du Bois and other people of color were particularly powerful projects that were ultimately excluded from postwar world politics and its diplomatic cul-tures. Yet even if demands for racial equality were shut down in Versailles, else-where the struggle was not over. Indeed, the tensions between competing strands of (inter)-nationalism—and, perhaps more importantly, within particular inter-nationalist projects—remained a distinctive feature of this era.

At the time of the armistice, Du Bois had been championing racial equality in the United States for several decades. His internationalist engagement with the world of Paris in 1919 and the new forms of global politics it inspired is representative of the ways in which "racial affiliation" beyond state borders was becoming an increasingly powerful political language—on both sides of the struggle for racial equality. Yet even though historical actors like Du Bois in the Americas, Europe, and Africa at times emphasized an active politics of transnational solidarity based on shared experiences of "being black," this project was not without its tensions. Rather, the early interwar period saw the emergence and articulation of competing and contrasting visions of black internationalism. These were most notoriously, but not only, those advocated by Du Bois and his nemesis, Marcus Garvey. Here, I use the term *internationalism* broadly to denote a form of political mobilization primarily, but not exclusively, intended as an intervention in the international arena. This mobilization unfolded within and beyond the existing institutional framework, most obviously interstate diplomacy and the League of Nations.[14] Of course, this politics was also transnational in its aim and tactics, "meaning that the perceptions and actions of the actors regularly transcended and crossed existing political boundaries."[15] In this chapter, I trace the problem of race and equality (and racial discrimination) from the defeat of the Japanese proposal for racial equality at the Paris Peace Conference to the mobilization of this idea by black personalities across the Atlantic—from African Americans as well as native elites in the colonial world, with particular emphasis on the Portuguese empire. Revisiting this black internationalist effort in the early interwar years is a fruitful exercise, since it affords us a point of entry into a political positionality that is otherwise displaced or sidestepped in national, imperial, or league-centric histories of the postwar period.

## Paris 1919 beyond Versailles: Racial Equality in a World of Empires

In the winter of 1919, Paris was seething with political effervescence. Politicians, diplomats, philanthropists, intellectuals, and pressure groups were drawn to the French capital, where representatives of the victorious powers convened to deliberate on the terms of the coming peace.[16] Beyond more pragmatic debates over territorial borders, geopolitics, or reparations, the war had also aroused more idealistic concerns over rights and good governance, in both domestic and world politics. In the aftermath of a conflict where Europeans, Africans, and Asians had fought side by side, the question of racial equality assumed epochal importance.[17] For those actors already involved in the struggle against racism and segregation, time seemed ripe for change. In the United States, for instance, the deployment of African American troops on the European front animated debates over discrimination at home.[18] But perhaps no other episode was as consequential to this early interwar diplomacy of race as the rise of Japan, a non-European and nonwhite power, to the club of victors gathering at Versailles. Of course, Japan's engagement with this issue was not new. Tokyo had already raised the problem of discrimination in the diplomatic arena regarding the treatment of Japanese citizens abroad, especially in California.[19] But at Versailles, the place it enjoyed at the negotiation table as a great power afforded Japan the political leverage to push this agenda further.

On February 13, 1919, a proposal submitted by the Japanese delegation to the peace conference requested that a clause securing "the equality of nations" and "the equal and just treatment" of citizens, regardless of race or nationality, be included in the covenant of the future League of Nations. Two months of negotiations followed, but the Japanese proposal was eventually defeated on April 11, 1919. The short-lived, yet complex career of racial equality at Versailles has already been the object of detailed study.[20] It is not my intention here to intervene in or revisit this debate. I raise the Japanese proposal as a point of entry into a moment of both possibility and closure. On the one hand, the fact that racial equality emerged in the negotiations as a political concern at all speaks to a political sensibility that resonated not merely within the Japanese delegation but also among many other actors in domestic and international politics at the time. For these actors, racial affiliation was becoming a fertile ground for political mobilization—within and beyond the framework of the modern nation-state.[21] On the other hand, we cannot overlook that this politics of transnational solidarity based on race coexisted with, and was limited by, national boundaries and the profound association between race and nationality, pervasive in much political thinking in this period. It is not a coincidence, then, that the Japanese proposal was largely discussed by the three main protagonists involved—the United States, the British Empire, and Japan itself—as a problem pertaining to the treatment of immigrants of color *within* nation-states rather than a defense of universal equality. In particular, Australia, as a British Dominion represented by Prime Minister William Hughes, was adamant in its opposition. It saw the equality bill as a clear threat and an affront to its restrictive and racially defined immigration policy.[22] Significantly enough, during the course of the negotiations the semantics of the debate shifted from racial equality as a general principle to the "equality of nations" and just treatment of their nationals within a particular institutional framework: the League of Nations.[23]

But if Paris 1919 embodied a triumphal moment for national self-determination where empires were crumbling (most visibly in central and eastern Europe and in the Middle East, where nation-states, old and new, were being drawn and set up), in the vast regions of the world occupied or administered by the victorious powers, empire was still alive and well. Of course, at Versailles empire was yet another restrictive force that undermined the political potentiality of racial equality as a transformative principle in world politics. The very composition of the British delegation—including one rotating seat assigned to the "white dominions" (and India) as representatives of the British Empire—had a strong impact on how the Japanese proposal was received and debated.[24] The same was true in other "imperial" delegations as well. Yet while it represented an underlying concern against which the issue had to be leveled, empire did not necessarily imply a negative approach to the problem of racial equality or the rejection of it as a legal or philosophical principle.[25] As I have argued elsewhere, to the

Portuguese representatives in Paris the Japanese proposal had little to do with immigration or universal equality.[26] Rather, it raised concerns about colonial administration on the ground, where racial discrimination was an entrenched practice and various forms of interracial collaboration were a necessity, including the thousands of "employees of African race" occupying the ranks of the civil service in Angola and Mozambique. With them in mind, the delegate Norton de Matos defended that "as a colonial nation, we have to face this problem with utter caution."[27] In fact, the general opinion within the delegation was that "such an important issue cannot be solved, from one moment to another, in such a definitive and general way."[28]

Indeed, caution was a dominant position among delegates and observers in Versailles, many of whom showed serious concerns about the future ramifications of having racial equality enthroned as a principle in domestic and international politics.[29] When the Japanese proposal was put up for a vote on April 11, 1919, Wilson's trusted adviser Colonel House passed on a warning to the president, noting that "the trouble is that if [the proposal] should pass, it would surely raise the race issue throughout the world."[30] We do not know if House had a specific case in mind, but his note can be broadly read as an anxious reference to the growing wave of demands for equality and political rights—including self-determination and nondiscrimination—everywhere, from African Americans seeking equal treatment at home to elites of color in the colonial world fighting for equality or, often, the realization of their rights as citizens of the empire. If none of these struggles was completely new, by the time the peace conference convened, these claims had gained momentum, prompted by the spread of Wilsonian ideas of popular legitimacy and self-determination to unexpected places.[31] In Paris itself, a Pan-African congress had convened in late February, bringing together delegates from the Caribbean, the United States, Europe, and Africa under the auspices of some of the most prominent figures in the non-white world, especially W. E. B. Du Bois and Blaise Diagne, a Senegalese deputy to the French parliament.[32] The congress adopted several resolutions intended to be presented to the victorious powers meeting in Paris, including various provisions to safeguard the welfare of "the natives of Africa."[33] The resolutions specifically mentioned the following areas: access to land and education; enjoyment of medical care and sanitary conditions; freedom of culture and religion; total abolition of slavery and forced labor; and the protection of natives' rights to participate in their own government. In addition, the League of Nations was called to supervise the implementation of these directives, as well as to advocate for the rights of "civilized negroes" everywhere.[34] For delegates to the Pan-African Congress, racial equality demanded a social policy of advancement of colored peoples, mostly through education, and the recognition of their political subjectivity and rights, both in the colonial world and the "civilized" West.

The resolutions of the Pan-African Congress suggest that black intellectuals on both sides of the Atlantic, saw 1919 as a moment of great political possibility that needed to be seized. Yet, delegates at Versailles were not ready to adopt racial equality or pan-African recommendations. With the Japanese proposal defeated, the politics of empire, race, and discrimination was neutralized by more philan-thropic concerns over social issues and native welfare. Demands for education, health, and, generally speaking, access to the benefits of "modern civilization" did not make their way into the delegates' agenda as issues of racial equality. Rather, concerns over social conditions in Africa were related to the internation-alization of colonial good governance, especially as expressed in debates of the mandate system advocated by the likes of Jan Smuts of South Africa.[35] Versailles was as much a defense of national sovereignty to those deemed fit to exercise self-determination as it was an extension of imperial control over those colo-nial peoples regarded as too primitive, or not ready, to do the same. The racially coded language of evolution and degrees of civilization was instrumental in de-fining "fitness" to self-government in the aftermath of the war. This is evident, for instance, in the design of the mandate system, which explicitly assigned degrees of political maturity to entire populations based on their assumed stage of social evolution.[36] In those areas where self-determination was denied, a reformed ver-sion of colonialism was offered as the entry ticket into the new world order. De-prived of racial equality, those "primitive peoples" were admitted to the world of the League of Nations, but through the backdoor—that is, as objects of colonial intervention, not as political actors in their own right.[37] As Adam Ewing has ar-gued, the Versailles system instituted a "more refined" form of white supremacy, for it "demarcated a clear line of separation between national citizens with rights and stateless subjects [such as native peoples] deemed unprepared for the exer-cise of those rights."[38]

The rise and fall of the race question in Paris in 1919, within and beyond the spaces of formal diplomacy, is indicative of the limitations and shortcom-ings of the world order that ensued from Versailles. Indeed, as Mark Mazower has argued, the dominant brand of internationalism leading up to the League of Nations ultimately required and strengthened the necessarily exclusionary politics of empire and white (that is, Anglo-American) world leadership.[39] The promises of international equality, national self-determination and popular sov-ereignty, tenets of the Wilsonian vision for a postwar future, were constrained in their scope and application by hierarchies of civilization and race. But as Erez Manela has pointed out, these impediments did not discourage emerging nation-alists in the colonial world to use the Wilsonian language to advance their own agendas, often challenging the association between civilization, sovereignty, and race on the way.[40] This is also true of the black internationalists involved in the pan-African movement and other forms of transatlantic dialogue.[41] In May 1919, Du Bois argued that "a League of Nations is absolutely necessary to the salva-tion of the negro race," for only international collaboration and dialogue between races could prevent future conflict. If the rejection of the Japanese proposal was "deplorable," it should serve as "an argument for and not against a Nation of Nations."[42] Only a few months later, in November, his disillusionment was pat-ent: "the proposed League is not the best conceivable—indeed, in some respects it is the worst. . . . Nevertheless, . . . let us have the League with all its autocracy and then in the League let us work for democracy of all races and men."[43] These words, expressing a sense of both hope and resentment, anticipated what was yet to come.

## "Black Gentlemen" Rising: Black Internationalism in a World of Borders

Before the start of the peace conference, Du Bois attempted to influence the American position in the negotiations by presenting to Secretary of State Robert Lansing a "memorandum on the future of Africa." Du Bois opened his case deploring old practices of colonial governance that disregarded "the welfare of the inhabitants" and allowed "unspeakable atrocities [to be] committed against natives," particularly as had recently been witnessed, before and during the war, in the German colonies. Yet, he recognized, sovereignty was not a viable solution to the colonial world, as "the principle of self-determination could not be wholly applied to semi-civilized peoples." In light of this impasse, Du Bois advocated the internationalization of Africa. Placed under the supervision of an international commission, the new government would promote the principles of civilization, modern culture, social reform, philanthropy, and respect for natives' rights and institutions. If this proposal reads remarkably congruent with dominant debates on colonial affairs circulating at the time, the twist introduced by Du Bois was that this move to internationalize Africa should be carried out in close collaboration with a geographically scattered yet tightly related group: the "educated classes" and "civilized" elements among "the Negroes" from the United States to the West Indies and colonial Africa.[44] Only then, he contended, would it be possible to "reconstruct Africa in accordance to the wishes of the Negro race."[45]

Du Bois's vision for a postwar future is telling of how the language of popular sovereignty, self-determination, and civilization could be appropriated in defense of a black internationalist project envisioning both the advancement of colonial peoples in Africa and the protection of equal rights to the African diaspora in the West. The Pan-African Congress of 1919 was yet another expression of this transnational politics of race, as it advanced a reformist agenda to colonial governance while demanding equal treatment "wherever persons of African descent are civilized."[46] Quite obviously, this platform tacitly dismissed the political subjectivity of the "uncivilized." Indeed, in the early interwar years, black internationalist politics was a game of "educated elites," or "black gentlemen," as described by Ed Junod.[47] Prominent figures, from intellectuals to politicians, defended racial equality in the name of the entire "negro world," yet most admitted that the colonial masses were not "ready" to exercise modern political rights, but needed to be "uplifted" through social policy, especially education. In Paris in 1919, black internationalists were not completely opposed to the imperial order but hoped to have a greater voice in defining the guiding principles of colonial reform, as well as greater access to the League of Nations as an international platform on which to push their agenda. The Versailles settlement dashed these aspirations. The internationalization of Africa it produced operated largely within the constraints of the dominant imperial system, neither allowing nor inviting the contribution of black internationalists. As Du Bois himself noted in disappointment, "in its present form [the league] is oligarchic, reactionary, restricted and conservative, and it gives Imperialism . . . unwarranted preponderance."[48] Du Bois's words convey a sense of frustration with the constitution of the league as an "imperialists' club."[49] Of course, the initial exclusion did not prevent these "black gentlemen" from confronting the organization in the following years.

In the early interwar period, black individuals and organizations had regarded the league as a promising political platform. The Permanent Mandate Commission was particularly appealing to black internationalist politics. It embodied the principles of "benign tutelage," or the "sacred trust of civilization," as established in Article 22 of the League's Covenant. As Veronique Dimier has argued, while the idea of mandate dictated that European rule should seek the well-being of native populations through social policy rather than the (economic) needs of the colonial powers, it also put in place, and generalized, indirect rule as a "democratic" form of colonial government. It was predicated on the idea of the devolution of authority to legitimate African leaders.[50] Arguably, it was this articulation of social reformism and political enfranchisement that made the framework of the league in general and of the Mandate Commission in particular appear so promising to various colored organizations.[51] Moreover, as René Claparéde of the Bureau International pour la Défense des Indigénes told Du Bois in 1921, the mandate system was creating standards of moral governance that could later serve to propel states everywhere, not only on mandated territories.[52] The commission allowed petitioners to voice their concerns and criticism of current policy through petitions, and to develop their internationalist visions and aspirations for colonial Africa, the epicenter of the "Negro world."[53] Indeed, successive Pan-African Congresses attempted to influence and exploit the league as a political space. In 1921, three demands were taken to Geneva on behalf of the congress held in London, Brussels, and Paris: that a section be created in the International Labour Office (ILO) to deal specifically with issues of "native negro labor"; that "a man of negro descent" be appointed to the Mandate Commission as soon as there was a vacancy; that the status of "civilized people of Negro descent" be considered more carefully, as the existence of discriminatory "laws and conventions" resulted in a "feeling of resentment, personal insult, and despair . . . among those very persons whose rise is the hope of the Negro race."[54] The resolutions also entreated the league to sponsor "an International Institute for the study of the Negro Problem, and for the evolution and protection of the Negro race."[55] The 1923 congress, held in London and Lisbon, demanded that blacks have a voice in government as well as access to land, education, and equal treatment before the law. The resolution once more requested that "a representative of the negro race" be appointed to the ILO and the Mandate Commission and that the league establish direct representation in the mandated territories so it could better investigate and report on local conditions.[56] Of course, black internationalists like Du Bois knew that Geneva had "little if any direct power" to address many of these demands. Yet they attempted to explore the league as a "vast moral power" or an international forum from which they could publicize their views and hopefully influence public opinion.[57]

In the early 1920s, attempts to engage with the league exposed profound fractures within black internationalism. Arguably the most critical point of contention was that between Du Bois's pan-Africanism and Marcus Garvey's (in)famous claim of "Africa to Africans." I cannot possibly do justice here to the complex history of how Garvey created a mass movement with ramifications on both sides of the Atlantic, nor can I explore all the points of controversy, dissonance, and rivalry between his version of diasporic politics and that promoted by the likes of Du Bois.[58] However, I bring up Garveyism here as an important counterpoint, not only in terms of political principles, but also regarding proposed policies and tactics. As other black personalities, Garvey was an obstinate critic of race relations in the United States. But his solution to this problem was predicated on the conflagration of race, territorial sovereignty, and nationality. If the United States was a "white man's country" where the black minority was violently discriminated against, then the members of the "negro race" in the diaspora, seen as representatives of a black nationality, should organize in an independent African state. In July 1922, Garvey's Universal Negro Improvement Association (UNIA), alongside the African Communities League, presented a petition to the League of Nations requesting that South Africa's mandate, Southwest Africa, be returned to the "black race," allowing its members to "live peaceably under the protection of their own racial government." Recalling the vital service rendered by black troops in the Great War, the petitioners noted that, at the peace conference, "no consideration has been given [to] us as a people." Now was the time to redress this problem. The petitioners, describing themselves as "negroes of the Western world," were "willing to place at the disposal of our brothers in Africa the culture and civilization . . . we have acquired."[59] The petition was not considered, as it failed to comply with the procedural norms and the substantive rules of the league.[60]

In the "return to Africa" ideal, internationalist claims are made in the name of a form of self-determination where race and nation overlap. But as the 1922 petition to the league goes to show, as a political project of global aspirations Garveyism also involved a colonizing and civilizing ethos. One of its ramifications was the rejection of European presence on the "black continent" altogether, as expressed in the slogan "Africa for the Africans." Garveyism became popular in the United States and abroad, where it prompted a wave of anticolonial sentiment, real and imagined.[61] To white elites in the United States, Europe, and the colonial world, it was perceived as much more radical and politically dangerous than Du Bois's proposals of cooperation within the established international order, so much so that those invested in the Pan-African Congresses on various occasions felt the need to stress their complete dissociation from it.[62] On June 23, 1921, Du Bois wrote to US secretary of state Charles E. Hughes to clarify that the congresses had "nothing to do with the so-called Garvey movement" but, in fact, "have had the cordial cooperation of the French, the Belgian, and the Portuguese governments and hope to get the attention and sympathy of all colonial powers."[63] The same was true on the other side. In 1921, for instance, Garvey asked the league to disregard the demands of the Pan-African Congress on the grounds that the latter did not represent the "masses of the negroes."[64] He also accused "Du Bois and his associates" of exploiting the congresses to their "own personal satisfaction" by promoting a dangerous policy of "social contact, comradeship and companionship with the white race."[65] Garvey was also critical of the presence of "white folk," often government or colonial officials, as spokesmen at the Pan-African Congresses. "It reminds me," he told his supporters, "of the conference of rats endeavoring to legislate against the cats and the secretary of the rats convention invites the cat to preside over the convention."[66]

The internationalism put forward by blacks in the Americas was not received with discomfort only by white colonial elites. The black or creole elites of the empire—be they French, Belgian, or Portuguese—could also be suspicious of their transatlantic brothers. The Pan-African Congress of 1921 displayed such tensions. For instance, as Paul Panda of the Union Congolaise [Congolese Union] told Du Bois, in Brussels a "hostile warfare was being waged against [the Congress]," because many thought "that the goal of our reunion is to start a revolutionary movement among the African colonies." Thus, the confirmation that Garvey would not take part in any shape or form was "welcome to our friends."[67] Likewise, when the Portuguese delegates sent by the Liga Africana [African League] returned to Lisbon, they were met with opposition and slogans like "long live Marcus Garvey!" and "away with fakers!"[68] In the early 1920s, the Partido Nacional Africano [African National Party] based in Lisbon was an important platform for Garveyist ideas in Portugal.[69] There is little indication of similar activities in Angola and Mozambique, and in these cases it is likely that South Africa or Rhodesia served as the centers of this line of thought.[70] Yet, even if some periodic manifestations show how appealing Garveyism was to some actors, in the Portuguese Empire it remained a mostly marginal, or momentary, position. In fact, most of the black organizations formed in Lisbon and in the colonies in the first decades of the twentieth century, such as the Liga Angolana [Angolan League], the Grêmio Africano [African Guild], and the Liga Africana, were "moderate, reformist, and *assimilado* in outlook."[71] This means that they were mostly seeking social reform and political accommodation within the structures of the empire rather than a rupture with them. In Mozambique, for instance, the local African elites writing in the incipient black press persistently denounced a plethora of colonial abuses, including forced labor, the generalized selling of alcohol, the lack of public education, or the exploitation of African women.[72] Yet, the solution to these problems was seldom a complete rupture with the empire. Rather, these elites frequently called for imperial reform and demanded their full recognition as equal citizens of the empire, including a certain level of local autonomy to manage their own "civilizing mission" in the ways they saw fit. To further their case at home, they engaged in dialogue with the colored organizations and their struggles staged elsewhere.[73] Of course, by claiming to act in the name of the social advancement of the "natives" and for the benefit of civilization, colonial elites could work to reinforce the boundaries of their social position, their status and distinction as "civilized" Africans. In that, they could better identify with the reformist views supported by Du Bois and the other "black gentlemen" attending the Pan-African Congresses. For instance, at the 1921 congress, Nicolau dos Santos Pinto defended that to attain "our dream and ambition to make Portuguese Africa . . . a prosperous country," it was necessary to transform the native masses, to "imbue them with a feeling for order, with economic foresight, teach them love of work and give them schools, many schools." If they were to succeed, Pinto noted, Portuguese Africans should unite, get together, "as our brothers have done in North America."[74]

It was indeed in the hope of "rousing the public opinion of the black Portuguese" that Pinto asked Isaac Beton, secretary general of the Pan-African Association, to hold the Third Pan-African Congress in Lisbon.[75] Du Bois suggested the West Indies instead, to ensure the "general participation of American negroes."[76] Financial constraints, however, rendered this suggestion unfeasible. After all, Beton remarked, what the congress needed were not numbers but delegates who were "aware of their duty toward the race, men who once returned to their respective countries will not lose interest entirely in the Pan-African Association."[77] The comment refers to the low numbers of paying members in the association, a problem already raised in earlier correspondence. Du Bois traced the lack of cooperation by black Americans to the ill treatment by French delegates at the earlier congress.[78] Be that as it may, Beton replied, one should "serve the Race according to their means," meaning that the burden to financially support the congress should fall on black Americans first, as a more organized and active community, especially if compared with the dispersed black French community.[79] Insufficient fundraising and lack of financial resources became a devastating problem, especially after the Board of Directors of Du Bois's National Association for the Advancement of Colored People (NAACP) declined to fund the incoming congress and to focus instead on "local American race problems," their primary area of interest.[80] The problem of communication among actors spread across different locations added to the list of challenges to the impending congress, including difficulties in coordinating with black organizations in Lisbon after the sudden death of Nicolau Santos Pinto on June 22, 1922.[81] Europe-based black personalities such as Paul Panda from Belgium and Blaise Diagne and Gratien Candace from France were accused of "strangling a manifestation that could improve the race."[82] Indeed, it was the sentiment that the Pan-African Association had been "strangled at birth" either by the "criminal apathy" of some or by the "despicable hostility" of others, that led to Beton's decision in early August to postpone the Third Congress indefinitely.[83] In the following weeks, Du Bois sent letters to personalities and organizations defending his view that holding the Congress as planned was vital to the pan-African cause. Upon Beton's refusal, Du Bois called the Congress himself as ranking member of the Executive Committee of the Pan-African Association.[84]

The 1923 congress finally took place in London on November 7–8 and in Lisbon on December 1–2. However, the events leading up to it had dented the image of a common cause by crudely exposing deep rifts within black internationalism along imperial and national lines. The confrontational exchange between Du Bois and Beton revealed not only different approaches to racial politics on both sides of the Atlantic but also the frustration and difficulties involved in sustaining a transnational project in a world of borders, from fundraising concerns to conference logistics. The painful experience as the head of the Pan-African Association led Beton to conclude that "we are not mature enough for an international front or for any action exclusively amongst ourselves."[85] Indeed, for many of the "black gentlemen" based in Europe or the colonies, the brand of social reformism promoted by the league and supported as a principle in most colonial circles was, strategically, a more viable option than black internationalism. The source of animosity, in Du Bois's reading, was that the leaders of the "French Negro group [saw] themselves as Frenchmen first and Negroes second." Quite appropriately, it was proposed that the now defunct Pan-African Association, whose Paris office had been closed before the congress convened, be made into a "Pan-African Committee for France and the French Colonies." Similar nationally bounded groupings should be created elsewhere, from Portugal to South Africa and Liberia.[86] The Lisbon session of the congress, though smaller in scope, was attended by eleven countries and by current and former colonial ministers. A presentation on the "work of the Negroes of San Thomé" had Du Bois impressed to the point of describing that colony as the "most independent and progressive" in Portuguese Africa.[87] This only goes to show the extent to which pro-empire sentiment could infiltrate the pan-African project, especially if we consider that only two years later São Tomé came under attack at the League of Nations as an emblematic case of the persistence of slavery and forced labor in modern colonialism. On that occasion, members of the Lisbon-based African National Party wore the nationalist mantle and addressed the league to defend Portugal against what was seen as a "defamatory campaign."[88] In France, too, some of the personalities who had supported black internationalism in 1919, such as Diagne and Candace, had now turned their back on the pan-African ideal.[89] The "black gentlemen" had drifted apart.

## Conclusion: For Common Action and Clear Vision

In the early interwar years, Wilsonian and Du Boisian internationalism were necessarily different, if not complete opposites. The first embraced a vision of peace predicated on continuing white world leadership and, as such, turned a blind eye to the problem of race and equality. The latter voiced the aspirations of "colored peoples" in general, and of the black diaspora in particular, to political enfranchisement and socioeconomic advancement. Both views, however, shared a crucial premise: the idea that "civilization"—or a "civilized status"—was the entry ticket into the world of rights, equality, and sovereignty. While for Wilson the profound differences in degrees of civilization between white men and colonized populations called for an exclusionary and paternalistic politics of colonial oversight (as embodied in the mandate system), for Du Bois they demanded an active policy of social advancement and integration, mostly through education. In Paris in 1919 and in the ensuing world order, both views coexisted and were championed by competing political forces. The black internationalist cause gained momentum even though racial equality was excluded from the Versailles settlement and the institutional framework of the league. In the early 1920s, Du Bois and other personalities associated with the pan-African movement persisted in their quest to engage, influence, and ultimately infiltrate an internationalist political culture that was fundamentally based on their exclusion (as well as the exclusion of the masses of the so-called Negro world).

Yet the forms of political mobilization thriving around the global experience of being black were not devoid of internal tensions. Overlapping conversations and strategic alliances among black personalities and organizations in several locations coexisted with national animosity, personal rivalry, and much misunderstanding. "Race" as a transnational political experience—or, in other words, "racial belonging" as a basis for a politics of comradeship across borders—had to be constantly negotiated and leveled against more provincial or divisive tendencies. Among them were claims associated with nationality or other territorial forms of political allegiance such as imperial citizenship. It is nearly a truism to point out that loyalties to the race, the nation, and the empire both required and animated different political dispositions and often contradictory, if not irreconcilable, goals. But the most interesting question is why and how competing "degrees of affinity" gained currency and came to be articulated as a meaningful political language—or eventually to be rejected as such.[90] The rise of black internationalism in Paris in 1919 relates to the potential of race as a ground for claim-making, both within and across national borders, in the aftermath of a world conflict in which people of African descent, and the African continent, played a crucial role.[91] In the world emerging after Versailles, the political potential of "race" was drastically curtailed. The pressing problem of racial equality was neutralized by a reformist agenda committed to a politics of uplifting "primitive races" through social policy rather than political enfranchisement. Black internationalists had to navigate a world of nations, empires, and mandates in which their transnational advocacy and political articulation in terms of race did not always resonate well with the people or institutions they were addressing.

Over the course of several Pan-African Congresses, some of the cracks in black internationalism assumed critical proportions. In consequence, to some of the personalities involved in the movement "racial belonging" gradually lost its currency and appeal as a meaningful political language, as the position of the French delegation at the 1923 congress clearly shows. Following these disagreements, Du Bois attempted to regain the support of his French counterparts by claiming that, even if "the future of the Negro race . . . calls for common action and clear vision," this does not mean that blacks need "to give up . . . national allegiances." After all, France had a critical role to play considering its achievements in putting in practice the principle of racial equality, by treating the "cultured black man as cultured."[92] If these words suggest that the Du Boisean vision of a common colored front, of black gentlemen rising, was crumbling under the weight of national or imperial loyalties, they also expose how Du Bois himself struggled to defend his internationalist dream in a world of borders. By 1923, the pressures of race, nation, and empire had all taken their toll.

## Notes

1. Woodrow Wilson, "Address to the Senate of the United States: A World League for Peace," January 22, 1917, *American Presidency Project*, accessed February 28, 2018, http://www.presidency.ucsb.edu/ws/?pid=65396.

2. Erez Maneli, *The Wilsonian Moment: Self-Determination and the International Origins of Anticolonial Nationalism* (Oxford: Oxford University Press, 2007), 22. For a general account of the various aspects of Wilson's political ideas, see Ross A. Kennedy, ed., *A Companion to Woodrow Wilson* (Malden, MA: Wiley-Blackwell, 2013).

3. Theodore Marburg, "Race and Sovereignty as Affected by a League of Nations," *Annals of the American Academy of Political and Social Science* 72 (July 1917): 142.

4. Ibid, 145.

5. Simon Nelson Patten, "Peace without Force," *Annals of the American Academy of Political and Social Science* 72 (July 1917): 31–40, 37.

6. Several authors and commentators have already emphasized Wilson's problematic complicity with racial discrimination in the United States, including by establishing segregation in public administration during his administration. See Gary Gerstle, "Race and Nation in the Thought and Politics of Woodrow Wilson," in *Reconsidering Woodrow Wilson: Progressivism, Internationalism, War and Peace*, ed. John Milton Cooper Jr. (Baltimore: Johns Hopkins University Press, 2008), 93–123; Jennifer D. Keene, "Wilson and Race Relations," in *A Companion to Woodrow Wilson*, ed. Ross A. Kennedy (London: John Wiley, 2013), 133–51; Henry Blumenthal, "Woodrow Wilson and the Race Question," *Journal of Negro History* 48, no. 1 (January 1963): 1–21. Eric S. Yellin, *Racism in the Nation's Service: Government Workers and the Color Line in Woodrow Wilson's America* (Chapel Hill: University of North Carolina Press, 2013). While Wilson's southern upbringing is commonly brought up in explaining his conservative outlook on racial matters, Pestritto has pointed out that racial hierarchy was deeply engrained in Wilson's understanding of politics and history, including by informing his notion of national self-determination or political rights as a privilege only accessible to those more advanced, or progressive, races. See Ronald J. Pestritto, *Woodrow Wilson and the Roots of Modern Liberalism* (Lanham, MD: Rowman & Littlefield Publishers, 2005): 43–45. Andrew Zimmerman also describes Wilson, along with Jan Smuts of South Africa, as "two of the world's most influential segregationists." See Andrew Zimmerman, *Alabama in Africa: Booker T. Washington, the German Empire, and the Globalization of the New South* (Princeton, NJ: Princeton University Press, 2010).

7. When trying to understand why the question of racial equality was such a thorny issue in the United States even at times of Wilsonian idealism, we must consider not only the plight of marginalized groups such as African or Native Americans in the country but also the international ramifications of US imperialism, from Haiti to the Philippines. In this sense, we may consider the Wilson's United States itself as an empire. See Mary A.

Renda, *Taking Haiti: Military Occupation and the Culture of US Imperialism, 1915–1940* (Chapel Hill: University of North Carolina Press, 2001); Edward S. Kaplan, *US Imperialism in Latin America: Bryan's Challenges and Contributions, 1900–1920* (Westport, CT: Greenwood Press, 1998); Paula A. Kramer, *The Blood of Government: Race, Empire, the United States, and the Philippines* (Chapel Hill: University of North Carolina Press, 2006).

8. Manela, *Wilsonian Moment*, 19–34.

9. On the global colour line, see Marilyn Lake and Henry Reynolds, *Drawing the Global Colour Line: White Men's Countries and the International Challenge of Racial Equality* (Cambridge: Cambridge University Press, 2008); Paul Gordon Lauren, *Power and Prejudice: The Politics and Diplomacy of Racial Discrimination* (Boulder, CO: Westview Press, 1996). Most notably, Zimmerman describes the Paris Peace Conference as a "Segregationist International." See Zimmerman, *Alabama in Africa*, 198–204.

10. As the chairman of the League of Nations Commission, Wilson decided that a unanimous vote was required on the racial equality question. This alone defeated the Japanese proposal, which counted on a majority of favorable votes. Norman A. Graeber and Edward M. Bennett, *The Versailles Treaty and Its Legacy: The Failure of the Wilsonian Vision* (Cambridge: Cambridge University Press), 56.

11. On how the black internationalists involved in the pan-African movement related to Wilsonian ideals, see Sarah Claire Dunstan, "Conflicts of Interest: The 1919 Pan-African Congress and the Wilsonian Moment," *Callaloo* 39, no. 1 (Winter 2016): 133–50.

12. Clarence G. Contee, "Du Bois, the NAACP, and the Pan-African Congress of 1919," *Journal of Negro History* 57, no.1 (January 1972): 13–28.

13. The "Salon de la Paix" (Hall of Peace) has been recently renamed to host the delegates of the peace conference. It was a room inside the Ministry of Foreign Affairs, also known as Quai d'Orsay, due to its location. For a fictional rendition, see Judith Claire Mitchell, *The Last Day of the War* (New York: Anchor Books, 2004), 119–20.

14. On a reading of black politics in this period as "transnational," see: Michelle A. Stephens, "Black Transnationalism and the Politics of National Identity: West Indian Intellectuals in Harlem in the Age of War and Revolution," *American Quarterly* 50, no. 3 (1998): 592–608.

15. Manela, *Wilsonian Moment*, 222.

16. This sense of Paris 1919 is captured by Du Bois himself. See W. E. B. Du Bois, "Opinion," *The Crisis* 18, no. 1 (May 1919): 7–9.

17. Lauren, *Power and Prejudice*, 75–88.

18. Adriane Lentz-Smith, *Freedom Struggles: African Americans and World War I* (Cambridge, MA: Harvard University Press, 2009).

19. Lake and Reynolds, *Drawing the Global Colour Line*, 166–89.

20. Naoko Shimazu, *Japan, Race and Equality: The Racial Equality Proposal of 1919* (London; New York: Routledge, 1998); Kristofer Allerfeldt, "Wilsonian Pragmatism? Woodrow Wilson, Japanese Immigration, and the Paris Peace Conference," *Diplomacy & Statecraft* 15, no. 3 (2004): 545–72; Noriko Kawamura, "Wilsonian Idealism and Japanese Claims at the Paris Peace Conference," *Pacific Historical Review* 66, no. 4 (November 1997): 503–26; Paul Gordon Lauren, "Human Rights in History: Diplomacy and Racial Equality at the Paris Peace Conference," *Diplomatic History* 2, no. 3 (1978): 257–77.

21. On how the Japanese proposal resonated abroad, see Yuichiro Onishi, "The New Negro of the Pacific: How African Americans Forged Cross-cultural Solidarity with Japan, 1917–1922," *Journal of African American History* 92, no. 2 (Spring 2007): 191–213; Reginald Kearney, "Japan: Ally in the Struggle Against Racism, 1919–1927," *Contributions in Black Studies* 12 (1994): 1–12.

22. Shimazu, *Japan, Race, and Equality*, 121–36. On the development of the "White Australia" policy, see Lake and Reynolds, *Drawing a Global Colour Line*, 136–56.

23. Several changes were made to the wording of the proposal during the negotiations, in a clear move to tone down the political sensitiveness of the issue in order to get it through. When the final amendment was presented to the League of Nations Commission, the Japanese delegate Baron Makino stressed these changes, affirming that the proposal merely regarded "the relationships between the nationalities forming the League." See Shimazu, *Japan, Race, and Equality*, 28.

24. The white dominions were crucial in shaping the British position on the racial equality question, in contrast with their otherwise modest contribution to other themes at the conference as a whole. See Shimazu, *Japan, Race, and Equality*, 14.

25. It is worth noting that two of the imperial delegations sitting at the negotiation table, France and Italy, voted in favour of the Japanese proposal. It would be interesting to analyze the debates within these delegations leading to this decision. Shimazu mentions, for instance, that the French delegation protested against Wilson's decision of requiring a unanimous vote on this matter and pointed out the hypocrisy of creating a league based on Wilsonian ideals while refusing to address a principle of "universal importance." There is some debate on the Portuguese vote, but the minutes of the Portuguese delegation, which I consulted at the Diplomatic Archives in Lisbon, document a favorable vote. Shimazu refers to Portugal as a nonregistered, thus contrary vote, while Japanese sources list Portugal as a vote in favor of the proposal. See Shimazu, *Japan, Race, and Equality*, 30 and 196 (note 107, chapter 1).

26. For a more detailed account of the Portuguese position, see Caio Simões de Araújo, "Race Problems, Social Issues: The Portuguese Empire and the Racial Equality Proposal, Paris 1919," in *The League of Nations' Work on Social Issues: Visions, Endeavours and Experiments*, ed. Magaly Rodríguez García, Davide Rodogno, and Liat Kozma (Geneva: United Nations Press, 2016), 33–46. For a discussion of debates on race in the Portuguese empire, see Miguel Bandeira Jerónimo, "The 'Civilising Guild': Race and Labour and the Third Portuguese Empire, c. 1870–1930," in *Racism and Ethnic Relations in the Portuguese Speaking World*, ed. Francisco Bethencourt and Adrian Pearce (Oxford: Oxford University Press, 2012): 173–99.

27. Portuguese Diplomatic Archives (Arquivo Histórico Diplomático, hereafter AHD), S-91-A, Sala-Livros, *Actas da Delegação Portuguesa na Conferência de Paz*, 1918–19, 92.

28. Ibid.

29. On how the American delegation considered the domestic repercussions of the proposal back home, see Allerfeldt, *Wilsonian Pragmatism*. On how similar calculations were made by other delegations, see Sean Brawley, *The White Peril: Foreign Relations and Asian Immigration to Australasia and North America 1919–78* (Sydney: University of New South Wales Press, 1995), 15–29.

30. Margaret MacMillan, *Paris 1919: Six Months That Changed the World* (New York: Random House, 2002), 320.

31. Manela, *Wilsonian Moment*.

32. On the political trajectory of Diagne, see Michael C. Lambert, "From Citizenship to Negritude: 'Making a Difference' in Elite Ideologies of Colonized Francophone West Africa," *Comparative Studies in Society and History* 35, no. 2 (April 1993): 239–62.

33. W. E. B. Du Bois, "The Pan-African Congress," *The Crisis* 17, no. 6 (April 1919): 273–74.

34. Ibid., 271–74. According to Du Bois's final report, with fifty-seven delegates, the national representation at the congress was composed as follows: United States (sixteen),

French West Indies (thirteen), Haiti (seven), France (seven), Liberia (three), Spanish Colonies (two), Portuguese Colonies (one), San Domingo (one), England (one), British Africa (one), French Africa (one), Algeria (one), Egypt (one), Belgian Congo (one), and Abyssinia (one).

35. Mazower pointed out that the mandate system was defended by Smuts as a way articulating the white Dominion's imperial interests and Wilsonian humanitarian requirements. See Mark Mazower, *No Enchanted Palace: The End of Empire and the Ideological Origins of the United Nations* (Princeton, NJ: Princeton University Press, 2008), 45–46. On the politics of imperial social reformism, see Miguel Bandeira Jerónimo, *The "Civilizing Mission" of Portuguese Colonialism, 1870–1930* (Basingstoke: Palgrave Macmillan, 2015).

36. Antony Anghie, *Imperialism, Sovereignty and the Making of International Law* (Cambridge: Cambridge University Press, 2005), 115–95. On Wilson's ideas about fitness to self-government, see Erez Manela, "People of Many Races: The World beyond Europe in the Wilsonian Imagination," in *Jefferson, Lincoln, and Wilson: The Dilemma of Race and Democracy*, eds. John Milton Cooper and Thomas J. Knock (Charlottesville: University of Virginia Press, 2010), 198.

37. Zimmerman, *Alabama in Africa*, 196–97.

38. Adam Ewing, *The Age of Garvey: How a Jamaican Activist Created a Mass Movement and Changed Global Black Politics* (Princeton, NJ: Princeton University Press, 2014), 110–11. For another reading of Versailles as a "failure of the Wilsonian Vision," see Graebner and Bennett, *Versailles Treaty*.

39. Mazower, *No Enchanted Palace*.

40. Manela, *Wilsonian Moment*, 61–62.

41. Dunstan, *Conflicts of Interest*; Stephens, *Black Transnationalism*.

42. "A League of Nations," *The Crisis* 18, no. 1 (May 1919): 10–11.

43. "The League of Nations," *The Crisis* 19, no. 1 (November 1919): 336–37.

44. On the internationalization of African and colonial affairs, see Bandeira Jerónimo, *"Civilizing Mission."*

45. W. E. B. Du Bois, "Memorandum on the future of America, November 19, 1918". W. E. B. Du Bois Papers (MS 312), (henceforth Du Bois Papers), Special Collections and University Archives, University of Massachusetts, Amherst Libraries.

46. Du Bois, "Pan-African Congress," 274.

47. Letter from Ed Junod, secretary of the Bureau International pour la Défense des Indigénes, to Sir Eric Drummon of the League of Nations, July 8, 1921. League of Nations Archives (henceforth LoNA), Box R 39, Mandates Section, Dossier no. 13940, Document no. 13940.

48. "League of Nations," *The Crisis* 19, no. 1 (November 1919): 336–37.

49. Susan Pedersen, *The Guardians: The League of Nations and the Crisis of Empire* (Oxford: Oxford University Press, 2015), 61.

50. Veronique Dimier, "On Good Colonial Government: Lessons from the League of Nations," *Global Society: Journal of Interdisciplinary International Relations* 18, no. 3 (2004): 279–99.

51. Du Bois later suggested that the Mandate Commission was a result of the 1919 Pan-African Congress's demand that the League of Nations "bring the status of African peoples under its purview." W. E. B. Du Bois, *In Battle for Peace*, ed. Henry Louis Gates Jr. (Oxford: Oxford University Press, 2007), 12.

52. Letter from René Claparéde to W. E. B. Du Bois, March 8, 1921, Du Bois Papers.

53. On the politics of petitioning to the League of Nations, see Pedersen, *The Guardians*, 77–103.

54. W. E. B. Du Bois, "The Negro and the League of Nations," ca. November 1921, draft of article concerning Du Bois's trip to Geneva as a representative of the Pan-African Congress, Du Bois Papers.

55. W. E. B. Du Bois, letter from Pan-African Congress to the League of Nations, ca. September 1921, Du Bois Papers.

56. Ida Gibbs Hunt, Rayford Logan and W. E. B. Du Bois, "The Third Pan-African Congress," *The Crisis* 27, no. 3 (January 1924): 120–22.

57. Du Bois, "Negro and the League of Nations."

58. There is a vast literature on Marcus Gravey and his version of black internationalism. For a recent and excellent account, see Ewing, *Age of Garvey*. Other interesting readings are Rupert Lewis, *Marcus Garvey: Anti-Colonial Champion* (Trenton, NJ: Africa World Press, 1988); Judith Stein, *The World of Marcus Garvey* (Baton Rouge: Louisiana State University Press, 1986); E. David Cronon, *Black Moses: The Story of Marcus Garvey and the Universal Negro Improvement Association* (Madison: University of Wisconsin Press, 1955). On the rivalry between Garvey and Du Bois, see Elliot P. Skinner, *African Americans and US Policy toward Africa, 1850–1924: In Defense of Black Nationality* (Washington, DC: Howard University Press, 1992).

59. Petition of the Universal Negro Improvement Association and African Communities League to the League of Nations, New York, July 20, 1922, in Robert A. Hill, ed., *The Marcus Garvey and Universal Negro Improvement Association Papers*, vol. 9 (Berkeley: University of California Press, 2006), 532–35.

60. Cronon, *Black Moses*, 148–49.

61. On the myth of Garvey as a "black liberator of Southern Africa," see the introduction to Hill, *Marcus Garvey*, vol. 10, lii–cxvi.

62. W. E. B. Du Bois, "A Second Journey to Pan-Africa," ca. December 7, 1921, Du Bois Papers. Colonial officials and diplomats stationed in the United States, Europe and (southern) Africa wrote profusely on the dangers of Garveyism and the political "agitation" it produced. See Hill, *Marcus Garvey*, vols. 9 and 10.

63. W. E. B. Du Bois to Charles Evans Hughes, US Secretary of State, New York, June 23, 1921, in Hill, *Marcus Garvey*, vol. 9, 3.

64. Telegram from Marcus Garvey to the secretary general of the League of Nations, September 9, 1921, LoNA, Box R 39, Mandates Section, Dossier no. 13940, Document no. 15499, "Pan-African Congress, August–September, 1921."

65. Telegram from Marcus Garvey to the secretary general of the League of Nations, August 3, 1921, LoNA, Box R 39, Mandates Section, Dossier no. 13940, Document no. 14410, "Congrés Pan-Africaine, Aout–Septembre, 1921."

66. "Negro World Report. The Pan-African Congress," Liberty Hall, New York, August 2, 1921, in Hill, *Marcus Garvey*, vol. 9, 138–39.

67. Letter from Paul Panda to W. E. B. Du Bois, July 11, 1921, Du Bois Papers.

68. "Echo of Pan-African Congress," *A Imprensa da Manhã*, September 20, 1921, in Hill, *Marcus Garvey*, vol. 9, 213. The congress had been attended by José de Magalhães representing the Lisbon-based *Liga Africana* and Nicolau dos Santos Pinto representing associations from the colonies, that is, the Liga dos Interesses Indígenas de São Tomé e Príncipe, the Liga Angolana, and the Grêmio Africano de Lourenço Marques, Mozambique.

69. José de Castro and José Luís Garcia, "A Batalha e a Questão Colonial," *Ler História* 27–28 (1995): 125–46.

70. On the spread of pan-African ideals in Mozambique, see Aurélio Rocha, *Associativismo e Nativismo em Moçambique: Contribuição par ao Estudo das Origens do Nacionalismo Moçambicano* (Maputo: Texto Editores, 2006).

71.  Douglas L. Wheeler, *Origins of African Nationalism in Angola: Assimilado Protest Writings, 1859–1929* (Los Angeles: University of California Press, 1968), 74. *Assimilado* refers to the small African elite who enjoyed citizenship rights under Portugal's indigenato system, the Portuguese policy of native administration by means of assimilation. Indigenato established that Africans could potentially acquire full citizenship rights if they met three criteria: have command of the Portuguese language, have a professional occupation and, as a consequence, be able to differentiate themselves from "common" Africans by adopting European culture and living "civilized" life. While the system was mostly codified in the late 1920s in Angola, Mozambique and the Portuguese Guinea, its roots are in the 1910s. In Mozambique, for instance, a colonial ordinance establishing the separate legal status to the assimilated African dates back to 1917. See Rocha, *Associativismo e Nativismo em Moçambique*, 129–31. For a more detailed analysis of indigenato and the imperial citizenship regime see Cristina Nogueira da Silva, "Natives Who Were 'Citizens' and Natives Who Were Indígenas in the Portuguese Empire, 1900–1926," in *Endless Empire: Spain's Retreat, Europe's Eclipse, America's Decline*, ed. Alfred McCoy, Josep Fradera, and Stephen Jacobson (Madison: University of Wisconsin Press, 2012), 295–305.

72.  Vlademir Zamparoni, "A Imprensa Negra em Moçambique: a trajetória de 'O Africano'—1908–1920," *África: Revista de Centro de Estudos Africanos* 11, no. 1 (1988): 73–86; Vlademir Zamparoni, "As 'Escravas perpétuas' & o 'Ensino prático': raça, gênero e educação no Moçambique colonial, 1910–1930," *Estudos Afro-Asiáticos* 24, no. 3 (2002): 459–82.

73.  Jeanne Marie Penvenne, "João dos Santos Albasini (1876–1922): The Contradictions of Politics and Identity in Colonial Mozambique," *Journal of African History* 37, no. 3 (1996): 419–64; Jeanne Marie Penvenne, "'We Are All Portuguese!' Challenging the Political Economy of Assimilation: Lourenço Marques, 1870–1933," in *The Creation of Tribalism in Southern Africa*, ed. Leroy Vail (Berkeley: University of California, 1989), 256–81.

74.  Nicolau dos Santos Pinto, "The Portuguese Negro," *The Crisis* 23, no. 6 (April 1922): 259–60.

75.  Letter from Isaac Beton to W. E. B. Du Bois, October 31, 1922, Du Bois Papers. The Pan-African Association had been created in Paris in 1921 to campaign for the advancement of the "negro race" and to promote the pan-African cause by organizing congresses every two years. The president and secretary were, respectively, Gratien Candace and Isaac Beton, both from Guadalupe.

76.  Letter from W. E. B. Du Bois to Isaac Beton, December 4, 1922, Du Bois Papers.

77.  Letter from Isaac Beton to W. E. B. Du Bois, December 21, 1922, Du Bois Papers.

78.  Letter from W. E. B. Du Bois to Isaac Beton, March 1922, Du Bois Papers.

79.  Original in French: "servir la Race selon ses moye." Letter from Isaac Beton to W. E. B. Du Bois, May 29, 1922, Du Bois Papers.

80.  W. E. B. Du Bois, "The Third Pan African Congress," 1923, Document enclosed in a letter sent from Du Bois to the editor of *African World*, Du Bois Papers. As Du Bois also told Ida Gibbs, the costs of his participation in the 1923 Congress were not covered by the NAACP but by the National Federation for Colored Women. See Letter from W. E. B. Du Bois to Ida Gibbs, September 27, 1923, Du Bois Papers.

81.  Letter from Rayford Logan to W. E. B. Du Bois, September 6, 1923, Du Bois Papers.

82.  Original in French: "étrangler une manifestation susceptible de profiter à la race." Letter from Isaac Breton to Jessie Fauset, August 9, 1923, Du Bois Papers.

83.  Original in French: "étranglée à sa naissance," "criminelle apathie," "ignoble hostilité." Letter from Isaac Beton to W. E. B Du Bois, August 3, 1923, Du Bois Papers.

84. Letter from W. E. B. Du Bois to José de Magalhães, August 28, 1928, Du Bois Papers.

85. Original in French: "nous ne sommes pas encore mûrs pour une entente internationale ni pour une action exclusivement entre nous." Letter from Isaac Breton to Jessie Fauset, August 9, 1923, Du Bois Papers.

86. W. E. B. Du Bois, "The Third Pan African Congress," *The Crisis* 27, no. 3 (January 1924): 122. Though reports in *The Crisis* magazine speak of the presence of French delegates at the Third Congress, there is some confusion whether France actually did send any representatives. See Brian Russell Roberts, *Artistic Ambassadors: Literary and International Representation of the New Negro Era* (Charlottesville: University of Virginia Press, 2013), 125–26.

87. W. E. B. Du Bois, "Pan-Africa in Portugal," *The Crisis* 27, no. 4 (February 1924): 170.

88. According to Bandeira Jerónimo's detailed study, the African National Party wrote to the league's secretary to refute the critical allegations against Portugal. To the same effect, the Party also participated in the Second General Assembly of the *Ligue Internationale pour la Defense des Indigènes*, held in Geneva in 1925. Bandeira Jerónimo, "*Civilizing Mission*," 185–86.

89. David L. Reed, "Rayford W. Logan: The Evolution of a Pan-African Protégé, 1921–1927," *Journal of Pan-African Studies* 6, no. 8 (March 2014), p. 23.

90. Nico Slate, "Introduction: The Borders of Race and Nation," in *Race, Ethnicity and the Cold War: A Global Perspective*, ed. Philip E. Muehlenbeck (Nashville: Vanderbilt University Press, 2012), ix–xvii.

91. Jennifer D. Keene, "W. E. B. Dubois and the Wounded World: Seeking Meaning in the First World War for African-Americans," *Peace & Change* 26, no. 2 (April 2001): 135–52.

92. W. E. B. Du Bois, "Memorandum to Messrs. Diagne, Candace and Their Friends on the Future of the Pan-African Congress," ca. December 1923, Du Bois Papers.

# Bibliography

Allerfeldt, Kristofer. "Wilsonian Pragmatism? Woodrow Wilson, Japanese Immigration, and the Paris Peace Conference." *Diplomacy & Statecraft* 15, no. 3 (2004): 545–72.

Anghie, Antony. *Imperialism, Sovereignty and the Making of International Law*. Cambridge: Cambridge University Press, 2005.

Araújo, Caio Simões de. "Race Problems, Social Issues: The Portuguese Empire and the Racial Equality Proposal, Paris 1919." in *The League of Nations' Work on Social Issues: Visions, Endeavours and Experiments*, edited by Magaly Rodríguez García, Davide Rodogno, and Liat Kozma, 33–46. Geneva: United Nations Press, 2016.

Bandeira Jerónimo, Miguel. *The "Civilizing Mission" of Portuguese Colonialism, 1870–1930*. Basingstoke: Palgrave Macmillan, 2015.

Blumenthal, Henry. "Woodrow Wilson and the Race Question." *Journal of Negro History* 48, no. 1 (January 1963): 1–21.

Brawley, Sean. *The White Peril: Foreign Relations and Asian Immigration to Australasia and North America 1919–78*. Sydney: University of New South Wales Press, 1995.

Castro, José de, and José Luís Garcia. "A Batalha e a Questão Colonial." *Ler História* 27–28 (1995): 125–46.

Contee, Clarence G. "Du Bois, the NAACP, and the Pan-African Congress of 1919." *Journal of Negro History* 57, no. 1 (January 1972): 13–28.

Cronon, E. David. *Black Moses: The Story of Marcus Garvey and the Universal Negro Improvement Association*. Madison: University of Wisconsin Press, 1955.

Dimier, Veronique. "On Good Colonial Government: Lessons from the League of Nations." *Global Society: Journal of Interdisciplinary International Relations* 18, no. 3 (2004): 279–99.

Du Bois, W. E. B. *In Battle for Peace*. Edited by Henry Louis Gates Jr. Oxford: Oxford University Press, 2007.

———. "Opinion." *The Crisis* 18, no. 1 (May 1919): 7–9.

———. "The Pan-African Congress." *The Crisis* 17, no. 6 (April 1919): 271–74.

———. "Pan-Africa in Portugal." *The Crisis* 27, no. 4 (February 1924): 170.

———. "The Third Pan African Congress." *The Crisis* 27, no. 3 (January 1924): 120–22.

Dunstan, Sarah Claire. "Conflicts of Interest: The 1919 Pan-African Congress and the Wilsonian Omen." *Callaloo* 39, no. 1 (Winter 2016): 133–50.

Ewing, Adam. *The Age of Garvey: How a Jamaican Activist Created a Mass Movement and Changed Global Black Politics*. Princeton, NJ: Princeton University Press, 2014.

Gerstle, Gary. "Race and Nation in the Thought and Politics of Woodrow Wilson." In *Reconsidering Woodrow Wilson: Progressivism, Internationalism, War and Peace*, edited by John Milton Cooper Jr., 93–123. Baltimore: Johns Hopkins University Press, 2008.

Gibbs Hunt, Ida, Rayford Logan, and W. E. B. Du Bois. "The Third Pan-African Congress." *The Crisis* 27, no. 3 (January 1924): 120–22.

Graeber, Norman A., and Edward M. Bennett. *The Versailles Treaty and Its Legacy: The Failure of the Wilsonian Vision*. Cambridge: Cambridge University Press.

Hill, Robert A., ed. *The Marcus Garvey and Universal Negro Improvement Association Papers*. Vols. 9–10. Berkeley: University of California Press, 2006.

Jerônimo, Miguel Bandeira. "The 'Civilising Guild': Race and Labour and the Third Portuguese Empire, c. 1870–1930." In *Racism and Ethnic Relations in the Portuguese Speaking World*, edited by Francisco Bethencourt and Adrian Pearce, 173–99. Oxford: Oxford University Press, 2012.

Kaplan, Edward S. *US Imperialism in Latin America: Bryan's Challenges and Contributions, 1900–1920*. Westport, CT: Greenwood Press, 1998.

Kawamura, Noriko. "Wilsonian Idealism and Japanese Claims at the Paris Peace Conference." *Pacific Historical Review* 66, no. 4 (November 1997): 503–26.

Kearney, Reginald. "Japan: Ally in the Struggle against Racism, 1919–1927." *Contributions in Black Studies* 12 (1994): 1–12.

Keene, Jennifer D. "W.E.B. Dubois and the Wounded World: Seeking Meaning in the First World War for African-Americans." *Peace & Change* 26, no. 2 (April 2001): 135–52.

———. "Wilson and Race Relations." In *A Companion to Woodrow Wilson*, edited by Ross A. Kennedy, 133–51. London: John Wiley, 2013.

Kennedy, Ross A., ed. *A Companion to Woodrow Wilson*. Malden, MA: Wiley-Blackwell, 2013.

Kramer, Paula A. *The Blood of Government: Race, Empire, the United States, and the Philippines*. Chapel Hill: University of North Carolina Press, 2006.

Lake, Marilyn, and Henry Reynolds. *Drawing the Global Colour Line: White Men's Countries and the International Challenge of Racial Equality*. Cambridge: Cambridge University Press, 2008.

Lambert, Michael C. "From Citizenship to Negritude: 'Making a Difference' in Elite Ideologies of Colonized Francophone West Africa." *Comparative Studies in Society and History* 35, no. 2 (April 1993): 239–62.

Lauren, Paul Gordon. "Human Rights in History: Diplomacy and Racial Equality at the Paris Peace Conference." *Diplomatic History* 2, no. 3 (1978): 257–77.

———. *Power and Prejudice: The Politics and Diplomacy of Racial Discrimination.* Boulder, CO: Westview Press, 1996.

"A League of Nations." *The Crisis* 18, no. 1 (May 1919): 10–11.

"The League of Nations." *The Crisis* 19, no. 1 (November 1919): 336–37.

Lentz-Smith, Adriane. *Freedom Struggles: African Americans and World War I.* Cambridge, MA: Harvard University Press, 2009.

Lewis, Rupert. *Marcus Garvey: Anti-Colonial Champion.* Trenton, NJ: Africa World Press, 1988

MacMillan, Margaret. *Paris 1919: Six Months That Changed the World.* New York: Random House, 2002.

Manela, Erez. "People of Many Races: The World beyond Europe in the Wilsonian Imagination." In *Jefferson, Lincoln, and Wilson: The Dilemma of Race and Democracy,* edited by John Milton Cooper, and Thomas J. Knock, 184–208. Charlottesville: University of Virginia Press, 2010.

———. *The Wilsonian Moment: Self-Determination and the International Origins of Anticolonial Nationalism.* Oxford: Oxford University Press, 2007.

Marburg, Theodore. "Race and Sovereignty as Affected by a League of Nations." *Annals of the American Academy of Political and Social Science* 72 (July 1917): 142–46.

Mazower, Mark. *No Enchanted Palace: The End of Empire and the Ideological Origins of the United Nations.* Princeton, NJ: Princeton University Press, 2008.

Mitchell, Judith Claire. *The Last Day of the War.* New York: Anchor Books, 2004.

Onishi, Yuichiro. "The New Negro of the Pacific: How African Americans Forged Cross-Cultural Solidarity with Japan, 1917–22." *Journal of African American History* 92, no. 2 (Spring 2007): 191–213.

Patten, Simon Nelson "Peace without Force." *Annals of the American Academy of Political and Social Science* 71 (July 1917): 31–40.

Pedersen, Susan. *The Guardians: The League of Nations and the Crisis of Empire.* Oxford: Oxford University Press, 2015.

Penvenne, Jeanne Marie. "João dos Santos Albasini (1876–1922): The Contradictions of Politics and Identity in Colonial Mozambique." *Journal of African History* 37, no. 3 (1996): 419–64.

———. "'We Are All Portuguese!' Challenging the Political Economy of Assimilation: Lourenço Marques, 1870–1933." In *The Creation of Tribalism in Southern Africa,* edited by Leroy Vail, 256–81. Berkeley: University of California, 1989.

Pestritto, Ronald J. *Woodrow Wilson and the Roots of Modern Liberalism.* Lanham: Rowman & Littlefield Publishers, 2005.

Reed, David L. "Rayford W. Logan: The Evolution of a Pan-African Protégé, 1921–1927." *Journal of Pan-African Studies* 6, no. 8 (March 2014): 27–53.

Renda, Mary A. *Taking Haiti: Military Occupation and the Culture of US Imperialism, 1915–1940* (Chapel Hill: University of North Carolina Press, 2001).

Roberts, Brian Russell. *Artistic Ambassadors: Literary and International Representation of the New Negro Era.* Charlottesville: University of Virginia Press, 2013.

Rocha, Aurélio. *Associativismo e Nativismo em Moçambique: Contribuição par ao Estudo das Origens do Nacionalismo Moçambicano.* Maputo: Texto Editores, 2006.

Santos Pinto, Nicolau dos. "The Portuguese Negro." *The Crisis* 23, no. 6 (April 1922): 259–60.

Shimazu, Naoko. *Japan, Race and Equality: The Racial Equality Proposal of 1919*. London; New York: Routledge, 1998.

Silva, Cristina Nogueira da. "Natives Who Were 'Citizens' and Natives Who Were Indígenas in the Portuguese Empire, 1900–1926." In *Endless Empire: Spain's Retreat, Europe's Eclipse, America's Decline*, edited by Alfred McCoy, Josep Fradera, and Stephen Jacobson, 295–305. Madison: University of Wisconsin Press, 2012.

Skinner, Elliot P. *African Americans and US Policy toward Africa, 1850–1924: In Defense of Black Nationality*. Washington, DC: Howard University Press, 1992.

Slate, Nico. "Introduction: The Borders of Race and Nation." In *Race, Ethnicity and the Cold War: A Global Perspective*, edited by Philip E. Muehlenbeck, ix–xvii. Nashville: Vanderbilt University Press, 2012.

Stein, Judith. *The World of Marcus Garvey*. Baton Rouge: Louisiana State University Press, 1986.

Stephens, Michelle A. "Black Transnationalism and the Politics of National Identity: West Indian Intellectuals in Harlem in the Age of War and Revolution." *American Quarterly* 50, no. 3 (1998): 592–608.

Wheeler, Douglas L. *Origins of African Nationalism in Angola: Assimilado Protest Writings, 1859–1929*. Los Angeles: University of California Press, 1968.

Yellin, Eric S. *Racism in the Nation's Service: Government Workers and the Color Line in Woodrow Wilson's America*. Chapel Hill: University of North Carolina Press, 2013.

Zamparoni, Vlademir. "A Imprensa Negra em Moçambique: a trajetória de 'O Africano'—1908–1920." *África: Revista de Centro de Estudos Africanos* 11, no. 1 (1988): 73–86.

———. "As 'Escravas perpétuas' & o 'Ensino prático': raça, gênero e educação no Moçambique colonial, 1910–1930." *Estudos Afro-Asiáticos* 24, no. 3 (2002): 459–82.

Zimmerman, Andrew. *Alabama in Africa: Booker T. Washington, the German Empire, and the Globalization of the New South*. Princeton, NJ: Princeton University Press, 2010.

CAIO SIMÕES DE ARAÚJO is a Mellon postdoctoral fellow at the Centre for Indian Studies in Africa at Wits University. He is the editor of *A Luta Continua, 40 Anos Depois: Histórias Entrelaçadas da África Austral*.

# 9 Persian Visions of Nationalism and Inter-Nationalism in a World at War

Timothy Nunan

It says everything about us, and nothing about the First World War, that commemoration of the event focuses on the battlefields of France and Belgium and little on the eastern front—and still less the "real" eastern front of Persia.[1] Yet understanding Persia's place in the reformation of the international order matters, and not only because it lends perspective on Tehran's current attempts to negotiate its place in the international system. Like their contemporaries from India, China, Egypt, and elsewhere, Persian intellectuals engaged with the discourses of self-determination that flowered during the war. But their engagements with internationalist thought were wide and varied. Persia entered the war as a joint protectorate of Britain and Russia but left it as a founding member of the League of Nations—after having been a subject of the Treaty of Brest-Litovsk and having withstood a socialist revolution. Reconstructing the engagement of Persian intellectuals and statesmen matters, then, for anyone interested in understanding the marketplace of ideas about internationalism that flourished beyond Versailles.

In taking up this task, this chapter relies on several indispensable works that help us understand the domestic "demand side" of Persian nationalism.[2] At the same time, scholarship in Iranian studies stands somewhat removed from works on the history of internationalism that emphasize how nationalism and internationalism were originally constitutive of, not opposed to, one another.[3] And in contrast to excellent work in, for example, Chinese history, it can sometimes ignore the fundamentally international context in which nationalisms were forged.[4] The contribution of what follows is, then, to underscore how seriously Persian nationalists like Sayyid Hassan Taqīzādeh (1878–1970) took the question of a legitimate international order that would provide the nation with the necessary breathing room to develop. Yet at the same time, I advance the conversation on internationalism by taking seriously the nonliberal internationalisms that attracted intellectuals betrayed by liberal imperialism.[5] The German Empire and later the Soviet Union were important vectors of internationalist thought that Persian actors engaged seriously with.[6] My goal then is to convince scholars of Iranian history and scholars of internationalism that they have much to learn from one another by looking outside the nation and beyond Western actors, respectively.[7] More broadly still, I aim to engage in debates about the extent to which colonial (here, semicolonial) actors viewed political sovereignty (as opposed to socialism, antiracism, Islamic revolution, or other goals) as their ticket to international society.[8]

In terms of sources, this chapter benefits from the writings and memoirs of key Persian intellectuals, such as Taqīzādeh's memoirs and the newspaper *Kāveh* that he edited under wartime German patronage, as well as the archives of the League of Nations. Certainly this is not a comprehensive treatment of Persia's Great War. Additional work could connect military developments on the ground with shifting internationalist discourses or focus more on the competition between Persian elites in Tehran, Berlin, and London. Consciously set aside here, too, is consideration of the industrial infrastructure of print and distribution that materially gave ideas feet.[9] Mine is an analysis that focuses on the intersection of elites, internationalist thought, and geopolitics.

## "The Profits of German Friendship"

How the most outstanding exponent of early twentieth-century Persian nationalism ends up being published in wartime Berlin demands explanation. Firstly, however, a brief primer: The nineteenth century was a geopolitical disaster for Persia. In the first half of the century, it surrendered its most populous and wealthiest territories in the Caucasus to the Russian Empire through the Treaties of Gulistan (1813, giving up most of present-day Georgia, Dagestan, and Azerbaijan) and Turkmenchai (1828, ceding present-day Armenia and parts of southern Azerbaijan). During the late nineteenth century, Persia fell under the domination of the British and Russian Empires. At the same time, however, Persian intellectuals demanded parliamentary government and a curtailment of foreign privileges. The movement secured a new constitution and a parliamentary assembly (the Majlis), but it had the bad timing of erupting at the same time as London and St. Petersburg sought détente in central Eurasia. A 1907 Anglo-Russian agreement partitioned Persia into zones of influence. And in 1911–12, Russian troops occupied Tehran and massacred both mullahs and reformers in Mashhad. British forces did nothing, increasing anti-British and anti-Romanov sentiment. When the Great War started, Persia declared its neutrality. However, western and northwestern Persia soon became a battlefield between Ottoman and German forces on one side and British and Russian forces on the other. As Taqīzādeh himself related in a series of public lectures at Columbia University in 1958, "The two neighboring powers and especially Russia reduced Iran to almost the state of a vassal country."[10] Indeed, the Sykes-Picot Agreement envisioned the annexation of not only parts of the eastern Ottoman Empire but also northwestern Persia to the Russian Empire.[11]

As the war engulfed precisely these areas—Persia's most populous and economically developed—Persian intellectuals sought to influence the war through collaboration with the Central powers. In Ottoman-occupied Kermanshah (a city in western Persia), some established the National Defense Committee and Council of Representatives, which claimed to represent the legitimate government of Persia.[12] Berlin, Vienna, and Istanbul engaged Persian intellectuals in the diaspora too. Prominent among such Persians abroad was Sayyid Hassan Taqīzādeh, originally trained for a career in the Shi'a *ulema* (clergy). On account of his own revolutionary activities, Taqīzādeh had been forced to emigrate to London and then to New York, where he was in 1914. Soon after the outbreak of the war, Taqīzādeh was invited to the Catskills retreat of 'Alīqolī Khān, a fellow Persian freemason and revolutionary.[13] Living at the resort with Khān and his American wife (herself a follower of the Baha'i faith) was an Indian revolutionary whom Khān was trying to enroll at West Point to obtain military training for his struggles against the British.[14]

Soon, Taqīzādeh received an invitation to meet with the German consulate in New York. There, the consul made clear his intent: "The German state had taken many prisoners from France, England, and Russia. A great number of them were Muslims, from Algeria to Tatarstan to India." Berlin, the consul continued, had separated out the Muslim prisoners to explain to them "the profits of German friendship and enmity towards the state that had dominated them." Taqīzādeh had been sought out as an agitator.[15] He accepted. After an Atlantic crossing via Rotterdam, Taqīzādeh soon discovered the broader context for his services. Indian revolutionaries had gathered together in the German capital, where "they had been given training in bombs, dynamite, horseback riding, and shooting."[16] However, moving the Indians from Germany to the subcontinent presented challenges. The Indians could travel through the Central powers' territory without problems but needed "accessories in Persia" to aid their transit. Hence, the Indians had encouraged the German consulate to hire diaspora Persians to found a newspaper that could both be distributed via the Ottoman front, sow sympathy for the German and Ottoman cause in the war, and, in doing so, smooth the Indians' transit through Persia into the Raj.[17]

Reaching back into his own constitutionalist networks, Taqīzādeh formed the newspaper *Kāveh*. Taqīzādeh and the intellectual Mohammad 'Ali Jamālzādeh would author some 80 percent of the newspaper's articles.[18] Publication commenced on January 16, 1916, launching a transnational enterprise that would combine war reporting, reviews of Orientalist scholarship, and essays on Persian literature and mythology—all key elements in the making of Persian nationalism and topics that scholars in Iranian studies have studied on their own terms. It is, however, less to these themes and more to the vision of international order embedded in *Kāveh* that I would now like to turn. Rather than dismissing *Kāveh* as an accessory to German imperialism, I will examine how it located the Persian cause in a "market of ideas" on internationalism in which Wilsonianism was a latecomer and far from the foreordained victor.

## Embracing Liberal Hegemony

Even before *Kāveh* began publication, Taqīzādeh was busy publishing brochures that give us a sense of where his engagement with internationalist thought began.[19] In one brochure, "Persia and the European War," published under the pseudonym "a Persian patriot," Taqīzādeh stressed Persia's destiny as the center of a string of independent Islamic states: the Ottoman Empire, Persia, and Afghanistan. "All but three of the many states that were founded by Mohammadan peoples on the soil of the former Caliphate Empire and preserved their existence for a long time," explained Taqīzādeh, "have been totally exterminated or made into the limp slaves, the constituent parts, of the European Great Powers that have made the extermination of any political life in Islam their goal."[20] As Taqīzādeh saw it, European powers sought to divide and rule by promising Tehran annexations of Najaf and Karbala, exacerbating divisions between "Kavus and Afrasiab, between Iran and Turan."[21] In contrast to the Allied powers, which together had ended the existence of no fewer than thirteen Muslim states, the Central powers had liberated Albania from the Serbian yoke.[22]

Flirt as these initial interventions of Taqīzādeh did with "Muslim world politics," they gradually gave way to a different vision of internationalism that located Persia in a different, more Eurocentric, frame.[23] One month before Taqīzādeh's brochure appeared, the liberal German politician Friedrich Naumann had published *Mitteleuropa*, in which he argued in favor of a zone of German liberal hegemony in central Europe.[24] With hundreds of millions of consumers organized in politically independent national entities—here states like a "liberated" Albania or the Kingdom of Poland (an autonomous puppet state established in November 1916)—Germany could form an economic bloc capable of competing with the United States or the British Empire while transitioning to social democracy at home. The point was to create a union of states east of Berlin under German economic hegemony, yet with Germany freed of the burden of including millions of Poles, Ukrainians, and White Russians—much less Albanians and Persians—into a liberal German polity itself.

With this in mind, it may make more sense why a Persian social democrat like Taqīzādeh examined the fate of the nations that had fallen to Russian imperialism, in particular Georgia, Poland, and Finland in the first issues of *Kāveh*.[25] These nations had rich histories (made legible through European Orientalists), but infighting and foreign intrigue had delivered them to the Romanovs. Germany, Taqīzādeh's articles implied, could promise a vision of self-determination that would allow states in the Russian limitrophe to thrive (Persia included). As the piece on Georgia emphasized, these countries' present was "Persia's tomorrow."

It is important to note, however, that according to Taqīzādeh, this vision would be achieved in tandem with European social democrats and not merely the kaiser's war machine. In the summer of 1916, for example, Taqīzādeh traveled to Copenhagen to meet the Danish critic Georg Brandes (1842–1927), who had authored an article in the newspaper *Politiken* criticizing czarist policy in Iran.[26]

For nineteen days, Taqīzādeh and Brandes drafted an article lambasting Russian policy in Persia that the former would later use in appeals to socialist parties. Brandes even sent the manuscript to Lenin and Trotsky, leading Taqīzādeh to believe that it had been "very effective." Yet—underscoring the linkage between Orientalism and internationalism—Taqīzādeh also used his time in the Danish capital to visit the Royal Copenhagen Library, where Avestan-language manuscripts taken from India by the Danish Orientalist Niels Ludvig Westergaard had been deposited. Taqīzādeh was fascinated by them but also noted that they had been placed "with great caution under the glass." European Orientalist scholarship, far from an instrument of epistemological domination, was a tool that could help make legible the nationhood that small nations needed to claim international recognition.

This vision of self-determination in harmony with, rather than opposed to, German liberal hegemony was, of course, not just limited to "Oriental" nations. Following his summer trip to Scandinavia, Taqīzādeh traveled to "liberated" Poland, that is, the puppet Kingdom of Poland recognized by Germany and Austria-Hungary as a national homeland. Reporting from festivities in Warsaw, Taqīzādeh noted the joy of the participants as Polish songs that had been forbidden under czarist rule were performed.[27] Far from being "wild" (*waḥshī*) a "killer of nations," or "imperialistic," Taqīzādeh explained, Germany and Austria-Hungary were "defenders of lesser nations."[28] In contrast, he explained, perfidious Albion had trampled on the rights of "small nations" like the Greeks, whose pro-German king the British had toppled through an intervention in Thessaloniki and the installation of a provisional revolutionary government. Skeptics who brand Taqīzādeh as a puppet have the burden of explaining why he would embrace liberal hegemony, rather than annexation, if he was so cynical. They also need to explain why this vision of liberal hegemony was less legitimate than the projects of Wilsonianism and Leninism that would displace it.

## Nations Big and Small

Persian investment in one vision of internationalism or the other was dependent on events on the ground. In April 1916, Ottoman forces besieged a British garrison in Kut al-Amarna, Mesopotamia, taking 13,309 prisoners.[29] *Kāveh* celebrated these events, but more significantly for the Persians, German and Ottoman forces recaptured Persian cities like Qaṣr-i Shirin and Kermanshah from Russian forces, allowing *Kāveh* reporters (and members of the National Defense Committee) to return to their hub in Kermanshah.[30] Yet by the end of the summer, offensives by Russian forces and Romania (which joined the war on the Entente side) nearly prompted Berlin and Vienna to sue for peace.[31]

The Romanian offensive offered a window into *Kāveh*'s prioritization of national self-determination versus the geopolitical concerns of the German, Austro-Hungarian, and Ottoman Empires. Many of the southwestern lands of the Austro-Hungarian Empire were populated by Romanians, although large cities such as Hermannstadt (today Sibiu) and Kronstadt (today Brasov) had German majorities as well as a substantial urban Hungarian population. Moreover, following the establishment of the Dual Monarchy, a diet based in Klausenburg (today Cluj-Napoca) that had allowed Romanians a certain amount of autonomy was dissolved. If one accepted that the Romanians were, too, a small nation oppressed by a larger nation (here the Hungarians), then the Romanian cause had certain parallels with the Persian one.

*Kāveh*'s coverage of the subsequent German and Austrian repulsion of the Romanian offensive, however, made clear the newspaper's limits when it came to national self-determination. Throughout the autumn of 1916, both German and Austrian forces operating from the northwest and Bulgarian and Ottoman forces in the south halted Romania's advances in Transylvania and an attempted crossing of the Danube on October 1. *Kāveh* was unsparingly pro-Austrian and pro-German in its coverage of the war, celebrating not only the liberation of Hermannstadt and Kronstadt from Romanian occupation but also the German-Bulgarian conquest of the port city of Constanta from Romanian and Russian armies.[32] This first article simply did not address the legitimacy of the Romanian national cause or the justification for occupying Romania's lone port. Then, following sensationalist reporting in the British *Daily Mail* that had described Romania, Serbia, Belgium, and Montenegro as "small nations" oppressed by Germany, a second article published in December offered a more full-throated defense of the war.[33]

*Kāveh* explained that Romania was the creation of Russian imperialism, a fake nation that had embellished its past by linking its history with that of Rome in an act of "self-righteousness."[34] Having sat on the sidelines of the war for two years, Romania now opportunistically sought to take advantage of the weakened state of Austria-Hungary in order to bring the "races" (*nezhādān*) of Transylvania into one state. However, *Kāveh* noted, the opposite would happen, as both Transylvania and "Romanian territory" were now destined to fall under the rule of a non-Romanian government. Presumably, because Romanians were not a "small nation," much less a nation at all, this was not imperialism. As for Constanta and the Dobruja more broadly, the piece defended their detachment from Romania on the grounds that they were really Ottoman territories: "It has not been long since a part of the colonies [i.e., the Dobruja] were Ottoman, and as the followers of Gladstone say, the crescent flags have eternally departed and 'sunsetted' (*ghorūb karde bud*)—all of this has importance especially for the Muslim East and Islam. This is why the Muslims of the world see with total pride that Muslim troops have been fighting shoulder to shoulder with the bravest troops of the world and the greatest nations of the world."[35] If this was not incendiary enough, the article's conclusion speculated about the possibility of the Central powers recognizing an independent Slav state that could emerge out of Siberia, led by the offspring of thieves, murderers, and exiles. If Petrograd could play the game of sponsoring irredentism in central Europe, then Berlin and Vienna could do the same in the territories of the Russian Empire. The article further cited an *ayat* from the Qur'an ("But the plan of the disbelievers is nothing but delusion") to denounce Russia's meddling.[36] In short, while the Romanian campaign might have offered an opportunity to reflect on how Berlin and Vienna were exploiting Persian nationalism for their own ends, *Kāveh* instead presented Romanian nationalism as a project of Russian imperialism. The point was not that "small nations" did not have a right to exist but rather that Romania did not meet these criteria—and perhaps that even if it did, the cause of defending the Ottoman Empire as a sovereign Muslim state overrode certain small nations' claims.

Soon, however, the Romanian campaign turned into a stalemate. Both Allied hopes of using the Romanian offensive to force Berlin and Vienna out of the war as well as the Central powers' expectations of a decisive victory over Bucharest were dashed. This in turn raised the question of whether the war might be halted. Newly appointed British prime minister David Lloyd George remained committed to victory, but American president Woodrow Wilson thought differently. As Wilson stressed in a speech on January 22, 1917, the American goal was a "peace without victory" that would ensure America's permanent role as "neutral arbiter and the source of a new form of international order."[37] The "equality of nations," he explained, "must neither recognize nor imply a difference between big nations and small, between those that are powerful and those that are weak."[38]

These concepts of "big" and "small" nations were part and parcel of the vocabulary of late nineteenth-century internationalism.[39] Many late nineteenth-century Anglophone thinkers viewed the nation "as a step away from the particular and towards the universal," since it represented a step away from tribalism toward the largest actually meaningful human collectivity—the nation—that could then interact with other nations.[40] Yet against the background of German and Italian national unification, the question of "small" nations was contested. Critics of "small nations" argued that good institutions were more important than nationality, and that self-esteem expressed itself most healthily within a "great nation"—better to be an English duke than an Albanian prince. The most dignified move for "small nations," later skeptics like Alfred Zimmern argued, would be economic integration into the blocs and pooled sovereignty in internationalist arrangements.[41]

The editorial board at *Kāveh* was well-versed in these debates, and its members read Wilson's speech with interest. We know this because they printed in their February 15, 1917, issue a telegraph they sent to President Wilson:

> Most esteemed Mister Wilson, the President of the United States of America (Washington):
> Your declaration to the grandees of the Congress about the sacred right of small nations has awakened hope and ebullition in the heart of the nation of Persia as to its future. We address you and the nation of America on the part of our own nation so that you may use your full influence for the benefit of those sacred principles and, from this noble feeling of humanity, consider the good condition and stability of the world, including the condition of the ancient races.[42]

Yet the *Kāveh* team was twisting Wilson's words. Wilson had spoken only about the nations' "size," not their "age." Persian nationalists repeatedly asserted that Persia's "age" entitled it to special consideration beyond its small "size." More broadly, this assertion of Persia as an "ancient race" equivalent to the Jews, Greeks, or Romans leveraged Persia into a legible European imagination, again with the help of Orientalist scholarship.

Always opportunistic, however, the editors at *Kāveh* exploited new wartime developments to find new interlocutors. Following mass strikes, the Russian czar Nicholas II abdicated, leading to a situation where a provisional government ruled in uneasy tandem with the Petrograd Soviet. Once the provisional government announced its intention to continue to fight with czarist war aims, the Soviet government announced a "Petrograd formula" of peace: self-determination, no annexations, and no indemnities. This was anathema to London and Paris, which feared that the Soviet government could undermine war efforts by rallying domestic labor and socialist support for peace with Berlin. When the Petrograd Soviet called for an international socialist conference in Stockholm on July 1, 1917, London and Paris canceled the passports of the socialist delegations that planned to travel there. And combined with American reluctance to throw its weight behind the Petrograd proposal, the conference was unlikely to end the war.[43]

What it did offer, however, was another platform for Taqīzādeh and the Persian cause. Taqīzādeh and Wahid ul-Mulk traveled to Stockholm for the July 1, 1917, conference.[44] Just as the conference started, Taqīzādeh appeared in the newspaper *Stockholms Dagblad*, as "a Persian patriot who addressed an appeal to the Russian government."[45] In it, he sympathized with the Soviet's proposal but emphasized the need for a Persian settlement, noting that St. Petersburg had for decades carried out a "damned policy that enforces an emigration of simple-minded Russian peasants and moves them to a foreign country for the undisguised purpose of the Russification of other countries and assimilating and absorbing foreign peoples." Drawing on the idea of "ancient races"—distinct from, but often appearing in tandem with the idea of "small nations"—Taqīzādeh claimed that the migration of one hundred thousand Russian peasants into Persia threatened to destroy a people that had, "all the way from Zoroaster's and Cyrus's days to the present time, uninterruptedly been a nation and a race and had one language and culture."[46] Taqīzādeh adopted a similar tack in a French-language communique to the Russian provisional government written from Stockholm in August, noting how the principles behind "the democratic spirit" that had triumphed over "the autocratic regime" in Russia forbade the use of force or violence against "foreign nations." And from the point of view of "history, its traditions, its language, its culture, its race, and its religion," Taqīzādeh explained, Persia was undoubtedly a nation foreign to Russia.[47] In short, even if the annihilation of "ancient races" was in any event deplorable, Russia's newfound embrace of a politics of peace forbade it from oppressing peoples whom Orientalist scholarship had unambiguously identified as distinct nations with their own right to develop without foreign interference or dilution.

Taqīzādeh and ul-Mulk adopted a different tack in their communiqué to the Stockholm conference. Their "Appeal of the Persian People" explained that without extending the protection accorded to "weak nations" like Poland also to

Persia, imperialist intrigue would turn "Persian soil into the scene of other murderous and bloody wars." The only solution that would prevent "the capitalists on the Thames and the Neva" from doing so "would be for Persia to become in Middle Asia what Switzerland is in Middle Europe: its own master with its own rights, untouchable independence, and a right to defend itself and cordon itself off from European covetousness."[48] Were the appeal to a Hobsonian anti-imperialism not enough, the pair situated Persia, and Shi'ism, within a Christian frame of reference. Referring to the 1911 Russian bombardment of the Imam Reza shrine in Mashhad, the manifesto stressed that the site held "the same meaning for Shi'ite Mohammadans as the Church of the Holy Sepulchre in Jerusalem for Christendom."[49] While something of an intellectual grab bag, the communiqué bolsters the argument of Rebecca Karl that political self-determination was not the only desideratum for colonial actors during the global moment of the late 1910s. The Persians recognized that global capitalist relations and a dismissal of the Islamic heritage had produced inequalities that political sovereignty alone would not remedy.

## "The Ukrainian Newborn": Brest-Litovsk

Such talk of economic hierarchy and religious communities aside, political sovereignty still remained very attractive—even if it was not Wilson who would deliver it to Persia. As Taqīzādeh himself recalled in his Columbia lectures, "there seemed to be very little hope for Iran as an independent state when an unexpected and great historical event changed the whole situation. This was the Russian Revolution of 1917."[50] Following the October Revolution, the Bolsheviks began troop withdrawals from Persian Azerbaijan, published the contents of the Sykes-Picot Agreement (whose visions of Russia annexing Persian Azerbaijan and eastern Anatolia were abandoned), and entered into peace negotiations with the Central powers. Yet perhaps more important than these immediate actions was the question of what kind of legitimate peace the Bolsheviks would pursue in the former czarist limitrophe. In late December, Bolshevik negotiating teams led by Leon Trotsky and German military commanders agreed to an armistice that de facto recognized the independence of the territories liberated by the Central powers since the beginning of the war: the Kingdom of Finland, the Kingdom of Lithuania, the Duchy of Courland, and the aforementioned Polish state. Yet many Bolsheviks criticized this as a sellout, demanding that the Allied powers apply self-determination to their own territories and colonies, while others argued for a war of revolutionary self-defense that would expose German liberal hegemony as a smokescreen for capitalist imperialism. Given that the proceedings at Brest-Litovsk were published as part of the Bolsheviks' diplomatic strategy, Iranian nationalists like Taqīzādeh followed Leon Trotsky and demanded the inclusion of Persia in the negotiations so that it would be a subject, and not only an object of negotiations.[51] As Taqīzādeh himself noted in his memoirs, it was no surprise that the Persian government in Tehran recognized the Bolsheviks as the legitimate government of Russia in December 1917, making it one of the few countries to have continuous relations with any government in Petrograd over the winter of 1917–18.[52]

All the same, any legitimate international order over the former czarist limitrophe would have to be reached in accordance with Berlin. More than having backed the Persian cause from the beginning of the war, Berlin had endorsed the rhetoric of self-determination at Brest-Litovsk. As Adam Tooze points out, Wilson's Fourteen Points (which appeared after the initial agreements at Brest-Litovsk) do not contain the word *self-determination* and instead speak in terms of the "interests" of people rather than their desires.[53] And as the Central powers grew more and more desperate for grain deliveries, Berlin and Vienna concluded a sensational "bread peace" (Brotfrieden) with the People's Republic of Ukraine, recognizing the Ukrainian state and setting out fair terms for commercial relations with the republic.[54] (The fact that the republic's representatives did not control Kiev was overlooked.) For many social democrats both within the German Reichstag as well as allies like Taqīzādeh, this was a liberal peace to be proud of. Nations like the Poles and Ukrainians received political and cultural autonomy but would find it in their self-interest to sign commercial treaties with Berlin and Vienna. The question remaining for those who dismiss this position, or Taqīzādeh's support for it, as militarist propagandizing, remains why many social democrats would go to jail *defending* eastern European independence—and why the line taken in German films and editorials of the era was in favor of Ukrainian sovereignty per se, not annexation or further aggression toward Soviet Russia.[55]

Writing as all this was taking place, Taqīzādeh hailed Ukrainian sovereignty as a model for Persia. "What surprising changes are afoot in the world today!" began an article in *Kāveh* titled "The Newborn Ukraine":

> With what quick steps does this old world turn! The neglected children of man hear that events are currently taking place in the world that seem like a breath of fresh air, or perhaps an exception, but tomorrow these issues become part of the normal events of life and become just another part of world affairs. At the same time that great teachers of the economic affairs of the world, or those famous people knowledgeable about geography or great statesmen in their cramped and dark negotiating rooms, sitting next to a pile of books old and new, write long articles, then gather in societies and circles to discuss with one another whether the economic situation, or the geographic reality, or the current political affairs of a country are such that this or that country can be independent, we [now] see that the aforementioned country has taken the great step of declaring its independence to the whole world, that it has uncoiled itself from internal relations with other countries, and that it has been released into freedom.[56]

A map depicted Ukraine (without Crimea but including the territory comprising the Kuban People's Republic, an anti-Bolshevik polity) as connecting an independent Poland with an independent "Caucasus." The point was now less the rights of "ancient races" and more the right of nations to form relations *regardless* of their "age" or "size." All that mattered was a friendly hegemon with whom to sign a bilateral treaty, and the nation could burst into international society.

Of course, the Bolsheviks had other opinions. During negotiations over the place of the now-independent Ukrainian People's Republic in a final peace treaty, Trotsky and other Bolshevik delegates refused to recognize the German-backed Ukrainian Rada, denouncing it as an illegitimate expression of bourgeois domination over the proletariat. While Bolshevik forces were marching on Kiev, Trotsky broke off the negotiations altogether, announcing a brash policy—the only time until then or since in diplomatic history—of unilateral abandonment of war and refusal to continue negotiations.[57] If the imperialists wanted to ravage Ukraine, their thinking went, better that they do so without the trappings of self-determination that Taqīzādeh had just celebrated. Reacting to the chaos at Brest, Woodrow Wilson offered little further clarity in his Fourteen Points by demanding the "evacuation of all Russian territory."[58] But the territories "liberated" by Germany from 1914 to December 1917 already had the ability to determine their fate. Wilson's refusal to distinguish between "Russian," and "Ukrainian" territory left American policy vague. Yet rather than halting the war and supporting the Ukrainian People's Republic, the German military command resumed the war against Soviet Russia on February 18. With the revolution on the line, the Bolsheviks walked back to the negotiating table and agreed to a more punitive (and the more famous) second Treaty of Brest-Litovsk on March 3, 1918.

The treaty prompted quite different reactions among German Social Democrats and Persian nationalists. The former despised it as a "treaty of violation," in contrast to the legitimate "treaty of bread." The SPD (Social Democratic Party of Germany) abstained from voting on the treaty in the Reichstag on March 22, while the USPD (Independent Social Democratic Party of Germany) voted against it. As the German military overthrew the Ukrainian People's Republic with a more compliant Hetmanate in April 1918, the original vision of a liberal hegemonic peace in the East vanished. Or at least it did for Ukraine: as the May 1918 issue of *Kāveh* celebrated, article 7 of Brest-Litovsk recognized the independence of Persia and Afghanistan and made them two of several states whose sovereignty Russia recognized (the others were Ukraine, Estonia, Livonia, Finland, and the Åland Islands).[59] But there was more good news for Persia: an addendum to article 7 forced both the Central powers and Russia to "abstain from any claims to Persian territory or spheres of influence in Persia." A subsequent article titled "Russia and Persia" celebrated the moment, noting that events of the year since Nicholas II's abdication had reversed two centuries of Russo-Persian relations.[60] Not only had Persia and fifty-five million Europeans gained their freedom, but there was a "strong possibility" that the peoples of "the states of southern Asia, like the Caucasus and Turkestan," would attempt to gain their "complete independence, or at least many of their rights and liberties."[61] Ukraine's yesterday had become Persia's present.

Granted, the order inaugurated by the Treaty of Brest-Litovsk was very much in flux. The Bolshevik negotiating team at the Brest fortress signed the treaty without so much as reading it, dismissing it as a *diktat* of imperialist diplomacy. (The Bolsheviks had already de facto unilaterally abdicated all czarist claims to Persian territory and established relations with the government in Tehran. Even if they dismissed the treaty as a scrap of paper, Brest-Litovsk did not confirm anything the Bolsheviks had not already given away in Persia.) The summer of 1918 saw the German army advance beyond the Brest-Litovsk line, as military brass like Erich Ludendorff envisioned the overthrow of the Bolshevik regime and the transformation of Russia into a subject of German hegemony. The General Staff even planned a joint invasion of Petrograd with now-independent Finland. Recognizing the weakness of his position, on August 27, Lenin signed a supplementary treaty to Brest-Litovsk that guaranteed German and Finnish support for the Bolshevik regime's survival in exchange for 6 billion marks ($1.46 billion) and Moscow's recognition of Georgian independence. Celebrating German imperialism where their German Social Democratic colleagues could not, the editorial team at *Kāveh* was thrilled. Echoing its initial pieces on Georgian nationhood, *Kāveh* celebrated the release of the Georgians and (also now independent) Armenians from eight hundred years of tyranny.[62] What a legitimate peace in the East looked like depended very much on whether one looked at it from Berlin or Tehran.

### From Brest-Litovsk to Paris

Legitimate or not, the peace in the East soon unraveled. The armistice that Germany signed with the Entente on November 11, 1918, annulled the Treaty of Brest-Litovsk. But what would replace it at the Paris Peace Conference was anyone's guess. Political entrepreneurs like Taqīzādeh, used to monopolizing the attention of German interlocutors, would now have to compete for the sympathy of the Americans, British, and French. The Persian government in Tehran had never abdicated, and it maintained relations with the Allied powers throughout the war. After Wilson had given his "peace without victory" speech, the Persian ambassador to Washington had noted his personal approval and emphasized to Wilson's Secretary of State Robert Lansing that Tehran looked forward to a seat "whenever a peace conference should take place."[63] Later that same year, in December 1917, the Persian ambassador repeated this demand, adding that he expected American assistance in revising the Treaty of Turkmenchai (1828) following the war.[64] Washington ignored this. The Inquiry, a study group that Wilson had commissioned to explore myriad territorial issues around the world, rejected the idea of territorial concessions to Persia (although reserving the possibility of "unifying" Azerbaijan within a Persian state).[65]

Given its very modest history of lobbying Washington, the Persian governmental team hesitated over the best way to make its case once in Paris. One draft of the territorial demands noted that the seasonal movement of nomadic tribes and the Persian watersheds of rivers in eastern Mesopotamia spoke for a limited annexation of territory from what was to become Iraq.[66] Another draft section asked for territory in the Caucasus on the basis of the majority of the population "being of the Aryan race, speaking Persian, and being Muslim" and analogies between the Caucasus (for Persia) and Alsace-Lorraine (for France) and Yugoslavia (for Serbia)—formulations that were dropped in lieu of more muted language of how these Caucasus territories "must be returned to Persia, for they had already been made part of Persia."[67] In another draft, the delegation argued that a strong, independent Shi'a Persia would serve as a bulwark against pan-Islamism and pan-Turanism.[68] Persia, a final draft explained, deserved rewards for remaining neutral as "a great Mussulman country" in a conflict in which Turkey had declared a "Holy War."[69]

Finally, the Persian government team issued its demands, an ambitious list of territorial annexations and sectarian protectorates.[70] In addition, the Persian government delegation demanded a cancelation of all debts to Russia, an assignment of war damages to the debt of Turkey, and some Persian share in German indemnities payments. These demands were issued not only to the great powers but also against other delegations, especially that of the Azerbaijan Democratic Republic. Even though its territorial demands implied the liquidation of the republic, Tehran demanded that no other country in the world should have the right to call itself "Azerbaijan" and urged an immediate border agreement with Turkey to avoid schemes to divide Baku and Tehran over the question of Azerbaijan.[71]

More significant, however, was the rival Persian delegation led by Taqīzādeh. One month after the Persian government issued its demands, in April 1919, Taqīzādeh issued "a brief statement of the Persian cause and the moderate aspiration of the people."[72] As the *Memorandum on Persia's Wishes and Her Aspirations* argued, "the Persian question [was] an important one for the World-Peace" due to Persia's location and sizable population. Returning to his established discourse of "ancient" nations, Taqīzādeh argued that "the Persian nation" was entitled to equal treatment because of its past contributions "to the world's civilization and human progress." Persia, he noted, had given refuge to both "the Children of Israel" and "the persecuted philosophers of Byzantium." Further, stressed the text, the "Wise Men of the East" (the Three Magi), whom Taqīzādeh identified as Persian, were among the very first to greet "the Great Peace-Preacher of the World."[73] And lest readers discount the need to return such acts of goodwill, the memorandum reminded them of the commonality between Persia and "her Western Indo-European brothers."[74]

As far as concrete demands were concerned, Taqīzādeh "merely" demanded the evacuation of foreign troops from Persia, the annulment of foreign treaties and capitulations, a loan of $100 million, and admission into the League of Nations.[75] Far from a budding Shi'a hegemon outfitted with a Kurdish colony and able to stand as a bulwark against Sunni fanaticism, Turkish adventurism, and Russian power, Taqīzādeh imagined a more modest polity integrated into international society not only through the League of Nations but also its deep links with a Judeo-Christian and Indo-European "West." Left unanswered in both the Persian government's and Taqīzādeh's proposals, however, was how Persian sovereignty would be guaranteed through the League of Nations. Problematic as the peace at Brest-Litovsk had been, it had at least been backed by German military and economic power, while the unilateral concessions granted to Persia from Petrograd were backed by the moral force of world anti-imperialist opinion. As the league's covenant was announced that summer, with Persia invited to join, what kind of sovereignty Persia could claim for itself under the new liberal international order remained an open question.

## Ironic Victory

These Persian proposals for the place of a sovereign Persia in the world belong to the realm of intellectual, not political history. Neither the British, nor French, nor Americans at Versailles heard their proposals. And as far as London was concerned, the overriding desideratum was that the Persian government sign a treaty guaranteeing British access to the oil reserves of the Persian Gulf. After six months of secret negotiations, on August 9, 1919, London and Tehran announced the signing of a blockbuster Anglo-Persian agreement that would turn Persia into a virtual British protectorate. Formalizing the specter of political independence with economic colonization, Persia was "pre-admitted" as a founding member of the League of Nations in November 1919.[76] As Taqīzādeh recounted in the Columbia lectures, it had become apparent that "Britain hastened to take Russia's place" in Persia "with the purpose of establishing a complete domination."[77]

Soon standing in the way of a British liberal hegemony over Persia, however, was not only Persian domestic opinion but also the Red Army. During the winter of 1919–20, the Red Army charged through the Caucasus, threatening to reconquer Baku from the Azerbaijan Democratic Republic and dislodge White Russian forces from the southern shore of the Caspian Sea. Élites from the Azerbaijan Democratic Republic petitioned the league to join a federal arrangement with Persia and be "separated from Russia whatever government is established."[78] Only a year earlier, the Azerbaijanis and the two Persian delegations had squabbled over the partition of greater Azerbaijan; now, the imperative to avoid Bolshevism was enough for the Azerbaijanis to demand that Persia annex the Azerbaijan Democratic Republic in order to protect it from Soviet rule.

It was in this geopolitical conjuncture that *Kāveh* reminded readers of the danger of Russian imperialism. Since 1916, the Persian writer Mohammad 'Ali Jamālzādeh had authored many of the newspaper's articles on Russo-Persian relations, themselves extracts from a bigger book on Russo-Persian relations from ancient times until the Russo-Persian War of 1722–23.[79] Finally published in 1920, it was reviewed in the January 1920 issue of *Kāveh* by Taqīzādeh with glowing praise.[80] Until very recently, Taqīzādeh noted, Persian history had been marked by clashes with the Turks and the Arabs. Russia, in contrast, barely registered in the Persian historical imagination. "If someone during the age of the Safavids had spoken of the risk of the Russians' proximity to Persia," wrote Taqīzādeh, "he would have been the object of laughter and ridicule. Behind the Caucasus Mountains and the shores of the Caspian Sea and the Black Sea, there they were, a half-barbarian people dwelling and toiling in abominably cold lands. The name of this nation had not been heard in the Orient of the world until the time of Vladimir I."[81]

Tragically for Persia, however, the Russians turned out to be a formidable nation. While the Russians were themselves colonized by "Mongol barbarians" under Ivan the Terrible and the Romanov Dynasty, the Russian Empire had begun to colonize the lands to its south. The pinnacle of the "confiscation, torture, invasion, violation, and murder" had been the Treaty of Turkmenchai (1828). If this process had continued indefinitely, Taqīzādeh wrote, soon "armed herds of barbarians from the shores of the Neva would have invaded the mountains of Luristan, the plains of Isfahan, the capital of Shah 'Abbas the Great, Mashhad, the capital of Nader Shah, Qom, Qazvin, Hamadan, and Kermanshah.[82] Who knows—if the Russian Revolution had not happened, perhaps they would have set foot onto the Pasargaedae and the waters [i.e., the Persian Gulf]?"[83] Bolshevism had initially seemed to mark a decisive break from the Russian imperial past, but by May 1920, the Russian threat had presented itself again, as the Bolsheviks had not only captured Baku (destroying the Azerbaijan Democratic Republic) but also launched the Soviet Caspian fleet toward Enzeli to destroy White Russian armies stationed there and to support the insurgency of Mirza Kuchek Khān, a guerrilla leader who had rebelled against Tehran for years.

The emergency in northern Persia prompted diverse reactions from Persians in Berlin and London. No friend of British or Russian imperialism, Muhammad Jamālzādah nonetheless explored the possibility of ideological community between the Bolsheviks and Persians in two long articles for *Kāveh*. Whereas "Bolshevism" or "socialism" had once only been the fanciful vision of a few utopians, wrote Jamālzādeh, the collapse of the Russian Empire and the October Revolution had led to the dissolution of centuries' worth of autocratic laws. The historical importance of Bolshevism in Russia, he stressed, was on the scale of "the Ancient Greeks' discoveries in science and philosophy, the appearance of the Nazarenes [i.e., Christians], the conquest of the Arabs, the invasion of the Mongols, the discovery of America, and the great uprising of France."[84] More than being confined to Russia, moreover, Jamālzādeh reminded readers that "what goes by the name of Bolshevism [had] manifested itself" in Hungary and Bavaria too.

Yet rather than rushing to judgment—so common with great historical events—Jamālzādeh instead sought to contextualize Soviet socialism in the longer durée. "The first manifestation and appearance of the socialist approach," he wrote, "was in Persia, and the first famous socialist of the world who acted on the strength of his conviction was Mazdak the Persian."[85] The name of Mazdak might not be familiar. But Mazdak was a sixth-century prophet and religious reformer who rebelled against the established Zoroastrian clergy of his time and preached for communal property. Mazdak's call threatened the Sassanid ruler Khosrow I so much that Mazdak and many of his followers were put to death. Jamālzādeh was not the first to highlight Mazdak as a champion of social justice and even socialism. Yet the move to highlight Mazdak as a socialist showed how the historical heritage of Persia could be endlessly refashioned in order to speak to new geopolitical circumstances. Jamālzādeh reviled Russian imperialism, but he found much in common with Soviet socialism. Still, as was once the case at the Stockholm conference, it remains less clear if Persian nationalists viewed global capitalism, rather than a lack of political sovereignty, as *the* fundamental obstacle to be overcome for securing their nation's place in the sun.[86] Nationalists like Taqīzādeh were fundamentally interested in sovereignty, although for them liberal internationalism was not necessarily its best guarantor—one need look no further than the conjunction of the Anglo-Persian Treaty and Persian entry into the League of Nations.

In the meantime, however, the Bolshevik threat continued to put severe pressure on the league and Persia's future. By the spring of 1920, with the Red Army on the verge of invading northern Persia, and rumors (true, it turned out) that the British had bribed the Persian government to sign the Anglo-Persian agreement, the government in Tehran was on the verge of implosion. Persia could become a viable bridgehead for world revolution in the way that Hungary and Bavaria had not. Fearful of Bolshevism, Tehran appealed to the logic of internationalization, via the League of Nations, that the British had unwittingly granted them. On May 19, 1920, the Persian government filed an appeal to the League of Nations demanding a meeting of the League Council (Britain, France, Italy, and Japan) to consider collective action to safeguard the peace in Persia.[87] London dithered—it was not clear whether it could conduct an intervention into Persia against a non-league member like the USSR. (Making things more complicated still was the fact that no members of the league even recognized the USSR at all, much less as a member of the league.[88]) More fundamentally, however, allowing the Persians to appeal to the League Council would force London and Paris to defend the idea of an independent Persian state when the very point of league membership had been to provide Tehran with an "independence safe for empire."[89] But on June 2, the league agreed to review the case to the council for a meeting on June 5.[90]

It was ironic timing. On the same day (June 5) that the League Council agreed that league members could intervene to defend Persia's territorial integrity, in northern Persia Kuchek Khān announced the formation of a Soviet Republic of Gilan that received Soviet support.[91] This placed the British in an extraordinary position. The dream of a Persian colony in all but name was disintegrating rapidly. But in order to save it, the British had to walk a fine line between discrediting the league as a fig leaf for imperialism or watching the Bolshevization of Persia.[92] Turning to the League Council to authorize an intervention offered a solution, but it also had the effect of treating Persia "as if" it were a sovereign state—the fiction that legitimized the league as something more than a cloak for British hegemony. As a certain Jean Monnet (then a thirty-two-year-old deputy secretary general of the league) made clear to Sir Eric Drummond, the Secretary-General of the league, much caution was needed before hearing Persia's claims vis-à-vis Soviet Russia, since "Persia is not considered as having actually complete independence."[93] But how could the league authorize London to intervene to protect Persian sovereignty if Persia was not really sovereign? Perhaps without realizing it, the Persian government had exploited the contradictions of the league by tak-ing its guarantees seriously.

Soon, however, the attempt to internationalize the war in northern Per-sia backfired. Mirza Kuchek Khān, the guerrilla leader of the Soviet Republic of Gilan, grew tired of Soviet meddling into his own revolution and fled into the wooded hills from which his *Jangal* (forest) movement took its name. Pan-icked over the prospect of a complete loss of influence in Tehran, in the late sum-mer the Bolsheviks sought negotiations with the Persian government. Moscow wanted above all to forestall that northern Persia could ever again be used as a staging ground against Soviet Russia—and an agreement that Tehran would tol-erate socialist parties.[94] The Persian government sent ʿAlīgholī Khān Moshaver Memalek, then the Persian ambassador to Istanbul, to negotiate the treaty with Moscow, which was signed on February 26, 1921. It was a major accomplish-ment for Tehran, helping to formalize much of what had been gained at Brest-Litovsk—then lost over the course of 1918–21. The treaty represented the first equal agreement that Persia had signed with any European state for centuries, and even Taqīzādeh, who was critical of the treaty, noted that it came as "a great relief" after years of occupation and interference. Not long after Persia had un-intentionally secured its status as an independent country through the league's logic of internationalization, it had also secured recognition of its sovereignty from Moscow.

Nevertheless, "after the treaty had been published," wrote Taqīzādeh in his memoirs, "I wrote an interpretation of it in the newspaper *Kāveh* and made some criticisms of it."[95] In *Kāveh*'s August 1921 issue, Taqīzādeh attacked articles 5 and 6 of the treaty, which allowed Soviet Russia the right of intervention "if a third party should attempt to carry out a policy of usurpation by means of armed in-tervention in Persia."[96] Taqīzādeh noted that the wording of the treaty gave Mos-cow alone the right to decide whether Persian territory was, in fact, being used to prepare an attack on Russia. As such, he explained, the treaty had placed Per-sia in the same situation as Belgium prior to the First World War.[97] Taqīzādeh also disliked the use of the phrase "according to international law and usage" as a benchmark in the treaty, suggesting it be replaced by "according to enforced international norms" or "in all countries." As Taqīzādeh observed, previously existing international law had, after all, made coup d'états in Persia an estab-lished international custom. While Persians would work with the great powers as needed, history had shown international law per se to be little more than a scrap of paper when it came to Persian sovereignty.

Irked by Taqīzādeh's criticism, the Persian government sent *him* to Moscow to negotiate the details of telegraph and transport treaties with the new Soviet gov-ernment. (The Treaty of Turkmenchai had made the Caspian in effect a Russian lake.) His departure marked the closure of *Kāveh* in Berlin, but even after a year and a half, the negotiations failed due to a new prime minister in Tehran.[98] In August 1923, Taqīzādeh departed for Berlin, where he would marry his German fiancée before departing back to Persia for a new chapter of a "stormy life" (as he titled his memoirs), this time as a deputy in the Persian parliament. Yet in spite of its deficiencies, the Russo-Persian Treaty of 1921 proved longer-lasting than Brest-Litovsk as a basis for Persia's place in the world. While Tehran unilaterally rejected articles 5 and 6 following the Islamic Revolution, it proved far more durable than either Brest-Litovsk or the League of Nations. What Eric Weitz dubs a "Bolshevik moment" had failed in the sense of spreading international revolution but succeeded in securing Persia, finally, into a new kind of international order marked by the league on the one hand and Moscow's support for postcolonial nationalisms on the other.[99]

## Conclusion

Miraculously, the First World War had turned Persia not into a colony but rather a member of international society. True, none of Persia's territorial demands—not to speak of its claims to protectorate status over Shi'a shrines beyond Persia's borders—had been fulfilled. Many aspects of Persia's position within the international system of the league still treated it as a protectorate, limiting, for example, the number of arms it was allowed to import.[100] Yet in contrast to the territorial settlement in much of the former Ottoman Empire produced by the Sykes-Picot Agreement, the borders within which Tehran was to accommodate itself have endured for more than a century. The British and the Soviets regarded Persian sovereignty as a malleable thing, but Persian elites working between London and Moscow had asked for as much sovereignty as the league or Kremlin would permit. Little by little, from Brest-Litovsk to Moscow, Persians had found creative ways to work debates about the new international order that the Great War had thrown onto the table.

What does looking "beyond Versailles" through the lens of Persia do for our understandings of this global moment more broadly? Firstly, it underscores the importance of looking beyond not only Versailles but also Wilsonianism to reconstruct the history of internationalism. Not only was Wilsonianism late to the debate about self-determination opened up between the Germans and the Bolsheviks at Brest-Litovsk, but for actors along the former czarist limitrophe, Bolshevik internationalism and German liberal hegemony were the only two options for a postwar order actually backed by force. While Persian actors appealed to the League of Nations as an arena to defend their sovereignty during the Bolshevik invasion of northern Persia in 1920, Taqīzādeh's later insistence on the crucial semantic difference between "enforced international norms" and "international law" is suggestive of how little faith Persian actors put into internationalism (as opposed to partnership with a great power) to defend their interests.

Secondly, it underscores the ways in which non-Western actors themselves thought broadly about what kind of legitimate international order would follow the war. As this piece has emphasized, Persian intellectuals thought globally. Taqīzādeh understood the Ukrainian sovereignty crisis of his time as a bellwether for global concepts of sovereignty and embraced the cause of German liberal hegemony over Poland, Finland, or Georgia, as Persia's. In his Columbia lectures, Taqīzādeh reiterated how Persian-language periodicals in India and the

Ottoman Empire served as incubators for Persian liberal thought, as well as the ways in which the Russian defeat at the hands of the Japanese emboldened Persian constitutionalists in the aftermath of 1905.[101] In this sense, bringing transnational approaches to bear on the study of nationalisms and internationalisms after the First World War does not constitute a back-projection of our understandings of "the global" onto those historical actors but only helps us re-create the connections that actors like Taqīzādeh took for granted.

Finally, however, Persia's experience reminds us that this global moment was full of broken promises—not just Wilson's—that have profound effects on the internationalist thought embedded within postcolonial nationalisms today. Every acknowledgement of Persian sovereignty achieved from 1918 to 1921 was violated, voided, or conditional. Brest-Litovsk was abrogated through the 1918 armistice (on the German side) and the invasion of Enzeli (on the Soviet side). While the British were very keen to defend the idea of Persian sovereignty under the aegis of the League of Nations when Soviet Russia appeared to threaten British interests in Persia, London violated the league covenant and Persian sovereignty when it jointly invaded Iran along with the Soviet Union in 1941. And as we have seen, while the Russo-Persian Treaty recognized Persian sovereignty, it also made explicit Moscow's right to intervene in Persia through articles 6 and 7. While this piece has, then, urged that we take seriously German and Bolshevik promises for international society, it is worth recalling that from the point of view of Tehran, these alternative visions of internationalism were as full of disappointments as Wilsonianism was for so many others.[102] At a time when Tehran's place in international society remains contested, understanding these early moments of promise—and betrayal—could scarcely be more urgent.

## Notes

1. In current Persian, the name for the country whose capital is Tehran is *Irān*, but because Western sources came into contact with Iran through Greek sources calling the country *Persis*—itself an exonym referring to the region of Pars in southwestern Iran—the country was called Persia well into the twentieth century. In 1935, Reẓa Shah Pahlavi requested foreign delegates to refer to the country by the name "Iran," a usage that had gained traction. However, the adjective *Persian* is still often used in cultural contexts ("Persian cuisine," "Persian music").

2. Keivandokht Ghahari, *Nationalismus und Modernismus in Iran in der Periode zwischen dem Zerfall der Qāǧāren-Dynastie und der Machtfestigung Reẓa Schahs. Eine Untersuchung über die intellektuellen Kreise um die Zeitschriften Kāweh, Iranšahr und Āyandeh* (Berlin: Klaus Schwarz Verlag, 2001); Afshin Marashi, *Nationalizing Iran: Culture, Power, and the State 1870–1940* (Seattle: University of Washington Press, 2008); Ali Ansari, *The Politics of Nationalism in Modern Iran* (Cambridge: Cambridge University Press, 2012); Ali Ansari, ed., *Perceptions of Iran: History, Myths, and Nationalism* (London: IB Tauris, 2014).

3. Glenda Sluga, *Internationalism in the Age of Nationalism* (Philadelphia: University of Pennsylvania Press, 2013); Mark Mazower, *Governing the World: The History of an Idea* (New York: Penguin, 2012), especially 48–54.

4. Sebastian Conrad, *What Is Global History?* (Princeton, NJ: Princeton University Press, 2016), 84. Rebecca E. Karl, *Staging the World: Chinese Nationalism at the Turn of the Twentieth Century* (Durham, NC: Duke University Press, 2002); Erez Manela, *The Wilsonian Moment: Self-Determination and the International Origins of Anticolonial Nationalism* (Oxford: University of Oxford Press, 2007).

5. Manela, *Wilsonian Moment*; Susan Pedersen, *The Guardians: The League of Nations and the Crisis of Empire* (Oxford: University of Oxford Press, 2015).

6. Afshin Matn-Asgari, "The Impact of Imperial Russia and the Soviet Union on Qajar and Pahlavi Iran: Notes toward a Revisionist Historiography," in *Iranian-Russian Encounters: Empires and Revolutions Since 1800*, ed. Stephanie Cronin (London: Routledge, 2013), 11–46.

7. For a useful parallel in Ottoman history, see Aimee Genell, "Empire by Law: Ottoman Sovereignty and the British Occupation of Egypt, 1882–1923" (PhD diss., Columbia University, 2013).

8. Rebecca E. Karl, "Review of *The Wilsonian Moment* by Erez Manela," *American Historical Review* 113, no. 5 (December 2008): 1474–76. See also Arno J. Mayer, *The Political Origins of the New Diplomacy* (New Haven, NJ: Yale University Press, 1959), and *Politics and Diplomacy of Peacemaking: Containment and Counterrevolution at Versailles, 1918–1919* (New York: Knopf, 1967).

9. James L. Gelvin and Nile Green, eds., *Global Muslims in the Age of Steam and Print* (Berkeley: University of California Press, 2013).

10. Hassan Taqīzādeh, "Lecture 2" from "The History of Modern Iran" Lecture Series, in *Maqālāt-I Taqīzādeh, Jald-I Hashtom, Neveshtehha-yī khārajī*, ed. Iraj Āfshār (Tehran: Shekufan, 1979), 221.

11. Sean McMeekin, *The Russian Origins of the First World War* (Cambridge, MA: Harvard University Press, 2011), 194–213.

12. The committee and the council were forced to move to another city in western Persia, Qaṣr-i Shirin and later Baghdad (then in the Ottoman Empire) following successful Russian advances toward Kermanshah in the summer of 1916. However, once Turkish forces reclaimed Kermanshah later that summer, the two institutions returned there. For more on this episode, see Jean Calmard, "Kermanshah IV: History to 1953," *Encylopeadia Iranica*, online edition, 2015, accessed October 19, 2018, http://www.iranicaonline.org/articles/kermanshah-04-history-to-1953

13. 'Alīqolī Khān (1856–1917) was a Persian revolutionary, founder of the French Masonic Lodge in Iran, and one of the leading figures in the Iranian Constitutional Revolution; Hassan Taqīzādeh, *Zendegī-yī Tufānī (Khāterāt-I Saidhassan Taqīzādeh)*, ed. Iraj Āfshār (Tehran: Muhammad 'Ali Ilmi, 1989), 175.

14. Ibid., 176.

15. Ibid., 181–82.

16. Ibid., 184.

17. Ibid., 183.

18. Sayyid Mohammad-Ali Jamāzādeh (1892–1997) was one of the pioneers of modern Persian prose fiction. One issue of interest, but beyond the bounds of this paper, is *Kāveh*'s war reporting. According to *Encylopedia Iranica*, two Persians, Reẓaqolī Khān Māfi Neẓam-al-Salṭāna (the chair of the National Defense Council in Kermanshah) and Sayyid Hassan Modarres (the head of the Council of Representatives) contributed the bulk of the paper's reporting from the Ottoman-Russian front but does not go into further detail about the transmission of such information from Mesopotamia and Iran to Berlin.

19. Hassan Taqīzādeh, *Persien und der europäische Krieg* (Berlin: Karl Curtius, 1915), in Politisches Archiv des Auswärtigen Amtes (PA/AA) R 19156.

20. Ibid., 39–40.

21. Ibid., 40, 42. Kavus was the mythological shah of Iran in parts of Ferdowsi's epic *Shāhnāmeh*, while Afrasiab was the ruler of a rival polity, Turan (often identified with Turkic invaders from central Eurasia).

22. Ibid., 43. The sixteen states identified as colonized were India, Egypt, Sudan, Morocco, Algeria, Tunis, Tripoli, Baluchistan, Bukhara, Khiva, the Crimea, Kazan, the Caucasus, Dagestan, Somaliland, and Oman. Albania (which became independent in 1913) was occupied by Bulgarian and Austrian forces from October 1915, when Taqīzādeh would have been finishing *Persia and the European War*, thus allowing for this conquest to be depicted as the liberation of a Muslim country.

23. For more on the idea of Muslim world politics, see Cemil Aydin, *The Idea of the Muslim World: A Global Intellectual History* (Cambridge, MA: Harvard University Press, 2017). While I do not have space in this essay to compare Taqīzādeh's vision of Muslim world politics with the ideas discussed by Aydin, it is worth noting that Taqīzādeh focused much more on issues specifically humiliating to Shi'a (i.e., the potential bargaining away of Karbala and Najaf) and placed a greater emphasis on the political possibilities available to still existing Muslim states (rather than the possibilities of the transnational mobilization of Muslims under British, French, or Russian rule).

24. Friedrich Naumann, *Mitteleuropa* (Berlin: G. Reimer, 1915).

25. "Nazarī betārikh ve dars 'abrat. Dāstān-I Gerjestān yā fardā-yi Irān," *Kāveh*, April 16, 1916; "Nazari beh tārikh ve dars 'abrat. Inferāẓ-I Lahistān yā Akhtrāt beh Irāniyān," *Kāveh*, May 5, 1916; "Nazari beh tārikh ve dars 'abrat. Sargozasht-I Fenlānd," *Kāveh*, June 15, 1916.

26. Taqīzādeh, *Zendegī-yī Tufānī*, 187.

27. "Āwalīn ruz-I isteqlāl-I Lahistān," *Kāveh*, November 15, 1916, 8.

28. Original: "madāf' ain-i malal-i saghir" in "Nashawad Lahastān," *Kāveh*, November 15, 1916, 1.

29. Eugene Rogan, *The Fall of the Ottomans: The Great War in the Middle East* (New York: Basic Books, 2015), 266.

30. "Suqut-i Kut al-Am'arnāh," *Kāveh*, May 16, 1916, 8; "Shekast-i Rushā dar Irān," *Kāveh*, July 15, 1916, 8.

31. Adam Tooze, *The Deluge: The Great War and the Remaking of Global Order, 1916–1931* (New York: Penguin, 2014), 46.

32. "Aūẓā'-ī rūmānī," *Kāveh*, October 16, 1916, 8.

33. "Rūmānī ham," *Kāveh*, December 1, 1916, 1–2.

34. Ibid., 2.

35. *Kāveh* was referring to William Ewart Gladstone (1809–1898), who campaigned against Benjamin Disraeli in part on the latter's meek response to the massacres of Bulgarians in the Ottoman Empire. The reference here is in all likelihood to Gladstone's 1876 pamphlet *Bulgarian Horrors and the Question of the East*, an anti-Turkish pamphlet which dramatized the massacres for British audiences.

36. The Qur'an, Al-Ghafir 40:25

37. Ibid., 53.

38. Woodrow Wilson, Speech before the United States Congress, January 22, 1917.

39. Georgius Varouxadis, "'Great' Versus 'Small' Nations: Size and National Greatness in Victorian Political Thought," in *Victorian Visions of Global Order: Empire and International Relations in Nineteenth-Century Political Thought*, ed. Duncan Bell

(Cambridge: Cambridge University Press, 2007), 136–58. My thanks to Ben Goossen (Harvard University) for drawing my attention to this piece.

40. Stuart Jones, *Victorian Political Thought* (Basingstoke: Palgrave, 2000), 49.

41. Alfred Zimmern, "The International Settlement and Small Nationalities" (1919), in Alfred Zimmern, *The Prospects of Democracy and Other Essays* (London, 1929), 116–34. Tellingly, the original setting for this text was as an address on Welsh self-determination within the United Kingdom.

42. "Talagrāf dād khuahi az taraf vatan parastān-i Irān beh Vilsun," *Kāveh*, February 15, 1917, 16.

43. Tooze, *Deluge*, 77.

44. Taqīzādeh, *Zendegī-yī Tufānī*, 188.

45. Taqīzādeh, "En persisk patriot, som riktar en vädjan till ryska regeringen," *Stockholms Dagblad*, June 29, 1917, reproduced in *Maqālāt-I Taqīzādeh*, vol. 8 (*Neveshtehhā-yi Siyāsī beh zabānhā-yi khārajī*), ed. Iraj Āfshār (Tehran, 1978), 707–13.

46. Ibid., 711.

47. Taqīzādeh, Letter to President of the Council of Ministers of the Provisional Government of Russia (August 1917), in *Maqālāt-I Taqīzādeh, Jald-I Hashtom, Neveshtehha-yī khārajī*, ed. Iraj Āfshār (Tehran: Shekufan, 1979), 300–1.

48. Hassan Taqīzādehand Wahid ul-Mulk, "Aufruf des persischen Volkes an den International Kongress der Sozialisten in Stockholm in Sommer 1917," in *Maqālāt-I Taqīzādeh*, vol. 8 (*Neveshtehhā-yi Siyāsī beh zabānhā-yi khārajī*), ed. Iraj Āfshār (Tehran, 1978), 714–17.

49. The Imam Reẓa Shrine in Mashhad contains the remains of the eighth Shi'a Imam and is one of the most important pilgrimage sites for Shi'a Muslims after Mecca, Karbala, and Najaf.

50. Taqīzādeh, "Lecture 2," 223–24.

51. On other Iranian nationalists and negotiations with the Bolsheviks, Rouhollah K. Ramazani, *The Foreign Policy of Iran, 1500-1941: A Developing Nation in World Affairs* (Charlottesville: University of Virginia Press, 1966, 146–63); Leon Trotsky, quoted in Victor Serge, *Year One of the Russian Revolution*, chapter 5, accessed February 28, 2018, https://www.marxists.org/archive/serge/1930/year-one/ch05.htm; for the proceedings of the conference itself, see Proceedings of the Brest-Litovsk Peace Conference. The Peace Negotiations Between Russia and the Central Powers. November 21, 1917–March 3, 1918 (Washington: Government Printing Office, 1918).

52. Taqīzādeh, *Zendegī-yī Tufānī*, 189; N. M. Mamedova, "Russia ii. Iranian-Soviet Relations (1917–1991)," *Encyclopædia Iranica*, online edition, 2009, accessed February 28, 2018, http://www.iranicaonline.org/articles/russia-ii-iranian-soviet-relations-1917-1991.

53. Tooze, *Deluge*, 119; Woodrow Wilson, Fourteen Points (January 8, 1918), accessed February 28, 2018, http://avalon.law.yale.edu/20th_century/wilson14.asp.

54. Among these were the requirement that grain deliveries be paid for on delivery with industrial goods (not on credit), the cession of the city of Chełm from the Kingdom of Poland (the aforementioned Polish entity existent from 1916 to 1918) to Ukraine, and the creation of a new province of Ruthenia in the Austro-Hungarian Empire with the recognition of cultural autonomy for Ukrainians therein (Tooze, *Deluge*, 132).

55. Klaus Epstein, *Matthias Erzberger and the Dilemma of German Social Democracy* (Princeton, NJ: Princeton University Press, 1959), 219–20, 237.

56. Aukrāīnī-yi Nowzād," *Kāveh*, March 15, 1918, 2.

57. Tooze, *Deluge*, 132.

58. Woodrow Wilson, Speech before the United States Congress, January 8, 1918.

59. "Vaqāi'a-yi Jang-i Farangistān," *Kāveh*, April 15, 1918, 8.

60. "Rus ve Irān," *Kāveh*, May 15, 1918, 1.

61. Ibid.

62. "Vaqāi'a-yi Jang-i Farhangistān," *Kāveh*, October 15, 1918, 16–7. In the same article, *Kāveh* dismissed the Czechoslovak army then fighting against the Bolsheviks as the expression of "ancient enmity" among Slavic peoples toward the Austrian state.

63. Mehdi Khan (ambassador of Persia to the United States), Message to Robert Lansing (January 15, 1917) in *Papers Relating to the Foreign Relations of the United States 1917—Supplement 1—The Great War* (Washington, DC: Government Printing Office, 1931), 14.

64. Persian Legation to US Department of State (December 17, 1918) in *Papers Relating to the Foreign Relations of the United States 1918—Supplement 1—The Great War* (Washington, DC: Government Printing Office, 1933), 897. The Treaty of Turkmenchai led to the annexation of the territories that now compose most of Armenia, Nakhchivan, and southeastern Azerbaijan from Persia by the Russian Empire.

65. Lawrence E. Gelfand, *The Inquiry: American Preparations for Peace, 1917–1919* (New Haven, CT: Yale University Press, 1963), 257.

66. League of Nations Archives, Prince Firuz Papers, Box II, "Droit aux Restitutions Territoriales, Demande de Rectifications de Frontières," 1.

67. Ibid., 5; League of Nations Archives, Prince Firuz Papers, Box II, "Claims of Persia Before the Conference of the Preliminaries in Paris," 9.

68. League of Nations Archives, Prince Firuz Papers, Box II, Untitled (Note on Pan-Islamism) (Undated, probably 1919 or 1920).

69. League of Nations Archives, Prince Firuz Collection, Box II, Alighali Khan and Mocbavorol Mamalek, "Request of the Persian Government to the President and Delegates of the Conference of the Preliminaries of Peace at Paris" (February 1919).

70. These included: (a) the Transcaspian Province of the former Russian Empire; (b) the territories lost in the Treaties of Gulistan and Turkmenchai; (c) all of Turkish Kurdistan; and (d) guarantees that Persia's interests in "the Holy Places" (Shi'a tombs and shrines) in Karbala, Najaf, Kazemin (al-Khadimiyah), and Samerah (Samarra) be taken into consideration (League of Nations Archives, Prince Firuz Papers, Box II, "Claims of Persia Before the Conference of the Preliminaries in Paris," 8–9).

71. League of Nations Archives, Prince Firuz Collection, Box II, Untitled Note (1919).

72. Hassan Taqizādeh, "Memorandum on Persia's Wishes and Her Aspirations Addressed to the Peace Conference of Paris" (The Hague, April 1919), in *Maqālāt-I Taqizādeh*, vol. 8 (*Neveshtehhā-yi Siyāsī beh zabānhā-yi khārajī*), ed. Iraj Afshar (Tehran, 1978), 722–28.

73. Ibid., 724.

74. Ibid., 725.

75. Ibid., 726–27.

76. League of Nations Archives, Box 1450, 28/2138, "Letter Conveying the Formal Accession of Persia to the League of Nations."

77. Taqīzādeh, "Lecture 2," 224.

78. League of Nations Archives, Box R564 11/2558 (Future of the Azerbaijan Republic), Letter from Persian Foreign Ministry to British Foreign Office (December 23, 1919).

79. Muhammad 'Alī Jamālzādeh, *Tārikh-i ravābit-i Rus va Īrān* (1920).

80. Hassan Taqīzādeh, "Tārīkh-i Ravābat-i Rus va Irān," *Kāveh*, January 22, 1920, Attachment, Page A.

81. Ibid., Attachment, Page A-B. Vladimir the Great was ruler of Kievan Rus' from 980 to 1015.

82. Isfahan was the capital of Iran from 1598 until 1736. Shah 'Abbas (1571–1629) is usually considered the greatest of the Safavid rulers of Iran. Under his reign, the capital of Iran was moved from Qazvin to Isfahan. Mashhad was the capital of Iran from 1736 to 1750. Nader Shah was the shah of Persia from 1736 to 1747. Qazvin was the capital of Safavid Iran from 1555 to 1598.

83. The Pasargadae was the capital of the Achamaenid Empire and contains the tomb of Cyrus the Great (600–530 BCE). It is located near Shiraz, in southern Iran (most of the other sites that Taqīzādeh referenced lie in northern Iran), which itself was capital of Iran from 1750 to 1782. (Hassan Taqīzādeh, "Tārīkh-i Ravābat-i Rus va Irān," *Kāveh*, January 22, 1920, Attachment, Page B).

84. "Bālshevism dar Irān-I Qadīm," *Kāveh*, March 21, 1920, 3–4.

85. Ibid., 4. Jamālzādeh's piece continued into a second part, titled "Bālshevīsm dar Irān-I Qadīm," *Kāveh*, May 21, 1920.

86. Karl, "Review of *The Wilsonian Moment*," 1475.

87. League of Nations Archives, Box R573 11/4374, Letter from Prince Firouz (Persian Foreign Minister) to Eric Drummond (secretary general of the League of Nations), May 19, 1920.

88. League of Nations Archives, Box R573 11/4576, Letter from Adrian-Joost van Hamel to Eric Drummond, June 1, 1920.

89. Susan Pedersen's term for Iraqi independence in *The Guardians*.

90. League of Nations Archives, Box R573 11/4624, Letter from Eric Drummond to Prince Firouz, June 2, 1920.

91. A full consideration of Kuchek Khān and Gilan is beyond the scope of this chapter. The classic work remains Cosroe Chaqueri, *The Soviet Socialist Republic of Iran, 1920–1921: Birth of the Trauma* (Pittsburgh: University of Pittsburgh Press, 1995). For one introduction to the literature, see Janet Afary, "The Contentious Historiography of the Gilan Republic in Iran: A Critical Exploration," *Iranian Studies* 28, nos. 1–2 (Winter-Spring 1995): 3–24. A recently published Russian collection offers many of the relevant archival documents from the Soviet side: M. A. Persits, ed., *Persidskiĭ mirovoĭ revoliutsii. Dokumenty o sovetskom vtorzhenii v Gilian (1920–1921)* (Moscow: Kvadriga, 2009).

92. On French opposition to the authorization of intervention, see League of Nations Archives, Box R573 11/4641 (containing numerous editorials from French dailies) and Box R573 11/4593.

93. League of Nations Archives, Box R573 11/4593, Letter from Jean Monnet to Eric Drummond (June 1, 1920)

94. Letter from L. M. Karakhan to the Central Committee of the Russian Communist Party (Bolsheviks) (January 6, 1921), Russian State Archive for Socio-Political History (RGASPI) f. 5, op. 3, d. 208, l. 5–6.

95. Taqīzādeh, *Zendegī-yī Tufānī*, 189.

96. "Ahdnāmeh-yī Irān va Rus," *Kāveh*, August 6, 1921.

97. Ibid., 15.

98. Taqīzādeh, *Zendegī-yī Tufānī*, 191.

99. Eric D. Weitz, "Self-Determination: How a German Enlightenment Idea Became the Slogan for National Liberation and Human Rights," *American Historical Review* 120, no. 2 (2015): 462–96, 485.

100. This happened later within the framework of a 1925 league effort to limit international arms trafficking placing severe restrictions on arms imports to the Persian Gulf and Arabian Sea. For more, see League of Nations Archives, Box R242 8/41051 and 8/42254.

101. Taqīzādeh, drafts of "The History of Modern Iran," in *Maqālāt-I Taqizādeh*, vol. 8 (*Neveshtehhā-yi Siyāsī beh zabānhā-yi khārajī*), ed. Iraj Afshar (Tehran, 1978), 199, 201.
102. Manela, *Wilsonian Moment.*

## Bibliography

Afary, Janet. "The Contentious Historiography of the Gilan Republic in Iran: A Critical Exploration." *Iranian Studies* 28, nos. 1–2 (Winter–Spring 1995): 3–24.

Āfshār, Iraj, ed. *Maqālāt-I Taqīzādeh, Jald-I Hashtom, Neveshtehha-yī khārajī.* Tehran: Shekufan, 1979.

Ansari, Ali, ed. *Perceptions of Iran: History, Myths, and Nationalism.* London: IB Tauris, 2014.

Aydin, Cemil. *The Idea of the Muslim World: A Global Intellectual History.* Cambridge, MA: Harvard University Press, 2017.

Calmard, Jean. "Kermanshah IV: History to 1953." *Encylopeadia Iranica.* Online edition, 2015. Accessed October 19, 2018. http://www.iranicaonline.org/articles/kermanshah-04-history-to-1953.

Chaqueri, Cosroe. *The Soviet Socialist Republic of Iran, 1920–1921: Birth of the Trauma.* Pittsburgh: University of Pittsburgh Press, 1995.

Conrad, Sebastian. *What Is Global History?* Princeton, NJ: Princeton University Press, 2016.

Epstein, Klaus. *Matthias Erzberger and the Dilemma of German Social Democracy.* Princeton, NJ: Princeton University Press, 1959.

Gelfand, Lawrence E. *The Inquiry: American Preparations for Peace, 1917–1919.* New Haven, CT: Yale University Press, 1963.

Genell, Aimee. "Empire by Law: Ottoman Sovereignty and the British Occupation of Egypt, 1882–1923." PhD diss., Columbia University, 2013.

Ghahari, Keivandokht. *Nationalismus und Modernismus in Iran in der Periode zwischen dem Zerfall der Qāğāren-Dynastie und der Machtfestigung Reža Schahs. Eine Untersuchung über die intellektuellen Kreise um die Zeitschriften Kāweh, Iranšahr und Āyandeh.* Berlin: Klaus Schwarz Verlag, 2001.

Jamālzādah, Muhammad 'Alī. *Tārikh-i ravābit-i Rus va Īrān.* 1920.

Jones, Stuart. *Victorian Political Thought.* Basingstoke: Palgrave, 2000.

Karl, Rebecca E. "Review of *The Wilsonian Moment: Self-determination and the International Origins of Anticolonial Nationalism* by Erez Manela." *American Historical Review* 113, no. 5 (December 2008): 1474–76.

———. *Staging the World: Chinese Nationalism at the Turn of the Twentieth Century.* Durham, NC: Duke University Press, 2002.

Khan, Mehdi (Ambassador of Persia to the United States), Message to Robert Lansing (January 15, 1917) in *Papers Relating to the Foreign Relations of the United States 1917—Supplement 1—The Great War,* 14. Washington, DC: Government Printing Office, 1931.

Mamedova, Nina Mamedova. "Russia II: Iranian-Soviet Relations (1917–1991)." *Encyclopædia Iranica.* Online edition, 2009. Accessed October 19, 2018. http://www.iranicaonline.org/articles/russia-ii-iranian-soviet-relations-1917-1991

Manela, Erez. *The Wilsonian Moment: Self-Determination and the International Origins of Anticolonial Nationalism.* Oxford: University of Oxford Press, 2007.

Matn-Asgari, Afshin. "The Impact of Imperial Russia and the Soviet Union on Qajar and Pahlavi Iran: Notes toward a Revisionist Historiography." In *Iranian-Russian*

Encounters: Empires and Revolutions Since 1800, edited by Stephanie Cronin, 11–46. London: Routledge, 2013.

Marashi, Afshin. Nationalizing Iran: Culture, Power, and the State 1870–1940. Seattle: University of Washington Press, 2008.

Mayer, Arno J. The Political Origins of the New Diplomacy. New Haven, CT: Yale University Press, 1959.

———. Politics and Diplomacy of Peacemaking: Containment and Counterrevolution at Versailles, 1918–1919. New York: Knopf, 1967.

Mazower, Mark. Governing the World: The History of an Idea. New York: Penguin, 2012.

McMeekin, Sean. The Russian Origins of the First World War. Cambridge, MA: Harvard University Press, 2011.

Naumann, Friedrich. Mitteleuropa. Berlin: G. Reimer, 1915.

Rogan, Eugene. The Fall of the Ottomans: The Great War in the Middle East. New York: Basic Books, 2015.

Pedersen, Susan. The Guardians: The League of Nations and the Crisis of Empire. Oxford: University of Oxford Press, 2015.

Persian Legation to US Department of State (December 17, 1918) in Papers Relating to the Foreign Relations of the United States 1918—Supplement 1—The Great War, 897. Washington, DC: Government Printing Office, 1933.

Persits, Moiseĭ Persits, ed. Persidskiĭ mirovoĭ revoliutsii. Dokumenty o sovetskom vtorzhenii v Gilian (1920–1921). Moscow: Kvadriga, 2009.

Sluga, Glenda. Internationalism in the Age of Nationalism. Philadelphia: University of Pennsylvania Press, 2013.

Taqīzādeh, Hassan. "En persisk patriot, som riktar en vädjan till ryska regeringen." Stockholms Dagblad, June 29, 1917, reproduced in Maqālāt-I Taqīzādeh, vol. 8 (Neveshtehhā-yi Siyāsī beh zabānhā-yi khārajī), edited by Iraj Āfshār, 707–13. Tehran: Sherkat-i Sahāmī-yi Ufsat, 1978.

———. Zendegī-yī Tufānī (Khāterāt-I Saidhassan Taqīzādeh). Edited by Iraj Āfshār. Tehran: Muhammad 'Ali Ilmi, 1989.

Tooze, Adam. The Deluge: The Great War and the Remaking of Global Order, 1916–1931. New York: Penguin, 2014.

Varouxadis, Georgius. "'Great' Versus 'Small' Nations: Size and National Greatness in Victorian Political Thought." In Victorian Visions of Global Order: Empire and International Relations in Nineteenth-Century Political Thought, edited by Duncan Bell, 136–58. Cambridge: Cambridge University Press, 2007.

Weitz, Eric D. "Self-Determination: How a German Enlightenment Idea Became the Slogan for National Liberation and Human Rights." American Historical Review 120, no. 2 (2015): 462–96.

Wilson, Woodrow. Speech before the United States Congress. January 22, 1917.

———. Speech before the United States Congress. January 8, 1918.

Zimmern, Alfred. "The International Settlement and Small Nationalities" (1919), in The Prospects of Democracy and Other Essays, 116–34. London: Chatto & Windus, 1929.

TIMOTHY NUNAN is Assistant Professor at the Center for Global History at the Free University of Berlin. He is author of Humanitarian Invasion: Global Development in Cold War Afghanistan.

# 10 "Emblems of Sovereignty"

## The Internationalization of Danzig and the Polish Post Office Dispute, 1919–25

### Marcus M. Payk

It is no coincidence that Günther Grass chose to have Oskar Matzerath, the antihero of his famous 1959 novel *The Tin Drum*, experience the outbreak of the Second World War inside the Polish post office in the Free City of Danzig. There are few other buildings—and few other cities—that so vividly symbolize the difficult and unfortunate compromises of Versailles. Because the newly constituted Polish state had been promised access to the Baltic Sea, the Allies decided to turn Danzig into an internationalized city and grant Poland various special rights with regard to the port, including its own postal service. Although the peacemakers tried to guarantee the German-speaking majority's right to self-determination by placing the city under the authority of the League of Nations, many observers saw nothing but a fragile construct. The Free City was soon regarded as a prime example of the foolishness and malice of the victorious nations. This view fostered, perhaps inevitably, nationalist outrage among the majority of Danzig's citizens, culminating in the violent "reunification" with Germany after 1939.[1]

Yet if the assumption that a direct line can be drawn from the "failed peace" to the outbreak of the Second World War is misleading, it would be just as wrong to assume the reverse—namely, that the internationalization of Danzig was an "exemplary model for the European postwar order" and a "prudent compromise."[2] This chapter attempts to draw a more differentiated picture. The fundamental problem was that the statehood of the Free City was at no time the result of the will of the city's collectivity but rather imposed from the outside and legalized through international treaties and bilateral agreements.[3] Using the example of the conflict over the introduction of a Polish postal service, this chapter illustrates how the indeterminate sovereignty of the city-state was negotiated between the conflicting interests of Danzig and Poland, between actors on the ground, national policy-makers, and the officials of the League of Nations. The aim is to show how individual provisions of the Versailles Treaty were implemented, appropriated, and instrumentalized in a concrete case. The phenomenon of the Free

City of Danzig—as an entity sui generis—moreover offers an unfamiliar perspective on the entire peace settlement, helping us to understand the notions of sovereignty, statehood, and legalism at the heart of the Paris system.

## Deciding on Danzig after the First World War

In the late eighteenth century, the Polish Rzeczpospolita disappeared from the map of Europe. Poland would be reconstituted as a nation-state only in the wake of the First World War. The "Polish question" was back on the agenda of European politics as soon as the Central powers installed a Polish regency kingdom in November 1916 as an independent satellite state. There was consensus in the western public arena that the formation of a new Polish state after one hundred years of foreign domination was not only politically and geostrategically necessary but, more than that, an act of historical justice and the realization of the promise of national independence and self-determination. In early 1917, Woodrow Wilson had proclaimed a "united, independent, and autonomous Poland" as an objective of the postwar order.[4]

After the United States entered the First World War, the call for an independent Poland was strongly reasserted and complemented with the observation that Poland needed access to the Baltic Sea. Being connected to international transport and trade routes, the Americans assumed, was essential for the re-created state to survive and to maintain its independence in the shadow of the powers that had partitioned Poland in the past—Germany, Austria, and Russia. However, the Allied diplomats and experts did not agree on whether it was indeed necessary to cede a German seaport city—and Danzig had been a candidate early on—to Poland. An alternative suggestion was to create a free port with guaranteed Polish rights of way and use.[5] US war aims and Wilson's Fourteen Points stated clearly enough that an "independent Polish state should be erected which should include the territories inhabited by indisputably Polish populations, which should be assured a free and secure access to the sea, and whose political and economic independence and territorial integrity should be guaranteed by international covenant."[6]

That this declaration produced more questions than answers became apparent after the armistice of November 11, 1918. Political instability, continued violence, and civil war in central and eastern Europe caused uncertainty among the Allies whether or not the preconditions for the establishment of a new Polish state were fulfilled. Although few questioned the overall objective of Polish independence, the borders of the new state were far from settled and it was unclear whether its sovereignty was sufficiently consolidated. As the Allied statesmen and diplomats gathered in Paris at the end of the year, the authority of the military leader Józef Piłsudski was much in question, in spite of his declaration of leadership over the Polish nation in November. It was unclear how far beyond Warsaw Piłsudski's influence reached. The impression of a chaotic situation with power struggles and unchecked violence was confirmed again and again in the weeks following the armistice—with anti-Semitic attacks in Lviv, Polish insurgents' violent capture of Poznan, and guerrilla actions of Polish militias at the Czechoslova-kian, Ukrainian, and Lithuanian borders.[7]

At the Paris Peace Conference, the "Polish question" became heavily con-tested. The representatives of the United States and Great Britain were for the most part skeptical of Piłsudski's regime and cautioned against overestimat-ing the stability of the new government in Warsaw or its political predictability.[8] French diplomats, however, regarded the political and military disorder in Po-land with greater leniency, seeing it mostly as a temporary problem. The reasons behind this confidence were of a geostrategic nature: a territorially saturated, economically independent Poland was the single most important building block in France's strategy of a "cordon sanitaire." This concept was based on the notion that a network of strong nation states in eastern Europe would keep in check any new German aggression, as well as the further expansion of Bolshevik Russia.[9]

The efforts of the Polish delegation of course need to be added to the picture of a primarily Anglo-Saxon and French conflict of interest over the future shape of eastern Europe. During the negotiations, Poland was able to achieve remarkable results that hardly anyone in Warsaw believed possible prior to the conference. But in the case of Danzig, despite tremendous efforts, Poland had to agree to a compromise, which to all appearances honored Wilson's promise of access to the Baltic Sea but fell drastically short of Poland's expectation of annexing the city. The report presented by the Commission on Polish Affairs on March 19 had pro-posed both the cession of most of western Prussia (the "Polish corridor") and the complete transfer of the seaport city to the Polish state. But when David Lloyd George and Woodrow Wilson refused to accept this plan, a fierce dispute over possible interim solutions erupted behind the scenes. On April 1, the Council of Four at the Paris peace conference decided to implement an earlier British pro-posal, detaching the city and its immediate vicinity from the German Empire and declaring it a Free City.[10]

Behind this plan of a "Free City of Danzig," initially referred to as "Free Han-seatic City," was the idea that the town and the port would be opened to accom-modate Poland's needs without falling under its sovereignty.[11] To achieve this, the economic infrastructure of Danzig and Poland would be intertwined—for example, by means of a shared administration of the port and its integration into the Polish customs area. Poland was moreover given the right to militarily defend Danzig and to represent it abroad. At the same time, the Allies underlined that the city would be an independent and autonomous polity "under the protection of the League of Nations," as formulated in article 102 of the Versailles Treaty.[12]

Yet no one in Paris laid out in detail how this internationalization would be achieved. Questions such as these were postponed to a subsequent treaty between Danzig and Poland, which the Allied powers committed themselves to broker. It is worth noting that the establishment of Danzig as a Free City was by no means historically unprecedented. For long stretches of time since the Middle Ages, the seaport had been independent. Between 1807 and 1814, Danzig even had been a Free City and nonstate entity under French influence, falling under Prussian rule only after Napoleon's defeat.[13] During the negotiations at the Paris Peace

Conference, another city-state served as a further role model: the Free City of Krakow. In contrast to Napoleonic Danzig, its autonomy had been decided only at the Congress of Vienna. But similar to Danzig after the First World War, the creation of the Free City of Krakow had been a compromise in the face of competing territorial claims. In the case of Krakow, the arrangement was successful enough to guarantee the thriving of the city under the protection of its guarantors Russia, Prussia, and Austria until 1846.[14]

## An Unhappy Compromise in an Unclear Situation

In the case of Danzig, the portents were anything but encouraging. From its inception, the Allied compromise sparked massive protest. Not surprisingly, they were the fiercest in Danzig itself. On April 25, when rumors of the peace conditions began to spread, several tens of thousands of people protested the decision. Across the German Empire, resistance was vehement, too. Again and again, protesters pointed out that the majority of the city's population spoke German and had a German cultural background. Some estimates indicated that more than 90 percent of the population was German. Hence, it was not easy to dismiss the claim that the forced separation from Germany violated the principle of self-determination. In a dramatic statement, the head of the German delegation at Versailles, Count Ulrich von Brockendorff-Ratzau, lamented in May 1919 that "the proposed rape of Danzig" not only represented a gross violation of the right to national self-determination but would also herald "an enduring state of war in the East."[15]

German outrage was met with Polish disappointment, as Poland had banked on the outright cession of Danzig. Even the subsequent demand that Poland be granted unlimited right to station troops in the city and control all port facilities found little support among the Allied decision-makers. Understandably, among Polish diplomats the impression took hold that their newly founded state held little credit with the British and the Americans, who were now attenuating all the promises they had made during the war. Particularly Britain's prime minister Lloyd George was said to harbor strong anti-Polish sentiments—a not quite fair assessment but one that turned him into a "public enemy" in Warsaw all the same.[16] In any case, after the negotiations at the Paris Peace Conference, a mixture of disappointed expectations and wounded pride came to dominate Warsaw's foreign policy, taking the eventual annexation of Danzig as an unspoken but self-evident long-term objective.[17]

Despite the discontent among the involved parties, when the Treaty of Versailles came into effect on January 10, 1920, Danzig was detached from Germany and became a condominium of the Allied powers—a decision the Supreme Council consisting of the principal Allied powers had confirmed once again a few days earlier.[18] After the withdrawal of the German armed forces, British and French troops entered the city on February 13. The British diplomat Sir Reginald Tower held authority over the city as the representative of the Allied powers. He reported to the Paris Ambassadors Conference, which had replaced the Supreme Council in early 1920. Shortly after, the League of Nations appointed him high commissioner according to article 103 of the Treaty of Versailles.[19] Although Tower left the German administration of the city untouched and agreed to keep the mayor, Heinrich Sahm, in office, he could not prevent strong anti-Polish sentiment from spreading across the city. In a report to Paris from August, Tower had to concede a sharp increase in violent clashes: "Cases of personal assault are unfortunately numerous. During the last week an organised 'Pole-hunt' appears to have taken place."[20]

From the viewpoint of the Warsaw government, however, the conflicts between the German majority and Polish minority were not the most pressing problem; rather, Poland was outraged about the delays in the clearance of shipments of ammunition and other important war materiel in the port of Danzig. Since February 1919, Poland had been engaged in a bitter war with Soviet Russia, and after a series of defeats, Warsaw was on the defensive. In May 1920, the Red Army had started an offensive that put massive pressure on Polish troops, pushing them back into their own territory.[21] The situation became even more serious for Poland's military leadership when the dockworkers of Danzig began to refuse to unload deliveries of arms and ammunition intended for the Polish army. On July 22, 1920, the mostly Social Democratic dockworkers launched an outright strike—ostensibly on pacifist grounds and in part out of solidarity with the Bolshevik revolutionaries but primarily due to bitter nationalist resentment toward Poland.[22]

This put the Allies in a difficult spot. Although they had been critical toward the aggressive expansionism of the young Polish state since late 1918, its looming defeat by the Bolsheviks would have been fatal for the European order they envisioned. Yet the options of the Allied representatives in Danzig to secure the Polish military supply line were limited. In the face of the hostile atmosphere in the city, it seemed unimaginable that the demands the Warsaw government had made of Tower and his top military official, General Richard Haking, would be put into practice: declaring Martial Law and allowing Polish workers to unload the ammunition shipments. Haking gauged that such a course of action would necessitate the complete Allied occupation of the city, requiring at least four battalions of reliable British and French troops.[23]

In the end, Tower and Haking were spared having to take a clear stance in the dispute over the arms shipments and position themselves against the nationalist machinations on either side. For one thing, Polish troops won an unexpected victory in mid-August, stopping the Red Army just before Warsaw (the so-called Miracle at the Wisła). What is more, the workers of Danzig were increasingly disillusioned about the dictatorial way the Bolsheviks were asserting their power in Russia and in the occupied territories. On August 31, 1920, the dockworkers decided to end the strike. At this point, local patriotism began to dominate, as workers cautioned that the "suicidal policy" of stopping arms shipments might pave the way for the Soviets to capture Danzig—or even Germany.[24]

## Convention and Constitution

At the very least, these quarrels in the spring and summer of 1920 showed the pressing need to define the future relations between Danzig and Poland. What was the value of the guaranteed access to the Baltic Sea if Warsaw could not count on this promise even at a moment of existential crisis? The condominium of the victors was thus to be replaced as soon as possible by a binding agreement that would clarify the international status of the city as well as its relationship with Poland. According to the provisions of the Treaty of Versailles, formal provisions had to be attained in two areas: First, Danzig and Poland had to reach a bilateral agreement following article 104 of the Versailles Treaty, in which all questions regarding cooperation in economic and financial relations, as well as transport, foreign representation, and military defense, would be settled in detail. Second, the formal status of Danzig as a political entity had to be spelled out by a constitution for the Free City, which would be guaranteed by the League of Nations.

Both goals should not be underestimated as mere procedural and legal clarification. On the contrary: highly detailed legal provisions and treaty arrangements were the hallmark of the Paris system and can be found throughout the peace treaties—from reparations to minority protection. It is evident that this special emphasis on international law on the one hand and on a domestic democratic-republican constitution on the other served to emphasize the Allies' claim of having defended law, justice, and the "sanctity of treaties" against the law-breaking behavior of the Central powers. This legalistic approach of the entire peace settlement should not distract from the fact that most of the regulations and formalistic arrangements favored the special interests of the victorious nations. But on the whole, the Allies felt the need to disperse any impression of arbitrary power politics and to create the appearance of a legally sound and just peace.[25]

Danzig exemplifies this notion of legalism. Securing the political independence of the Free City and regulating its relationship with Poland were thought to require a strong formal and contractual basis. All legal regulations were aimed at minimizing the political conflicts and defining as clearly as possible the bounds within which all involved parties—Danzig and Poland, but also the League of Nations and, at least indirectly, Germany—could act. The experience of the striking dockworkers in the summer of 1920 had shown the Allies the urgency of clearly laying down the rights and obligations of both sides regarding the use of the port. The first step was the formulation of a convention between Danzig and Poland in which the general provisions of the Treaty of Versailles were to be specified in greater detail, setting up the terms of cooperation in various areas. Already in November 1919, the Allies had agreed to the Polish delegation's request to move these negotiations from Warsaw to Paris, whereas the first talks among technical experts were to take place in Danzig itself.[26] But neither during these expert talks nor during the following negotiations between representatives of Poland and Danzig in May 1920 did the parties even come close to an agreement. The Polish side interpreted the unspecific stipulations of the Versailles

Treaty in a way that most closely approximated their initial aim of annexing the city. For example, they insisted on permanently stationing troops there and turning the port into a Polish naval base. In effect, this would have superseded the independence of Danzig, as would the proposal of gradually introducing Polish legislation and jurisdiction. Danzig, for its part, emphasized the city's independence and demanded that Poland be allowed to interfere in all areas of municipal administration only with the consent—and ultimately only by invitation—of the city's government. This restriction would have effectively rendered the promised access to the sea worthless.[27]

That both sides were so at odds with each other and fought for their interests in such an uncompromising way caused much consternation among the Allies. In Paris, the bilateral negotiations between the delegates from Danzig and Poland continued until September, at which point Lord Derby, the British representative to the Ambassadors Conference, pushed for a different solution.[28] A commission of Allied experts was called on to draft a new convention by elaborating on the original compromises the peacemakers had formulated in Paris. On October 15, this draft was presented to the dismayed delegates of Poland and Danzig, who were asked to agree to it within a week, since the founding of the Free City was already set for October 23. The refusal of the Polish side made it impossible to meet this date. Its leader, Ignacy Paderewski, tried to intervene by turning to the French authorities, but the delegates from Danzig signed the contract on November 9 in a formal ceremony in the French Foreign Ministry on the Quai d'Orsay. This convention, which later came to be known as the Treaty of Paris, came into effect on November 15, marking the birth of the Free City.[29]

Objectively, there was no reason for the delegation from Danzig to complain about the convention. Its position that the Free City constituted an independent international entity had been explicitly confirmed, although the limits of its sovereignty and the extent of Polish rights were laid out in greater detail than before. This legal framework did not bring a lasting peace, however. Even though the Polish delegation signed the contract on November 18, new inconsistencies, flaws, and ambivalences allowing for conflicting interpretations soon became apparent. Already a few months later, a supplementary agreement had to be formulated. This new convention, which was signed in Warsaw on October 24, 1921, further refined the principles and provisions ruling Danzig-Polish affairs.[30] Whereas the Treaty of Versailles had regulated relations in nine articles, the Treaty of Paris contained forty articles, and the new Treaty of Warsaw an additional 244 articles. Among its subject matters were regulations regarding the right of citizenship and jurisdiction as well as rules for the Danzig stock exchange, the recognition of certificates and diplomas, or fishing rights. If we broaden our perspective beyond these foundational treaties to include the decrees of the high commissioners, the decisions of the Council of the League of Nations as the executive body of this international organization, or the pronouncements of the Permanent Court of International Justice in The Hague, we will see why the relations between Danzig and Poland were indeed labeled as an impenetrable "legal labyrinth."[31]

The Allies saw the need to legally define not only the international relations of the Free City—that is, its relations to Poland and the international community—but also its domestic order. Article 103 of the Treaty of Versailles explicitly demanded a constitution for Danzig. This was not only in line with the tradition of constitutionalism since the eighteenth and nineteenth centuries, which had checked monarchs' and governments' arbitrary rule with the will of the citizens, but also conformed to the proclaimed right of national self-determination. Wilson, who had popularized the term and the ideals associated with it like few others, never defined self-determination as merely connected to the idea of the independence of nation states—or even just national autonomy. Rather, for the American president the term referred to the right of self-government and hence to democratic representation and participation, which he saw as the necessary precondition for the peaceful resolution of conflicts and for balancing individual interests. A democratic system would in turn stem not only domestic repression but also international aggression.[32]

The democratic constitution for Danzig was certainly no compensation for the city's separation from Germany. But it was a crucial element underlining the city's independence and diffusing unrest and internal conflicts. Allowing for the political participation of the local population, so the Allies' rationalized, would curb protest and increase the internal legitimacy of the Free City. Consequently, the Allies agreed that a constitution could not be forced onto Danzig from the outside but rather had to be worked out by the city's citizens themselves. It would, however, require the subsequent approval by the high commissioner, in order to fall under the protection of the League of Nations.[33]

The drafting of Danzig's constitution did, in fact, follow these principles. Since September 1919, the city government had drawn up several drafts. In January, the newspaper of the Social Democratic Party declared the question of the constitution the most pressing political problem in Danzig, as a constitution would prevent the city from becoming a "playground of international capital."[34] But it was not until late spring, after the Allies had taken command, that the constitutional process was formally initiated. Tower set the date for elections to a constitutional assembly on May 16, 1920. The assembly came together for the first time on June 14. A subcommittee with seventeen members, among them an Allied delegate with an advisory vote, was formed to draw up a draft. On August 20, the constitution was passed. Tower formally declared his acceptance and immediately passed it on to the League of Nations.[35]

In Geneva, however, Danzig's constitution was not dealt with immediately. In a first step, Ishii Kikujirō, the Japanese delegate to the Council of the League of Nations, was named rapporteur on Danzig and instructed to examine the proposal. His report from November 1920 underlined the centrality of internal order for the Free City's stability. The constitution would create a "stable and peaceful political situation" and prevent "germs of disorder, inadequate government, anarchy or disregard of international obligations" from thriving.[36] At the heart of this view was the conviction that the League of Nations could guarantee Danzig's existence as an internationalized territory only if it was not governed by despotism and arbitrary rule. In this view, the polity of the Free City was grounded not in any sense of nation or national belonging but rather in republican self-determination and good and just governance.

The Council of the League of Nations discussed the Ishii report on November 17, only two days after the formal creation of the Free City. It largely agreed with its findings and formally declared the league the guarantor of Danzig's constitution. Again, there were several critical interventions, and behind the scenes in Geneva, the Polish delegates made another attempt at a blank check for the city's military protection. There were even rumors about turning Danzig into a Polish mandate.[37] Although the League of Nations commissioned the constitutional assembly in Danzig to clarify certain points, the city's sovereignty and neutrality were explicitly confirmed. In case of war, the League of Nations even reserved the right to name a state for Danzig's protection, although it was clear to everyone that Germany was considered the potential aggressor and Poland the defender.

The Council of the League of Nations' decision to guarantee the protection of Danzig and its constitution concluded at least for the time being the establishment of the Free City as an internationalized territory. Some amendments and clarifications were added to the constitution until it finally took effect on June 14, 1922. In the years that followed, each change had to be confirmed by the League of Nations. All in all, however, the constitution and the framework of international treaties and conventions created a legal foundation that would secure Danzig's independence and allow for amenable relations with Poland—or so the Allies hoped. But this hope turned out to be an illusion. It was precisely the minute legal and contractual regulation of the relations between Poland and Danzig that turned out to be highly prone to engender conflict. The "constant paragraph war" placed a heavy burden on the relationship between these two unequal entities.[38]

## The Polish Post Office Dispute

Particularly in the first half of the 1920s, conflicts between the Free City of Danzig and Poland were carried out in the form of bitter legal disputes. There were strong tensions surrounding the building of a Polish ammunition depot on the Westerplatte Peninsula, which was planned in response to the dockworkers' strike but built only in 1924, after tough negotiations. But the most striking example of the legalistic battles between Danzig and Poland is the dispute over the introduction of Polish postal services in the city. This was not a remote issue or simply a technical question. The promised access to the sea always implied Poland's connection to global communication networks. Moreover, the postal service was a state monopoly and therefore an expression and attribute of state sovereignty. In the case of the Free City, its sovereignty could never simply be taken for granted—in fact, the dispute over a Polish post service reveals how fragile and unstable a construct Danzig's sovereignty was.[39]

The controversy over Poland's right to establish "postal, telegraphic and telephonic communication between Poland and the port of Danzig" (according to article 103, section 3 of the Treaty of Versailles) began even before the creation of the Free City. After the Polish postal service had received a temporary office for the examination of packages in April 1920, shortly after the Allies took power, the Treaty of Paris granted Poland the right to open a post office on the port's premises (articles 29–32). This office was to deliver only to Poland and overseas, but the Treaty of Warsaw from October 1921 granted Poland the right to define the extent of the necessary infrastructure (articles 149–68). To run its postal service, Poland received the building of the former military hospital on Heveliusplatz near the port. Initially, the Polish postal administration did not use this building but established itself even closer to the port and rented several storehouses directly at the docks.[40]

Behind the scenes, however, a fierce dispute ensued over the degree to which the Polish postal service would be allowed to expand its operations throughout Danzig. Haking, who had been promoted to League of Nations high commissioner in early 1921, had already rebuffed Polish demands twice. On May 25, 1922, Haking made the formal decision that the Polish postal service had to limit itself to the port, and on January 6, 1923, he again confirmed that no additional post office would be allowed to open in the city.[41] This should have settled the matter for Danzig, but the Poles duly pointed out that the treaties and agreements did not clearly define the demarcation between the port and the city. In fact, all of Danzig could be regarded as a harbor city in the sense of one "administrative unit."[42] This viewpoint was based on a previous decision by the high commissioner. In a dispute over the railroad, Haking had defined the area of the port rather generously.[43] Thus, the Polish side was optimistic that it was operating on a sound legal basis when it began to set up its offices toward the end of 1924 in the building on Heveliusplatz, conveniently located in Danzig's downtown between the Radunia and Motława Rivers. The administration of Danzig's own postal services had informed the Senate already in late October 1924 of the Polish intentions to establish a competing service, including offices open to public business.[44]

In early 1925, the conflict escalated. At daybreak on January 5, a snowy Monday morning, the Polish post set up ten letterboxes in the center of Danzig. Although they contained a notice in Polish and German indicating that they delivered only to Poland, there was nevertheless an outcry in the German-speaking public—particularly since the Senate claimed only to have been informed about these plans on January 3. Charges of "new attempts at Polinization" were quickly leveled.[45] Almost immediately the letterboxes were damaged in nighttime actions: "nationalist hotspurs" daubed the Polish notices and the state emblem with tar.[46] Other sources indicate that the red letterboxes were covered with black and white horizontal stripes—making the appearance of the box reminiscent of the colors of the defunct German Kaiserreich.[47] The Polish side protested this willful damage of property vehemently but was even more outraged over the defiling of its national symbol: the white eagle on a red background. The Polish representative in Danzig, Henryk Strasburger, demanded an official apology, and the government in Warsaw went as far as to threaten military intervention if the authorities in Danzig were unable to enforce order in the city and prevent any further actions such as these.[48]

Even without these threats Mayor Sahm and his administration were determined not to let this conflict turn into a demonstration of political power but instead to treat it as an international legal dispute. The Senate insistently appealed to the city's population to "act within the bounds of the law and abstain from any illegal activities. These kinds of spontaneous and criminal acts . . . complicate the situation of the Free City of Danzig and harm its interests."[49] Though not without "intense inner aversion," Sahm formulated a note to Poland containing an apology for the defiling of the Polish national emblem.[50] Most importantly, the machinery of the League of Nations was set in motion. Mervyn MacDonell had taken over the office of high commissioner from Haking in February 1923. He was a British career diplomat who had until then behaved very cautiously. In the dispute over the letterboxes, he initially attempted to resolve the crisis informally. When it became apparent that these mediating efforts came to nothing, the Senate of Danzig quickly demanded that the high commissioner formally investigate Poland's actions. Haking's decisions from 1922 and 1923 strengthened the Free City's conviction that it was in a legally advantageous position.[51]

Indeed, MacDonnell confirmed the Senate's position in a resolution on February 2. The Polish side could no longer challenge Haking's original decisions, MacDonnell argued, particularly as it had not protested them at the time. MacDonnell thus prohibited the Polish postal administration from expanding its operations to the entire territory of the Free City and opening offices that offered its services to the local population. Yet this decision did little to cool down the situation. While Danzig's administration welcomed the high commissioner's pronouncement and immediately passed it on to the press—which published it with often triumphant nationalistic undertones—Polish officials harshly criticized the ruling. Shortly afterward, Strasburger filed an official complaint to the high commissioner. In a memorandum, he again outlined Poland's legal stance and demanded that the case be handed over to the League of Nations for a final decision.[52]

In Geneva, officials of the League of Nations had recognized early on that this local dispute had to be understood within the larger context of the conflict between Danzig and Poland. Probably the most enlightening analysis was formulated by Joost van Hamel, the Dutch head of the league's legal department. In an internal note, he voiced his doubts whether Haking's decisions could really be regarded as the final resolution of the dispute. Furthermore, he illuminated the bigger picture and underlying dimensions of the conflict. The letterboxes, he claimed, were "emblems of the sovereignty" of a state, thus equating the state's postal services with state power. In this sense, the conflict was a direct consequence of the question of who could ultimately claim territorial sovereignty in Danzig.[53]

This interpretation raised a problem that went all the way back to the initial decision to internationalize the city and that could not be entirely resolved in legal terms. Although the government of Danzig unwaveringly asserted its sovereignty, the Polish side was unwilling to treat Danzig as a completely in-dependent state and interact with the city on the basis of sovereign equality.[54] That was the price of the Allied compromise of 1919. The internationalization of Danzig created political uncertainties and ambiguities that could not be entirely resolved by means of legal arrangements and international treaties. It was almost inevitable that doubtful cases and gaps in the regulations would continuously emerge, with each side naturally trying to exploit them to their advantage. While the Free City clung to the League of Nations and wanted to avoid cooperation with Poland as much as possible, the Polish government persistently attempted to strengthen its presence in Danzig. But what raised the most concern among the Allies was the impression that Warsaw was looking for an opportunity to create a fait accompli. In early February 1925, MacDonnell turned to the secretary gen-eral of the League of Nations, Eric Drummond, to express his deep concern that the postal conflict could offer the Polish government—or at least a few irrespon-sible hardliners—a pretext for a military intervention leading to the ultimate an-nexation of Danzig. He claimed to have reliable information regarding the secret movement of Polish troops along the Free City's border. As MacDonnell wrote to Geneva, "local Poles here make no secret of their belief that those troops would have been used if the Senate had not apologized or if they had moved the boxes at my request."[55] Six weeks later, he repeated this warning to the new rapporteur for Danzig at the League of Nations, the Spaniard José Quiñones de León. Irregular Polish troops numbering up to fifty thousand soldiers stood ready, the high com-missioner claimed to know, and were waiting to invade the Free City at the next opportunity.[56]

MacDonnell's warnings went largely unnoticed in Geneva, Paris, and London.[57] Danzig was far away and western European governments were busy with other international problems, for example the dispute over the withdrawal of troops from the Rhineland and Germany's entry into the league.[58] Still, ad-dressing the dispute through all the formal procedures of the League of Nations was not just a makeshift solution or a ruse to gain time for political maneu-vering. Rather, it confirmed the legalistic structures of the Paris system. Follow-ing Poland's appeal, the Council of the League of Nations discussed the matter on March 13. The meeting took place in Geneva with the participation of represen-tatives from both sides: Mayor Sahm for Danzig, Strasburger and Foreign Min-ister Aleksander Skrzyński for Poland.[59] Both parties clashed hard, with Sahm forfeiting much sympathy by insisting on speaking only German. Still, the Coun-cil of the League of Nations did not take sides. Even though MacDonnell's deci-sion of February 2 was revoked, the case was now passed on to the Permanent Court of International Justice (PCIJ) in The Hague, which was asked to address the underlying legal issues in an advisory opinion.[60]

Although Heinrich Sahm had proposed precisely this course of action already in confidential talks in January, he must have been sorely disappointed by the re-sults it yielded.[61] On May 16, the judges in The Hague rejected Danzig's position and confirmed the Polish one in every particular. Haking's previous decisions were not binding, the court argued, and existing treaties and agreements in fact did allow Poland to offer public postal services from the port with its own delivery infrastructure.[62] At its next meeting on June 11, the Council of the League of Nations adopted the PCIJ's advisory opinion and called in an expert commission to delineate a clear boundary between port and city as prescribed by the court. In July, these experts arrived to survey the local conditions, and as a result the territory of the port was demarcated very generously to include six of the ten locations where the Polish postal service had already installed letterboxes in January.[63] On September 19, 1925, the Council of the League of Nations adopted the recommendations of the expert commission.[64] The Polish post office at Heveliusplatz was now internationally authorized.

## Conclusion

That Poland prevailed in the end is perhaps less remarkable than the way the entire dispute played out. Although protagonists from all sides were aware of the political background, they could act only within the legal framework created by the Treaty of Versailles and the subsequent treaties and agreements on Danzig. Or, to put it the other way around, at no point could the conflict over the sovereignty of the Free City be carried out openly. It was always embedded into a legalistic and normative structure that factored out basic problems. It is indicative that no other territorial dispute went to court in The Hague more often than the one between Danzig and Poland.

However, sophisticated as the legal regulations and formal procedures may have been, they did not, in fact, lead to a more peaceful coexistence of Danzig and Poland. On the one hand, the Paris system created an international legal regime that, for the most part, was not open to political change. The dominance of the victors did not allow for the integration of the losers, nor did it allow for a revision of the decisions reached in 1919–20. On the other hand, Danzig had been constituted as a Free City exclusively on the basis of treaties, conventions, constitutions, and court rulings—mostly under international supervision and often against the will of the local population. In this regard, Danzig ran counter to the Paris system, which usually assumed independence the other way around: First, it presumed the existence of political entities such as nations or peoples as essentialized givens of the international order. Then, in a second step, it assigned to these entities clear-cut borders, unambiguous categories of citizenship, and a predictable government. The Free City did not easily fit into this system, which is why despite all efforts, its status in the international community could never conclusively be resolved.

Not surprisingly, the Nazi regime chose to latch on to the postal dispute in the 1930s. Nazism presented itself as a revolutionary movement aiming to overthrow Versailles, challenging the "bourgeois" belief in treaties and legal arrangements, and defying the diplomatic routines of the League of Nations. In this sense, the Free City, and specifically the Polish post office there, were symbolically highly charged places where the Nazis' revisionism gave way to open warfare. Already at the outbreak of the Second World War, in the early hours of September 1,

1939, German SS troops attacked the building on Heveliusplatz, in which approximately sixty Polish postal workers had barricaded themselves. While the presence of military staff among them provided a pretext for the assault, it is clear that the German action was less a necessary act of war than a symbolic destruction of the order of Versailles. Whereas the Polish government had pursued a strategy of gradually undermining and slowly incorporating the Free City into Poland, the Nazi regime aimed to destroy all contractual obligations, agreements, and legal duties with brute force.[65]

Still, it would be inappropriate to see the failure of the Free City of Danzig as inevitable. The very fact that a violent clash was avoided for almost twenty years, despite the many contested issues, showed that the distinctive legal framework regulating the relationship between Danzig and Poland offered a forum for alternative forms of negotiation and conflict resolution. It is hard to ignore, however, that the acceptance of the League of Nations or the authority of the PCIJ always depended on the political interests at stake. While Poland grudgingly accepted the Allies' decision to internationalize Danzig, and Germany pursued a strict policy of revisionism behind the scenes, among the great powers only Great Britain and, in a very limited sense, France were willing to invest politically into the experiment of the Free City. But this willingness waned considerably in the course of the 1930s. "Pourquoi mourir pour Dantzig?" was a French political slogan on the eve of the Second World War.[66] Already in the 1940s, the disenchanted conclusion many people drew was that the deeper meaning of the Free City was to caution against embarking on similar experiments in the future. It was precisely the rules regarding the protection by the League of Nations that turned out to be insufficient: "They showed how not to act if similar situations should arise in the future."[67] In fact, internationalization did not figure into the few comparable territorial disputes after 1945, for example in the case of Trieste at the Italian-Yugoslavian border.[68] Only after 1989 did the idea of an "international territorial administration" emerge anew: for example, in Kosovo or in East Timor.[69] These territories have often been compared to the historical example of the Free City, and the long-term success or failure of these new attempts has yet to be assessed. But as the case of the internationalization of Danzig shows, legalistic constructs and normative regimes can frame the question of political sovereignty, but they can never resolve it.

## Notes

1. Roger Moorhouse, "'The Sore That Would Never Heal': The Genesis of the Polish Corridor," in *After the Versailles Treaty: Enforcement, Compliance, Contested Identities*, ed. Conan Fischer and Alan Sharp (London: Routledge, 2008); Lutz Oberdörfer, "Die Danzig/Korridor- und die Memelfrage in Versailles und den ersten Nachkriegsjahren," in *Preußische Landesgeschichte: Festschrift für Bernhart Jähnig*, ed. Udo Arnold, Mario Glauert and Jürgen Sarnowsky (Marburg: Elwert, 2001); Hans Viktor Böttcher, *Die Freie Stadt Danzig: Wege und Umwege in die europäische Zukunft. Historischer Rückblick, staats- und*

*völkerrechtliche Fragen*, 3rd ed. (Bonn: Kulturstiftung der Dt. Vertriebenen, 1999); Anna M. Cienciala, "The Battle of Danzig and the Polish Corridor at the Paris Peace Conference of 1919," in *The Reconstruction of Poland, 1914–1923*, ed. Paul Latawski (New York: St. Martin's Press, 1992); John Brown Mason, *The Danzig Dilemma: A Study in Peacemaking by Compromise* (Stanford, CA: Stanford University Press, 1947); Albert Brödersdorff et al., eds., *Die Entstehung der Freien Stadt Danzig: Fünf Aufsätze* (Danzig: Kafemann, 1930).

2. Peter Oliver Loew, *Danzig: Biographie einer Stadt* (Munich: Beck, 2011), 186.

3. Nathaniel Berman, *Passion and Ambivalence: Colonialism, Nationalism, and International Law* (Leiden: Martinus Nijhoff, 2012), 209–14, 223–30. For a different take see Elizabeth M. Clark, "Borderland of the Mind: The Free City of Danzig and the Sovereignty Question," in *German Politics and Society* 35 (2017): 24–37.

4. Woodrow Wilson, Address to the Senate of the United States, January 22, 1917, in *Papers Relating to the Foreign Relations of the United States* (hereafter *FRUS*), *1917: Supplement 1, The World War* (Washington, DC: US Government Printing Office, 1861ff.): 24–29, 27. For more on the background see Włodzimierz Borodziej, *Geschichte Polens im 20. Jahrhundert* (Munich: Beck, 2010), 97–119; Marian Leczyk, *Druga Rzeczpospolita 1918–1939: Społeczeństwo, Gospodarka, Kultura, Polityka* (Warsaw: Książka i Wiedza, 2006), 13–59; Paul Latawski, ed., *The Reconstruction of Poland, 1914–1923* (New York: St. Martin's Press, 1992); Norman Davies, *God's Playground: A History of Poland*, vol. 2 (Oxford: Clarendon Press, 1981), 378–92.

5. See Mieczysław B. Biskupski, "Re-Creating Central Europe: The United States 'Inquiry' into the Future of Poland in 1918," *International History Review* 12, no. 2 (1990): 249–79, 257–68.

6. Woodrow Wilson, Address to Congress, January 8, 1918, in *The Papers of Woodrow Wilson*, vol. 45, ed. Arthur Link (Princeton, NJ: Princeton University Press, 1966–94), 534–39, 538.

7. See Czesław Brzoza/Andrzej Sowa, *Historia Polski 1918–1945* (Krakow: Wydawnictwo Literackie, 2006), 17–50; Mikulas Fabry, *Recognizing States: International Society and the Establishment of New States since 1776* (Oxford: Oxford University Press, 2010), 126–27; Piotr J. Wróbel, "The Revival of Poland and Paramilitary Violence, 1918–1920," in *Spießer, Patrioten, Revolutionäre: Militärische Mobilisierung und gesellschaftliche Ordnung in der Neuzeit*, ed. Rüdiger Bergien and Ralf Pröve (Göttingen: V&R Unipress, 2010). See also Robert Gerwarth, *The Vanquished: Why the First World War Failed to End, 1917–1923* (London: Allen Lane, 2016); Jochen Böhler, Włodzimierz Borodziej, and Joachim von Puttkamer, eds., *Legacies of Violence: Eastern Europe's First World War* (Munich: Oldenbourg, 2014).

8. Davies, *God's Playground* 2:393–94.

9. Peter Jackson, *Beyond the Balance of Power: France and the Politics of National Security in the Era of the First World War* (Cambridge: Cambridge University Press, 2013), 235–43; Olivier Lowczyk, *La fabrique de la paix: Du Comité d'études à la Conférence de la paix, l'élaboration par la France des traités de la Première guerre mondiale* (Paris: Economica, 2010), 318–21. As a classic interpretation also Piotr Stefan Wandycz, *France and Her Eastern Allies, 1919–1925: French-Czechoslovak-Polish Relations from the Paris Peace Conference to Locarno* (Minneapolis, MN: Lund Press, 1962).

10. Volker Prott, *The Politics of Self-Determination: Remaking Territories and National Identities in Europe, 1917–1923* (Oxford: Oxford University Press, 2016), 134–40; Benjamin Conrad, *Umkämpfte Grenzen, umkämpfte Bevölkerung: Die Entstehung der Staatsgrenzen der Zweiten Polnischen Republik 1918–1923* (Stuttgart: Steiner, 2014), 152–55; Leczyk, *Druga Rzeczpospolita*, 60–75; Kay Lundgreen-Nielsen, *The Polish Problem at the*

*Paris Peace Conference: A Study of the Policies of the Great Powers and the Poles, 1918–1919* (Odense: Odense University Press, 1979), 233–47; Mason, *Danzig Dilemma*, 35–61.

11. James Headlam-Morley, *A Memoir of the Paris Peace Conference, 1919* (London: Methuen, 1972), 69.

12. Mason, *Danzig Dilemma*, 77–89.

13. See Loew, *Danzig*, 38–182.

14. Davies, *God's Playground*, 2: 334–39; Meir Ydit, *Internationalised Territories from the "Free City of Cracow" to the "Free City of Berlin"* (Leiden: A. W. Sythoff, 1961), 22.

15. "Observations of the German Delegation on the Conditions of Peace of 29 May 1919," in *FRUS, 1919*, 6:836. For additional context cf. Christoph Martin Kimmich, *The Free City: Danzig and German Foreign Policy 1919–1934* (New Haven, CT: Yale University Press, 1968), 12–44.

16. Norman Davies, "Lloyd George and Poland, 1919–20," *Journal of Contemporary History* 6, no. 3 (1971): 132–54, 132.

17. Lundgreen-Nielsen, *Polish Problem*, 245–47.

18. It was not until January 6, 1920, that the Supreme Council decided on the general outline of the transition of German sovereignty to the Allied main victors, which was summarized in an agreement with the Germans that was signed on January 9.

19. Jürgen Heideking, *Areopag der Diplomaten: Die Pariser Botschafterkonferenz der alliierten Hauptmächte und die Probleme der europäischen Politik 1920–1931* (Husum: Matthiesen, 1979), 76; Gerhard Paul Pink, *The Conference of Ambassadors* (Geneva: Geneva Research Centre, 1942), 52–54. On the high commissioners in Danzig, see Wolfgang Ramonat, *Der Völkerbund und die Freie Stadt Danzig 1920–1934* (Osnabrück: Biblio-Verlag, 1979), 93–116.

20. Reginald Tower to George Curzon, Report of August 12, 1920, in *Documents on British Foreign Policy, 1919–1939: First Series* (hereafter *DBFP*), vol. 11, ed. Ernest L. Woodward and William N. Medlicott (London: Her Majesty's Stationery Office, 1947–1986), 472.

21. Norman Davies, *White Eagle, Red Star: The Polish-Soviet War, 1919–20 and "the Miracle on the Vistula"* (London: Pimlico, 2003), 121–96.

22. Moorhouse, "Sore That Would Never Heal,"191–92; Mason, *Danzig Dilemma*, 116–17.

23. Richard Haking to George Curzon, telegram on August 6, 1920, in *DBFP*, 11:442.

24. "Entschluß der Danziger Hafenarbeiter!," *Danziger Volksstimme*, September 1, 1920, 2.

25. Marcus M. Payk, *Frieden durch Recht? Der Aufstieg des modernen Völkerrechts und der Friedensschluss nach dem Ersten Weltkrieg* (Munich: De Gruyter/Oldenbourg, 2018).

26. Protocol, November 25, 1919, in *FRUS, 1919*, 9:336.

27. Mason, *Danzig Dilemma*, 90–92.

28. Lord Derby (Edward Stanley) to George Curzon, letter from September [15], 1920, in *DBFP*, 11:562f.

29. Heideking, *Areopag*, 78–84; Mason, *Danzig Dilemma*, 92–93.; Ernst Ziehm, "Die Verwaltung Danzigs durch die interalliierten Hauptmächte und die Konstituierung der Freien Stadt Danzig," in *Die Entstehung der Freien Stadt Danzig: Fünf Aufsätze*, ed. Albert Brödersdorff et al. (Danzig: Kafemann, 1930), 40–41. The text of the Treaty of Paris in League of Nation Treaty Series, vol. 6 (1921), 190–207.

30. League of Nation Treaty Series, vol. 116 (1931), 5–155.

31. Mason, *Danzig Dilemma*, 93. For an overview over the legal foundations, see ibid.; Böttcher, *Freie Stadt*, 93–128; John K. Bleimaier, "The Legal Status of the Free City of

Danzig 1920–1939: Lessons to be Derived from the Experiences of a Non-State Entity in the International Community," *Hague Yearbook of International Law* 2 (1989): 69–93.

32. Trygve Throntveit, "The Fable of the Fourteen Points: Woodrow Wilson and National Self-Determination," *Diplomatic History* 35 (2011): 445–81. On Wilson's interest in constitutions, see Thomas J. Knock, *To End All Wars: Woodrow Wilson and the Quest for a New World Order* (New York: Oxford University Press, 1992), 3–14.

33. Berman, *Passion and Ambivalence*, 224–25.

34. "An die werktätige Bevölkerung der Freien Stadt Danzig!," *Danziger Volksstimme*, January 17, 1920, 1.

35. Ziehm, "Die Verwaltung Danzigs," 38–39.

36. Ishii Kikujirō, "Report to the League Council, November 17, 1920," in *League of Nations Council: Minutes of the Thirteenth Session* (Geneva: League of Nations, 1921), 3.

37. Strutt to League of Nations, telegram November 13, 1920, in League of Nations Archive Geneva (hereafter LoNA), R139.

38. Ydit, *Internationalised Territories*, 190.

39. See also Clark, "Borderland of the Mind," 27–29.

40. Albert Gallitsch, "Die Landespostdirektion Danzig und ihre postalischen Beziehungen zu Polen," *Archiv für das Post- und Fernmeldewesen* 8, no. 3 (1956): 190–209; Adolf Weidenmann, *Der Danzig-Polnische Poststreit* (Aschaffenburg: Waillandt, 1931).

41. Ibid., 19–29.

42. Mason, *Danzig Dilemma*, 159.

43. Gallitsch, "Landespostdirektion Danzig," 199.

44. Gallitsch, "Landespostdirektion Danzig," 198–99; Weidenmann, *Der Danzig-Polnische Poststreit*, 34–35.

45. "Neue Polonisierungsmanöver," *Danziger Volksstimme*, January 6, 1920, 3.

46. "Die polnische Post," *Danziger Volksstimme*, January 7, 1925, 3.

47. Mason, *Danzig Dilemma*, 153; Weidenmann, *Der Danzig-Polnische Poststreit*, 14.

48. Ramonat, *Völkerbund*, 155.

49. "Die Ruhe bewahren!," *Danziger Volksstimme*, January 19, 1925, 1.

50. Heinrich Sahm, *Erinnerungen aus meinen Danziger Jahren: 1919–1930* (Marburg/Lahn: Johann-Gottfried-Herder-Institut, 1958), 100.

51. Gallitsch, "Landespostdirektion Danzig," 199.

52. Henryk Strasburger, memorandum of February 20, 1925 (translation), LoNA, R167.

53. Joost van Hamel to Erik Colban, Minute, March 7, 1925, LoNA, R167.

54. Böttcher, *Freie Stadt*, 93–115; Kimmich, *Free City*, 54–6. For an exploration of "sovereign equality," see Gerry J. Simpson, *Great Powers and Outlaw States: Unequal Sovereigns in the International Legal Order* (Cambridge: Cambridge University Press, 2004).

55. Mervyn MacDonnell to Eric Drummond, letter of February 5, 1925, LoNA, S332.

56. Mervyn MacDonnell to José Quiñones de León, letter of March 25, 1925, LoNA, S332.

57. Alexander Cadogan to Eric Drummond, letter of March 5, 1925, LoNA, S332.

58. Zara Steiner, *The Lights That Failed: European International History 1919–1933* (Oxford: Oxford University Press, 2007), 355, 387–430.

59. Cf. Sahm, *Erinnerungen*, 104–106.

60. League of Nations, *Official Journal* (1925), 469–72; Ramonat, *Völkerbund*, 156–57. On the founding of the PCIJ, see Ole Spiermann, *International Legal Argument in the Permanent Court of International Justice: The Rise of the International Judiciary* (Cambridge: Cambridge University Press, 2005).

61. See Erik Colban, Record of Conversation with M. Sahm on January 17, 1925, January 18, 1925, LoNA, S332.

62. Polish Postal Service in Danzig, Advisory Opinion, May 16, 1925, in *Publications of the Permanent Court of International Justice (PCIJ), Series B 11* (Leiden, 1925), 41.

63. The documents and maps of the expert commission at LoNA, R168. See also Gallitsch, "Landespostdirektion Danzig," 200–203.

64. League of Nations, Official Journal (1925), 1371–77.

65. On the dispute over the Polish post office: Dieter Schenk, *Die Post von Danzig: Geschichte eines deutschen Justizmords* (Reinbek: Rowohlt, 1995).

66. Henry Kissinger, *Diplomacy* (New York: Simon & Schuster, 1994), 573.

67. Mason, *Danzig Dilemma*, 88.

68. Glenda Sluga, *The Problem of Trieste and the Italo-Yugoslav Border: Difference, Identity, and Sovereignty in Twentieth-Century Europe* (Albany: State University of New York Press, 2001).

69. Carsten Stahn, *The Law and Practice of International Territorial Administration: Versailles to Iraq and Beyond* (Cambridge: Cambridge University Press, 2008); Ralph Wilde, "From Danzig to East Timor and Beyond: The Role of International Territorial Administration," *American Journal of International Law* 95, no. 3 (2001): 583–606.


# Bibliography

Berman, Nathaniel. *Passion and Ambivalence: Colonialism, Nationalism, and International Law*. Leiden: Martinus Nijhoff, 2012.

Biskupski, Mieczysław B. "Re-Creating Central Europe: The United States 'Inquiry' into the Future of Poland in 1918." *International History Review* 12, no. 2 (1990): 249–79.

Bleimaier, John K. "The Legal Status of the Free City of Danzig 1920–1939: Lessons to Be Derived from the Experiences of a Non-State Entity in the International Community." *Hague Yearbook of International Law* 2 (1989): 69–93.

Böhler, Jochen, Włodzimierz Borodziej, and Joachim von Puttkamer, eds. *Legacies of Violence: Eastern Europe's First World War*. Munich: Oldenbourg, 2014.

Borodziej, Włodzimierz. *Geschichte Polens im 20. Jahrhundert*. Munich: Beck, 2010.

Böttcher, Hans Viktor. *Die Freie Stadt Danzig: Wege und Umwege in die europäische Zukunft. Historischer Rückblick, staats- und völkerrechtliche Fragen*. 3rd ed. Bonn: Kulturstiftung der Dt. Vertriebenen, 1999.

Brödersdorff, Albert, Walther Recke, Theodor Rudolph, L. Foerster, and Ernst Ziehm, eds. *Die Entstehung der Freien Stadt Danzig: Fünf Aufsätze*. Danzig: Kafemann, 1930.

Brzoza, Czesław, and Andrzej Sowa, *Historia Polski 1918–1945*. Krakow: Wydawnictwo Literackie, 2006.

Cienciala, Anna M. "The Battle of Danzig and the Polish Corridor at the Paris Peace Conference of 1919." In *The Reconstruction of Poland, 1914–1923*, edited by Paul Latawski, 71–94. New York: St. Martin's Press, 1992.

Clark, Elizabeth M. "Borderland of the Mind. The Free City of Danzig and the Sovereignty Question." In *German Politics and Society* 35 (2017): 24–37.

Conrad, Benjamin. *Umkämpfte Grenzen, umkämpfte Bevölkerung: Die Entstehung der Staatsgrenzen der Zweiten Polnischen Republik 1918–1923*. Stuttgart: Steiner, 2014.

Davies, Norman. *God's Playground: A History of Poland*. Vol. 2. Oxford: Clarendon Press, 1981.

———. "Lloyd George and Poland, 1919–20." *Journal of Contemporary History* 6, no. 3 (1971): 132–54.

———. *White Eagle, Red Star: The Polish-Soviet War, 1919–20 and "the Miracle on the Vistula."* London: Pimlico, 2003.

Fabry, Mikulas. *Recognizing States: International Society and the Establishment of New States since 1776*. Oxford: Oxford University Press, 2010.

Gallitsch, Albert. "Die Landespostdirektion Danzig und ihre postalischen Beziehungen zu Polen." *Archiv für das Post- und Fernmeldewesen* 8, no. 3 (1956): 190–209.

Gerwarth, Robert. *The Vanquished: Why the First World War Failed to End, 1917–1923*. London: Allen Lane, 2016.

Headlam-Morley, James. *A Memoir of the Paris Peace Conference, 1919*. London: Methuen, 1972.

Heideking, Jürgen. *Areopag der Diplomaten: Die Pariser Botschafterkonferenz der alliierten Hauptmächte und die Probleme der europäischen Politik 1920–1931*. Husum: Matthiesen, 1979.

Ishii Kikujirō. "Report to the League Council, 17 November 1920." In *League of Nations Council: Minutes of the Thirteenth Session*. Geneva: League of Nations, 1921.

Jackson, Peter. *Beyond the Balance of Power: France and the Politics of National Security in the Era of the First World War*. Cambridge: Cambridge University Press, 2013.

Kimmich, Christoph M. *The Free City: Danzig and German Foreign Policy 1919–1934*. New Haven, CT: Yale University Press, 1968.

Kissinger, Henry. *Diplomacy*. New York: Simon & Schuster, 1994.

Knock, Thomas J. *To End all Wars: Woodrow Wilson and the Quest for a New World Order*. New York: Oxford University Press, 1992.

Latawski, Paul, ed. *The Reconstruction of Poland, 1914–1923*. New York: St. Martin's Press, 1992.

Leczyk, Marian. *Druga Rzeczpospolita 1918–1939: Społeczeństwo, Gospodarka, Kultura, Polityka*. Warsaw: Książka i Wiedza, 2006.

Link, Arthur, ed. *The Papers of Woodrow Wilson*. Vol. 45. Princeton, NJ: Princeton University Press, 1966–94.

Loew, Peter O. *Danzig: Biographie einer Stadt*. Munich: Beck, 2011.

Lowczyk, Olivier. *La fabrique de la paix: Du Comité d'études à la Conférence de la paix, l'élaboration par la France des traités de la Première guerre mondiale*. Paris: Economica, 2010.

Lundgreen-Nielsen, Kay. *The Polish Problem at the Paris Peace Conference: A Study of the Policies of the Great Powers and the Poles, 1918–1919*. Odense: Odense University Press, 1979.

Mason, John Brown. *The Danzig Dilemma: A Study in Peacemaking by Compromise*. Stanford, CA: Stanford University Press, 1947.

Moorhouse, Roger. "'The Sore That Would Never Heal': The Genesis of the Polish Corridor." In *After the Versailles Treaty: Enforcement, Compliance, Contested Identities*, edited by Conan Fischer and Alan Sharp, 185–95. London: Routledge, 2008.

Oberdörfer, Lutz. "Die Danzig/Korridor- und die Memelfrage in Versailles und den ersten Nachkriegsjahren." In *Preußische Landesgeschichte: Festschrift für Bernhart Jähnig*, edited by Udo Arnold, Mario Glauert, and Jürgen Sarnowsky, 85–98. Marburg: Elwert, 2001.

*Papers Relating to the Foreign Relations of the United States.* Washington, DC: US Government Printing Office, 1861ff.

Payk, Marcus M. *Frieden durch Recht? Der Aufstieg des modernen Völkerrechts und der Friedensschluss nach dem Ersten Weltkrieg.* Munich: De Gruyter/Oldenbourg, 2018.

Pink, Gerhard Paul. *The Conference of Ambassadors (Paris 1920–1931).* Geneva: Geneva Research Centre, 1942.

Prott, Volker. *The Politics of Self-Determination: Remaking Territories and National Identities in Europe, 1917–1923.* Oxford: Oxford University Press, 2016.

Publications of the Permanent Court of International Justice (PCIJ), Series B 11. Leiden: 1925.

Ramonat, Wolfgang. *Der Völkerbund und die Freie Stadt Danzig 1920–1934.* Osnabrück: Biblio-Verlag, 1979.

Sahm, Heinrich. *Erinnerungen aus meinen Danziger Jahren: 1919–1930.* Marburg/Lahn: Johann-Gottfried-Herder-Institut, 1958.

Schenk, Dieter. *Die Post von Danzig: Geschichte eines deutschen Justizmords.* Reinbek: Rowohlt, 1995.

Simpson, Gerry J. *Great Powers and Outlaw States: Unequal Sovereigns in the International Legal Order.* Cambridge: Cambridge University Press, 2004.

Sluga, Glenda. *The Problem of Trieste and the Italo-Yugoslav Border: Difference, Identity, and Sovereignty in Twentieth-Century Europe.* Albany: State University of New York Press, 2001.

Spiermann, Ole. *International Legal Argument in the Permanent Court of International Justice: The Rise of the International Judiciary.* Cambridge: Cambridge University Press, 2005.

Stahn, Carsten. *The Law and Practice of International Territorial Administration: Versailles to Iraq and Beyond.* Cambridge: Cambridge University Press, 2008.

Steiner, Zara. *The Lights That Failed: European International History 1919–1933.* Oxford: Oxford University Press, 2007.

Throntveit, Trygve. "The Fable of the Fourteen Points: Woodrow Wilson and National Self-Determination." *Diplomatic History* 35 (2011): 445–81.

Wandycz, Piotr S. *France and Her Eastern Allies, 1919–1925: French-Czechoslovak-Polish Relations from the Paris Peace Conference to Locarno.* Minneapolis, MN: Lund Press, 1962.

Weidenmann, Adolf. *Der Danzig-Polnische Poststreit.* Aschaffenburg: Waillandt, 1931.

Wilde, Ralph. "From Danzig to East Timor and Beyond: The Role of International Territorial Administration." *American Journal of International Law* 95, no. 3 (2001): 583–606.

Woodward, Ernest L., and William N. Medlicott, eds. *Documents on British Foreign Policy, 1919–1939: First Series.* London: Her Majesty's Stationery Office, 1947–86.

Wróbel, Piotr J. "The Revival of Poland and Paramilitary Violence, 1918–1920." In *Spießer, Patrioten, Revolutionäre: Militärische Mobilisierung und gesellschaftliche Ordnung in der Neuzeit,* edited by Rüdiger Bergien, and Ralf Pröve, 281–304. Göttingen: V&R Unipress, 2010.

Ydit, Meir. *Internationalised Territories from the "Free City of Cracow" to the "Free City of Berlin."* Leiden: A. W. Sythoff, 1961.

Ziehm, Ernst. "Die Verwaltung Danzigs durch die interalliierten Hauptmächte und die Konstituierung der Freien Stadt Danzig." In *Die Entstehung der Freien Stadt*

*Danzig: Fünf Aufsätze*, edited by Albert Brödersdorff, Walther Recke, Theodor Rudolph, L. Foerster, and Ernst Ziehm, 33–45. Danzig: Kafemann, 1930.

MARCUS M. PAYK is Professor of Modern History at Helmut Schmidt University in Hamburg. He is author of *Frieden durch Recht? Der Aufstieg des modernen Völkerrechts und der Friedensschluss nach dem Ersten Weltkrieg.*

# Index

Czechoslovakia, Czechs, 7, 18, 20, 32n18, 38–42, 44, 46–48, 50–51, 124, 127, 129, 132, 134, 136–137, 138n5, 139n10, 217
Czechoslovakian National Council, 40–41, 49

Dagestan, 209n22
*Daily Mail* (newspaper), 194
Dalmatia, 17
Danzig, 6, 9–11, 17, 21–22, 66, 69, 215–217, 219–228
Danzig Polytechnic University, 66
Davion, Isabelle, 7, 20
Deak, John, 9
Declassé, Théophile, 85
democracy, democratic practices, 21–22, 30, 40, 50–51, 60, 127, 156
Denmark, Danes, 16, 21, 26, 192
deportation, 5
Derby, Lord (Edward Stanley), 221
Diagne, Blaise, 170, 176–177, 181n32
Dimier, Veronique, 173
diplomacy, diplomats, 1–4, 6, 10, 16, 18, 22, 26, 39–40, 42, 44–45, 48, 53n23, 61, 66, 87–88, 90, 92–93, 125, 161n51, 165, 167–168, 171, 183n62, 197, 199–200, 216–218, 221, 225, 227
Disraeli, Benjamin, 209n35
Dmowski, Roman, 18, 32n10, 44
Drummond, Eric, 204, 226
Du Bois, W. E. B., 10, 167–168, 170–179, 181n34, 182n51, 183n54, 184n80

East Prussia, 16–17, 19–22, 24, 26–27, 62, 66
East Timor, 228
eastern Europe, 1–2, 6–7, 16–21, 38–39, 41, 43, 46, 51, 59, 64, 66, 106, 147, 169, 198, 216–217
Eastern Galicia, 17
Eastern Silesia, 42
economics, economists, 25, 42, 44, 66, 93, 114, 166, 195, 198, 217, 220
education, 47, 104, 131, 135, 139n16, 170–173, 175, 178
Egypt, 6, 8, 77–87, 88–93, 96n41, 96n52, 97n52, 99–103, 105–114, 143, 146, 182n34, 189, 209n22
    British occupation of, 8, 77–81, 83–89, 91–94, 101 101
    Capitulations, 77, 79, 81–82, 84–85, 87, 90, 92, 101–102, 110, 113, 201
    Electoral Law (1900), 102–104
    independence (1922), 89, 92, 107–108. *See also* Anglo-Egyptian Treaty (1936)
    mixed courts, 84, 105, 111, 114, 118n39

National Courts, 102, 105
nationality laws, 100–101, 105–107, 109–114, 118n41, 120n81
Ellguth-Turawa, 24
Enlightenment, 31n2
Entente Cordiale (1904), 89
Entente Powers (First World War), 32n10, 43, 48–50, 82, 85, 89, 139n8, 185n85, 193, 200. *See also* Allied Powers
Eritrea, 152
Estonia, 199
Ethiopia, 152, 155, 161n51
ethnic cleansing, 3, 5, 18, 60
ethnicity, ethnic identity, 5–7, 19, 21, 26, 44–45, 47, 62, 101, 111, 120n77, 125, 132, 135, 149
ethnonationalism, 20, 26–27, 61, 64, 67–68
Eupen-Malmedy, 17, 19
European Union, 31
Ewing, Adam, 171

Farah, Georges, 105
fascism, fascists, 3, 9, 145, 148–157, 159n31, 160n40
Fezzan, 144
Finland, 192, 197, 199–200, 206
First World War, 1, 6–7, 9–11, 16, 18, 20–22, 24, 29–31, 32n10, 33n22, 38–40, 46, 59–62, 64, 67, 69, 77, 92–93, 94n4, 100, 102, 104, 108, 117n25, 138n3, 143–144, 153, 155–156, 165–166, 174, 189–191, 205–207, 215
Fiume, 10, 17
Foch, Ferdinand, 48
Folwark, 27
Foucault, Michel, 99, 115n2
France, French, 3, 7, 19–20, 23, 28, 30, 38–44, 47–50, 54n64, 77, 79, 85, 89, 110, 112, 114, 115n9, 146, 152, 155, 158n17, 170, 174–178, 181n25, 182n34, 185n86, 189, 200–203, 217–219, 221, 226, 228
Franco-Prussian War (1870–71), 20
French Revolution, 31n1
Frýdek, 42, 44
Frysztat district, 38, 42
Fu'ad I (king), 112

Galicia, 5, 124
Garvey, Marcus, 174–175, 183n58, 183n62
Genell, Aimee, 8, 104
General Government, 33
Generalplan Ost, 59
Geneva, 11, 223, 225–226
geography, geographers, 62, 66, 70
Georgia, 190, 192, 200, 206

Germany, Germans, 2–3, 7, 16, 18–29, 33n22, 38, 46, 54n54, 59, 61, 63–66, 68, 70–71, 78–81, 85, 90, 115n9, 124, 128–133, 135–137, 139n8, 147, 149–151, 153, 172, 189–191, 193–195, 198–201, 203–204, 206, 215–217, 219, 222, 224, 228, 230n18
German Revolution (1918), 23
Ghali, Paul, 111
Gladstone, William Ewart, 209n35
Gniezno, 63
governmentality, 99
Grabski, Władysław, 49–50
Grass, Günther, 215
Great Britain, British, 2–3, 8, 28, 30, 33n28, 39, 41, 43–44, 47–48, 50, 54n64, 56n103, 77–89, 91–92 100, 102, 104, 106–107, 110, 143, 146, 152, 181n24, 182n34, 189, 200, 202–204, 206, 217–219, 226, 228. *See also* British Empire
Foreign Office, 77–85, 87–88, 90, 92–93, 96n45
Greece, Greeks, 71, 97n52, 105, 110, 117n25, 193, 196, 203
Grenard, Fernand 43–44
Grey, Edward, 77, 79, 82–86
Guadalupe, 184
Gulistan, Treaty of (1813), 190

Habsburg Empire. *See* Austro-Hungarian Empire
Hague, The, 11, 221, 226–227
Haiti, 182n34
Haking, Richard, 219, 224–226
Hamel, Joost van, 225
*Heimat*, 25
Henrys, Prosper, 43, 49
Hermannstadt/Sibiu, 193–194
Hindenburg, Paul von, 30
history, historians, 4, 11, 23, 28, 40, 59, 61–63, 66–68, 78, 100, 103, 117n28, 126–127, 179n6
Hitler, Adolf, 30, 154
Hughes, William, 169, 174
humanitarianism, 4, 182n35
Hungary, Hungarians, 16, 21–22, 24, 26, 90, 125, 194, 203–204
Hurst, Cecil, 90

imperialism, 4, 146, 150, 173, 179n7, 189, 191–195, 197, 199–200, 202–204
India, 102, 158n5, 169, 189, 191, 193, 206, 209n22
Institute for Research on Recent Polish History, 67

Institute for the Study of Ethnic Affairs, 67
Inter-Allied Commissions (IACs), 22–24, 26, 33n34, 43, 45, 47, 49–50
International Labour Office (ILO), 173
international law, 6, 77, 88, 93, 112, 115n8, 165, 205–206, 220
international relations, 2, 4, 85, 165, 222
internationalism, 6, 10, 18, 92, 101–102, 115n7, 117n23, 165–168, 171–175, 177–179, 180n11, 183n58, 189–193, 195, 204, 206–207
Iran, 6, 10, 190–192, 207n1, 210n51, 212n82. *See also* Persia
Islamic Revolution, 206
Iraq, 200
Ireland, 153
Ishii Kikujirō, 222–223
Islam, Muslins, 80–84, 88, 101, 107, 111–113, 143, 145, 151–153, 156–157n2, 191, 194, 197, 201, 209n23, 210n49
Istanbul, 79, 191, 205
Istria, 124, 144, 147, 153
Italo-German agreement (1939), 161n49
Italy, Italians, 2–3, 9, 20, 28, 30, 39, 41, 45, 110, 124, 127–128, 132–133, 143–148, 150–153, 155–156, 181n25, 195, 204
1938 racial laws, 152, 156
Ivan the Terrible, 203

Jamālzādeh, Mohammad 'Ali, 191, 202–204, 208n18
Japan, Japanese, 2–3, 9–10, 13n21, 47, 97n52, 168–171, 180n10, 180n21, 181n23, 181n25, 204, 207, 222
Jews, 67, 103–105, 107, 112, 118n38, 133, 145, 152–153, 156–157, 160n38, 160n40, 161n57, 196
Johannisburg county, 27
Junod, Ed, 172

Kamil, Husayn, 80, 82–83, 84–87, 91, 95n27, 106
Karch, Brendan, 7, 147
Karl I (kaiser), 124
Karl, Rebecca, 197
Karviná, 47–48
Kashubes, 68
Kauffman, Jesse, 7
*Kāveh* (newspaper), 10, 190–196, 198–200, 202–203, 205, 208n18
Kazan, 209n22
Kemal, Mustafa, 109
Kermanshah, 191, 193, 203, 208n12
Keynes, John Maynard, 3

Piast dynasty, 62, 68–69, 74n30
Picon Stephen, 38
Piłsudski, Józef, 32n10, 67, 216–217
Pinto, Nicolau dos Santos, 176
plebiscites, 1, 7, 16–17, 19–22, 24, 26, 29, 31,
    32n10, 39, 44–45, 47–48, 50–51, 109
  Austria (1938), 30
  Carinthia (1919), 22, 24, 29
  East Prussia (1920), 24
  Rhineland (1936), 30
  Saarland (1935), 30
  Schleswig-Holstein (1920), 29
  Sopron (1921), 22, 24, 29
  Upper Silesia (1921), 7, 17, 22–24, 27–28
Pleß, 27
Poland, Poles, 1–2, 7, 10–11, 16, 18–19, 21–29,
    32n10, 33n22, 38–51, 54n64, 59–61, 63–70,
    124, 127, 129, 132, 134, 192–193, 196, 198,
    206, 210n54, 215, 217–223, 225–228
  constitution (1791), 23
Polanians, 68–69
police, 22, 24, 29, 33n34, 47
Polish Miners' Union, 41, 44
Polish National Assembly, 42
Polish National Committee, 40–41
Polish Socialist Party, 62, 67
Polish Uprising (1920), 23, 29
Polish-Czechoslovak War (1919), 42–43
Polish-German border dispute, 61–62
Polish-Lithuanian Party, 62
Polish-Soviet War (1919–21), 24–25, 50
Pomerania, 62, 66–70
population transfers, 60. See also deportation
Portugal, Portuguese, 1, 10, 168, 170, 174–177,
    181n25, 181n26, 182n34, 184n71, 185n88
Portuguese Guinea, 184n71
Posen, 8, 21, 33n22, 62, 65
postcolonial nationalism, 206–207. See also
    anticolonialism; colonialism; nationalism
postwar order. See new world order
Poznań University, 66
Poznan, 217
Prague, 46, 48
press, 2, 25, 42, 46, 81, 118n36, 136, 167, 175, 225
prisoners of war, 48, 128, 191, 193
propaganda, 7, 17, 24–26, 29, 31, 34n58, 46, 66–
    68, 70, 83, 155
Protestantism, Protestants, 21, 26–27, 41,
    51, 103
protests, 23–24. See also violence
Prussia, 16, 21, 27, 33n22, 63, 64, 67–69, 115n9,
    217–218. See also East Prussia; West
    Prussia

Qasr-I Shirin, 193
Quai d'Orsay, 38–39, 42–44, 167, 180n13, 221
Quiñones de León, José, 226

race, 5, 10, 59, 61, 71, 88, 99, 101, 110, 116n16,
    120n77, 125, 137, 156, 165–166, 168–179,
    179n6, 181n26, 184n75, 194–196, 198, 201
Rava, Maurizio, 153
Realpolitik, 17, 40, 51
Red Army, 49–50, 202, 204, 219
referenda, 30–31, 40, 45–46, 49–51. See also
    plebiscites
religion, 8–9, 23, 25–26, 51n3, 61, 85, 88, 99–
    101, 112, 115n7, 120n81, 145, 147–148, 170,
    196–197
Renner, Karl, 32n9, 129
revanchism, 35n70
revolutionary upheaval, 3
Rhineland, 30, 226
Rhodesia, 175
right of residence, 47, 132–134
riots. See protests
Rodd, Rennell, 90, 96n52, 97n52
Roman Empire, 31n1, 94n5, 146, 155, 157, 194,
    196
Romania, Romanians, 33n19, 125, 127, 129, 132,
    193–195
Romer, Eugeniusz, 62
Rotterdam, 191
Rudnicki, Mikołaj, 66
Rushdi, Husayn, 79–80, 82, 85
Russia, Russians, 18, 20–21, 25, 62, 64–65, 67,
    77, 79, 82, 90, 96n41, 128, 189–190, 193–
    197, 199–205, 216–217, 219. See also Soviet
    Union
  White Russians, 192, 202–203
Russian Revolution, 1, 64, 197, 203
Russo-Persian Treaty (1921), 206–207
Russo-Persian War (1722–23), 202, 206
Ruthenia, Ruthenians, 124, 210n54
Rybnik, 27

Saar Deutsche Front, 30
Saarland, 10, 17
Sahm, Heinrich, 225–226
Saint-Germain, Treaty of (1919), 2, 22, 125, 137,
    139n8
Sajovic, Rudolf, 135, 137
Salonica, Armistice of (1918), 41
San Domingo, 182n34
Sanusiyya, 143, 158n5
Schleswig-Holstein, 16–17, 21, 26, 29, 31n3
schlonsak (dialect), 19

CPSIA information can be obtained
at www.ICGtesting.com
Printed in the USA
BVHW032347010419
544346BV00003B/6/P

9 780253 040916